Understanding Early Childhood
Mental Health

Understanding Early Childhood Mental Health

A Practical Guide for Professionals

edited by

Susan Janko Summers, Ph.D.

and

Rachel Chazan-Cohen, Ph.D.
George Mason University
Fairfax, VA

·P A U L·H·
BROOKES
PUBLISHING C? ®

Baltimore • London • Sydney

Paul H. Brookes Publishing Co.
Post Office Box 10624
Baltimore, Maryland 21285-0624
USA

www.brookespublishing.com

Typeset by Integrated Publishing Solutions, Grand Rapids, Michigan.
Manufactured in the United States of America by
Sheridan Books, Inc., Chelsea, Michigan.

The individuals described in this book are composites or real people whose situations are masked and are based on the authors' experiences. In all instances, names and identifying details have been changed to protect confidentiality.

Classroom Assessment Scoring System and CLASS are trademarks of Robert C. Pianta.

Library of Congress Cataloging-in-Publication Data

Understanding early childhood mental health: a practical guide for professionals/edited by Susan Janko Summers and Rachel Chazan-Cohen.
   p.   cm.
  Includes bibliographical references and index.
  ISBN-13: 978-1-59857-075-5
  ISBN-10: 1-59857-075-7
  1. Early childhood education—United States.   2. Child development—United States.   3. Child mental health—United States.   4. Developmental psychology.   5. Social learning.   I. Summers, Susan Janko. II. Chazan-Cohen, Rachel.
LB1139.25.E89 2012
372.210973—dc23   2011035085

British Library Cataloguing in Publication data are available from the British Library.

2015   2014   2013   2012   2011

10   9   8   7   6   5   4   3   2   1

Contents

About the Editors

Susan Janko Summers, Ph.D., is an educational ethnographer who has studied and written about child maltreatment, infant mental health, children with disabilities, and children and families at risk in the contexts of culture, community, and educational settings. She earned interdisciplinary master's and doctoral degrees with an emphasis on early childhood special education at the University of Oregon. She is keenly interested in the effects of mindfulness and meditation on emotional health and social relationships.

Rachel Chazan-Cohen, Ph.D., is Associate Professor of Applied Developmental Psychology at George Mason University in Virginia. Previously, she was a senior research analyst and Coordinator of Infant and Toddler Research in the Office of Planning Research and Evaluation in the Administration for Children and Families, U.S. Department of Health and Human Services. She trained in developmental and clinical psychology at Yale University, where she earned a doctoral degree, and at Tufts University, where she earned a master's degree. She is particularly interested in the biological, relational, and environmental factors influencing the development of at-risk children and, most especially, on the creation, evaluation, and refinement of intervention programs for families with infants and toddlers.

About the Contributors

Linda S. Beeber, Ph.D., R.N., is an advanced-practice psychiatric mental health nurse and Francis Fox Term Professor at the University of North Carolina at Chapel Hill School of Nursing. As Principal Investigator, she has studied in-home, interpersonally based psychotherapy for depressive symptoms in Early Head Start mothers (supported by grants from the National Institute of Mental Health and the Administration for Children and Families [ACF], U.S. Department of Health and Human Services [DHHS]). She also developed and tested a curriculum for Early Head Start staff to identify, support, and refer caregivers (e.g., mothers, fathers, grandparents, foster parents) who have depressive symptoms (supported by the ACF, DHHS). Her interest is in bringing effective, culturally congruent mental health care to parents and children who are living with limited resources and in challenging conditions.

Allison B. Boothe, Ph.D., is a clinical psychologist who specializes in infant and early childhood mental health. She is the statewide director of Louisiana's Quality Start Mental Health Consultation Program, which provides mental health consultation to child care centers throughout the state as part of the child care quality rating and improvement system. Dr. Boothe codesigned and co-established the health consultation model used in Louisiana. Dr. Boothe has clinical and research interests in children who have experienced maltreatment and their parents, clinical interventions, and mental health consultation to child care centers.

Neil W. Boris, M.D., is Professor in the Department of Psychiatry and Behavioral Sciences at Tulane University School of Medicine in Louisiana. After completing residency training at Brown University, Dr. Boris received a Career Development Award sponsored jointly by the National Institute of Mental Health and the American Academy of Child and Adolescent Psychiatry. His wide-ranging clinical work has focused on young children who have experienced maltreatment, children with life-threatening illnesses, and children whose parents have substance-abuse problems. His research, focusing on the social and emotional development of high-risk children under 5 years of age and including studies of early intervention programs serving high-risk families in the United States and the impact of community-based programs for orphans in Rwanda and Malawi, has been published in more than 50 peer-reviewed journals and dozens of chapters in leading texts.

Regina Canuso, M.S., PMHCNS-BC, a psychiatric mental health nurse, gained expertise in infant–toddler mental health as a Head Start nurse, then as Health and Mental Health Coordinator for Early Head Start, and later as Mental Health Coordinator for Head Start and Early Head Start in Syracuse, New York. She created a mental health program within the Syracuse Early Head Start and forged a collaborative relationship with Dr. Linda Beeber to test parent–child mental health interventions. In addition to being a consultant to the Onondaga County, New York, Health Department's Healthy Start, where she founded and chaired its Mental Health Committee, she completed a National Head Start Fellowship that focused on identifying depression in parents of children in early childhood education programs. Her passion has always been to promote two-generation mental health with low-income, vulnerable mothers and their young children.

Nicole Denmark, B.A., is a doctoral candidate in the Department of Human Development at the University of Maryland, College Park. Ms. Denmark graduated from Reed College, and worked for two years as an Early Head Start teacher. Her research interests focus on parenting and low-income children's social development in low-income, minority, and immigrant populations. She is particularly interested in using this research to help inform home visiting and other early childhood programs for minority populations. Ms. Denmark is currently working on her dissertation on parenting among Central American immigrant mothers of children enrolled in Head Start. Her work is funded by a Head Start Scholars Award from the U.S. Department of Health and Human Services.

Melissa Duchene, B.S., is a doctoral student in the Department of Human Development at the University of Maryland, College Park. Her current research focuses on examining the relation between parenting and the social skills of children with autism. Ms. Duchene received her bachelor of science degree in psychology from the University of Central Florida.

Sherryl Scott Heller, Ph.D., is an applied developmental psychologist and a senior mental health consultant on a statewide initiative focused on improving the quality of child care centers through the development of a quality rating system and mental health consultation services. She edited *A Practical Guide to Reflective Supervision* (ZERO TO THREE, 2009) with Linda Gilkerson of the Erikson Institute in Chicago. Dr. Heller has long-standing clinical and research interests in parenting, child care, the effects of violence and maltreatment on child development, attachment, and attachment disturbances in very young children; gender development and disturbances; perinatal loss; and reflective supervision.

Brenda Jones Harden, Ph.D., is a psychologist whose work spans early childhood policy, practice, and research arenas. For more than 30 years she has focused on the developmental and mental health needs of young children at environmental risk, with a specific emphasis on preventing maladaptive outcomes in these populations through early childhood intervention programs. Dr. Jones Harden is currently Associate Professor in the Early Childhood Education program of the Department of Human Development, University of Maryland, College Park. She received her doctoral degree in developmental and clinical psychology from Yale University.

Angela Walter Keyes, Ph.D., is an applied developmental psychologist and a senior mental health consultant on a statewide initiative focused on improving the quality of care provided to children under age 5 in group care settings. This initiative has at its core a focus on fostering children's social-emotional development as well as teaching techniques to modify children's challenging behaviors in a positive way. Dr. Keyes provides reflective supervision to the mental health consultants who provide services to child care centers that are working toward improving the quality of care they provide. She is trained in infant mental health and has coauthored a book chapter on reflective supervision. Dr. Keyes coteaches a course on multiculturalism and cultural competence in clinical practice to psychology interns and psychiatry residents.

Neena M. Malik, Ph.D., received her B.A. from Yale University in 1988 and her Ph.D. in child and family clinical psychology from the University of Denver in 1997. Currently she is Psychology and Postdoctoral Training Director in the Division of Psychology, Department of Pediatrics, at the University of Miami, Miller School of Medicine. Prior to her work at the University of Miami, Dr. Malik conducted research and interventions in collaboration with Miami's juvenile courts. Since moving to the University of Miami, Dr. Malik has conducted research in the areas of infant and toddler exposure to trauma and violence, family functioning, and youth at risk. She has published and presented in areas such as infant mental health, parent–child and family relations, children's exposure to trauma and violence, domestic violence, marital functioning and child adjustment, and family functioning and risk behaviors in gay youth.

Colleen I. Monahan, B.A., is currently a doctoral student in the Department of Human Development at the University of Maryland, College Park. She has a B.A. in psychology from Syracuse University. She has worked as a research technician in a psychophysiology lab at the University of Buffalo, researching electroencephalogram/event-related potentials and substance use disorders. Ms. Monahan's research interests include early child development and the impact of environmental risk factors on young children's developmental outcomes.

Timothy F. Page, Ph.D., is Betty J. Stewart Associate Professor of Social Work Practice with Children and Director of the Louisiana State University's School of Social Work doctoral program. His current research and scholarly activity is in the area of attachment-based narrative assessments with children, an attachment-based parenting intervention for high-risk families, and caseworker training in infant mental health. His primary interest is in the area of how early caregiving relationships promote emotional security and the foundation for healthy development among infants and young children and how social work interventions with children and parents can address risks and provide corrective experiences for compromised development. He earned his doctorate in social welfare from the University of Wisconsin–Madison.

Jane Squires, Ph.D., is Professor of Early Intervention/Special Education, Director of the Early Intervention Program, and Director of the University Center for Excellence in

Developmental Disabilities and the Center on Human Development at the University of Oregon. She oversees research and outreach projects in the areas of developmental screening, social-emotional competence, early identification of developmental delays, and the involvement of parents in monitoring their young children's development. She currently directs a systems change grant focused on improving identification, treatment, and referral of substance-exposed newborns and teaches master's and doctoral courses on early intervention and prevention, early childhood foundations, curriculum, and assessment.

Deborah Roderick Stark, M.S.W., is a nationally recognized expert in child and family policy and programs. Working with public and private agencies, she has developed programs that provide children and families coordinated support services to enhance their life experience. She received her B.A. from Wellesley College and her M.S.W. from the University of California at Berkeley. As Special Assistant to the Commissioner of the Administration on Children, Youth and Families of the U.S. Department of Health and Human Services during the Clinton administration, she designed and implemented Congress's 1993 Family Preservation and Support initiative and the 1994 Early Head Start program. Prior to this, she was a policy analyst for the bipartisan National Commission on Children.

Jamell White, M.S., M.S.W., is a doctoral student in the Department of Human Development at the University of Maryland, College Park. She is a therapist and case manager specializing in children with autism spectrum disorders and other developmental disabilities. Ms. White obtained her bachelor's degree in psychology from the University of Maryland, a master's degree in social work from the National Catholic School of Social Service, and a master's degree in special education from The Johns Hopkins University. Her research areas of interest include the impact of disabilities on family functioning and the social and emotional development of young children with disabilities.

Meryl Yoches, B.A., is a doctoral student in the Department of Human Development with a specialization in developmental science and a concentration in early childhood at the University of Maryland, College Park. Her research interests include the intersection of child development and public policy, especially child care and preschool programs for low-income families. She received her B.A. at Connecticut College, where she majored in psychology and minored in human development.

Foreword

The history of this book is connected to a larger history occurring in the early childhood field, a history that includes researchers and programs like yours. Slightly more than 15 years ago researchers, program directors, evaluators, and administrators assembled in Washington, D.C., to design an evaluation of Early Head Start (EHS), a newly established early childhood program for low-income families with children ages birth to 3. Using a competitive grant review process, the U.S. Department of Health and Human Services Administration for Children and Families selected 17 university-based research team sites to participate in the national evaluation. Each site also received additional funds for local site-specific data collection, and each was required to have a university partner with a local EHS program. The national contractor, Mathematica Policy Research, Inc., coordinated the cross-site data collection. Although many researchers attending the initial meeting were already acquainted, many were not, and few had established relationships with their community partners or those from other sites. So began a journey toward a large-scale successful collaboration that has contributed to the literature on low-income children's development as well as the important role that early education and development programs can play in the lives of children and their families.

The researchers represented a diversity of disciplines, including child psychiatry, pediatrics, anthropology, sociology, early childhood education, psychology, nursing, social work, developmental disabilities, family finance, community psychology, evaluation science, and linguistics. More than once, our federal agency program director, Esther Kresh, decisively kept us on task as we moved through countless debates and discussions about assessment instruments, tracking strategies, time lines, informed consent issues, and all other essential matters related to a longitudinal study involving several thousand families and a multisite, multiteam network. We soon learned that keeping to task, working hard, and advancing the study were secondary to a far more important aspect of human dynamics, namely, relationships. If we were to be successful, we needed to become a team, albeit one with diverse approaches and views. In short, we needed to develop trusting relationships and, led by our federal project officer, Esther Kresh, and later by her successor, Rachel Chazan-Cohen, we succeeded.

What began as a 3-year study became an ongoing 15-year collaboration. Along the way we crafted more than a research and evaluation team; we became an evaluation family. We experienced what all families do: New members entered into our kinship system (graduate students and early career faculty members), members of our family married and had their own families grow, members of our family achieved personal successes, and some developed health problems. The shared joy at pictures of new babies and grandbabies, career changes, and professional successes were no more or less shared than our concern when colleagues developed health problems or our grief when we lost members of our EHS consortium family. Each member of our family came to realize that the trusting relationships that we developed were the glue that held us together during both good and difficult times. Indeed, the infant mental health core dictum, *relationships matter*, was key to our success, as was our ability to exercise reflective supportive practices during the most difficult times involving loss. Although initially only one of the home-visiting EHS program sites, the Michigan site with which I was affiliated, used an infant mental health approach, the relationship-focused attention to caregiver–infant interactions increasingly became an integral component of many more programs, regardless of their home- or center-based context. The increasing incorporation of infant mental health relationship approaches into EHS programs is especially gratifying. For slightly more than 30 years I served as president or executive director of state and international infant mental health organizations. As Executive Director of the International Association for Infant Mental Health and then its successor, the World Association for Infant Mental Health, I helped to develop 50 infant mental health Affiliate Associations across the globe. The growing understanding around the globe that the quality of caregiver–infant relationships has a powerful impact on human development—from the organization of synaptic neural networks to intersubjective mental concepts of self and other—provides a clear justification for inclusion of the infant mental health relationship framework into any early childhood rearing and/or educational context.

Perhaps it should not be surprising, therefore, that continued investments in the relationship-based approach to early interventions has led to dynamic changes in such early intervention efforts in the 21st century. The national evaluation of EHS provided solid evidence that home-visiting interventions have potential for producing lasting effects on the quality of mother–child relationships. But EHS was not doing enough to support the mental health of children and their families and did not provide a systematic examination of infant mental health practices. Something new was needed, and something new was provided. The Administration for Children and Families funded five University–EHS partnerships and a university early intervention program in order to gather information about the effectiveness of infant mental health practices within EHS programs and about how programs might produce sustainable changes in parent–infant interactions. Seasoned investigators with their program partners used a mixed-method approach to directly document the effectiveness of mental health approaches to early intervention. *Understanding Early Childhood Mental Health: A Practical Guide for Professionals* is one result of their efforts and, considered within the context of practice and child outcomes, it is perhaps the most important result. Through *Understanding Early Childhood Mental Health,* Susan Janko Summers, Rachel Chazan-Cohen, and their colleagues provide an exemplary and transformative blend of scientific, clinical, and practical knowledge to guide EHS teachers, home visitors, and support professionals in their collaborative quest to place infants and toddlers firmly on the resilient side of social-emotional development. *Understanding Early Childhood Mental Health* not only embraces a systems view of early development, it provides alternate pathways and the effective skills needed to guide infants and their caregivers toward positive mental health and the enhancement of adaptive behavior.

In our efforts to build resilient developmental pathways at Michigan State University, we have constructed a framework to guide community systems change efforts beginning at the prenatal period and extending through the child's ultimate entry into the workforce (Fitzgerald, Allen, & Roberts, 2010). The concept of a risk-to-resilience continuum is core to the model. The framework posits that resilience during the first few postnatal years is built from caregiving contexts that provide ongoing nurturing relationships with the same adults; experiences responsive to individual differences in such characteristics as temperament; physical protection, safety, and regulation of daily routine; developmentally appropriate practices related to perceptual-motor, cognitive, social stimulation, and language exposure; limit setting (discipline), structure (rules and routines), and expectations (for positive outcomes); and stable, supportive communities (violence free) and culture (a sense of rootedness and connectedness). Moreover, the risk-to-resilience continuum recognizes the neurobiological underlying structural and functional organization of the nervous system particularly with respect to stress regulation (e.g., hypothalamic, pituitary, adrenal axis), effortful control (e.g., prefrontal cortex), imitative behavior (e.g., mirror neurons), and mental representations of experience (Fitzgerald, Wong, & Zucker, in press; Fonagy, Luyten, & Strathearn, 2011). From the opening chapter defining infant mental health (Stark & Chazan-Cohen) to the final chapter on evaluating program effectiveness (Summers), authors weave their way through the risk-to-resilience continuum, not from the arcane perspective of scientists, but from a practice perspective, one designed to cross knowledge domains and provide frontline caregivers with the background and skills necessary to implement infant mental health practices and, thereby, guide infants and toddlers onto resilient developmental pathways.

In the first decade of the 21st century, significant strides have been made in translating knowledge from developmental science into practice, particularly with respect to the earliest years. Many years ago, the distinguished developmental psychologist Harriet Rheingold suggested rather boldly that there should be formal efforts to teach parenting skills to prospective parents. Many years later with equal boldness she anticipated contemporary emphasis on building positive behaviors to enhance resilience skills:

> In fact, parents, like the rest of us, tend to ignore what goes right and fasten on what goes wrong. Not only a good start to mental health but a better start can come from recognizing and rewarding such behaviors at their onset. If we wait until we think children are ready to be taught them, we pay the penalty of a lost opportunity. (Rheingold, 1988, p. 1)

Reading *Understanding Early Childhood Mental Health* and putting its messages into practice will help us move forward in our collective efforts to support caregivers and promote optimal development for all infants and very young children.

Hiram E. Fitzgerald, Ph.D.
University Distinguished Professor
Michigan State University

REFERENCES

Fitzgerald, H.E., Allen, A., & Roberts, P. (2010). Campus-community partnerships: Perspectives on engaged research. In H.E. Fitzgerald, C. Burack, & S.D. Seifer (Eds), *Handbook of engaged scholarship: Contemporary landscapes, future directions: Vol. 2. Community-campus partnerships* (pp. 5–28). East Lansing: Michigan State University Press.

Fitzgerald, H.E., Wong, M.M., & Zucker, R.A. (in press). Early origins of alcohol use and abuse: Mental representations, relationships, and the risk-resilience continuum. In N. Suchman, M. Pajulo, & L.C. Mayes (Eds), *Parenting and substance addiction: Developmental approaches to intervention.* New York: Oxford University Press.

Fonagy, P., Luyten, P., & Strathearn, L. (2011). Borderline personality disorder, mentalization, and the neurobiology of attachment. *Infant Mental Health Journal, 32,* 47–69

Rheingold, H.L. (1988). The infant as a member of society. *Acta Paediatrica, 77,* 9–20.

Acknowledgments

Anyone who has conducted research in applied settings knows the true benefit of their work comes not just from learning *about* programs and people, but also from learning *with* and *from* them. We are grateful to our research partners in Early Head Start and early intervention programs across the nation who shared their time, experiences, and expertise with us. They helped broaden and deepen our questions and the meaning of our work. We also wish to thank our partners at work—the many colleagues and students who contributed their ideas and talents. Finally, we wish to thank our partners at home who give our lives meaning—our families.

To Early Head Start programs, personnel, and families

Partnerships and Pragmatics

Editor's Introduction

Susan Janko Summers

There is a basic human connection. Like water, we flow together.

—Oliver Stone (2009)

he preceding words may sound sentimental, poetic, or perhaps even cliché. But they are also profoundly true and grounded in science. Humans are linked to one another not only by habit and necessity. We are linked by our five senses, our mental concepts about ourselves and others, our sensations, our behaviors, and by the electrical and chemical activities in our brains that underlie these. The human brain is structured to support social connections, and social relationships comprise the environment in which the social brain develops and becomes so structured. We flow together like water, and we are also the water through which we flow.

Consider just a few of the many seen and unseen things occurring among infants and parents that support human connection.

- There is evidence that the brain chemistry of expectant fathers, like expectant mothers, changes during pregnancy making *both* parents more likely to bond with their newborns (Friedman, 2009).

- Just a few hours after birth, an infant shows a preference for her mother's face over others' faces (Field, Cohen, Garcia, & Greenberg, 1984). In turn, an infant's gaze makes her mother feel calm and stimulates the mother to nurture her baby.

- Less than an hour after birth, infants open their mouths and stretch out their tongues, reflexively imitating an adult model. Then infants imitate from memory 24 hours later—an early form of communication (Meltzoff & Moore, 1994). When infants imitate, mirror neurons in the brain are activated, a precursor to the infant's later ability to understand, react to and move with, or attune to caregivers.

- Skin-to-skin contact, or "emotional touch," such as kissing an infant's downy head or stroking a child's back as he or she falls asleep, soothes emotions, activates hormones, decreases blood pressure, leads to mild sedation, and aids the autonomic nervous system (Cozolino, 2006).

- When parents and babies play interactional games such as Peek-a-boo, a release of chemicals in the baby's and the parents' brains enhances energy and a sense of elation (Schore, 1997).

Psychologist Allan Schore (2001) tells us infant mental health is better defined as "psychoneurobiological" than as solely psychological (Schore, 2001). Infant and caregiver brains regulate one another during moment-to-moment interactions (Cozolino, 2006). In other words, through human interactions and relationships, our brains are built and rebuilt. During the first years of life, an infant's brain experiences critical or sensitive periods of particularly rapid growth and forms the neural networks and structural systems that influence functioning for the rest of life. During this time, primary caregivers are all important in shaping infant social and emotional development. In Cozolino's words, "Caregiver nurturance sets us on a course of physical and psychological health—or when it is lacking, disease and mental illness" (2006, p. 8).

At the heart of caregivers' nurturance is an ability to create a safe physical and emotional space surrounding their baby—a space in which the baby is free to grow, explore, and just be in the world. And at the heart of educators' work with infants and families is the job of creating that same kind of safe space. This type of space is relatively free from noise, demands, stress, and judgments. It is a space where educators and home visitors are psychologically present, consistently caring, listening with focused attention, and helping caregivers to observe their children carefully and to think about their parenting reflectively.

The authors of this book have experience creating just that kind of safe space and mindful attention with families, with programs, and with one another through their work on the Early Promotion and Intervention Research Consortium.

PARTNERSHIPS

In October 2000, the federal Early Head Start Program sponsored an Infant Mental Health Forum and began the Early Head Start Mental Health Initiative. The Initiative instituted policy and provided funding aimed at supporting research and innovative practice that would encourage the social and emotional development of young children and would support optimal caregiver–child relationships that make these possible. Out of this Initiative came the work of the Early Promotion and Intervention Research Consortium and a research agenda based upon partnerships with local programs.

For more than 5 years, the authors of this book worked with Early Head Start and early intervention programs to study infant mental health services for infants and families experiencing difficult life circumstances and to address the mental health problems that frequently accompany those circumstances (research on early intervention programs was funded by the U.S. Department of Education's Field Initiated Studies). *Understanding Early Childhood Mental Health: A Practical Guide for Professionals* is based upon their collaborative work. The five university-program partners conducted studies that included different populations and used different training and intervention models but common measures. Their research goals were to understand the risks to mental health that children and families experience, how organizations provide professional development and intervention, and how different interventions lead to differing outcomes for infants and their caregivers. To learn more about Consortium studies see Table 1.

The Consortium worked hand in hand in the field with Early Head Start and early intervention program personnel on the challenging task of incorporating infant mental health services in their day-to-day work. Although outcome studies are critically important to guide and support evidence-based practices in the field, they rarely show the reality of *how* researchers and programs work together. The complicated answer to the *how* question matters greatly in terms of whether research agendas make real differences to programs and to the children and families they serve.

To supplement the outcome studies the Consortium conducted, in my role as qualitative researcher for the Consortium, I interviewed the Consortium researchers about their partnerships with community programs in order to understand the *how* of their work. When I asked one researcher how her partnership project began, she explained to me that prior to the research she had been a mental health consultant to an Early Head Start program. She told me she had felt "wildly ineffective at actually helping most of the children or creating any sort of institutional change."

The honesty and forthrightness of her answer (and also her humor) was typical among the many researchers and program partners I interviewed. It seemed to say to me that there was unusual trust and respect present in their partnerships that permitted open, honest communication. When I further questioned the same researcher to learn how Consortium researchers went about nurturing trust during their collaboration with one another and with programs, she talked about how relationships exist within a space. Her words recall the space early childhood professionals hope caregivers will create for their children: "The space between people is a vibrant, living, flexible, real thing. And if that can be healthy, all things are possible."

Openness, honesty, and attention are the foundations for growth and change when people and programs endeavor to do something novel—something that they do not completely understand and that scares them a little, even while they know it is important.

But when early childhood programs create a space where honesty may occur, personnel may not always like what they hear. This Early Head Start program director talks openly about her experience incorporating infant mental health services prior to her research partnership and the changes program staff and researchers brought to her organization through their partnership.

> I went on the experience I had with the mental health specialist that was part time here. I really felt as though her idea of us was that it was just a lot of adolescent teenagers and the staff, the ignorant staff that was here and had no clue what to do, and they needed someone in the mental health field to tell them. And all I saw was her pushing pills and degrading the parents and the staff. I didn't see any support. . . . [Now when I think about infant mental health] I see support, nurturing,

Table 1. Consortium projects, participants, and outcomes

Project partners	Participants	Intervention model	Family risks/characteristics	Outcomes
Early Head Start and University of Oregon	Early Head Start staff	On-site mentoring, including infant mental health consultation, reflective supervision, and observation and review of videos of home visits	Predominately Caucasian, some Hispanic and mixed race; rural–suburban; regional economic instability	Increased staff competence and confidence and infant and toddler social-emotional competence
Early Head Start and University of Maryland	Early Head Start staff	Staff training and ongoing reflective supervision in promoting healthy infant and toddler interactions	African American; urban; poverty and family violence	Increased staff competence and confidence, increased infant and toddler social-emotional competence
Early Head Start and University of North Carolina	Early Head Start Spanish-speaking newly acculturating mothers with symptoms of depression	In-home, modified interpersonal therapy delivered by nursing–Early Head Start team with bilingual interpreters	Predominately Mexican; rural–suburban; destabilizing pressures of immigration and rapid acculturation	Reduced maternal depression, improved mother–child interactions, and improved infant and toddler social-emotional competence
Early Head Start and Tulane University	Early Head Start adolescent mothers	Two group-parenting interventions (Circle of Security compared with teacher-led Nurturing Parent curriculum)	African American adolescent mothers; urban–suburban; poverty and family violence	Increased parental sensitivity to infant cues for attachment and exploration
Early Head Start and University of Miami	Early Head Start parents and at-risk infants and toddlers	Specialized assessment of high-risk families followed by parent–infant/toddler psychotherapy	African American, Haitian, Caribbean, Hispanic/Latino; urban; poverty; neighborhood and family violence; pressures of immigration and rapid acculturation	Stronger parent–child attunement and attachment

Source: Beeber et al. (2007).

guidance, partnership. We work together to resolve whatever problems we have. And whatever those problems are, we can work through them. It's not as big as we see it or we make it out to be. Because there is support, and there are many people out there willing to help.

Her strong words and the missed understandings and opportunities they represent—although not necessarily true for all early education programs striving to incorporate infant mental health services—illustrate what people working in programs already know: there is often an uneasy relationship between mental health professionals and early childhood educators. The work of infant mental health, and this book, is equally about the importance of professional partnerships as it is about essential infant–caregiver relationships.

PRAGMATICS

More than one participant in these research studies reported feeling ineffective in his or her efforts to include infant mental health practice in his or her early education program. As one highly trained and experienced early interventionist told us, "You deal with [a multitude of family issues] all the time, but never really feel you've necessarily been trained to do it." Similar experiences motivated these researchers and programs to partner in these projects and to address these important questions: What makes mental health practice so difficult for educators? And what should be done about this?

Research shows that early childhood educators do not receive adequate foundational preservice graduate or undergraduate training in assessing social-emotional development and regulatory problems (Hadadian, Tomlin, & Sherwood-Puzzelloc, 2005; Steele, 1995). Shonkoff and Phillips, authors of the groundbreaking book *From Neurons to Neighborhoods*, noted that "the incapacity of many early childhood programs to address these concerns and the severe shortage of early childhood professionals with mental health expertise are urgent problems" (2000, p. 5). These inadequacies in the profession are worth careful consideration because social-emotional development and regulation—in addition to being of great importance in and of themselves—are closely linked to all developmental areas, especially cognitive development. It is also worth considering that early educators and interventionists are in uniquely intimate relationships with infants, toddlers, and their caregivers—often in their living rooms—on a regular basis. Not only do early educators have ample opportunity to observe social-emotional development and the caregiver contexts in which they occur (Chazan-Cohen, Jerald, & Stark, 2001), they can hardly avoid doing so. Educators Gilbert Foley and Jane Hochman cautioned that although "psychotherapy, specifically dyadic (infant–parent) psychotherapy, is the domain of specialized mental health professionals and may require additional specialized training and supervision . . . all staff can and do have an impact on infant, family, and infant-family emotional well-being" (2006, p. 129). It is of utmost importance to infant mental health that the influence educators have on children and families comes from a place of clear understandings, good intentions, and skillful interactions. But these are easier said than done.

Perhaps the challenges associated with infant mental health work are made clearer by the words of people working to incorporate infant mental health practices in their day-to-day practice. One challenge is that the roles and responsibilities associated with mental health care are outside the traditional boundaries of early educators' training and expertise. In a qualitative research study in one of the five Consortium sites (Summers, Funk, Twombly, Waddell, & Squires, 2007), a home visitor reminded her interviewer several times during an interview that "I'm not a mental health worker. I'm a toddler teacher." In contrast, an infant mental health mentor to several Early Head Start and early intervention programs told us that the educators and interventionists she worked with were willing to broaden traditional professional roles and to learn about infant mental health. In their day-to-day work, however, those willing educators and interventionists were not always able to recognize important indicators of mental health. Note what the mentor says about the home visitors she works with when they review video of home visits together. "They don't know what they see. . . . They don't know attachment and bonding. If you put a video on, and you ask questions, they don't know what it looks like." Without adequate training and support, it is unreasonable to expect that educators *would* be able to recognize children's social-emotional developmental markers, or attachment and bonding, or attunement and regulation behaviors among caregivers. This lack of knowledge and skills does not escape the notice of the educators themselves. As one home visitor told us, "I know intuitively when I'm not having an impact. I just don't know why."

In addition to training, the rawness of mental health issues and the difficult circumstances surrounding them also challenge early childhood educators and interventionists. Another mentor talked about the challenges to home visitors in terms of both their discomfort with mental health issues, and the absence of support to deal with those issues.

> I have had so many home visitors say, "Well, why do I want to talk to [families about mental health] when I don't think there is anybody out there that's going to be able to help them. And then what do I do?" And that's really valid. So then the home visitor is in more of a mode of "Let's try and contain it and just get these educational things done."

Even before the near collapse of America's financial system and subsequent record unemployment, many families in the Consortium studies experienced chronic stress and challenging circumstances that are perhaps best expressed by the words of one Consortium researcher. These words provide a feeling not only of the children's and families' life circumstances, but also how these influenced program staff and on the researchers.

> It's a wonder to me that they are not all depressed. The atmosphere is harsh. The resources are mean. . . . On a day-to-day basis, these families live in violent neighborhoods. They have people firing guns through their walls. They have drug dealing going on in their front porches. They have abusive partners, and abusive other people. They are crowded into spaces that are dark. And they experience constant sickness. . . . When you look at all the contextual factors, the stressors are very intense. It is like, "Do I feed my children, or do I pay the rent? Do I get medication for this asthmatic child, or do I keep the electricity on?" Huge, really harsh choices.

Despite—or perhaps because of—the discomfort program personnel must feel working with families in such difficult circumstances, there seems to be a general willingness among most educators and interventionists to incorporate infant mental health into their work, as illustrated in this interview excerpt with one of the Consortium researchers.

Eleven ways to support infant mental health in Early Head Start, education, and intervention programs

1. **Educate teachers, home visitors, and supervisors about social and emotional development and caregiver–child relationships.** Although emotions and social relationships are ordinary parts of life experienced by all, they are challenging to assess and to observe in the context of relationships. Educators must be able to recognize behavioral markers of social and emotional development and of positive caregiver–child interactions and to respond in helpful ways to children and families' psychological and social developmental needs. (See Chapter 1.)

2. **Make sure that all staff acquire and use skillful communication strategies.** Assessing development; assessing high-risk situations; understanding individual experiences and perspectives; establishing, maintaining, and modeling healthy relationships; offering support and guidance—these all are necessary for encouraging infant mental health, and all depend on skillful communication. (See Chapters 7 and 14.)

3. **Reach prospective parents early.** Every prospective parent and new parent needs—and often welcomes—information, education and developmental guidance. During these periods of family receptivity and of rapid and critically important infant development, support is more likely to make great and positive differences in infant development and parent–child relationships and to prevent later problems and distress. (See Chapters 6 and 7.)

4. **Establish protocol for recognizing and responding to exceptional needs.** As a regular part of program operation, early identification of mental health problems such as maternal depression, family violence, and failure to thrive, combined with follow-up services or referrals, will ensure access to the expertise and support infants and their families need, minimizing suffering and preventing further problems. (See Chapters 2, 3, and 5.)

5. **Establish protocol for recognizing and responding to child and family strengths as well as risks.** All human beings possess character strengths and virtues that when supported will lead them to happier lives and better relationships. Whenever possible, caregivers should take concrete steps to recognize and support child and family strengths, mediate and minimize risks, and mobilize support systems. (See Chapters 4, 5, and 7.)

6. **Provide a therapeutic environment.** Parents and children experiencing chronically difficult life circumstances may be bereft of models of communication and support for positive emotions. Programs can provide a culture of caring and communication and places of sanctuary—if only temporary—from stress-producing circumstances. (See Chapters 8, 9, 10, and 13.)

7. **Foster healthy nutrition and daily living patterns in families.** Positive mental health is supported by good physical health and positive environmental supports, including clean air and water; freedom from noise and crowding; sanitary surroundings; access to health and dental care; regular daily routines; and access to positive activities such as spiritual and religious practice, educational opportunities, and community participation. (See Chapters 9, 10, and 13.)

(continued)

(continued)

8. **Allocate sufficient time and resources to qualified mental health staff or consultants.** Many children and families experience chronic life and relationship problems on a day-to-day basis that compromise their daily happiness and long-term well-being. Children's and families' psychosocial needs should be reasonably and ethically met within the educational program whenever possible; when child and family needs extend beyond the program's scope and professional and ethical boundaries, provisions for outside services should be made. (See Chapters 9 and 10.)

9. **Make reflective supervision an ongoing practice.** Effective education depends upon teachers' and home visitors' ability to think critically and solve problems. Reflective supervision models, including mentoring, support continuous growth in knowledge, skill, and compassion—qualities that are fundamental to optimal growth and healthy relationships. (See Chapters 11 and 14.)

10. **Provide support to teachers, home visitors, and supervisors for compassion fatigue and secondary stress.** In order for program personnel to have healthy personal relationships with co-workers, and to support healthy relationships among children and families experiencing challenging circumstances, those program personnel must maintain their own mental health. (See Chapter 12.)

11. **Gather broad evidence to show that a program works—and how it works— by starting a conversation with families, staff, and community.** The essence of good program evaluation is recognizing what matters most to families, staff, and community and including their input in an evaluation to complement evidence-based practice. Some of what matters can be readily measured by standardized tests and observations. Other things must be measured in ways that deepen understanding of how the program is experienced by families and staff, how it benefits and is valued by the surrounding culture and community, and how it may offer services that are helpful and meaningful. (See Chapter 14.)

I think we have probably met with every single home visitor who is doing [infant mental health] intervention, and I always hustle them about the importance of infant mental health, how everything they do with the mother is contributing to infant mental health, and that we are going to work with them on some more focused ways for them to do it. And they all seem to really appreciate it. So something really good is coming . . . probably through the training and performance standards. It is not a new message to them. They just need to know how to do it. Or how what they are already doing is related.

One mental health consultant's experience with the program staff she mentored was similar to that of the researcher quoted earlier. The consultant told us with regard to the gap between staff willingness and performance, "The difference is between the wanting and the doing."

Through their partnerships with people and programs performing the day-to-day practice of infant mental health, the Consortium has learned some things about *what* to do and *how* to do it. The box beginning on the previous page provides an overview of these eleven ways to support infant mental health in Early Head Start, education, and intervention programs. It is the authors' hope that what the Consortium learned from their research and from their program partners helps to make real and important differences in infant mental health services in early education.

EARLY PROMOTION AND INTERVENTION RESEARCH CONSORTIUM PUBLICATIONS

Administration on Children, Youth, and Families. (2000). *A commitment to supporting the mental health of our youngest children: Report from infant mental health forum.* Washington, DC: U.S. Department of Health and Human Services.

Beeber, L.S., Chazan-Cohen, R., Squires, J., Jones Harden, B., Boris, N., Heller, S.S., & Malik, N.M. (2007). The Early Promotion and Intervention Research Consortium (E-PIRC): Five approaches to improving infant/toddler mental health in Early Head Start. *Infant Mental Health Journal, 28*(2), 130–150.

Beeber, L.S., Holditch-Davis, D., Perreira, K., Schwartz, T., Lewis, V., Blanchard, H., Canuso, R., & Goldman, B. (2010). Short-term, in-home intervention reduces depressive symptoms in Early Head Start Latina mothers of infants and toddlers. *Research in Nursing and Health, 33*(1), 60–76.

Beeber, L.S., Lewis, V., Cooper, C., Maxwell, L., & Sandelowski, M. (2009). Meeting the "now" need: PMH-APRN-interpreter teams provide in-home mental health intervention for depressed Latina mothers with limited English proficiency. *Journal of the American Psychiatric Nurses Association, 15*, 249–259.

Beeber, L.S., Perreira, K.M., & Schwartz, T. (2008). Supporting the mental health of mothers raising children in poverty: How do we target them for intervention studies? In S.G. Kaler & O. M. Rennert (Eds.) *Reducing the impact of poverty on health and human development* (Vol. 1, pp. 86–100). New York: Wiley-Blackwell.

Chazan-Cohen, R., Jerald, J., & Stark, D. (2001). A commitment to supporting the mental health of our youngest children. *Zero to Three, 22* (1), 4–12.

Chazan-Cohen, R., Stark, D.R., Mann, T.L., & Fitzgerald, H.E. (2007). Early Head Start and infant mental health. *Infant Mental Health Journal, 28*(2), 9–105.

Heller, S.S., & Gilkerson, L. (Eds.). (2009). *A practical guide to reflective supervision.* Washington, DC: ZERO TO THREE Press.

Jones Harden, B., Denmark, N., & Saul, D. (2010). Understanding the needs of staff in Head Start programs: The characteristics, perceptions, and experiences of home visitors. *Children and Youth Services Review, 32*, 371–379.

Malik, N.M., Boris, N., Heller, S.S., Jones Harden, B., Squires, J., Chazan-Cohen, R., Beeber, L.S., & Kaczynski, K.J. (2007). Risk for maternal depression and child aggression in Early Head Start families: A test of ecological models. *Infant Mental Health Journal, 28*(2), 171–191.

Summers, S.J., Funk, K., Twombly, L., Waddell, M., & Squires, J. (2007). The explication of a mentor model, videotaping, and reflective supervision in support of infant mental health. *Infant Mental Health Journal, 28*(2), 216–236.

Westbrook, T., Jones Harden, B., Holmes, A., Meisch, A., & Vick Whittaker, J. (in press). Physical discipline use and toddler behavior problems in low-income, African American families. *Early Education and Development.*

REFERENCES

Beeber, L.S., Chazan-Cohen, R., Squires, J., Harden, B.J., Boris, N.W., Heller, S.S., & Malik, N. (2007). The Early Promotion and Intervention Research Consortium (E-PIRC): Five approaches to improving infant/toddler mental health in Early Head Start. *Infant Mental Health Journal, 28*(2), 130–150.

Chazan-Cohen, R., Jerald, J., & Stark, D.R. (2001). A commitment to supporting the health of our youngest children, *Zero to Three, 22*(1), 4–12.

Cozolino, L. (2006). *The neuroscience of relationships: Attachment and the developing social brain.* New York: W.W. Norton.

Field, T., Cohen, D., Garcia, R., & Greenberg, R. (1984). Mother-stranger face discrimination by the newborn. *Infant Behavior and Development, 7,* 19–25.

Foley, G.M., & Hochman, J.D. (Eds.). (2006). *Mental health in early intervention: Achieving unity in principles and practice.* Baltimore: Paul H. Brookes Publishing Co.

Friedman, R.A. (2009, December 8). Postpartum depression strikes fathers, too. *New York Times,* p. D6.

Hadadian, A., Tomlin, A.M., & Sherwood-Puzzelloc, C.M. (2005). Early intervention service providers: What do they say about their infant mental health training needs? *Early Child Development and Care, 175*(5), 431–444.

Meltzoff, A.N., & Moore, M.K. (1994). Imitation, memory, and the representation of persons. *Infant Behavior and Development, 17,* 83–99.

Schore, A.N. (1997). Early organization of the non-linear right brain and development of a predisposition to psychiatric disorders. *Development and Psychopathology, 9,* 595–631.

Schore, A.N. (2001). Effects of a secure attachment relationship on right brain development, affect regulation, and infant mental health. *Infant Mental Health Journal, 22*(1–2), 7–66.

Shonkoff, J.P., & Phillips, D.A. (Eds.). (2000). *From neurons to neighborhoods: The science of early childhood development.* Washington, DC: National Academies Press.

Steele, L. (1995). Integrating infant mental health practices into Part H: Evolution of a local early intervention program. *Infants and Young Children, 11*(1), 73–83.

Stone, O. (2009, December 4). Excerpt from interview on *Bill Moyers Journal.* Retrieved July 11, 2011, from http://www.pbs.org/moyers/journal/12042009/transcript1.html

Summers, S.J., Funk, K., Twombly, L., Waddell, M., & Squires, J. (2007). The explication of a mentor model, videotaping, and reflective supervision in support of infant mental health. *Infant Mental Health Journal, 28*(2), 216–236.

I

Understanding Infant Mental Health

Development and Relationships

Susan Janko Summers

Those reading *Understanding Early Childhood Mental Health: A Practical Guide for Professionals* are probably already convinced of the importance of supporting infant mental health through early childhood education and intervention. Perhaps practitioners wish to relieve the suffering of a young child and the child's caregiver after they experienced trauma. Perhaps practitioners have witnessed firsthand how children's social-emotional problems influence their behavior and learning in other areas such as language or early literacy skills. Or perhaps they are familiar with research that shows how adverse conditions experienced during early childhood—such as exposure to abuse; emotional neglect; or caregivers with drug, alcohol, or mental health problems—greatly increase the likelihood that children will experience increased psychosocial and even serious health problems throughout their lifetimes. (See, e.g., Centers for Disease Control and Prevention, n.d.)

Even practitioners who are convinced of the importance of infant mental health may be uncertain about how to begin to effectively incorporate principles of infant mental health in their daily practice. Some practitioners in our partnership programs expressed their reluctance to tackle something so huge. In fact, the only way to begin to change something as big and important as infant mental health is through small, intentional, and informed acts in daily practice with children and families. This first section of *Understanding Early Childhood Mental Health* provides guidance to individual practitioners in recognizing important indicators of healthy social and emotional development and caregiving relationships.

In Chapter 1, Roderick Stark and Chazan-Cohen situate social-emotional development in the contexts of global child health and development and in family and culture. Chapter 1 also provides an overview of the professional field of infant mental health and identifies the challenges that early childhood professionals and programs are likely to encounter when designing and delivering infant mental health services. In Chapter 2 and Chapter 3 respectively, Malik presents practical information to help early childhood professionals recognize and respond to challenging child behavior such as anger or depression, and Beeber and Chazan-Cohen describe ways to recognize and respond to maternal depression. In Chapter 4, authors Monahan, Beeber, and Jones Harden present models of risk and resilience as a foundation for understanding how development is influenced by a child's individual and family ecology. In Chapter 5, the ways exposure to chronically stressful or traumatic circumstances affects child development, psychological well-being, and caregiving relationships are described by Yoches, Summers, Beeber, Jones Harden, and Malik. Finally, Squires's Chapter 6 and Boris and Page's Chapter 7 describe how early childhood programs can go about assessing early social-emotional development and caregiver–child relationships as the foundation for designing infant mental health interventions.

REFERENCE

Centers for Disease Control and Prevention. (n.d.). *Adverse Childhood Experiences Study (ACES)*. Retrieved June 15, 2011, from http://www.cdc.gov/ace/outcomes.htm

1

Understanding Infant Mental Health

Deborah Roderick Stark and Rachel Chazan-Cohen

*M*ost children come into the world with 10 fingers, 10 toes, and everything in between preprogrammed for success. If they are born with sufficient capabilities and experience a "good enough" caregiving environment, they are usually on an optimal path. They quickly learn about empathy when they cry and find loving hands that cuddle and soothe them. They learn about reciprocal relationships when they coo and receive a happy coo in return. They learn about trust when a plea for help is responded to promptly and consistently. And they learn about safety when, as the result of a smile or a cry, there is a kind gesture and reassuring touch that tells them all is okay. Above all, they learn that they are special and others delight in their being.

For these children, forming a secure emotional attachment with their parents and caregivers is natural and rewarding. This attachment provides the springboard for healthy exploration of their environment so that they can learn about the world around them and then return to their secure base when they are stressed or need to decompress. These children are developing healthy senses of self and others, which are critical components to positive social-emotional development and mental health.

But some children, due to circumstances beyond their control, experience social–emotional challenges that compromise their development. Whether these challenges are physiological or environmental, they alter the normal trajectory of child development. Such children may have a challenging temperament, be difficult to console, resist physical contact, or have trouble sleeping and calming themselves. They may have parents who are stressed due to poverty, lack of resources, lack of social support, or mental illness. For some children, these challenges pose minimal risk and can be easily addressed with limited intervention. For others, the challenges can jeopardize development, significantly altering their physical, social, and emotional growth and future potential. These children and their parents often need access to more specialized, targeted mental health services and supports delivered by infant mental health specialists.

Increasingly, early care and education providers encounter infants, toddlers, and young preschoolers in their care who have emotional challenges and for whom the regular child care environment is not sufficiently prepared to address their complex needs, as in the following examples.

Jared, a 15-month-old boy, has not been himself lately. His mother reports that he cries for long periods each night before bed. She also says that he has developed a new habit of throwing his food on the floor, so he makes a mess of himself and the apartment and barely eats. She is tired of cleaning up his messes and frustrated that he's wasting food. When he does finally eat, he often throws up what he has eaten. His child care provider has noticed that he seems more tired and less easy to console when frustrated. His frequent outbursts startle the other children in the program, especially the younger ones. Rocking him and playing soft music seem to provide some relief, but it is difficult for the provider to hold just Jared for long periods when there are other children in her care who need her attention as well.

Jared's mother is the primary contact with the provider, dropping Jared off each morning and picking him up in the evening after her shift as a clerk at a local convenience store. Since losing his job due to downsizing, Jared's father has started picking Jared up 1 or 2 days a week, but not until very late in the day. Jared has difficulty with separation at drop-off but seems indifferent in the evenings when either his mother or father picks him up. The child care provider has talked with Jared's parents about his outbursts and the strategies they are trying to use to console him and has asked that Jared's parents try to ensure that he gets enough sleep each night. Jared's mother appears frustrated and overburdened and comments that getting him to sleep longer is easier said than done.

Sophie, a 6-month-old girl and the third child in her family, is failing to gain weight. Her mother compares Sophie's size and listlessness to the development of her older children, who at a similar age were spirited bundles of joy. Sophie's mother is concerned but not sure what to do. She asked the pediatrician for help. Blood tests for common childhood illnesses all came back negative. The pediatrician suggested that Sophie's disposition might just be different from her older sisters' and recommended supplementing with formula to see if Sophie would start gaining weight. Unsatisfied, Sophie's mother turned to the early intervention (EI) program in her community to see if she could persuade it to conduct a developmental assessment. Other family members thought she was overreacting, suggested that Sophie was just going to be a smaller child, and dismissed her concern that something was wrong. Following her instinct and with persistence, her mother ultimately learned that Sophie was challenged by failure to thrive.

Box 1.1. Approaches to intervention in early education settings

Promotion is what parents and caregivers do in their everyday interactions with infants when they listen attentively, respond contingently, and provide the security of a stable caregiving environment and social relationships.

Prevention is what parents and caregivers do when they provide guidance and redirection of emerging behaviors that might grow into issues of emotional or behavioral concern.

Treatment is what mental health professionals provide to address a mental health issue that requires a systematic and sometimes therapeutic intervention.

For most children and parents, intervention at the promotion level is sufficient—although at times of transition, stress, or loss, a higher degree of intervention might be required. For children and families living with several risk factors, a more proactive prevention intervention that offers anticipation, guidance, and support can keep children on the track of healthy development and happy social relationships. Treatment is called for during times of difficulty for any family and for those experiencing toxic or constant levels of stress.

Jared and Sophie are not unique. Although the actual incidence and prevalence of infant mental health problems for all infant and toddler populations are difficult to gauge, Neena Malik and her colleagues at the University of Miami reported that 71% of children attending Early Head Start programs had experienced at least one trauma in their young lives. These traumas included serious illness or injury, a prolonged separation from their primary caregiver, homelessness, death of a close relative, and violence in home or community (Malik, 2007). Furthermore, the Early Head Start Research and Evaluation Project, a national study of 17 Early Head Start programs, found that more than half of mothers were struggling with feelings of depression at the time they enrolled their children in the program (U.S. Department of Health and Human Services, 2006). Exposure to these kinds of traumas and difficult life circumstances place children and caregivers at increased risk for mental health problems. Fortunately, advances in practice and research are helping to demystify infant mental health and are pointing the way to promising interventions that can support the continuum of early social and emotional development through promotion, prevention, and treatment. This book is intended to help early childhood and intervention practitioners and administrators understand the latest in both research and practice so that they and their programs are better able to appropriately and effectively respond to the children and families in their care.

THE MEANING OF MENTAL HEALTH

Professor of child psychiatry Dr. Charles Zeanah defined infant mental health as "the state of emotional and social competence in young children who are developing appropriately within the interrelated contexts of biology, relationship and culture" (Zeanah & Zeanah,

2001, p. 13). This definition stresses that infants are imbedded within physical, psychological, social, and cultural contexts, and these multiple contexts must be taken into consideration when assessing a child's social and emotional functioning. Dr. Zeanah went on
to say that assessment of social and emotional development must also center on the
whole child. Development trajectories across domains (i.e., areas of related developmental skills such as language skills or cognitive skills) are important for understanding
infant competence, because development in one area, or domain, influences and is influenced by skills in another developmental domain. For example, exposure to trauma
may affect a child's emotional state, which may in turn affect the child's willingness
to communicate with others despite the child's possession of language skills. Further
complicating the understanding and recognition of infant mental health problems, a
child's mental health can be compromised by factors internal to the child, such as chronic
physical illness, or external factors, such as neglectful caregiving, that increase the risk
of suffering.

THE IRONY OF INFANT MENTAL HEALTH

The juxtaposition of the words *infant* and *mental health* cause many to stop and to wonder. The word *infant* brings to mind something fresh, promising—a new beginning. The
words *mental health* conjure up the image of impaired mental health or mental illness and
bring to mind something wanting, sorrowful, debilitating. And in our culture of individual
strength and achievement, the words *mental health* may even bring to mind something
shameful. How could these words be combined? How could something so fresh and new
also be sorrowful and debilitating? Painful to acknowledge as it may be, infant mental
health issues exist, and are scarring the futures of many. Psychiatrist Robert Emde has
eloquently voiced that infants are suffering and that because of discomfort, adults often
try to deny this suffering, thereby compromising children's well-being (Chazan-Cohen,
Jerald, & Stark, 2001).

Educators can no longer turn a blind eye to this suffering or hope that things will get
better in time. To reduce the immediate suffering and long-term negative consequences
of impaired infant mental health, it is necessary to focus on mental health promotion and
treatment for the youngest, most vulnerable children and their families.

ENVIRONMENTAL INFLUENCES
ON INFANT MENTAL HEALTH

The work of developmental psychologist and Head Start cofounder Urie Bronfenbrenner
serves as a reminder that children develop within the contexts of family and community
and that they affect, and are affected by, relationships and experiences within each context. Parents and families are aware that family and community contexts are influenced
by broader, more diffuse economic and political contexts. To the infant, the caregiver is
the essential partner and the most influential context. The caregiving context exerts extraordinary power in the infant's day-to-day life, for there is no other stage in the human
life cycle during which a child is totally dependent upon caregivers for basic survival. The
immediate well-being—and ultimate development—of infants is highly contingent upon

the security of their relationships and experiences and the health and stability of the broader environment in which they live.

Compromised Development

Infants are complex beings with development occurring along multiple dimensions at varying rates. From social and emotional development to cognitive, linguistic, and physical development, each infant forges his or her own path. Whereas developmental milestones provide a guide for the trajectory of "average" development, parents, caregivers, and pediatricians all recognize that it is highly individualized for each child. As noted, they also realize the interrelatedness of these dimensions, so that an infant lagging in emotional development may also experience a compromised ability to engage in cognitive tasks and vice versa. In addition, although individual children develop at their own rates, the nature of developmental change for infants and toddlers is continuous and the rate of change is typically very rapid.

In fact, in the groundbreaking book *From Neurons to Neighborhoods* (2000), Jack Shonkoff and Deborah Phillips highlighted the brain's plasticity (or potential for change) and the critical role that early experiences play in shaping the brain's development. The brain grows more rapidly during the first 3 years than at any other time; therefore, a child's earliest experiences have long-term effects. Furthermore, caregiving interactions literally build the healthy brain architecture, or neurological structures and connections, necessary for future healthy development. As Dr. Shonkoff (2006) stated,

> Recurrent and excessive stress in the absence of protective relationships results in persistent activation of the body's stress-management systems, which includes the continuous elevation of serum cortisol. These increased hormone levels undermine the immune response and disrupt brain architecture by impairing cell growth and interfering with the formation of healthy neural circuits. (p. 2188)

Whereas some stress even promotes positive development, high levels of stress can be detrimental. Strong, supportive, positive environments can make even ongoing stress tolerable; however, toxic stress can lead to irreparable damage. Shonkoff (2006) used *toxic stress* to refer to

> Strong, frequent, and/or prolonged activation of the body's stress-management systems in the absence of the buffering protection of adult support. Precipitants include extreme poverty, recurrent physical and/or emotional abuse, chronic neglect, severe maternal depression, parental substance abuse, and family violence. (p. 2189)

Biological Challenges

For some infants, biological challenges threaten their social and emotional development and can also make parenting more challenging. Infants born at very low birth weight, who have other early medical complications such as chronic medical conditions, or who are one of multiple births (e.g., twins, triplets) can be more difficult to parent and are at higher risk for mental health issues—even for experiencing abuse. Temperament is an important biological factor that can also pose challenges. Just as there are some infants who naturally have a permanent carefree smile, there are others who are exceedingly difficult to console, who may fear new things or physical contact, or who find particular textures, smells, and sounds repulsive. (See Chapter 2 for more information on temperament.) In all of these cases, an innate biological challenge causes the infant duress and interferes with the development of relationships that facilitate strong mental health.

Challenging Relationships

The relationships infants have with their parents and other caregivers influence their overall development and emotional well-being. Strong, nurturing relationships facilitate healthy emotional development, including an infant or toddler's ability to organize experiences and cope with stress. Weak and indifferent relationships lead to a compromised sense of self and emotional insecurity. Infants who do not form secure attachments with their primary caregivers are more challenged in that they spend more energy and attention worried about having their desires understood and basic needs met, resulting in less energy to devote to learning from people and objects in their environments.

Although the strength of relationships is important, so too is the health and emotional well-being of the adult with whom the child is most closely attached. A growing number of studies highlight a direct correlation between maternal depression and troublesome infant mental health issues (Beardslee, 2002; Coyl, Roggman, & Newland, 2002; Field, 1998; National Scientific Council on the Developing Child, n.d.). Clearly, not all depressed parents have trouble parenting. However, research shows that depression tends to be associated with less sensitive and responsive parenting, taking the form of parents disengaging from their child or behaving in a harsh or angry way. It is this parenting that results in poorer outcomes for children, which underlines the dire need to develop, support, and fund interventions focused on the dyad so that both the infant and his or her mother receive comprehensive mental health services. Fathers should not be left out of the treatment mix, as their active, supportive involvement can bring about positive results for all. Furthermore, although most research has not focused on fathers, paternal depression is likely to affect the child directly as well as the family environment (National Academy of Sciences, 2009). (See Chapter 7 for more about parent–child attachment.)

Lacking the coping mechanisms to diffuse frustration, some infants and toddlers express their emotions in ways that might be interpreted as inappropriate aggression or incontrollable behavior. All too often parents and other caregivers equate such disruptive behavior with defiance and grow frustrated with the child's outbursts. Left unchecked, infant frustration fuels caregiver frustration and can spiral into an emotionally harmful relationship for both infant and caregiver.

In very extreme cases where infants' relationships with their primary caregivers are marked by abuse, neglect, and trauma, the child's emotional well-being can be severely compromised. When children's sense of personal safety is threatened, their sense of trust is crushed. Research shows that those children exposed to violence or neglect in the earliest years are more likely to display problem behaviors and lag significantly behind their peers in language and cognitive development (U.S. Department of Health and Human Services, n.d.). Chapters 3 and 5 discuss experiences that pose challenges to the

Box 1.2. Stress in early childhood

What happens when human beings experience psychological stress? Their brains naturally produce chemical and neural responses. These responses are designed to help human survival during times of stress. But the same responses may also result in negative outcomes such as physical health problems and compromised brain development. As journalist and public policy expert Dorian Friedman explained in an important publication by the National Scientific Council on the Developing Child,

> Whether stressful events are toxic, tolerable, or positive depends on how much of a bodily stress response they provoke and how long that response lasts. These, in turn, depend on whether the stressful event is controllable, whether the child has safe relationships to turn to for support, and how often and for how long the body's stress system has been activated in the past. (n.d., p. 3)

Friedman described toxic stress as resulting from "stressful events that are chronic, uncontrollable, and/or experienced without the child having access to support from caring adults" (p. 3).

Whereas most early intervention and Early Head Start programs are designed to address risk factors that children and families are experiencing, the stress that accompanies risk is also important for programs to consider. Although programs may not always be able to immediately address or eliminate all sources of risk in a child's or family's life, helping to build supportive caregiving relationships is key in minimizing toxic stress and making it tolerable for children and families. In fact, tolerable stress may even have positive outcomes, such as deepening compassion and strengthening the child's ability to deal with future adversity.

development of a secure parent–child relationship: maternal depression and traumatic experiences. Chapter 7 reviews the assessment of parent– and caregiver–child relationships.

At-Risk Environments

Many have noted that the physical and psychosocial environments surrounding children and families also influence children's emotional and physical health and well-being. According to the National Center for Children in Poverty, of the more than 12 million infants and toddlers younger than age 3 in the United States, 44%—5.6 million children—live in low-income families. More than half of those—2.9 million children—live in poor families (Wight & Chau, 2009).

Although federal poverty statistics are important for understanding the scope of the problem in society, they do not convey the impact of poverty on human beings in their day-to-day lives. Children living in poverty are less likely than their peers to have comprehensive health insurance, less likely to have access to high-quality early childhood opportunities, and more likely to experience social and emotional challenges (Wagmiller & Adelman, 2009). Likewise, their parents, who are likely to have been reared in poverty as well, live with the stresses of needing to provide shelter, food, and resources for their children.

Professor Gary Evans (2004) at Cornell University's College of Human Ecology studies the effects of cumulative risk on children living in poverty:

> Poor children confront widespread environmental inequities. Compared with their economically advantaged counterparts, they are exposed to more family turmoil, violence, separation from their families, instability, and chaotic households. Poor children experience less social support, and their parents are less responsive and more authoritarian. Low-income children are read to relatively infrequently, watch more TV, and have less access to books and computers. . . . The air and water poor children consume are more polluted. Their homes are more crowded, noisier, and of lower quality. Low-income neighborhoods are more dangerous, offer poorer municipal services, and suffer greater physical deterioration. (p. 77)

Dr. Evans (2006) warned that the accumulation of multiple environmental risks, compared to exposure to a single risk, increases the likelihood of related relationship problems—such as elevated child aggression and social withdrawal and less responsive parenting—and developmental problems—such as reduced IQ and increased hyperactivity, impulsivity, and aggression from exposure to environmental toxins such as lead or mercury.

Special mention must also be made of infants and toddlers who have entered the child welfare system. Infants account for the fastest-growing age group of children in foster care. Most EI programs have served children who are receiving child welfare services or who have been removed from parental care. An infant with a mental health challenge who is also uprooted from family and thrust into an out-of-home placement can suffer further trauma. This is not to say that the out-of-home placement is inappropriate but rather that the emotional upheaval created by such a change for any child can be immense and will require attention from programs serving these children.

Social isolation creates another set of environmental risks for infants and their parents. Compared to a generation ago, infants and their parents are more likely to be living far from extended family. This distance can create a vast ravine, leaving new parents isolated and alone at a time when they want guidance and support to navigate parenthood.

THE CHALLENGE OF INTEGRATING MENTAL HEALTH SERVICES INTO EARLY EDUCATION AND INTERVENTION PROGRAMS

Recognizing and addressing mental health needs of children has long challenged early education and intervention programs, child care programs, and school systems. Since the late 1990s, advances have been made, yet programs continue to find the challenges outlined in this section daunting.

Stigma

Stigma associated with the notion of impaired mental health is a huge challenge for caregivers and parents alike. Despite all that the mental health community has done over the years to attempt to dispel the negative connotation of mental health issues, far too many people still lack the full understanding and appreciation of social and emotional development (U.S. Department of Health and Human Services, 1999). For some cultural groups, the stigma of mental health challenges can be so severe that families may be looked down upon; they might be shunned or isolated, left to wonder why and how they will recover and support their child. For all practical purposes, stigma becomes discrimination, and the result is all too often a real misunderstanding of what the infant needs and how families and caregivers can best be supported in meeting those needs.

Reluctance to Intervene

For many early childhood programs, staff may feel reluctant to intervene in what they believe is a private and autonomous relationship between parent and child. They may witness the distraught infant who cries uncontrollably as the parent arrives for pick-up at the end of a long workday. Or they may experience the infant who is reluctant to form a relationship with anyone, seemingly indifferent to the parent as well as the staff. They may overhear unhappy exchanges between parents while also noticing a change in the infant's behavior or sleep patterns at the program. In any of these instances, caregivers can choose to look the other way and not intervene, or they can choose to do something and make a genuine connection with the parent, acknowledge the potential challenge, and determine whether additional support could be helpful for the infant and the family.

Gaps in Training, Mentoring, and Reflective Supervision

Despite a growing body of research on infant mental health and expanding opportunities for training through national organizations and early childhood professional development programs, few early childhood program educators and administrators receive the formal training—preservice or in service—they need to fully understand, appreciate, and appropriately respond to infant and family mental health challenges. Without a staff who understand the continuum of promotion, prevention, and treatment and the role that they play in this continuum, programs are unable to fully address the mental health challenges experienced by the infants and families in their program. Furthermore, without supervisors and program administrators who are also schooled in infant mental health, it is a challenge for programs to carry out such practices. Most communities do not have the resources to support programs, and they lack referral sources for those families who require specialized services.

The role of early childhood programs is first and foremost to promote mental wellness in the child by supporting the parent–child relationship and providing supportive and consistent caregiving relationships for children in settings that are safe for exploration and learning. By working directly with children to optimize their coping and problem-solving strategies, and by working with parents to support them in their parenting roles, programs can also prevent issues from arising. However, there will always be a sizable portion of children and families who, at some point, are going to need additional help and support. Trusted early childhood program staff can be central in helping families recognize a problem and in providing links to services, if needed. Therefore, staff need to be aware of problems or issues that might arise during these formative years, be able to recognize signs of trouble, feel confident in taking the first steps with families toward getting help, and have someplace to turn to for additional specialized services.

Lack of Funding

Even when programs are fortunate to have staff who are fully trained and capable of providing the full continuum of mental health services and supports to infants and their families, the funding streams that programs have access to will not reimburse for mental health services. Federal and state funding for early childhood services barely cover the cost of quality child care, let alone the added costs for potentially longer-term supports and services needed by infants and families with mental health challenges. For those children who qualify for Medicaid's Early Periodic Screening, Diagnosis, and Treatment, the program will pay for some initial services but not ongoing treatment. Ensuring that funding is available for treating children and caregivers is essential. Private insurance is increasingly likely to cover some mental health services but still will not cover the full cost of care.

Mental Health Needs of Early Childhood Personnel

The emotional challenges experienced by early childhood and EI personnel who provide services to high-risk populations and in high-risk communities cannot be underestimated. The experiences, environment, and conditions in which they work can have a negative impact on their own mental health—from stress to fear and depression. For caregivers to be effective in the delivery of high-quality early childhood services, their own mental health needs must be examined and addressed. Programs must recognize this challenge and provide a host of supports (e.g., mentoring, reflective supervision) and services (e.g., counseling, therapy)—either directly in house or through referrals—in order to support the mental health needs of staff.

Benefits of Integrating Mental Health Services into Early Education and Intervention Programs

When mental health services are integrated effectively in early childhood programs, the developmental trajectory for children is improved, peer relations among children are enhanced, parent–child and intrafamily relationships are more satisfying, and there is decreased maternal depression. For caregivers, this integration translates into increased competence and confidence in addressing the needs of very young children and their families and a less stressful program environment. For programs, this integration means a stronger commitment to and match for real child, family, and community needs that is driven by a desire to understand the unique situation of each child and family and to respectfully work in partnership with the family to strengthen the overall, long-term development of the child.

This book provides background information on the contributions of the child, parent, and caregiver–child relationship, as well as the contextual factors influencing infant mental health. It then addresses how to assess children and the parenting relationship and proposes effective strategies that can be used to enhance infant mental health. We strongly believe that engaging in the strategies described in this book will lead to important benefits to children, parents, and program staff.

STRESS IN EARLY CHILDHOOD

What happens when human beings experience psychological stress? Their brains naturally produce chemical and neural responses. These responses are designed to help human survival during times of stress. But the same responses may also result in negative outcomes such as physical health problems and compromised brain development. As journalist and public policy expert Dorian Friedman explained in an important publication by the National Scientific Council on the Developing Child,

> Whether stressful events are toxic, tolerable, or positive depends on how much of a bodily stress response they provoke and how long that response lasts. These, in turn, depend on whether the stressful event is controllable, whether the child has safe relationships to turn to for support, and how often and for how long the body's stress system has been activated in the past. (n.d., p. 3)

Friedman described toxic stress as resulting from "stressful events that are chronic, uncontrollable, and/or experienced without the child having access to support from caring adults" (p. 3).

Whereas most EI and Early Head Start programs are designed to address risk factors that children and families are experiencing, the stress that accompanies risk is also important for programs to consider. Although programs may not always be able to immediately address or eliminate all sources of risk in a child's or family's life, helping to build supportive caregiving relationships is key in minimizing toxic stress and making it tolerable for children and families. In fact, tolerable stress may even have positive outcomes, such as deepening compassion and strengthening the child's ability to deal with future adversity.

REFERENCES

Beardslee, W.R. (2002). *Out of the darkened room. When a parent is depressed: Protecting the children and strengthening the family.* Boston: Little, Brown.

Beeber, L.S., Chazan-Cohen, R., Squires, J., Jones Harden, B., Boris, N., Heller, S.S., et al. (2007). The Early Promotion and Intervention Research Consortium (E-PIRC): Five approaches to improving infant/toddler mental health in Early Head Start. *Infant Mental Health Journal, 28*(2), 130–150.

Chazan-Cohen, R., Jerald, J., & Stark, D. (2001). A commitment to supporting the mental health of our youngest children. *Zero to Three, 22*(1), 4–12.

Coyl, D.D., Roggman, L.A., & Newland, L.A. (2002). Stress, maternal depression, and negative mother-infant interactions in relation to infant attachment. *Infant Mental Health Journal, 23*(1–2), 145–163.

Evans, G. (2004). The environment of childhood poverty. *American Psychologist, 59*(2), 77–92.

Evans, G. (2006). Child development and the physical environment. *Annual Reviews of Psychology, 57,* 423–329.

Field, T. (1998). Maternal depression effects on infants and early interventions. *Preventive Medicine, 27*(2), 200–203.

Friedman, D. (n.d.). *Stress and the architecture of the brain.* Retrieved June 14, 2011, from www.begin withthebrain.com/resources/stress_article.pdf

Malik, N. (2007, June). *Trauma exposure and intervention in Early Head Start families.* Paper presented at the 11th Annual Birth to Three Institute, Washington, DC.

National Academy of Sciences, Board on Children, Youth and Families. (2009). *Depression in parents, parenting, and children: Opportunities to improve identification, treatment, and prevention.* Retrieved June 14, 2011, from http://www.iom.edu/Reports/2009/Depression-in-Parents-Parenting-and-Children -Opportunities-to-Improve-Identification-Treatment-and-Prevention.aspx

National Scientific Council on the Developing Child. (n.d.). *Maternal depression can undermine the development of young children.* Working paper #8. Cambridge, MA: Harvard University Center on the Developing Child.

Shonkoff, J.P. (2006). A promising opportunity for developmental and behavioral pediatrics at the interface of neuroscience, psychology, and social policy: Remarks on receiving the 2005 C. Anderson Aldrich Award. *Pediatrics, 118*(5), 2187–2191.

Shonkoff, J.P., & Phillips, D.A. (2000). *From neurons to neighborhoods: The science of early childhood development.* Washington, DC: National Academies Press.

U.S. Department of Health and Human Services. (1999). *Mental health: A report of the Surgeon General.* Rockville, MD: Author. Retrieved June 14, 2011, from http://www.surgeongeneral.gov/library/mental health/home.html

U.S. Department of Health and Human Services, Administration for Children and Families. (n.d.). *Infants and toddlers in the child welfare system: Findings from the NSCAW study.* Washington, DC: Author. Retrieved June 14, 2011, from http://www.acf.hhs.gov/programs/opre/abuse_neglect/nscaw/ reports/infants_todd/infants_todd.html

U.S. Department of Health and Human Services, Administration for Children and Families. (2006). *Depression in the lives of Early Head Start families: Research to practice brief.* Washington, DC: Author. Retrieved June 14, 2011, from http://www.acf.hhs.gov/programs/opre/ehs/ehs_resrch/reports/ dissemination/research_briefs/4pg_depression.html

Wagmiller, R.L., & Adelman, R.M. (2009). *Childhood and intergenerational poverty: The long-term consequences of growing up poor.* Retrieved June 14, 2011, from http://www.nccp.org/publications/ pub_909.html

Wight, V.R., & Chau, M. (2009). *Basic facts about low-income children.* National Center for Children in Poverty, Mailman School of Public Health, Columbia University. Retrieved from http://www.nccp .org/publications/pub_892.html

Zeanah, C.H., & Zeanah, P.D. (2001). Towards a definition of infant mental health. *Zero to Three, 22,* 13–20.

The Challenging Child

Emotional Dysregulation and Aggression

Neena M. Malik

For some people, it is hard to imagine that a person as small as an infant or toddler could cause so much trouble that he or she somehow manages to terrorize a whole early childhood program. For others, unfortunately, the experience of such a child is very well known. There is no question that even an infant, toddler, or early preschool-age child can be so difficult to manage that program staff breathe a sigh of relief on the days that child is not in school. Such children have the potential to be loveable, fun, and often just as sweet as their age-mates, but when they become upset, it can take an army to contain them and calm them down. These are very challenging children.

This chapter focuses on the difficult behaviors that challenging children can display and explains how to recognize these children and to understand and manage their challenging behaviors. It also suggests how early childhood programs can recognize both the vulnerabilities and the difficulties these young children experience and can work to help them develop and behave in more healthy, prosocial ways.

WHAT IS EMOTION DYSREGULATION?

Before defining *dysregulation,* it is helpful to understand what *emotion regulation* means. The concept of emotion regulation is just this: To survive and thrive, all living beings need an organized, coherent response to stressful events and experiences. It is the organization and coherence of that response that is labeled emotion regulation. In very young children, emotion regulation refers to their ability, in the context of some negative experience, to engage their own coping and communication skills and to manage their reactions to experiences that make them unhappy, hurt, afraid, angry, or frustrated. Reactions can be either overt or covert. *Overt reactions* are those that are externalized (i.e., can be seen) and include both physical and behavioral reactions. *Covert reactions* are the internalized, subjective experiences of feelings, and though they are often unseen by others, they are very powerful to the person experiencing them.

Infants' and toddlers' coping and communication skills are limited, of course. Infants are not expected to be able to regulate themselves very well at all. Infant mental health experts do, however, expect that infants who are on the right developmental trajectory toward emotion regulation will be able to make their distress known to caregivers. Perhaps more important, infants and toddlers must be able to accept the care and soothing that caregivers offer in order to return to a state of peacefulness, calm, and alertness after a distressing experience.

What is *emotion dysregulation*? A way to think about emotion dysregulation is that it functions as an opposite of emotion regulation. This may be seen in a number of ways. First, emotion dysregulation is the lack of an organized response to a stressful or upsetting event. This means that for infants and toddlers who have not developed a pattern of adaptive responding when something difficult happens, they are just simply overwhelmed by the negative emotions they experience. Second, some infants and toddlers lack the ability to direct or control behaviors and feelings associated with a stressful or upsetting experience. These children not only feel overwhelmed, but they act in ways that show that their feelings and behaviors are not within their control. It is this lack of control, or lack of regulation, that is the observable hallmark of emotion dysregulation in young children.

One of the most destructive observable behaviors in the context of dysregulation is aggression. Aggression tends to be a very common part of a young child's dysregulated response to frustration and anger, particularly during toddlerhood and the preschool years. Some aggression in young children is considered normative. When aggression is hard to control, however, or when it is not gradually replaced by emerging emotion and behavior regulation skills, there may be cause for concern.

Emotion regulation is a capacity that develops during the early childhood years; therefore, developmental experts do not expect toddlers and preschoolers to be fully in control of their reactions. Again, they even expect some aggression as a way of solving problems in young children. There are, however, a number of capacities that toddlers, and even infants, exhibit that show they are on the right path in terms of their development of emotion regulation. It is equally important to know what is expected based on a child's age and what might be a red flag or evidence of risk for early emotional regulation problems. Understanding age and risk factors is critical because the earlier problems are detected, the more intervention can help. Emotion regulation is an important emerging skill related to a host of other important functions in childhood, including the ability to pay attention and focus, make and keep friends, solve social problems, tolerate frustration, and even do well academically.

THE DEVELOPMENT OF EMOTION REGULATION

Studies of infant and toddler emotion regulation show that there are a number of core processes and abilities in infancy that may be related to the later development of emotion regulation. These include aspects of parent–child interaction involving the behavior of both parents and infants, the closeness of the parent–child relationship, and the infant's ability to share attention and enjoyment with caregivers. In toddlerhood, as cognitive and language capacities grow, children begin to develop more effective ways to tolerate frustration, use distraction, and use language to ask for help, among other capacities. All of these are important building blocks for the development of organization and coherence in emotion regulation.

The Importance of Parents and Caregivers

One of the most robust findings in studies of infant development is that when parents and their infants—from the time of birth until infants can talk, and even beyond—have a warm, positive relationship, and when parents model good emotion regulation, infants are likely to show progress toward developing those skills. Good predictors of a child's emerging capacities are reflected in parenting behavior. These include the extent to which parents display positive emotion, support their infant, do not become overwhelmed by their infant's negative emotion, and help soothe their infant when he or she is crying or upset. These behaviors, when displayed by any caregiver who spends a considerable amount of time with an infant, including parents and other daily care providers, are important for a number of reasons.

First, infants are born with an immature nervous system. This means that for the first several months of life, the world can be an overwhelming place. It is filled with sounds, sights, smells, objects, and movements with which an infant must become familiar. Without any ability to survive on his or her own, an infant must rely on caregivers to whom he or she can become accustomed. Because the world seems overwhelming, infants are easily startled, overstimulated, and sometimes scared. Because they cannot talk, when infants have a need of any kind, they cry. It is important for caregivers to become familiar with their infants and for infants to become familiar with their caregivers, so that rhythms and routines can be established. Caregivers begin to know the particular cries and displays of fussiness or discomfort, wants and needs, and preferences of their infants. This familiarity is important because it allows a caregiver to know 1) when an infant is upset, 2) what might be causing the upset, and 3) how to soothe the infant. It is the caregiver's soothing coupled with an acknowledgement and acceptance of an infant's distress that constitute "modeling" good emotion regulation.

Caregivers as Emotion Regulators for Infants

As noted above, infants are not expected to control their own emotions or expressions of emotion. Instead, their caregivers must do it for them. Negative emotions are dysregulating to infants even on a physical level; therefore, physical contact and soothing are the primary means for caregivers to model and provide emotion regulation for their infant. Rocking, holding, stroking, and speaking softly and sympathetically to an infant provides the infant with a safe, calm, accepting, and peaceful environment—a safe place and plenty of time to calm down. Holding an infant close to an adult body also serves to cocoon the infant in a smaller physical and social environment where the infant can block out much of what is bothering him or her or, if the discomfort is internal, use the calm physical presence and contact of the caregiver to help relax physically.

A critical part of a caregiver's job in modeling emotion regulation is to not become overwhelmed by the infant's display of negative emotion. This can be very challenging for some caregivers. Depression, illness, personal stress, physical or emotional discomfort, exposure to trauma, and difficult feelings about the infant can all get in the way of a caregiver being able to tolerate and accept the distress of an infant. One of the reasons taking care of a young child is among the most difficult jobs lies in the very nature of caring for an infant. Infants cannot take care of themselves and they cry a lot. Infants are not in control of their emotions and behavior. For many parents and caregivers, tolerating, let alone accepting, negative emotion and behavior can be a tremendous challenge. In order to help a child internalize the ability to regulate emotion and solve distressing situations without aggression and other difficulties, however, a parent or caregiver must be able to do just that: accept the child's negativity in order to help the child move beyond it.

Infant Capacities on the Pathway to Developing Emotion Regulation

Although during infancy caregivers do most of the work in regulating their child's emotions, there are some interesting research findings suggesting that infant capacities are important for later emotion regulation development. Researchers studied *joint attention*—that is, the infant's ability to share a focus on and enjoyment of an object or experience with a caregiver, even before the infant developed language skills (Morales, Mundy, Crowson, Neal, & Delgado, 2005). An example of joint attention is when an infant can follow the gaze of a caregiver toward an object or direct a caregiver's gaze to an object that the child may be interested in. Joint attention to an object or experience, and the social aspect of sharing enjoyment of or interest in an object or experience, is a capacity that can begin to emerge even at age 6 months and is an important precursor for future social and relationship skills that require taking another's perspective.

One of the findings of the study conducted by Morales and colleagues (2005) was that early joint attention in the form of following a caregiver's gaze at 6 months helped predict a child's ability to actively and independently cope with a frustrating situation at 24 months. The frustrating situation went like this: A child was presented with an attractively wrapped present and was told that he or she could have it but that he or she had to wait for 6 minutes. Children who were able to show better joint attention capacities at age 6 months were also, at 24 months, shown to distract themselves by purposefully playing with other toys by themselves or actively recruiting their parents to play with them, rather than focusing on the present or becoming upset by having to wait to receive it.

Additional factors in infant capacities related to the later development of emotional regulation include an infant's ability to express emotion, accept soothing from a caregiver, and learn to engage in self-soothing. Some of these skills are related to the quality of the parent–child interaction, including the quality of their attachment, but some are related to what can be called *infant temperament*. (See Chapter 7 to learn more about attachment.) Temperament is thought to be a child's natural tendencies, biologically based, in terms of activity, attention, and reactivity. Children who are more active and reactive than others may be harder to soothe. Children who are able to both sustain and be flexible in their attention may be easier to soothe. Both sustainability and flexibility

Box 2.1.   What is temperament?

Temperament is broadly defined as biologically, constitutionally based individual differences in characteristic behavioral or response style. Temperament remains generally consistent across settings, experiences, and time and can be seen from very early on in life. Ideas about temperament go back nearly 2,000 years.

Currently, professionals draw on the work of two sets of research to help us understand temperament. Thomas and Chess, in their landmark New York Longitudinal Study, described nine dimensions of behavioral responding that they believed to be relatively stable and consistent characteristics of children and that had an impact on children's development over time (Thomas, Chess, Birch, Hertzig, & Korn, 1963). These nine dimensions are approach-withdrawal, adaptability, quality of mood, intensity of reaction, distractibility, persistence or attention span, rhythmicity, threshold of responsiveness, and activity level.

Later it was realized that there was significant overlap among many of these characteristics and it became difficult to measure each of the nine dimensions separately. More recently, work has focused on the definitions of Rothbart and Posner (2006), who have described temperament as differences in reactivity and self-regulation. They have suggested that reactivity and self-regulation can be measured by examining three domains: emotionality, motor activity, and attention. They propose that reactivity is the characteristic way in which a child physiologically responds to stimuli and that self-regulation, including emotionality, activity, and attention, are ways in which children show the world how they are dealing with their reactions and responses.

There are also recent efforts to measure the activity of the brain and nervous system in order to understand the neurobiological underpinnings of temperament (Henderson & Wachs, 2007). These promising studies are beginning to show how individuals of different temperaments, even during infancy, may physiologically respond to experiences and situations around them.

Thomas and Chess (1977) initially described temperament on a continuum from "easy" to "difficult" children. These characterizations are used today and are thought to have a potential influence on children's development. For example, easy children are likely to be low in reactivity and high in self-regulation, including high sociability. Difficult children are likely to be high in reactivity and negative emotionality and may be socially inhibited. Research is not yet entirely clear regarding children's developmental outcomes related to easy versus difficult temperament, but it is becoming more clear that temperament may be an important predictor of adjustment and areas of internalizing and externalizing problems (Sanson, Hemphill, & Smart, 2004).

One of the most important concepts in temperament research is "goodness of fit" (Thomas & Chess, 1977). While an infant's temperament may be observed as early as 3 months of age, perhaps more important than the infant's temperament over time is whether there is a good fit between the infant's temperament and the caregiver. Although a difficult child may have a hard time adjusting, that difficulty may be mitigated by an easygoing, low-reactivity parent. A difficult child who has a difficult parent, however, may be more at risk, because the parent is likely to become dysregulated when the child is dysregulated and therefore less able to help that child re-regulate and engage with the world in a positive way. The match between a child's temperament and the personality and parenting behavior of the caregiver is called "goodness of fit." The "goodness of fit" concept makes it clear that both a child's *and* a parent or caregiver's temperament are important for understanding how children will develop.

of attention are thought to be important precursors of emotion regulation. *Sustainability of attention* means that when a child is upset, a caregiver may distract him by engaging his continued interest in another object or experience and thus help him become calmer. *Flexibility* is also important, because if the child is not able to shift attention away from one object to another and remains fixated on the object or experience that is upsetting, it will be more difficult to soothe that child (Sethi, Mischel, Aber, Shoda, & Larrea Rodriguez, 2000; Sheese, Rothbart, Posner, White, & Fraundorf, 2008). Shifting attention is one of the earliest observable signs of emotion regulation in very young children, which emerges well before more advanced social-communication abilities, such as language.

Emerging Emotion Regulation in Toddlers

As children grow and develop language and they become cognitively more mature, they begin to be more sophisticated in their expressions, including their expressions of distress. At this point, when children are able to walk and begin to talk, they also begin to show signs of aggression. Aggression is a normative behavior in the course of the development of emotion regulation. Relatively quickly, however, as language and other control capacities begin to develop, aggression should begin to fade. By 4 or 5 years of age, there should be little left of aggression as a regulation strategy. Even in toddlerhood, aggression should not be the most common strategy for regulation of emotion and behavior, because adults typically make it very quickly clear to young children that aggression is not an accepted form of emotional and behavioral expression. When caregivers are able to provide acceptance of a child's angry or frustrated emotions but show a disapproval of a child's aggressive behavior, the child will use more prosocial emotion regulation strategies. Those strategies for emotion regulation include use of language, comfort seeking, and what researchers Walter Mischel and colleagues (Sethi et al., 2000) called cooling strategies. *Cooling strategies* refer to attention- and distraction-type coping mechanisms.

Cooling Strategies

One of the ways that toddlers are able to begin showing signs of emotion regulation is through strategic deployment of attention, what Mischel and colleagues described as strategies to cool the emotional impact of a frustrating experience (Sethi et al., 2000). As we described above, an infant's abilities to sustain and be flexible with attention are precursors of this skill. When something frustrating occurs and cannot be solved alone (a common experience for toddlers), the child either needs to wait for someone to help solve the problem or needs to move on to a different experience altogether. Either way, emotion and behavior regulation are required in the form of shifting attention away from the "hot" experience and selectively and purposefully engaging in a different activity, which serves to "cool" the child. This is actually a complex task that requires a cognitive, attention, and physical shift away from something that is upsetting, and for many young children, it is not easy to do. Being able to demonstrate the ability to shift attention is a hallmark of emotion regulation in young children.

Toddler Language and the Leveraging of Caregiver Support

Toddlers' emerging use of language is one of the clearest ways they can begin to ask for and receive help when they are distressed. When something is frustrating or distressing, a young child who can use language effectively is able to focus an adult's attention on his or her needs by asking, "Can you help me?" or even reporting, "I'm mad." Just as in the case in infancy, and perhaps even more so because toddlers can be both demanding of assistance and stubborn in insisting that "I can do it," caregivers need to be sensitive to the child's emotional expressions. Caregiver sensitivity, coupled with a sense of how to be helpful and calming while allowing a child to gain a sense of mastery over what is upsetting, is a difficult but very important balance to strike in helping a child learn to internalize emotion regulation.

When toddlers encounter very difficult experiences, we expect them to behave much like infants—we expect them to cry. That cry signals a need for comfort that is fairly obvious to most adults. As toddlers begin to develop language to describe their inner experiences, they can also signal the need for comfort. For example, a 3-year-old may feel very frightened, but he may not actually cry. If that child is able to go to an adult and say, "That scared me," it is likely that the adult will instinctively comfort the child. Toddlers, just like infants, often need physical contact and soothing in order to recover from negative experiences. Generally, the more intense the experience, the more physical comforting will be required, including holding, rocking, and using a soothing voice, just as is done in infancy. When less intense experiences are encountered, caregivers can then leverage the verbal capacities of children and help talk them through the difficult experience. Toddlers whose language skills are slow to emerge typically experience more challenges with emotion regulation development. They cannot easily direct adult behavior or express internal states. In an already distressing situation, this difficulty compounds the negativity and frustration a toddler may feel, leading to dysregulation.

The Importance of Culture

There are many ways caregivers engage with infants and toddlers and help them internalize the capacity to regulate emotions. We have discussed several of these, including modeling of emotion regulation and soothing behavior. The process also has important cultural aspects of which to be aware. For example, researchers are beginning to examine how the development of emotion regulation capacities in young children may vary based on culture (Feldman, Masalha, & Alony, 2006). These researchers have found that for some infants in certain cultures (in this study, the Palestinian culture), the infant's development of skillful emotion regulation is related to continuous physical contact (e.g., being held) along with neutral and nonnegative emotional displays from the parent, as well as concrete assistance in completing tasks as children become toddlers. Yet for children from other cultures (focusing in this study on Israeli families), infants do not need to be held to develop the same regulation skills. In contrast, they prefer more face-to-face interactions, affectionate touching, and indirect forms of assistance in completing tasks as they become toddlers. These interaction patterns in the Israeli families studied led to greater development of emotional regulation skills in their children, whereas the earlier patterns of interactions encouraged greater emotion regulation development in Palestinian toddlers.

So we see that there is more than one way to provide the "right" kinds of support for children's social and emotional development. In both cultures, parent involvement and care is clearly a very strong part of how children develop the capacity in later toddlerhood for beginning to control and appropriately express their emotions. The optimal patterns of day-to-day interaction, however, may vary significantly across cultural groups. Core caregiving capacities to tolerate and accept negative emotion, and to offer soothing behaviors, are likely to exist across cultures. Acceptance of negativity and, as children become older, the ways in which caregivers provide support and assistance in the face of negativity, are very likely to vary somewhat across groups, depending on the values and customs of various cultural groups.

EMOTION DYSREGULATION AND AGGRESSION

Many parents, for a variety of reasons, have difficulty accepting negativity in their children and helping them express and manage their emotions. Children themselves may be vulnerable due to temperament, biological difficulties, or difficult experiences. In these situations, children are likely to be at risk for emotional dysregulation. Once on a trajectory of dysregulation, it can be very difficult for a child to correct himself or herself developmentally. Many adults have difficulties with dysregulated emotions in young children. Because children's emotional dysregulation problems are so hard for adults to manage, they tend to build upon themselves and escalate. However, as we will discuss later, there are strategies caregivers can use to help children who have moved off of an appropriate developmental trajectory get back on course in terms of regulation. Before learning ways of helping to manage dysregulation, it is useful to explore the number of ways dysregulation may occur.

Internalizing–Externalizing Continuum of Negative Affect

Development specialists describe two ends of a continuum of negative emotion experience and expression. All people have negative feelings. Ideally, even at a young age, these feelings can be appropriately expressed and responded to by adults. When children are unsure of adult responses and assistance, or if for some other reason they are unable to appropriately express negative feelings, those feelings may be turned inward. Alternatively, they may be expressed outwardly in inappropriate ways.

This inward or outward expression of emotion forms a continuum of experience and behavior that is referred to as *internalization* of feeling on one end of the continuum to *externalization* on the other. At the internalization end, children's feelings are not easily observed by others because those feelings are driven inward and may be expressed only in subtle ways. There are a number of internalized emotions and behaviors, including fears, worries, somatic or physical complaints, anxiety, depression, and withdrawal from others. At this end of the continuum, it can be said that children are *overcontrolled* in terms of emotion regulation. At the other end of the continuum, where children are *undercontrolled,* they may exhibit externalizing behaviors including attention problems, hyperactivity, oppositional and defiant behavior, and aggression. In the middle of the continuum, there is *appropriate control,* or regulation, of emotion and behavior. This distinction between internalizing and externalizing problems in emotion and behavior regulation has been recognized for several decades (e.g., Achenbach & Edelbrock, 1978).

Internalizing Problems in Early Childhood

Young children exhibit internalizing problems in a number of ways. The most obvious of these ways is through fears and anxiety. Normatively, infants and toddlers certainly have fears—fear of new people when infants are about 6 months or older, fear of the dark, fear of new places, fear of very loud noises, fear of surprising experiences, to name a few. At times, those fears persist beyond the age expected or persist despite consistent reassurance that seems to be understood by the child. In addition, at times, caregivers may be unable to soothe and comfort a scared child. When such things happen and the fear begins to have an impact on the kinds of experiences to which a child will tolerate exposure, they can be described as internalizing problems. Clinginess with a parent or caregiver, especially in new circumstances or with new people, is certainly normal with infants and young toddlers. After a "warm-up" period, however, during which the caregiver stays close, shows calm, and demonstrates that the new experience is safe, a child then should begin to be able to explore a new environment or interact with new people. A child who cannot do that may be suffering from overcontrolled emotion dysregulation. In such instances, what may be happening is that a child, even if she wants to participate in experiences, feels so overwhelmed by her negative feelings that the only way to handle them is to overly control herself by withdrawing or isolating herself from experiences. Shutting out the world means that fewer experiences, bad or good, will ensue, leading to a reduction in the possibility of further fear-invoking stimuli. If she is unable to use skills to show adults how she feels and get comfort, it is likely that those feelings will create such internal turmoil that there will be little energy left to relax and interact with others.

Excessive worrying; sadness; complaints about headaches, stomachaches, or other body aches; or a tendency to withdraw and self-isolate instead of socially engage are all examples of internalizing emotional dysregulation. These experiences are all normative when they are limited and are not typical of the child's behavior. It is when these behaviors are so frequent that they limit the child's capacity to interact with the world, or when the child is very hard to soothe when these behaviors are present, that dysregulation is indicated. At times, overcontrolled, internalizing young children can be easily overlooked. They are called "tough" or "independent," because they seem to be able to take care of themselves without needing adult soothing or assistance. These are children for whom educators and caregivers should have significant concern, however, because what is really happening is not that they do not need assistance, but that they are ill equipped to ask for assistance. It may be that their life experiences have already taught them not to count on adults for help. Instead, these children may feel that they have to be self-reliant. When very difficult things happen, however, a child who is unable to adequately express his pain or has difficulty asking for help is unlikely to have that pain or hurt easily resolved. Instead, that pain lingers, staying mostly hidden, causing the young child to become isolated. Again, he may look independent. For a young child who has been hurt or has gone through a difficult experience, however, not being able to resolve that hurt can create a period of great vulnerability and sensitivity, which may be so acute that the only way a child can manage those feelings is by shutting down. Over time, such dampening of emotion can cause significant problems with depression, social and peer problems, self-esteem issues, and long-term emotion and behavior regulation issues.

Externalizing Problems in Early Childhood

We tend to be much more aware of emotion dysregulation in young children when they are overt in their expressions of distress, such as tantrums, defiance, inability to control their behavior or hyperactivity, and aggression. When these problems occur, it is not just the child himself who is affected; all nearby are also affected and may be the recipients of a defiant act or the victims of an angry or aggressive outburst. During infancy, under-controlled emotional dysregulation is likely to take the form of excessive, angry crying and opposition, such that even young infants may stiffen and squirm away when a caregiver is trying to soothe them. Because this takes a toll on a caregiver, it may make the caregiver upset as well, which then in turn creates a difficult situation when trying to calm a wildly distressed infant. As children grow older and are able to use language more effectively, they may become more defiant. They may refuse to listen, refuse to comply with requests, and have a tantrum when pressed to cooperate. These children are likely to have low frustration tolerance, crying easily and becoming very upset when they cannot complete a task or activity in which they are interested. They may be quick to give up on themselves, as they are unable to tolerate the frustration and sadness they feel at not being competent. All of these behaviors, on occasion, are completely normal for infants and toddlers. Concern about emotion dysregulation issues should be present when these behaviors are typical ways a child responds to difficulty rather than ways he or she occasionally responds—for example, when not feeling well, not getting enough sleep, or going through a rough time for other reasons (e.g., a parental illness or divorce).

Aggression

Perhaps the most difficult of all externalizing, undercontrolled behaviors is aggression. Primarily, aggression occurs because there are many ways in which toddlers find their goals blocked. They are unable to reach an object, complete a task, explain what they want, understand their own reactions or the actions of others, cope with something that scares them, or posses a toy with which someone else is currently playing. A natural human tendency when a goal is blocked is to attempt a solution that will remove the obstacle. Because toddlers often feel frustrated by not being able to master experiences, or when they are required to share people or possessions, their aggression is usually in the form of throwing or breaking frustrating objects, or hitting, pushing, or sometimes biting frustrating people—usually their peers. Because aggression is such a highly disruptive behavior that can have truly painful consequences for others—both psychologically and at times physically—others may have a difficult time liking an aggressive child. Caregivers may feel rejected by the hostility that such children demonstrate, and other children may become fearful and disinterested in playing with a child who is unpredictable or who may predictably become violent. Decades of research has shown that aggressive children are among the most at risk of all vulnerable children, as they are at high risk for being disliked by peers throughout childhood, may become delinquent, and have a host of interpersonal and academic difficulties (Parker & Asher, 1987).

It is important to remember that, particularly for young children, aggression does not come out of a desire or intent to harm. It may seem that way to others, especially other children. However, as noted above, aggression is an issue with frustration tolerance and blocked goals more than anything else during the toddler years. The dysregulation that ensues can seem very purposefully hurtful, but it virtually never is with young children. It is important to remember that aggression in a young child is an expression of pain, discomfort, and distress, albeit a highly aversive expression. The problem, of course, is that aggression serves to push people away, rather than inviting them to help and engage in soothing, support, and problem solving.

PROGRAM STRATEGIES FOR ADDRESSING THE NEEDS OF DYSREGULATED CHILDREN

As anyone who has had responsibility for a child who is dysregulated knows, the challenges presented by these children can be enormous. Often, these children need one-to-one attention. Perhaps not all the time, but when these children are upset, the degree of their distress often requires a singular focus on them, either to help them stop crying or to help them stop causing disruptions. The challenges presented by children with emotion dysregulation can be overwhelming and exhausting. With early detection and enough support, however, many of the difficulties children experience and exhibit can be ameliorated.

Screening for Dysregulation

A number of screening tools can be used to help a program understand when children might be at risk for difficulty. The Ages & Stages Questionnaires®: Social-Emotional: A Parent-Completed, Child-Monitoring System for Social-Emotional Behaviors (ASQ:SE; Squires, Bricker, & Twombly, 2002) is one such tool that can be used with children as young as 6 months of age. It is easy to give to parents or caregivers, easy to score, and gives a score that provides a very good indication of risk for social, emotional, and dysregulation difficulties. Other tools that can be given to caregivers, including parents and teachers, focus on specific behaviors such as tantrums in children who are a bit older, such as the Child Behavior Checklist (for children 1½–5 years of age; Achenbach & Rescorla, 2000). Additional measures can be used to assess social and emotional functioning in infants and toddlers from 12 to 36 months (Infant Toddler Social Emotional Assessment; Carter & Briggs-Gowan, 2000) and children ages 2–6 years (Devereux Early Childhood Assessment [DECA-C]; LeBuffe & Naglieri, 2003). In addition, one of the best ways to understand if a child is at risk is to observe him or her. Watch as he or she tries new experiences, deals with frustration, negotiates toys and playground space with peers, and expresses sadness, worries, fears, and needs for help or comfort. Observe the ways the child both asks for help and is able—or unable—to accept help and comfort.

Preventive Strategies

Among the most important ways to help a child get back on the right developmental pathway for emotion regulation is to strengthen the relationships he or she may have with important adult caregivers. A child who has difficulty asking for help, expressing needs, and accepting comfort is a child who is very vulnerable to emotion dysregulation. Young children, however, are unlikely to have had such devastating experiences in their short lives that they are already completely turning their backs on adults, with no hope that adults will help them with difficult feelings and events. Consistency and predictability is truly the key here. Even though it may be difficult, and it often will be, taking a consistent stance of nurturance, acceptance of feelings, and comforting will eventually show an infant or toddler that a caregiver can be trusted to help and soothe them. This stance of nurturance and consistent acceptance of feelings is critical, especially because it needs to be combined with logical and developmentally appropriate consequences for problem behaviors. In a child who has experienced trauma or abuse, this can literally take months. The process is rarely unsuccessful, however, as young children truly do need adults to help them survive and navigate the difficult experiences of growing up. Young children need to feel cared for, loved, and liked. They need to be praised for good behavior. They also need to be given consistent and appropriate behavioral structure and have their feelings accepted when they are engaging in dysregulated behavior. In other words, they need to know that even though their behaviors are not accepted, their feelings are accepted, and who they are as people is accepted. These are all critical elements of using important caregiving relationships with a child to help them learn to better regulate their emotions and behavior.

Predictability and consistency are truly important elements of a young child's life that function as anchors in the child's growing ability to self-regulate. When children can predict what will happen in their homes or classroom environments, or if they have warnings and gentle reminders before transitions are to occur, they are much more likely to be able to marshal their resources to deal with what is happening in their lives and what will come next. When their environments are chaotic—as can be the case in high-risk environments—the internal experiences, both emotionally and physically, of infants and toddlers are chaotic as well. (Learn more about risk and resilience in Chapter 4.) Dealing with the situational and internal chaos makes dealing appropriately with difficult events a very challenging task.

Intervention Strategies

Sometimes preventive strategies are not enough and young children's dysregulated behavior requires additional intervention. Interventions can take place in the classroom or with parents, and ideally in both settings. In classroom-based behavior management, a behavioral specialist can come into a classroom, observe the child, and develop and implement strategies to help the child improve regulation. Typically, the specialist will suggest tools for educators to use when children become upset, such as creating a quiet space for children to regain composure, separating dysregulated children from other children who might be typical triggers for them in certain play areas, and sticker charts to help track and encourage good behavioral control. Specialists may also recommend to educators that they do not ignore a child when he or she is truly dysregulated or just send him or her to a quiet corner but instead engage in comforting, soothing, and calming interactions with the child. This strategy can be difficult to implement consistently in a classroom, but it is likely to be one of the most effective strategies to help improve a dysregulated child's emotional and behavioral control.

Parenting is challenging with a dysregulated child, and parenting interventions can help both the causes and consequences of both under- and overcontrol in young children. If a child's dysregulation is due, even in part, to parental inconsistency or difficulty with negative emotions, interventions can be very potent in correcting difficulties in the parent–child relationship. Most of these interventions, such as Eyberg's Parent–Child Interaction Therapy (Zisser & Eyberg, 2010), focus on helping parents become more consistent in two major areas of parenting. The first is enjoying their children: following their lead in play; praising them; and showing the children that they love them, care for them, like them, and respect them. The second area is in appropriate, effective, and consistent structure and discipline. Teaching parents to show consistent love, nurturance, and structure with children is a hallmark of parenting interventions for social and emotional development.

Because dysregulated young children are so challenging, it is also important to understand the emotional foundations of dysregulation. These have been briefly mentioned already in this chapter and are discussed more thoroughly in later chapters of this book (see Chapters 5 and 7 for discussions of trauma and attachment difficulties). The most important thing to remember about children whose behavior inflicts suffering on others, either by withdrawing and seeming to reject adult care or by becoming aggressive or angry, is that they are children who are themselves suffering. Young children do not have the social and cognitive sophistication required to engage in behaviors for the express purpose of making another person suffer. When they are overwhelmed, those feelings either go inward or they come out. If they are not coming out in a healthy way, they are being internalized in an unhealthy way or they are being externalized in an equally dysfunctional but more overt manner. Despite the fact that many dysregulated children are difficult to reach and relate to, reaching them on an emotional level and nurturing them in a consistent way is in fact exactly what they need to get back on a healthy developmental course.

Caring for Staff Who Care for Dysregulated Children

There is no harder job than helping children grow and develop. It requires constant attention, caring, and attunement to a child's needs. Most educators are in the business of helping children because it is so very rewarding to see children develop and to be part of that process. However, educating challenging, dysregulated children is often difficult to describe as rewarding. Training staff in what makes a child dysregulated and teaching educators to have empathy for these young children is the first step in dealing constructively with these children. The second step is helping caregivers understand how important they are to these children, because the children themselves have challenges in expressing that very simple and important reality. Helping staff regain a sense of control over their own emotions and their classrooms is also important, because it can often feel like dysregulated children consume all of teachers' time and dominate classroom dynamics.

The training issues just discussed are important to address, but they are not enough. The reality must be acknowledged that it is terribly difficult, both physically and emotionally, to have dysregulated children in a classroom. Often, dysregulated children are unhappy, whether they are internalizing or externalizing, and this is heartbreaking for educators who care about these children and work to make them happy and healthy on a daily basis. Classroom staff need ongoing support, supervision, and assistance, often in the form of additional staff members in the classroom. Both teachers and parents may need consultation from mental health professionals to help them manage their own feelings and their children's emotional and behavioral difficulties.

CONCLUSION

Infants and toddlers cannot survive, let alone thrive, without important adults in their lives. The capacities they have to provide adults with signals about their needs start out in a primitive way. Although infants and toddlers rapidly develop those capacities, the fragility and vulnerability present when they experience feelings of fear, hurt, anger, frustration, and rejection are significant, and remain so for quite some time—certainly well into childhood. After all, even adults need help from those close to them during difficult times and circumstances. The first step toward helping dysregulated children is recognizing that they are signaling a need with every ability they have, however limited and strained such abilities may be. As challenging as infants and toddlers may be at times, it is highly unlikely that they have yet given up on adults helping them, even if it may appear as though they have. Not giving up on these challenging but promising children may be the first and most important key to helping them get back to not just surviving, but thriving.

REFERENCES

Achenbach, T.M., & Edelbrock, C.S. (1978). The classification of child psychopathology: A review and analysis of empirical efforts. *Psychological Bulletin, 85,* 1275–1301.

Achenbach, T. M., & Rescorla, L. A. (2000). *Manual for the ASEBA preschool forms & profiles.* Burlington, VT: University of Vermont, Research Center for Children, Youth, & Families.

Carter, A., & Briggs-Gowan, M. (2000). *Infant Toddler Social and Emotional Assessment.* New Haven, CT: Yale University, Connecticut Early Development Project.

Feldman, R., Masalha, S., & Alony, D. (2006). Microregulatory patterns of family interactions: Cultural pathways to toddlers' self regulation. *Journal of Family Psychology, 20,* 614–623.

Henderson, H.A., & Wachs, T.D. (2007). Temperament theory and the study of cognition–emotion interactions across development. *Developmental Review, 27,* 396–427.

LeBuffe, P.A. & Naglieri, J.A. (2003). *The Devereux Early Childhood Assessment Clinical Form (DECA-C): A measure of behaviors related to risk and resilience in preschool children.* Lewisville, NC: Kaplan Press.

Morales, M., Mundy, P.C., Crowson, M.M., Neal, A.R, & Delgado, C.E. (2005). Individual differences in infant attention skills, joint attention, and emotion regulation behavior. *International Journal of Behavioral Development, 29,* 259–263.

Parker, J.G., & Asher, S.R. (1987). Peer acceptance and later personal adjustment: Are low-accepted children "at risk"? *Psychological Bulletin, 102,* 357–389.

Rothbart, M.K., & Posner, M.I. (2006). Temperament, attention, and developmental psychopathology. In D. Cicchetti & D.J. Cohen (Eds.), *Developmental psychopathology: Vol. 2. Developmental neuroscience* (2nd ed., pp. 465–501). Hoboken, NJ: John Wiley & Sons.

Sanson, A., Hemphill, S.A., & Smart, D. (2004). Connections between temperament and social development: A review. *Social Development, 13,* 142–170.

Sethi, A., Mischel, W., Aber, J.L., Shoda, Y., & Larrea Rodriguez, M. (2000). The role of strategic attention deployment in development of self-regulation: Predicting preschoolers' delay of gratification from mother–toddler interactions. *Developmental Psychology, 36,* 767–777.

Sheese, B.E., Rothbart, M.K., Posner, M.I., White, L.K., & Fraundorf, S.H. (2008). Executive attention and self-regulation in infancy. *Infant Behavior & Development, 31,* 501–510.

Squires, J., Bricker, D., & Twombly, E. (with Yockelson, S., Davis, M.S., & Kim, Y.). (2002). *Ages & Stages Questionnaires®: Social-Emotional (ASQ:SE): A parent-completed, child-monitoring system for social-emotional behaviors.* Baltimore: Paul H. Brookes Publishing Co.

Thomas, A., & Chess, S. (1977). *Temperament and development.* New York: Brunner/Mazel.

Thomas, A., Chess, S., Birch, H.G., Hertzig, M.E., & Korn, S. (1963). *Behavioural individuality in early childhood.* New York: New York University Press.

Zisser, A., & Eyberg, S.M. (2010). Treating oppositional behavior in children using parent-child interaction therapy. In A.E. Kazdin & J.R. Weisz (Eds.), *Evidence-based psychotherapies for children and adolescents* (2nd ed., pp. 179–193). New York: Guilford Press.

3

Maternal Depression

Linda S. Beeber and Rachel Chazan-Cohen

hen you hear the word *depression,* someone you know may spring to mind. It might be someone from your child care program—a new mother who does not seem interested in her beautiful infant, a mother of several children who has recently become frequently irritable and angry, a father who is withdrawn and cannot seem to get himself organized since he lost his job. It might be one of your staff colleagues who has been missing work lately. It could even be you.

Depression is the most frequently encountered mental health threat to parents, young children, and the staff who serve them. In Early Head Start programs, for example, at the time of enrollment, nearly half (48%) of mothers with children 1 year or younger reported depressive symptoms. One third of mothers with 1-year-olds and one third of mothers with 3-year-olds were depressed. Depression was chronic for 12% of the mothers (U.S. Department of Health and Human Services [DHHS], 2006). In the general population, about 12% of women experience depression in any given year, but among women living in poverty, the incidence of depression climbs to about 25% (Harvard University Center on the Developing Child, 2009; Knitzer, Theberge, & Johnson, 2008). Of these, the majority will not receive professional care (Vesga-Lopez et al., 2008). As you will learn, untreated maternal depression occurring prenatally and through the first years of life has serious and important long-term developmental consequences for children.

In this chapter, we explore ways to recognize depression and present practical ideas about how early childhood education and intervention programs can address depression in order to make immediate changes in the lives of children and families, and long-term differences in children's social, emotional, and cognitive development. Much of the chapter's content is based on our experiences with staff members in Early Head Start research partner programs and on transcripts from parents in the focus groups that preceded our depression intervention studies in Early Head Start programs (Beeber et. al., 2010).

DEPRESSION IS MORE THAN SADNESS

Depression—a sad mood that does not go away and is accompanied by changes in thinking, energy level, social functioning, and body functions—can range from mild to severe and can last for weeks, months, years, or an entire life. At present, the exact causes of depression are unknown. Many of the proposed causes, such as biological alterations, genes, emotional trauma, and exposure to stressful experiences, are beyond the power of early childhood programs to change. However, it is well known that depressed parents respond favorably to support if their symptoms are recognized and appropriate help is offered. The first step in recognizing depression is to distinguish it from the deep and sometimes lasting feelings of sadness that accompany losses and disappointments.

The sad mood that is at the heart of depression is often expressed through flattened facial expression, low or monotone voice, loss of a sense of humor, tearfulness, or even a tearless, emotionless state. A depressed person exhibits loss of enjoyment in the things that once brought pleasure. Depression invades and changes the quality of thinking. A depressed person may constantly replay thoughts about being bad, guilty, unworthy, or ugly. These thoughts are so strong that the person may seem distracted and unable to organize his or her day or make decisions. Depression disturbs sleep and body functions. A depressed person may wake up before dawn and be unable to get back to sleep, or conversely, may sleep too much. Other symptoms and signs include eating disturbances such as loss of appetite and under- or overeating, chronic constipation, loss of energy, headaches and other chronic pain, slowed movement, irritability, withdrawal from others, thoughts of dying, and preoccupation with thoughts of suicide (American Psychiatric Association, 2000). If enough of these symptoms are present and reach severe levels, a mental health professional can make a formal diagnosis of clinical depression. As illustrated later in this chapter, parents with less severe symptoms of depression are also of great concern.

Depression can be lethal. According to the National Institute of Mental Health (2009), suicide related to depression is the third most frequent cause of death in teens and young adults between the ages of 15 and 24. For every death by suicide, there are four nonfatal attempts. For those who work with infants and toddlers, the infrequent but catastrophic possibility of infanticide also exists and must be considered when assessing any depressed parent (Spinelli, 2004).

Grief, a sister of depression, is sometimes mistaken for depression. However, grief differs from depression in several ways. First, there is a universal quality to grief that makes it recognizable across cultures and languages. A grieving person who is "keening" (lamenting vocally) is unmistakable. An onlooker's heart goes out to him or her, and people have deep, ingrained ways of offering comfort. A depressed person is often a mystery. Those around him or her feel confused and are uncertain what to do. Grief is oceanic and sweeps over a person at inopportune times, whereas at other times he or she feels quite normal. Depression is unrelenting and omnipresent. Grief brings tears. Depression may be tearless and devoid of emotion. All of these differences are important in distinguishing these two states. The distinction is important, because grief is self-limited and will resolve with support and compassion, whereas depression may go on indefinitely and is less likely to resolve without treatment.

Early Childhood Program Staff
Will See Many Depressed Parents in Their Work

Depression is the most prevalent threat to mental health and the leading cause of lost productivity in the world, according to report by the World Health Organization (2006). Parents and families served by early childhood programs struggle on a daily basis with the issues that increase risk for depression, including poverty, unemployment, limited ability to speak English, family and relationship stress, substandard housing, exposure to violence, single parenthood, and physical illness or disability. Parents exposed to multiple risk factors develop serious depressive symptoms and depression at a much higher rate than the rest of the population. For example, studies conducted in Early Head Start programs have found more than 50% of mothers with moderate to severe symptoms of

---

Box 3.1.   Mental health risk factors in mothers of infants and toddlers

Economic hardship is one of the most powerful risk factors for depression. Low-income mothers are at high risk, with 40%–59% scoring in the severe range on standard depressive symptom measures (Lanzi, Pascoe, Keltner, & Ramey, 1999). If the mother is young, has several young children, has low education, and is the primary wage earner in a low-paying job, her risk quadruples (Brown & Moran, 1997). Furthermore, low-income mothers are twice as liable as middle-class mothers to have persistent depressive symptoms lasting for a year or longer (Lyons-Ruth, Connell, Grunebaum, & Botein, 1990; Lyons-Ruth, Wolfe, & Lyubchik, 2000), and it is the chronic nature of maternal depressive symptoms that appears crucial in the subsequent appearance of developmental and behavioral problems in the child (Field et al., 2000). Depressive symptoms have a greater effect on low-income mothers because the difficulties that any depressed mother would have in interacting with her infant or toddler are intensified by the additional problems that accompany poverty (Belle & Doucet, 2003). For example, dependence on public or borrowed transportation can make an emergency initiate a cascade of related problems (Beeber & Canuso, 2005). Illness, particularly chronic maternal or childhood illness, is a frequent source of unplanned emergencies (Silver, Bauman, & Weiss, 1999). Acquiring resources such as child support may require repeated interactions with the judicial or public assistance system. Further, with welfare-to-work programs, low-income mothers must balance parenting and work outside the home without the same advantages as middle-class mothers (e.g., an in-home washer and dryer). Because poverty inflicts its greatest damage on children under age 3 (Duncan & Brooks-Gunn, 2000), depressive symptoms that prevent a mother from staying employed, attending school, and helping her child use enrichment programs ultimately take a deeper toll by blocking her exit from poverty at the point in her child's life when it matters most.

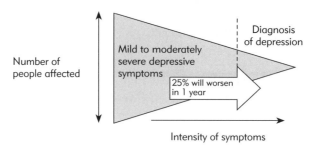

Figure 3.1. Diagnosis of depression.

depression (Beeber, Perreira, & Schwartz, 2008; DHHS, 2006). Early childhood programs that serve similar high-risk families can expect to see many parents who are suffering. Further, ongoing economic and social problems in the United States will likely increase the number of families who have one or more members suffering from depression.

Early education and intervention programs will encounter many more parents with less severe forms of depression than those whose symptoms are so severe that they need immediate treatment or hospitalization. These parents might not have the particular symptoms that are needed to qualify for a clinical diagnosis of depression, yet their functioning is impaired. Why is this important?

1. *Mild to moderate depressive symptoms have as great a negative impact on infant and toddler development as the most severe forms of clinical depression* (Hammen, 1991). It is the potential benefit for the child that justifies spending the time and resources to identify and help a depressed parent as quickly as possible.

2. *Less severe forms of depression can develop into clinical depression.* As Figure 3.1 illustrates, within a year of the first appearance of symptoms, approximately 25% of people with milder forms of depression (in the large part of the triangle) will develop more severe forms of depression (small part of the triangle; Simon, Ormel, VonKorff, & Barlow, 1995). Offering help to parents with depressive symptoms may allow them to make important, needed changes before severe, debilitating depression occurs—while they still have enough energy and motivation.

3. *Less severe forms of depression may not be accompanied by some of the key signs associated with depression.* As a consequence, programs often overlook parents who are struggling. A good example is the irritable, angry mother whose sadness and pain are overshadowed by her critical outbursts toward her child and toward program staff. Besides her tensions with others, the caregiver and the mother may not recognize that she has other key signs—distractibility, indecisiveness, disrupted sleep, and low energy. Because so many more parents experience milder forms of depression, programs may miss suffering parents. Grandparents, foster parents, and relatives who serve as primary caregivers for infants and toddlers can also suffer depressive symptoms. The Early Head Start study on depression mentioned earlier in this chapter (DHHS, 2006) reported that 18% of fathers with 2-year-old children had depressive symptoms and 16% of fathers with 3-year-old children had depressive symptoms. However, most studies of depression and depressive symptoms have

focused on mothers. For that reason, we use the term *mother* except where there is specific research that has involved fathers, grandparents, and other primary caregivers of young children.

A MOTHER'S DEPRESSION IS POTENTIALLY HARMFUL TO HER INFANT OR TODDLER

To the uneducated observer, a mother who interacts with her infant or toddler by playing, singing, tickling, and teaching is simply enjoying her child. Researchers know, however, that every mothering interaction builds the neurological, emotional, and social capacities of the infant or toddler. Even the ability of the mother to alter the pitch of her voice through *motherese* (or "baby talk") is an essential building block for the infant's early language development. Depressive symptoms in the mother typically result in one of two interactional patterns. Depression may "blunt" a mother by stifling her conversation and eye contact, keeping her voice at a monotone, slowing down her playfulness, and

Box 3.2. How depressive symptoms have an impact on mothering

Depressive symptoms can impair mothering (Hammen, 1991) by dulling or slowing the mother's response or by provoking irritable and intrusive responses that do not match the infant's or toddler's cues (Weinberg, Beeghly, Olson, & Tronick, 2008). The mother whose symptoms blunt her responses may withdraw or have shorter, less frequent interactions with the child, touch the child less often, and/or respond less sensitively to the child's signals (Zeanah, Boris, & Larrieu, 1997). Some mothers respond so slowly that their actions no longer correspond to the cues given by the infant or toddler (Bettes, 1988; Breznitz & Sherman, 1987). This response lag interferes with the mother's ability to regulate crying in the infant and to assist the toddler to regulate activity and tantrums (Cicchetti, Rogosch, Toth, & Spagnola, 1997; Toth, Rogosch, Manly, & Cicchetti, 2006). Depressive symptoms blunt these mothers' expression of joy and positive affect as well as their affective availability. Such mothers talk more slowly and less often with their children, using flat voice tones that impair language acquisition, attentiveness, affect regulation, and arousal in the infants or toddlers. Depressive symptoms also diminish the mother's game-playing with the infant and dampen her ability to reward her toddler for good behavior. Some mothers with depressive symptoms interact with their infants and toddlers irritably and intrusively, in a highly stimulating, highly controlling but erratic manner. The mother's irritability appears to originate in part from unrealistic expectations of the child, critical judgments of the child's behavior, and a low sense of parenting self-efficacy. Because symptomatic intrusive mothers do not act in response to their infant's cues, the maternal contingency that infants rely on to learn is lost. Overall, such a mother's interactions fail to foster learning and behavioral regulation (Beardslee & Gladstone, 2001; Field, Diego, & Hernandez-Reif, 2009; Keren, Feldman, & Tyano, 2001; O'Hara, 2009).

dampening her joy and enthusiasm toward the infant or toddler. Depressive symptoms may also disrupt a mother's responsiveness, creating irritable, intrusive, or rough patterns of mothering and preventing her from being a sensitive, supportive presence. If depressive symptoms persist in disrupting her mothering, her infant may show signs of distress, including difficulty eating or sleeping, looking distressed or sad, and not vocalizing or exploring through play. Her toddler may have language delays, sleep problems, tantrums, oppositional behaviors, and difficulty socializing. Developmental milestones may be delayed throughout the first 3 years. These delays are serious, especially in infants and toddlers with other challenges such as growing up in economically distressed families and dangerous neighborhoods.

The "Face" of Depressive Symptoms Varies Among Mothers

Every mother is unique, and the way in which she expresses depressive symptoms in the setting of a child care program will be influenced by such factors as her trust level and comfort with staff, her cultural background, and her temperament (for example, whether she tends to be expressive or stoic). Although staff will usually recognize the classic depressed mother with easily recognizable symptoms, here are some "faces" they might miss:

- *A mother who looks sad and tearful, or conversely, emotionless and tearless.* The low or sad mood that is at the heart of depressive symptoms or clinical depression may or may not be visible. Sometimes mothers can even be viewed as being dull or having intellectual impairments because they do not respond by changing their faces to smile, laugh, or animate their speech.

- *A mother who looks like she is struggling to enjoy her infant or toddler.* The inability to show joy and pride in the infant or toddler, even when staff members take note of how beautiful the child is, can be a tip-off. For most mothers, their role is of central importance, and their children bring them joy and pleasure even in the midst of harsh circumstances. Most nondepressed mothers can put their worries and sad feelings aside in the presence of the infant or toddler.

- *A mother who is overly critical or has unrealistic expectations of the infant or toddler.* Depression can produce expectations of a child that reflect the mother's preoccupation with her deep sense of hopelessness and failure. These perceptions can be expressed as shortcomings of the child or beliefs that justify her own sense of failure as a mother. For example, a mother may think, "He is a bad child just like I was."

- *A mother who seems distracted or overly apologetic.* Depression can produce persistent thoughts of guilt, apprehension, or doom. Mothers may have gloomy thoughts that persistently interfere with their ability to organize their work and carry it out. Mothers may demonstrate this symptom by being disorganized, having lapses in attention, being forgetful, or seeming unable to hear and understand what is being said to them. Mothers may try to explain their behavior in self-deprecating ways with negative statements such as, "I guess I'm stupid" or, "I'm just lazy."

- *A mother who is reluctant to leave home or socialize with other mothers.* Mothers are usually eager for the information and social support they get from other mothers. A mother who continually refuses to become involved with mothers like herself may be in need of a closer evaluation for depressive symptoms.

- *A mother who looks tired and is gaining or losing weight.* Mothers who cannot get enough sleep or who sleep too much may be experiencing symptoms of depression. Mothers lose sleep for many reasons, such as childbirth, having a new infant, or other life circumstances such as overcrowded living spaces, noise, or older children who are sick. However, if a mother wakes in the night or early morning for no reason, or if she cannot get back to sleep after being awakened, more investigation is needed. Many women gain weight rather than lose weight when depressed due to overeating as a comfort measure and to reduced energy for exercise and activity.

- *A mother who is sluggish or slow, or conversely, easily irritated or angered by minor issues or her child's needs.* Depressive symptoms drain energy, both through disrupting sleep and through slowing of movement and thinking. Noise, especially crying, is highly irritating to mothers who are depressed. The needs of others easily overwhelm mothers whose energy is already depleted. These changes fuel mothers' irritable, angry, and rough responses to their children.

- *A mother who reports continual illness and chronic physical pain such as headaches, stomach disturbances, and menstrual difficulties.* The physical signs of depressive symptoms can be intense and persistent. Although these symptoms need to be evaluated by a health provider in case they are related to serious health problems, continual reports of these problems may signal that depression is present. For some cultures, talking about physical illness and seeking help for sickness is more acceptable than seeking help for mental health problems.

- *A mother who conceals her symptoms and puts on a happy face.* Many cultures and families do not condone openly sharing issues such as depression. Fears of being seen as "crazy" or losing custody of a child may keep mothers from being open about their struggles with depression. Some mothers who hold strong religious beliefs may feel as if they are failing if they admit that their faith is not sufficient to keep depression at bay. Mothers who have emigrated from countries with few mental health resources may associate admission of symptoms with being forcibly removed from the family and hospitalized. Each mother will need to resolve her previous beliefs about mental health in order to acknowledge depression and, if needed, accept help for it. She is more likely to do this in the protective envelope of a trusting, consistent relationship.

Infants and Toddlers React to Their Mothers' Depression

Child development scientists have shown that infants and toddlers react to depression in their mother. Initially, infants may protest or try to elicit a different reaction, but over time, they try to compensate by developing protective patterns such as withdrawal or heightened attention-gaining activity. These patterns, combined with the interference caused by the mother's depressive symptoms, lead to a lessening of developmental stimulation that results in visible changes in the child. The reactions of the infant and toddler are specific enough that they can be used as ways of alerting clinicians and programs that a closer assessment of the mother is needed. Here are some signals in an infant or toddler that should be followed up:

- *An infant or toddler who has language and developmental delays.* An infant who is not babbling or vocalizing, or who diverts vocal energy into crying and fussing, may not be receiving adequate vocal stimulation from a depressed mother. Bilingual children often lag behind monolingual children in language acquisition. If a child is exposed to both languages simultaneously and is showing language delays, the child must be evaluated carefully to determine whether delays are attributable to dual languages, to caregiving, or to both. The lack of early babbling and vocalization in the bilingual infant and slow formation of early word sounds in the toddler may reflect low verbal exchange and prompting by their symptomatic mothers. Other developmental milestones such as large and fine motor skills may be sacrificed if the mother is not playing with and stimulating the child.

- *An infant who is irritable and difficult to calm and soothe.* Depressed mothers have great difficulty with their infants' irritability and crying and may not be successful in helping the infant learn to calm down and accept comfort.

- *An infant or toddler with feeding problems, weight loss, or rapid or excessive weight gain.* Feeding is a mutual activity that requires a mother to be sensitive and responsive to the child's cues. Depression affects a mother's ability to sensitively read cues and respond warmly and contingently, which can result in disruption of the normally smooth and pleasurable rhythm of feeding. Infants may regurgitate their food and have slowed weight gain. Some mothers with depressive symptoms may conserve their energy by using feeding or food as the primary way to calm the infant or occupy the toddler and may leave infants unattended with a propped bottle of milk or high-sugar juice or in a highchair with finger food. If mothers are socially withdrawn, the child may spend long periods of time in passive play. Reduced physical activity may lead to excessive weight gain, and poor nutrition may contribute to behavior changes and dental problems.

- *A toddler with behavior problems.* Toddlers of depressed mothers have been observed to have severe tantrums, biting, and difficulty in social settings. Depression interferes with the mother's energy level, decisiveness, creative thinking, and consistent limit setting—all of which are needed to help the toddler learn to modulate frustration and strong feelings. The mother who develops depression may have experienced excessively harsh treatment from her own parents that included abuse and corporal punishment. These mothers have no working model of how to be effective, compassionate parents. In fact, mothers in our studies have felt that to deny any gratification was to return to their harsh past. As a result, they set no limits on their toddlers at all. To further complicate matters, the mothers' depressive symptoms were often organized around their disrupted self-worth. They interpreted their toddler's behavior as evidence of their failure as a parent.

- *An infant or toddler who is neglected or abused.* Research studies have provided strong evidence linking depression in parents to incidents of child neglect or abuse (Zuravin, 1989). However, in our studies with Early Head Start parents, we observed very few instances of neglect or abuse. Most depressed mothers made certain that the infants and toddlers were cared for and protected no matter how little energy they

---

Box 3.3. Impact of mothers' depression on child behavior and development

Infants of symptomatic mothers look less often at the mother, vocalize less, and show more negative affect and less play and exploratory behavior (Cohn, Matias, Tronick, Connell, & Lyons-Ruth, 1986; Cohn & Tronick, 1989; Field, 1998; Field et al., 1988). Also, because the infant-directed speech of symptomatic mothers lacks the qualities that facilitate associative learning, their infants lag in performance on standardized language and mental development scales, and these lags persist into the toddler era—especially if maternal symptoms last longer than 6 months (Breznitz & Sherman, 1987; Field, 1998; Kaplan, Bachorowski, & Zarlengo-Strouse, 1999; Lang et al., 1996; Lyons-Ruth et al., 1990; Murray, 1992; Murray, Fiori-Cowley, Hooper, & Cooper, 1996; Murray, Kempton, Woolgar, & Hooper, 1993). Toddlers of symptomatic mothers demonstrate less participation in social activities and more negative affect, including severe temper tantrums (Cicchetti et al., 1997; Gross, Conrad, Fogg, Willis, & Garvey, 1995; Hart, Jones, Field, & Lundy, 1999; Needlman, Stevenson, & Zuckerman, 1991; Radke-Yarrow, Nottelmann, Belmont, & Welsh, 1993). Compared with children of nonsymptomatic mothers, infants and toddlers of symptomatic mothers have shown more negative and less positive affect, less sustained attentiveness, high activity levels, noncompliance, language delays, and tantrums (Field et al., 2009; Needlman et al., 1991). These infant or toddler behaviors have been correlated with subsequent preschool and school adjustment issues (Campbell, Shaw, & Gilliom, 2000). When economic hardship is added to the context, maternal depressive symptoms, even at mild to moderate levels (Campbell, Morgan-Lopez, Cox, & McLoyd, 2009; Hammen, 1991), are an additional challenge for a low-income infant or toddler that may culminate in persistent language delays, cognitive impairments, later childhood misconduct and learning disorders, school failure, and more susceptibility to mental health issues, depression, and suicide in adolescence and adulthood (Beardslee & Gladstone, 2001; Black et al., 2002; Brennan, Hammen, Katz, & Le Brocque, 2002; Campbell, Matestic, von Stauffenberg, Mohan, & Kirchner, 2007; Campbell et al., 2009; Cummings & Davies, 1994; Goodman & Gotlib, 1999; Halligan, Murray, Martins, & Cooper, 2007; Jackson, Brooks-Gunn, Huang, & Glassman, 2000; Lovejoy, Graczyk, O'Hare, & Neuman, 2000). As they reach preschool and school age, children reared by mothers with depressive symptoms are at higher risk than other children for depression, school adjustment problems, behavior problems such as aggression and conduct disorders, and speech and learning problems (Beardslee & Gladstone, 2001; Black et al., 2002; Brennan et al., 2002; Cogill, Caplan, Alexandra, Robson, & Kumar, 1986; Cummings & Davies, 1994; Goodman, Adamson, Riniti, & Cole, 1994; Gross et al., 1995; Harnish, Dodge, & Valente, 1995; Jackson et al., 2000; Klimes-Dougan et al., 1999; Lang et al., 1996; Lovejoy et al., 2000; Murray, Hipwell, Hooper, Stein, & Cooper, 1996; Murray et al., 1999).

---

had. Some mothers funneled all of their energy into parenting and neglected other aspects of their life. Although coping behaviors are a strength, the lack of visible signs of parenting difficulties or neglect or abuse in the child may also prevent programs from recognizing symptoms and offering help to a depressed mother.

Depressed Mothers in Early Childhood Programs

Depressed mothers may alert early childhood program staff or their health providers by behaving in ways that reflect the negative effects of depression on energy levels, activity levels, and thinking, such as being overcritical, distracted, or disorganized. These patterns may lead programs to mistakenly label depressed mothers as "noncompliant" or "difficult," further alienating staff from establishing trusting relationships with those mothers. Such mothers may drop out of programs or be reported for child neglect, alienating them further from would-be helpers. Here are some signals from parents that should be followed up by program staff in helpful and supportive ways:

- Not following through on program expectations
- Neglecting to schedule and keep child health care or other appointments (e.g., applying for the federal Women, Infants, and Children program or job training)
- Not using child enrichment materials or suggested activities with their child
- Frequent absences from home-visiting appointments or child care center attendance
- Consistently late drop-off and pick-up from early education or child care programs
- Decreased attendance in activities they previously enjoyed
- Coming late or leaving early from activities
- Looking inattentive or withdrawn during a program activity
- Expressing frequent criticism of activities
- Decreased involvement in activities they previously attended
- Frequent complaints about program activities or staff behavior

Depression During Pregnancy and the Postpartum Period—Opportunities for Intervention

Many early studies of depression in mothers were conducted during the period after childbirth, or the *postpartum period*. The term *postpartum depression* captures attention—especially when the media has tied it to the rare incidences of infanticide committed by depressed mothers. Strictly speaking, *postpartum depression* is used to describe depression occurring during the 6 weeks following childbirth (American Psychiatric Association, 2000). However, research verifies that the majority of mothers with postpartum depression were depressed prior to delivery, and that the pattern of depression continues past the postpartum period just after childbirth. In fact, some researchers have proposed changing the term to *perinatal depression* (Tronick & Reck, 2009). In our studies, we have observed that the period of time between 12 and 24 months postdelivery, generally not considered part of the postpartum period, is a time of high vulnerability to depression. However, pregnancy and childbirth do bring women into contact with health providers and early childhood professionals, creating an opportunity for mothers to be evaluated and offered treatment for depression.

Some key signs of depression during the antepartum period before childbirth, or the postpartum period after childbirth, include the following:

- *A mother who has severe vomiting, malaise, fatigue, and other symptoms that persist past the first trimester of pregnancy.* Most early symptoms resolve, and whereas other causes need to be investigated, persistence of severe symptoms is associated with current depression and predictive of postpartum depression.

- *A mother who does not appear invested in her pregnancy.* A mother may be depressed if she misses prenatal appointments, eats poorly, gains less than optimal weight, has vitamin deficiencies, or lacks interest in hearing the fetus's heartbeat, viewing an ultrasound image, or preparing for the infant's arrival. These dimensions are easily assessed during prenatal visits.

- *A mother who persistently engages in self-endangering activities.* Smoking, excessive activity, or self-endangerment provide cues that a mother may be depressed.

- *A mother who expresses dread or a belief that the pregnancy will have a bad outcome.* Persistent fears that the fetus is malformed, even with contrary assessment information,

Box 3.4.　Depression matters long before an infant is born

Although much attention has been paid to depression after the birth of the infant, new evidence is showing that depression during pregnancy has a direct impact on the developing fetus. Changes in depressed mothers' brain chemistry have been linked to slower fetal growth, a weakened immune system, and changes in the infant's brain structure that may increase vulnerability to stress after birth (Harvard University Center on the Developing Child, 2009). Although these studies are exploratory, nonetheless, the potential for maternal depression to change the biological development of infants and toddlers, especially those with other vulnerabilities, underscores the importance of effective early intervention (Tucker-Drob et al., 2011). Depressed mothers are liable to have unhealthy habits during the pregnancy, such as smoking, illegal drug use, and poor nutrition and have more nausea, stomach pain, and other physical symptoms (Marcus & Heringhausen, 2009). Depressed mothers also are less likely to make regular visits to their maternity care provider and have more complicated birth outcomes such as early delivery, a low-birth-weight infant, and a surgical delivery (Marcus & Heringhausen, 2009). Despite the prevalence (one in eleven infants is born to a depressed mother), one study estimated that 86% of depressed mothers did not get treatment during their pregnancy even when there are effective treatments for depression (Marcus & Heringhausen, 2009). Evidence is consistent that antidepressant therapy is safe during and after pregnancy. However, many mothers are reluctant to take medication for fear of harming the infant. Yet, treatment is still possible—fewer than 6 months of "talking therapy" treatments such as interpersonal psychotherapy and cognitive-behavioral therapy have been shown to be effective in reducing the symptoms of depression. After the symptoms of depression are under control, however, many mothers need additional help to positively interact with their child (Forman et al., 2007). Comprehensive programs that offer parenting support as well as a positive environment for the child are ideal for promoting positive outcomes when depression has been present during pregnancy (Harvard University Center on the Developing Child, 2009).

enduring fear of dying during delivery, or other beliefs about the fetus that are extreme and unfounded may be cues of current depression or risk of depression during the postpartum period.

- *Depression that appears within 4 weeks of delivery with severe and continual symptoms.* Compared with the transient shifts in mood new mothers may experience (sometimes known as "baby blues"), depression is more severe and lasts indefinitely, and the mood alterations do not change in response to diversions. Transient depressive symptoms are common during the postpartum period (with 85% of mothers experiencing them), generally appearing within 2–3 days after delivery and disappearing in 1–2 weeks (American Psychiatric Association, 2000). A mother's transient symptoms can disappear with a visit from a beloved friend, an outing, or a positive mood-inducing distraction.

When mothers show more persistent symptoms of depression, it is unwise to wait and see if those symptoms will pass on their own. Mothers interact more frequently with health providers and early childhood professionals during pregnancy and childbirth, and these relationships provide unique opportunities to help. Even in the midst of stressful issues and depression symptoms, a mother may hold out hope that her unborn child will have a happy, successful life. In fact, her motivation to accept help may be higher than at any other time in her life. In our work with Early Head Start programs serving expectant mothers, we have found that if help for depression is offered in the context of doing the best for her child, a mother can accept it better than if it were presented as a treatment for her mental health problem.

Most childbirth education curricula include information about depression and the importance of a mother's symptoms to her infant's cognitive and emotional development. Parenting guidance and child enrichment curricula generally do not include information on maternal depression. Programs such as Early Head Start establish a partnership with mothers in the antepartum period. Preparing mothers for the possibility of depression can begin the process of trust-building that will allow a mother who has been harboring depression to reach out and receive needed treatment and support.

Moving from Concern to Action with Depressed Mothers

Early childhood educators and home visitors—especially those whose primary areas of expertise are child health or development—may feel unprepared to help mothers experiencing depression. Staff may express their discomfort by arguing that their role does not include providing support for parental mental health concerns. However, there is strong evidence to demonstrate that infant and toddler mental health cannot be separated from parental mental health. There is also a growing recognition among early childhood and early intervention (EI) programs that in order to truly address the best interests of children, they must also serve the best interests of their parents. For example, federal Head Start and Early Head Start Performance Standards for supporting parental mental health were derived in part from compelling data on depression in Early Head Start families. Most programs and providers serving infants, toddlers, and their families have incorporated principles of infant mental health into their program expectations. In our work with EI and Early Head Start program partners, we found that staff embraced the importance of a mental health threat such as maternal depression. However, all of the programs with which we worked were uncomfortable about the next step—what to do when they encountered maternal depression. As we tested a mental health intervention that we embedded into the larger Early Head Start curriculum in order to address maternal depression in these programs, it became obvious to us that programs needed three things to be effective: 1) staff education and explicit skills training; 2) program-level policies, procedures, and referral resources; and 3) ongoing reflective supervision by and for supervisors and administrators. (To learn more about how organizations can support staff in addressing mental health issues, see Chapters 12 and 13.)

What Early Childhood Educators Need in Order to Reach Out to Depressed Parents

Throughout our research with programs, staff articulated their discomfort about working with depressed mothers. Even very skilled and experienced staff members told us they felt uncomfortable broaching the topic of depression with a mother, worrying that they would "make things worse" by talking about it. Here are some of the ways that two Early Head Start staff members expressed their worry when we asked how they felt about helping depressed parents:

> You know, it would be nice to know how to exactly approach parents. Because in the past, where there was a question about their welfare, you know? That you [were] just uneasy, then you would go to talk to the parents to kind of figure out what's going on. And then they get spooked because there's something really going on and they don't want anybody to know, so they up and they pull the child and relocate to a different center. Just so that, you know, it doesn't come home. You don't want to scare anyone away.

> You know, if you say anything toward [parents], they take offense. So I have to . . . watch what I say . . . because I don't want to make them mad at me. You walk a fine line, because you have two relationships . . . you have a relationship with the child and your relationship with the parents, too.

Staff members were haunted by children at risk whose parents abruptly took them out of the program. We understood their anguish, especially if staff had been involved with the parents and had to make a difficult referral, such as to child protective services. It became clear that staff needed to know how to approach parents, and they also needed to know how to work with parents who might not respond positively to an offer for help. Staff needed to practice essential communication skills such as attentive listening and reflecting—skills that were hard for them because they were used to "doing," not listening. Just as staff needed the right words to discuss child development issues and challenges with parents, they also needed to develop a vocabulary of mental health terms and to express their concerns in ways that were not frightening for parents. For example, when talking to a parent about a developmental concern, instead of pointing out a "developmental lag," staff learned to use less directive approaches that asked parents to reflect on their observations of the child, usually around a problem area. Likewise, when mental health issues arose, program staff quickly learned to refocus sensitive conversations on the parent's feeling and issues as a preliminary step to acknowledging parents' depressive symptoms (Beeber, 2009). (To learn more about active listening skills and communication with parents and caregivers, see Chapters 8 and 9.)

Staff also knew that regular program contacts such as pick-up and drop-off might be their only opportunity to talk with parents. In the process of recruiting mothers who showed signs of depression, staff learned to use these brief contacts as well as scheduled parent–teacher conferences or family goal-setting meetings as a place and time to do depression screening. We successfully worked with teachers and home visitors to build their knowledge of the way infants and toddlers demonstrate changes when a parent is depressed. We helped them increase their alertness to these patterns in their regular observations of the child. An Early Head Start staff member describes her growing awareness:

> We do daily anecdotal notes where if something comes up, you know . . . then we can go back and . . . piece together what's going on during this time frame where these things are happening . . . and, you know, day by day . . . you don't pay that [much] attention to it. But . . . if you go back and you're reading like, 2, 3 weeks at a time . . . it's like, "Oh, yeah!" You start putting them together. Something will jump out at you where he did that last week, and he did that this week, and . . . [keeping notes] is really helpful.

We repeatedly observed that the relationship between the staff person—usually someone with direct contact such as a home visitor, family advocate, or a teacher—and the depressed parent was the medium through which the parent could accrue the greatest mental health benefit (Beeber, Lewis, Cooper, Maxwell, & Sandelowski, 2009). If a parent was referred to the program's mental health consultant or to a provider outside the program, the encouragement and praise of the staff person made the difference in whether the parent remained in treatment. Thus, we began to develop ways of helping early education program staff partners support a parent after they had begun to get treatment for depression. We believe that it is the strong staff support of parents that bridges the gap between referral and a parent's actual participation in treatment.

Staff readily acknowledged that they had experienced depression in their personal lives that left them with a range of reactions, from being uneasy about engaging with depressed parents to feeling highly compassionate toward them. Staff expressed worry that they would become "burned out" from getting too close to parents who were depressed. In our research projects in which Early Head Start staff worked as intervention partners, we needed to build in debriefing time to be certain that staff were able to remain emotionally whole. Our experiences led us to believe that mental health work must be accompanied by a support structure such as reflective supervision for all staff—administrators as well as direct service staff. We explore this further as we discuss program structures that help support parents who are depressed or who have other mental health issues in Chapters 11 and 12.

CONCLUSION

Maternal depression is a serious illness with consequences for parent health and functioning, for child development and well-being, and for the parent–child relationship. Maternal depression is a common risk for mothers of young children, and early childhood education and intervention programs in contact with depressed mothers are in a unique position to help. However, to help, programs must first be able to recognize maternal depression. This chapter describes common behaviors of depressed mothers and their children and discusses the influence of depression on family engagement in program services. Once programs recognize depression, staff needs support to effectively address this topic with families and provide the services families need.

REFERENCES

American Psychiatric Association. (2000). *Diagnostic and statistical manual of mental disorders* (4th ed., text revision). Washington, DC: Author.

Beardslee, W.R., & Gladstone, T.R. (2001). Prevention of childhood depression: Recent findings and future prospects. *Biological Psychiatry, 49*(12), 1101–1110.

Beeber, L.S. (2009). Depressive symptoms in Latina mothers. *Head Start Bulletin, 80,* 57–59.

Beeber, L.S., & Canuso, R. (2005). Strengthening social support for the low-income mother: Five critical questions and a guide for intervention. *JOGNN-Journal of Obstetric Gynecologic and Neonatal Nursing, 34*(6), 769–776.

Beeber, L.S., Holditch-Davis, D., Perreira, K., Schwartz, T., Lewis, V., Blanchard, H., Canuso, R., & Goldman, B. (2010). Short-term, in-home intervention reduces depressive symptoms in Early Head Start Latina mothers of infants and toddlers. *Research in Nursing and Health, 33*(1), 60–76.

Beeber, L.S., Lewis, V., Cooper, C., Maxwell, L., & Sandelowski, M. (2009). Meeting the "now" need: PMH-APRN-interpreter teams provide in-home mental health intervention for depressed Latina mothers with limited English proficiency. *Journal of the American Psychiatric Nurses Association, 15,* 249–259.

Beeber, L.S., Perreira, K.M., & Schwartz, T. (2008). Supporting the mental health of mothers raising children in poverty: How do we target them for intervention studies? *Annals of the New York Academy of Sciences, 1136,* 86–100.

Belle, D., & Doucet, J. (2003). Poverty, inequality, and discrimination as sources of depression among USA women. *Psychology of Women Quarterly, 27,* 101–113.

Bettes, B.A. (1988). Maternal depression and motherese: Temporal and intonational features. *Child Development, 59*(4), 1089–1096.

Black, M.M., Papas, M.A., Hussey, J.M., Dubowitz, H., Kotch, J.B., & Starr, R.H., Jr. (2002). Behavior problems among preschool children born to adolescent mothers: Effects of maternal depression and perceptions of partner relationships. *Journal of Clinical Child and Adolescent Psychology, 31*(1), 16–26.

Brennan, P.A., Hammen, C., Katz, A.R., & Le Brocque, R.M. (2002). Maternal depression, paternal psychopathology, and adolescent diagnostic outcomes. *Journal of Consulting and Clinical Psychology, 70*(5), 1075–1085.

Breznitz, Z., & Sherman, T. (1987). Speech patterning of natural discourse of well and depressed mothers and their young children. *Child Development, 58*(2), 395–400.

Brown, G.W., & Moran, P.M. (1997). Single mothers, poverty and depression. *Psychological Medicine, 27*(1), 21–33.

Campbell, S.B., Matestic, P., von Stauffenberg, C., Mohan, R., & Kirchner, T. (2007). Trajectories of maternal depressive symptoms, maternal sensitivity, and children's functioning at school entry. *Developmental Psychology, 43*(5), 1202–1215.

Campbell, S.B., Morgan-Lopez, A.A., Cox, M.J., & McLoyd, V.C. (2009). A latent class analysis of maternal depressive symptoms over 12 years and offspring adjustment in adolescence. *Journal of Abnormal Psychology, 118*(3), 479–493.

Campbell, S.B., Shaw, D.S., & Gilliom, M. (2000). Early externalizing behavior problems: Toddlers and preschoolers at risk for later maladjustment. *Development and Psychopathology, 12*(3), 467–488.

Cicchetti, D., Rogosch, F.A., Toth, S.L., & Spagnola, M. (1997). Affect, cognition, and the emergence of self-knowledge in the toddler offspring of depressed mothers. *Journal of Experimental Child Psychology, 67*(3), 338–362.

Cogill, S.R., Caplan, H.L., Alexandra, H., Robson, K.M., & Kumar, R. (1986). Impact of maternal postnatal depression on cognitive development of young children. *BMJ (Clinical Research Edition), 292*(6529), 1165–1167.

Cohn, J.F., Matias, R., Tronick, E.Z., Connell, D., & Lyons-Ruth, K. (1986). Face-to-face interactions of depressed mothers and their infants. *New Directions for Child Development,* (34), 31–45.

Cohn, J.F., & Tronick, E. (1989). Specificity of infants' response to mothers' affective behavior. *Journal of the American Academy of Child and Adolescent Psychiatry, 28*(2), 242–248.

Cummings, E.M., & Davies, P.T. (1994). Maternal depression and child development. *Journal of Child Psychology and Psychiatry and Allied Disciplines, 35*(1), 73–112.

Duncan, G.J., & Brooks-Gunn, J. (2000). Family poverty, welfare reform, and child development. *Child Development, 71*(1), 188–196.

Field, T. (1998). Maternal depression effects on infants and early interventions. *Preventive Medicine, 27*(2), 200–203.

Field, T., Diego, M., & Hernandez-Reif, M. (2009). Depressed mothers' infants are less responsive to faces and voices. *Infant Behavior and Development, 32*(3), 239–244.

Field, T., Healy, B., Goldstein, S., Perry, S., Bendell, D., Schanberg, S., et al. (1988). Infants of depressed mothers show "depressed" behavior even with nondepressed adults. *Child Development, 59*(6), 1569–1579.

Field, T., Pickens, J., Prodromidis, M., Malphurs, J., Fox, N., Bendell, D., et al. (2000). Targeting adolescent mothers with depressive symptoms for early intervention. *Adolescence, 35*(138), 381–414.

Forman, D.R., O'Hara, M.W., Stuart, S., Gorman, L.L., Larsen, K.E., & Coy, K.C. (2007). Effective treatment for postpartum depression is not sufficient to improve the developing mother-child relationship. *Developmental Psychopathology, 19*(2), 585–602.

Goodman, S.H., Adamson, L.B., Riniti, J., & Cole, S. (1994). Mothers' expressed attitudes: Associations with maternal depression and children's self-esteem and psychopathology. *Journal of the American Academy of Child and Adolescent Psychiatry, 33*(9), 1265–1274.

Goodman, S.H., & Gotlib, I.H. (1999). Risk for psychopathology in the children of depressed mothers: A developmental model for understanding mechanisms of transmission. *Psychological Review, 106*(3), 458–490.

Gross, D., Conrad, B., Fogg, L., Willis, L., & Garvey, C. (1995). A longitudinal study of maternal depression and preschool children's mental health. *Nursing Research, 44*(2), 96–101.

Halligan, S.L., Murray, L., Martins, C., & Cooper, P.J. (2007). Maternal depression and psychiatric outcomes in adolescent offspring: A 13-year longitudinal study. *Journal of Affective Disorders, 97*(1–3), 145–154.

Hammen, C. (1991). *Depression runs in families.* New York: Springer-Verlag.

Harnish, J.D., Dodge, K.A., & Valente, E. (1995). Mother-child interaction quality as a partial mediator of the roles of maternal depressive symptomatology and socioeconomic status in the development of child behavior problems. Conduct Problems Prevention Research Group. *Child Development, 66*(3), 739–753.

Hart, S., Jones, N.A., Field, T., & Lundy, B. (1999). One-year-old infants of intrusive and withdrawn depressed mothers. *Child Psychiatry and Human Development, 30*(2), 111–120.

Harvard University Center on the Developing Child. (2009). *Maternal depression can undermine the development of young children: Working paper no. 8.* Retrieved January 17, 2010, from http://developingchild.harvard.edu/library/reports_and_working_papers/working_papers/wp8/

Jackson, A., Brooks-Gunn, J., Huang, C., & Glassman, M. (2000). Single mothers in low-wage jobs: Financial strain, parenting, and preschoolers' outcomes. *Child Development, 71*(5), 1409–1423.

Kaplan, P.S., Bachorowski, J.A., & Zarlengo-Strouse, P. (1999). Child-directed speech produced by mothers with symptoms of depression fails to promote associative learning in 4-month-old infants. *Child Development, 70*(3), 560–570.

Keren, M., Feldman, R., & Tyano, S. (2001). Diagnoses and interactive patterns of infants referred to a community-based infant mental health clinic. *Journal of the American Academy of Child and Adolescent Psychiatry, 40*(1), 27–35.

Klimes-Dougan, B., Free, K., Ronsaville, D., Stilwell, J., Welsh, C.J., & Radke-Yarrow, M. (1999). Suicidal ideation and attempts: A longitudinal investigation of children of depressed and well mothers. *Journal of the American Academy of Child and Adolescent Psychiatry, 38*(6), 651–659.

Knitzer, J., Theberge, S., & Johnson, K. (2008). *Reduce maternal depression and its impact on young children: Toward a responsive early childhood policy framework.* New York: National Center for Children in Poverty.

Lang, C., Field, T., Pickens, J., Martinez, A., Bendell, D., Yando, R., et al. (1996). Preschoolers of dysphoric mothers. *Journal of Child Psychology and Psychiatry and Allied Disciplines, 37*(2), 221–224.

Lanzi, R.G., Pascoe, J.M., Keltner, B., & Ramey, S.L. (1999). Correlates of maternal depressive symptoms in a national Head Start program sample. *Archives of Pediatrics and Adolescent Medicine, 153*(8), 801–807.

Lovejoy, M.C., Graczyk, P.A., O'Hare, E., & Neuman, G. (2000). Maternal depression and parenting behavior: A meta-analytic review. *Clinical Psychology Review, 20*(5), 561–592.

Lyons-Ruth, K., Connell, D.B., Grunebaum, H.U., & Botein, S. (1990). Infants at social risk: Maternal depression and family support services as mediators of infant development and security of attachment. *Child Development, 61*(1), 85–98.

Lyons-Ruth, K., Wolfe, R., & Lyubchik, A. (2000). Depression and the parenting of young children: Making the case for early preventive mental health services. *Harvard Review of Psychiatry, 8*(3), 148–153.

Marcus, S.M., & Heringhausen, J.E. (2009). Depression in childbearing women: When depression complicates pregnancy. *Primary Care, 36*(1), 151–165.

Murray, L. (1992). The impact of postnatal depression on infant development. *Journal of Child Psychology and Psychiatry and Allied Disciplines, 33*(3), 543–561.

Murray, L., Fiori-Cowley, A., Hooper, R., & Cooper, P. (1996). The impact of postnatal depression and associated adversity on early mother-infant interactions and later infant outcome. *Child Development, 67*(5), 2512–2526.

Murray, L., Hipwell, A., Hooper, R., Stein, A., & Cooper, P. (1996). The cognitive development of 5-year-old children of postnatally depressed mothers. *Journal of Child Psychology and Psychiatry and Allied Disciplines, 37*(8), 927–935.

Murray, L., Kempton, C., Woolgar, M., & Hooper, R. (1993). Depressed mothers' speech to their infants and its relation to infant gender and cognitive development. *Journal of Child Psychology and Psychiatry and Allied Disciplines, 34*(7), 1083–1101.

Murray, L., Sinclair, D., Cooper, P., Ducournau, P., Turner, P., & Stein, A. (1999). The socioemotional development of 5-year-old children of postnatally depressed mothers. *Journal of Child Psychology and Psychiatry and Allied Disciplines, 40*(8), 1259–1271.

National Institute of Mental Health. (2009). *Suicide in the US: Statistics and prevention.* Retrieved September 15, 2009, from http://www.nimh.nih.gov/health/publications/suicide-in-the-us-statistics-and-prevention/index.shtml

Needlman, R., Stevenson, J., & Zuckerman, B. (1991). Psychosocial correlates of severe temper tantrums. *Journal of Developmental and Behavioral Pediatrics, 12*(2), 77–83.

O'Hara, M.W. (2009). Postpartum depression: What we know. *Journal of Clinical Psychology, 65*(12), 1258–1269.

Radke-Yarrow, M., Nottelmann, E., Belmont, B., & Welsh, J.D. (1993). Affective interactions of depressed and nondepressed mothers and their children. *Journal of Abnormal Child Psychology, 21*(6), 683–695.

Silver, E.J., Bauman, L.J., & Weiss, E.S. (1999). Perceived role restriction and depressive symptoms in mothers of children with chronic health conditions. *Journal of Developmental and Behavioral Pediatrics, 20*(5), 362–369.

Simon, G., Ormel, J., VonKorff, M., & Barlow, W. (1995). Health care costs associated with depressive and anxiety disorders in primary care. *American Journal of Psychiatry, 152*(3), 352–357.

Spinelli, M.G. (2004). Maternal infanticide associated with mental illness: Prevention and the promise of saved lives. *American Journal of Psychiatry, 161*(9), 1548–1557.

Toth, S.L., Rogosch, F.A., Manly, J.T., & Cicchetti, D. (2006). The efficacy of toddler-parent psychotherapy to reorganize attachment in the young offspring of mothers with major depressive disorder: A randomized preventive trial. *Journal of Consulting and Clinical Psychology, 74*(6), 1006–1016.

Tronick, E., & Reck, C. (2009). Infants of depressed mothers. *Harvard Review of Psychiatry, 17*(2), 147–156.

Tucker-Drob, E.M., Rhemtulla, M., Harden, K.P., Turkheimer, E., & Fask, D. (2011). Emergence of a Gene x socioeconomic status interaction on infant mental ability between 10 months and 2 years. *Psychological Science, 22*(1), 125–133.

U.S. Department of Health and Human Services, Administration for Children and Families. (2006). *Research to practice: Depression in the lives of Early Head Start families.* Washington, DC: Author.

Vesga-Lopez, O., Blanco, C., Keyes, K., Olfson, M., Grant, B.F., & Hasin, D.S. (2008). Psychiatric disorders in pregnant and postpartum women in the United States. *Archives of General Psychiatry, 65*(7), 805–815.

Weinberg, M.K., Beeghly, M., Olson, K.L., & Tronick, E. (2008). Effects of maternal depression and panic disorder on mother-infant interactive behavior in the face-to-face still-face paradigm. *Infant Mental Health Journal, 29*(5), 472–491.

World Health Organization. (2006). Conquering depression. *Mental Health and Substance Abuse Facts and Figures.* Retrieved July 2, 2009, from http://www.searo.who.int/en/Section1174/Section1199/Section1567/Section1826_8101.htm

Zeanah, C.H., Boris, N.W., & Larrieu, J.A. (1997). Infant development and developmental risk: A review of the past 10 years. *Journal of the American Academy of Child and Adolescent Psychiatry, 36*(2), 165–178.

Zuravin S. (1989). Severity of maternal depression and three types of mother-to-child aggression. *American Journal of Orthopsychiatry, 59*(3), 377–389.

Finding Family Strengths
in the Midst of Adversity

*Using Risk and Resilience
Models to Promote Mental Health*

Colleen I. Monahan, Linda S. Beeber, and Brenda Jones Harden

*E*arly childhood education and intervention programs are designed to strengthen and support families so that, in turn, families can provide the most optimal, nurturing environments for their infants and toddlers. This approach sounds simpler than it often is in day-to-day work with families. We often puzzle as to why one family with everything going for it struggles with basic functions whereas another family experiencing massive adversity uses program resources to thrive and grow.

In this chapter, we discuss the characteristics that account for some of the differences in a family's capacity to cope with adverse situations. These characteristics can be identified as *risk*—that is, individual characteristics, events, and circumstances that endanger or compromise health and development—and *resilience*—that is, individual qualities, relationships, or resources that protect children and families against risk and help them cope, adapt, and even thrive despite experiencing adversity. In our work with families, risk and resilience are in constant interaction, with thriving families maintaining an ever-changing balance between the two. When risk and resilience are understood, early childhood professionals are better able to create programs that tip the balance in favor of preventing bad consequences and help families muster their strengths to raise socially skilled and emotionally healthy infants and toddlers.

USING RISK AND RESILIENCE MODELS IN EARLY PREVENTION AND INTERVENTION PROGRAMS

Early childhood programs frequently aim to serve children and families experiencing risk factors such as economic hardship, neglect, abuse, and parental mental health issues (Laucht et al., 2000). In fact, Head Start programs, stemming from President Lyndon B. Johnson's War on Poverty, were founded upon the premise that the negative effects that one important risk factor, poverty, has on young children can be reduced or eliminated through early education and that the trajectory of their lives can be improved (Vinovskis, 2005). Since that time, early childhood education and intervention programs have expanded to reach out to infants and toddlers experiencing an array of risk factors, including prematurity, low birth weight, and developmental problems associated with perinatal complications (i.e., complications that occur before and just after childbirth) (Adams, Hillman, & Gaydos, 1994). More recently, risks associated with poor mental health outcomes are being addressed in early childhood settings. Let's take a look at exactly what "risk" means to children and families, and what risks families of infants and toddlers commonly experience.

Risk has been generally defined as exposure to conditions that increase the likelihood of negative developmental outcomes for an infant or toddler (Brooks-Gunn, 1990). Risk was first widely recognized by educators and interventionists through a groundbreaking conference at the University of North Carolina in 1974. Dr. Theodore Tjossem (1976) of the National Institutes of Health edited a volume outlining intervention strategies for infants and young children experiencing risk, and he advanced a concept of risk that remains helpful today in thinking about what risk is and how programs might address risk. Dr. Tjossem proposed three categories of risk:

Established risk refers to infants with diagnosed medical conditions, such as Down syndrome or autism, known to result in developmental limitations. The goal of intervention for established risk conditions is to support children in developing to their full potential despite some relatively set limitations. Early intervention (EI) programs funded by the federal Individuals with Disabilities Education Act of 1990 (PL 101-476) and later amendments are examples of programs designed to address established risks experienced by young children.

Environmental risk refers to "early life experiences including maternal and family care, health care, opportunities for expression of adaptive behaviors, and patterns of physical and social stimulation" sufficiently limiting to infants and young children that, if they are not addressed, greatly increase the probability of poor health and development outcomes (Tjossem, 1976, p. 5). This is the kind of risk—poverty, lack of health care, stressed caregivers, for example—that most frequently comes to mind regarding the word *risk*. The goal of intervention for environmental risk conditions is to find ways to minimize and mediate risk conditions and to promote child and family strengths among those experiencing those conditions. Head Start, Early Head Start, child abuse prevention and treatment programs, and the Strengthening Families Programs are all examples of approaches that aim to ameliorate the negative effects of environmental risks.

Biolological risk is the final risk category described by Tjossem, and it refers to infants with a history of perinatal, neonatal, and early developmental events that suggest harm to the child's developing nervous system. This kind of risk may be seen among children exposed in utero to drugs, alcohol, or environmental toxins, or among children suffering chronic health problems such as asthma, for example. The goal of intervention with biological risk is to intervene as early as possible—preferably before a child's birth—to prevent or interrupt exposure to harmful events and to provide circumstances that counter and heal any harm resulting from exposure to those risk-producing conditions. Public health nurse home visiting programs, and components of Head Start and Early Head Start programs that address health, nutrition, and caregiver–child relationships, are examples of programs seeking to prevent or remediate biological risks.

Dr. Tjossem pointed out what early educators and interventionists know too well from their day-to-day work with families: risk factors often occur together and interact with and influence one another. Take, for example, an adolescent girl who becomes pregnant at age 15. She lacks prenatal health care for herself and her infant. Perhaps she is resistant to receiving health care because she uses drugs and alcohol recreationally and does not want to be found out. Both the lack of health care and her substance abuse place her infant at biological risk. This young woman leaves high school, cannot find work, and does not have a supportive family (her mother's current partner has been sexually abusive to the young woman)—all examples of environmental risk. When her infant is born, she may have a fragile nervous system and an inability to regulate emotions and physical states due to drug and alcohol exposure. The infant will enter a world where her single mom is without parenting experience, good role models, or family support, and where her mother is experiencing economic stress that will likely continue. The need for comprehensive, competent, and coordinated supports and services is readily apparent. However, to achieve these goals without families—and programs—feeling or being overwhelmed, it is helpful for educators to understand risk factors and how they interact, then to look for ways to identify and integrate services to strategically and manageably address multiple risks. As research on the resilience of persons experiencing even great hardship in their lives clearly shows, it is equally important to see this young woman in

Box 4.1. Family economic stress model

The *family economic stress* model, an extension of ecological systems theory, describes the impact of economic hardship on family processes as a function of the personal characteristics of individual family members, including the parent and child. The model identifies parent psychological distress as an important mediator between economic hardship and parenting. For low-income parents, such chronic stressors as single parenthood, life stress, financial worries, and the constant struggle to make ends meet are proposed to take a toll on their mental health, in turn diminishing their capacity to be sensitive and supportive parents (Mistry, Vandewater, Huston, & McLoyd, 2002). Empirical tests of the family stress model across a variety of contexts have demonstrated its utility in modeling the mediated relationship of income and hardship to family and child well-being (Conger et al., 2002; Mistry et al., 2002).

her entirety—not as an "at-risk mother" but as a young woman experiencing difficult circumstances, a young woman with attributes and assets who, given other circumstances, can grow to the benefit of herself and her child.

COMMON RISKS FOR
FAMILIES OF INFANTS AND TODDLERS

America has not made the great progress in eliminating poverty that it had hoped for. Rather, economic hardship is increasingly a risk factor in families of young children. According to the National Center for Children in Poverty (Chau, 2009), 19% of all children and 21% of children younger than age 6 in the United States live in families with incomes below the federal poverty level. Between 2000 and 2007, the number of children of all ages who were poor increased by 15%. During the same period, the number of infants and toddlers who were poor increased by 22%. Furthermore, an estimated 550,000 young children live in homeless families (National Center on Family Homelessness, 2003), and more than 150,000 children younger than age 6 live in foster care (U.S. Department of Health and Human Services [DHHS], 2003).

Substantiated abuse and neglect is also a risk for families, with more than 175,000 infants and toddlers identified as victims (Gaudiosi, 2003). An estimated 1.4 million to 4.2 million young children experience intimate partner violence (Edleson, 1999). Families also struggle when a parent suffers from a mental health or behavioral issue. In the United States, 10% of all young children live with a parent who abuses or has a dependence upon alcohol or drugs (National Household Survey on Drug Abuse, 2003). More than 300,000 young children (half of whom are infants and toddlers) have an incarcer-

---

Box 4.2.   Poverty

A substantial body of research links poverty with immediate threats to children's health and emotional well-being and to long-term negative developmental consequences. These linkages are particularly strong for children whose families experience deep poverty, who are poor during early childhood, and who are trapped in poverty for extended periods of time (Anderson Moore, Redd, Burkhauser, Mbwana, & Collins, 2009). Poverty places children at increased risk for a host of problems, beginning at conception (Halpern, 2000). Poverty significantly heightens the risk of exposure to physical health problems such as asthma, malnutrition, and elevated blood levels (Klerman, 1991); mental health problems (Gore & Eckenrode, 1996; McLoyd, 1990); inattentive or erratic parental care (Halpern, 1993); removal from the home and placement in foster care due to abuse and neglect (Halpern, 2000); and impairments in cognitive development and achievement (Duncan, Klebanov, & Brooks-Gunn, 1994; Levin, 1991). When compared with children from more affluent families, children from low-income families are more likely to have low academic achievement (McLoyd, 1998), drop out of school, and have behavioral and emotional problems (Duncan, Yeung, Brooks-Gunn, & Smith, 1998).

Box 4.3. Foster care

Nationwide, there are approximately 500,000 children in the U.S. foster care system. All are at exceptionally high risk for poor psychosocial outcomes (Child Welfare League of America, 2003). Research indicates that foster children tend to score lower on social-emotional measures than would be expected from a sample of children experiencing similar high-risk conditions but who are not in foster care (U.S. Department of Health and Human Services [DHHS], 2001). Compared with children who do not experience placement in foster care, foster children demonstrate higher rates of depression, poorer social skills, lower adaptive functioning, and more externalizing behavioral problems such as aggression and impulsivity (DHHS, 2001). Moreover, an estimated 20,000 adolescents age out of the foster care system each year and, as adults, face disproportionately high rates of unemployment, incarceration, dependence on public assistance, substance abuse, and nonmarital childbirth (Child Welfare League of America, 2003).

ated parent (Johnson & Waldfogel, 2002). Remarkably, in a recent study of Early Head Start parents, half of the parents experienced elevated symptoms of depression at the time of enrollment into the program (Early Head Start Research and Evaluation Project, 2003). Finally, families with infants and toddlers who are born with health and developmental problems may have additional risks. For example, parents of children with disabilities frequently struggle with depression (Singer, 2006).

RESILIENCE AND PROTECTIVE FACTORS

It should be clear that, although researchers may categorize risk conditions and label those categories so that we might more easily talk about and understand how risk functions, we would never wish to categorize and label people as "at-risk." Individuals often thrive despite the most challenging life circumstances. In fact, this is more often the rule than the exception. The concept of an individual thriving despite adversity is known as *resilience*, and research on resilience looks for individual characteristics that make them resilient. *Protective factors*, a related concept, refers to individual and environmental characteristics that support a person's positive response (or resilience) despite difficult life circumstances and biological or established risk (Werner, 1990).

Child psychologist Emmy Werner conducted a longitudinal study of children on the Hawaiian island of Kauai. She followed 698 children from the perinatal period through ages 1, 2, 10, 18, 31/32, and 40, monitoring the long-term effects of a number of biological, psychological, and social risk factors and documenting characteristics and circumstances that made the children resilient. Dr. Werner found that, even among the children exposed to biological risk conditions (e.g., perinatal complications), child outcomes "depended, increasingly, on the quality of the child-rearing environment and the emotional support provided by family members, friends, teachers, and adult mentors" (2004, p. 492).

Box 4.4.   An ecological model of human development

Developmental psychologist Urie Bronfenbrenner famously described developmental psychology as "the science of the strange behavior of children in strange situations for the briefest possible periods of time" (Bronfenbrenner, 1979, p. 513). Dr. Bronfenbrenner, with humor, was criticizing the way psychologists tried to understand child development without considering the relevant psychological, social, and physical surroundings that helped to shape the child.

Ecology is the study of relationships between organisms (including children) and environments (Garbarino, 1990). Dr. Bronfenbrenner proposed a model of *human ecology* emphasizing the multiple, interdependent environments in which children develop, and the progressive, mutual accommodations that children make in relationship to those multiple social and physical environments over their lifetimes (Bronfenbrenner, 1979). This theory, which has been tested and confirmed by numerous studies, posits that among the four nested and interacting ecologies exerting influence on children's development, the most important are *microsystems*, or settings that contain the complex of relationships children have with important others, such as family, peers, and other adults.

According to Bronfenbrenner (1979), the most influential environment for a child's development is the child–caregiver relationships occurring in microsystem settings. To ensure that children experience optimal developmental outcomes, a human ecology model maintains that it is essential for children to experience protective and nurturing caregiving environments. However, because it is known that change in any one subsystem influences changes in the system as a whole, a human ecology model also maintains that, in order for children to experience protective and nurturing caregiving environments, it is essential that educators, communities, and societies give attention to protecting and nurturing those caregiving environments.

The poorest outcomes for children by the time they reached age 40 "were associated with prolonged exposure to parental alcoholism and/or mental illness—especially for the men" (Werner, 2004, p. 492).

Dr. Werner's work, important for early education and intervention, found three types of protective factors present in the lives of children who were resilient despite their having experienced multiple risk conditions. First, children with easy temperaments, intelligence, health, and vigor tended to draw mostly positive responses from others, and these positive responses supported better developmental outcomes. Note that Dr. Werner points out that "research on resilient children has shown us that they had a least one person in their lives who accepted them unconditionally, regardless of temperamental idiosyncrasies, physical attractiveness, or level of intelligence" (1990, p. 113). (See Chapter 2 for information about the challenging child and the concept of "goodness of fit" between children and caregivers.) Second, family socialization that encouraged children to be trustful, independent, and autonomous, and to take initiative, supported better developmental outcomes. Within extended families, affectionate ties with alternative caregivers, including grandparents and siblings, helped buffer stress for children in difficult life circumstances. Third, external support systems, such as friends, schools, and teachers that reinforced the child's competence and provided the child with a positive set of values providing stability and meaning to their lives supported better developmental outcomes (Werner, 1990).

ASSESSING AND ADDRESSING RISK CONDITIONS

Historically, several theoretical models have guided thinking and research about risk and resilience, including Urie Bronfenbrenner's model of human ecology (1979), Arnold Sameroff and Michael Chandler's transactional model of development (1975), and several models related to these, including the family economic stress model and mediator models. Summary descriptions of these models are presented in this chapter.

The work of Arnold Sameroff and colleagues conducting the Rochester Longitudinal Study of the effects of risk on children points to specific risk factors that predict poor child outcomes (Sameroff, Seifer, Barocas, Zax, & Greenspan, 1987). These risk factors include the severity and chronicity of maternal mental illness, maternal anxiety, maternal behavior (e.g., depressed spontaneity in smiling, vocalizing, and touching), maternal education less than high school, parental perspectives about child rearing (e.g., rigid versus flexible attitudes, beliefs, and values), family size of four or more children, family social support, minority group status, and stressful life events (including loss of job, death, or physical illness). This work indicated that the best predictors of child outcomes were the number and combinations of risk factors.

Acknowledging as educators and interventionists that we cannot effectively and responsibly address child development issues if we do not also address the contexts and conditions that influence development, programs may use specific protocols or tools to assess risk. Several approaches to assessing risk, as well protective factors, are presented later in this chapter.

As we have noted, risk factors often occur in clusters, and risk categories interact. For example, poverty, low educational level, minority status, single motherhood, stressful life events, and large family size often appear as a single package (Sameroff, Seifer, Baldwin, & Baldwin, 1993). Programs may in good faith offer interventions that they believe to be helpful, but if interventions do not truly match the needs of families experiencing these conditions, they may add additional stress that overwhelms families. Educators can be more effective if, rather than focusing on a single factor in isolation, they understand how multiple risks affect families. For example, economic hardship is a risk factor that affects many families, but most often it occurs in tandem with other risks. A family experiencing economic hardship may also have problems affording transportation to the grocery store or to mandated child protective services meetings. The parents may experience situational depression related to the chronic worry of providing for their children's basic need for food, clothing, and shelter. Perhaps one of the children in the family has persistent respiratory problems and the family experiences many sleepless nights caring for their child, sometimes rushing to the emergency room for treatment because they cannot afford health care. Educators might find themselves assessing the risk this family is experiencing by asking,

- Is the number of problems they have at once so overwhelming that we need to reduce the family's burden?

- Are some of the problems worse than others, requiring us to tackle specific issues before we can address others?

- Is one particular problem creating other problems leading us to strategically focus on the first problem?

- Or are the problems so intertwined that we can start anywhere—maybe let the family choose what to fix first?

Each of these approaches aims at different goals and will lead staff and families down different paths. The cumulative risk and additive risk models discussed in this chapter present the theories behind each of these approaches. Each of the theories is supported by convincing evidence that either approach will be helpful. The most important

Box 4.5.   A transactional view of family risk

The *transactional model of child development* was first proposed by developmental psychologists Arnold Sameroff and Michael Chandler in 1975 in their seminal article, "Reproductive Risk and the Continuum of Caretaking Causality." At the time this article was written, research attempting to predict developmental outcomes for young children experiencing high-risk conditions tended to focus either on characteristics of the environment or characteristics of the child, and researchers assumed a direct causal relationship between risk and poor outcomes. Few research studies attempted to understand developmental outcomes based on characteristics of both the child *and* the psychological, social, and physical environments. Further, few studies considered that interactions occurring between the child and the psychological, social, and physical environment would influence child outcomes.

In a transactional approach, developmental outcomes are viewed as a function of neither the individual alone nor the experiential context alone. Developmental outcomes are instead seen as a product of the *mutual* contributions of the actively participating child *and* the caregiver that gradually shape the child, the caregiver, their relationship, and the larger caregiving context over time. Within the transactional model, the development of the child is seen as a product of the continuous, dynamic interactions of the child and the experience provided by his or her family and social context. The child and his or her individual characteristics are seen as contributing to and influencing relationships with caregivers, in contrast to the concept of the child as a passive partner shaped by caregivers. In addition, the characteristics of primary caregivers are seen as exerting a powerful and pervasive influence on child outcomes.

The continuum Sameroff and Chandler (1975) first described may be seen, on one end, as environments that are so lacking in necessary psychosocial, health, education, and economic resources that even minor pre- and perinatal problems are difficult to address. On the other end of the continuum, environments are sufficiently supportive that they allow compensations for almost any biological risk factor to prevent transformation into a disabling condition. The transactional model is an effort to provide a comprehensive view of how nature and nurture work together in a continuous flow, perpetually reorganizing and restructuring the child's inner and outer worlds through complex interactions over time (Sameroff & Fiese, 2000).

Box 4.6. Assessing and addressing risk

The national Strengthening Families Program identifies the following five factors that serve to protect children and make their development more resilient in the presence of risk: parent resilience, social connections, knowledge of parenting and child development, concrete support in times of need, and social and emotional competence of children (Horton, 2003). These protective factors correspond directly to the goals of infant mental health. The Center for the Study of Social Policy (Langford, n.d.) offers specific strategies education and intervention that programs may use to support and promote protective factors, including facilitating friendships and mutual support, strengthening parenting, responding to family crises, linking families to services and opportunities, facilitating children's social and emotional development, observing and responding to early warning signs of child abuse or neglect, and valuing and supporting families. In order to address some of these, programs may wish to formally or informally assess risk present in a family's life and identify resources available to them.

Before deciding *whether* to assess risk among children and families attending an early education or intervention program, it is wise to clarify *why* the program wishes to assess risk. Prior to choosing assessment instruments and designing assessment processes, program professionals should make certain that they have a legitimate need to know this information and that they know how it will be used to benefit children and families. Some common reasons for assessing risk include:

- Documenting individual circumstances as a part of ongoing program demographic and descriptive data collection (this information may be required by program funding sources)

- Identifying risk conditions in order to make referrals for needed services

- Identifying risk conditions, strengths, and resources in order to design specific in-program services

Once a program has established a need for this information, it should consider how it might gather assessment information in a way that respects individual and family privacy. It must consider the sensitive feelings and emotions that questions about risk may raise for families. When communicating with families, early childhood educators should emphasize that they wish to learn about any life circumstances the family may be experiencing rather than personal characteristics that may make parenting challenging. Educators should also be aware that normative parenting in modern Western culture may differ from normative parenting in other cultures. It is important for educators to learn parents' and caregivers' perspectives and compare how they might differ from their own or the program's perspectives without judging or evaluating. It is essential to interview parents and caregivers in their fluent language; in a private space; in an open, impartial, and unhurried manner; and using jargon-free language. (See Chapter 7 to learn more about communicating with families.)

It should be clear that, because risk factors and conditions are complex and interrelated, assessing risk is not necessarily a straightforward process. Some examples of approaches to assessing risk include focusing on aspects of the home environment (Dunst & Leet, 1994; Evans & Wachs, 2010; Freidman & Wachs, 1999), social support and networks, community resources, and difficult life circumstances (Dunst & Leet, 1986).

(continued)

Box 4.6.   *(continued)*

If a program gathers information about specific risk conditions, it should make certain that it has identified available resources to address each of these within the program and in the community. In-program resources might include parenting education, developmental screening and guidance, health care screening, nutrition education and resources, infant mental health consultation, early intervention specialists, and child care services. In-community resources might include food sources, housing sources, clothing and equipment sources, child care subsidies, health care, domestic violence, substance abuse, mental and behavioral health programs, and respite care.

The *additive* and *cumulative* risk models described in this chapter provide programs with guidance in selecting specific strategies to help address risk. It is important to make delivery of services as seamless as possible for already overburdened families by using consultants when possible and by coordinating schedules, transportation, and child care when necessary. In addition, whenever possible, programs should work to make identified needs and services an integral, normalizing, and positive part of the program rather than something that identifies families as "needy" or "inadequate." For example, school or community gardens that involve children and families in planning, planting, harvesting, and preparing meals together can address hunger, nutrition education, nutritional needs, and a sense of community. Family education groups that promote knowledge of child development and resources might also have a caregiver-to-caregiver component that promotes friendships and supportive communities.

lesson is that, once a particular approach has been chosen, the approach should be continued and reviewed periodically with the family to see how it is working. Otherwise, the family can become confused if suddenly or randomly the approach switches from "let's reduce the pressure on you" to "we have to solve this problem first."

The following example shows how an Early Head Start program staff member worked with an extended family member who had stepped in to care for her infant niece when the child's parents were both incarcerated for substance abuse and crime. Initially, the aunt felt overwhelmed, but she responded beautifully to the "too many at once" approach guided by an additive theory of multiple risk (Ackerman, Izard, Schoff, Youngstrom, & Kogos, 1999). The following is her description of how the Early Head Start staff person helped her to reduce her load by tackling each problem one at a time as it presented:

Aunt: I've got a 2-year-old and I've got to think about the finances, and I've got to think about the child care. And I've got to think about my own sanity, and I've got to think about, "Where's my niece?" you know, day, after day, after day, after day. That's not easy.

Interviewer: So your Early Head Start family advocate really helps out by helping you manage more effectively. . . . How does she do that?

Aunt: She sets up her physical therapy. She sets up her—well, whatever she needs. She sets it up, tells me where to go, runs me there. And her last statement is always to say, "How can I help you?" You know. So it's wonderful. I love it. Nobody ever asks me, "How can I help you?"

Box 4.7. Cumulative risk models and additive risk models

Cumulative risk models, originally described by child psychiatrist Dr. Michael Rutter in 1979, are based upon the premise that it is not just any one risk factor that matters for child outcomes but rather an accumulation of risk factors that can adversely affect the course of child development (Rutter, 1979; Sameroff, Bartko, Baldwin, Baldwin, & Seifer, 1998). That is, the number of risk factors present in a child's life, rather than the type of risk factors, has the greater influence on the child's development. In this model, the influence of risk factors is cumulative, and the presence of more risk factors is related to a higher certainty of negative outcomes (Seifer, Sameroff, Baldwin, & Baldwin, 1992).

Research using the cumulative risk model has found numerous relationships between the accumulation of risk factors and child outcomes. Compared with children who experience fewer risk factors, children who experience a greater number of risk factors are more likely to be victims of physical abuse and maltreatment (Woodward & Fergusson, 2002), experience lower levels of responsive parenting (Popp, Spinrad, & Smith, 2008), have less stimulating home environments (Brooks-Gunn, Klebanov, & Liaw, 1995), score lower on tests of language skills (Hooper, Burchinal, Roberts, Zeisel, & Neebe, 1998; Stanton-Chapman, Chapman, Kaiser, & Hancock, 2004), and have lower levels of academic achievement (U.S. Department of Health and Human Services [DHHS], 2002; Gutman, Sameroff, & Eccles, 2002). Based upon this model, research has found relationships between the accumulation of risk factors and children's health, cognitive development, behavior problems, emotional well-being, and school achievement. In one study of low-income children's language development, for example, researchers found that cumulative risk was associated with preschool children's language scores, especially for girls (Stanton-Chapman et al., 2004). Measuring maternal risk factors (e.g., prenatal tobacco use, medical history), paternal risk factors (e.g., less than 12 years education), and childbirth risk factors (e.g., low birth weight, preterm birth), the authors found that on average, a girl's Preschool Language Scale (PLS-3) total score decreased 2.3 points with each risk factor she experienced. The accumulation of multiple risk factors thus appears to increase the negative effects of poverty on children's language development.

In another example, the Early Head Start Research and Evaluation Project (DHHS, 2002) examined risk indices that reflect some combination of demographic, child, family, and environmental risks. For example, items on the risk index included the following: being a single parent, receiving public assistance, being neither employed nor in school or job training, being a teenage parent, and lacking a high school diploma or general equivalency diploma. The report found that 26% of the families enrolled in Early Head Start experienced four or more of these risk factors and that the subsample of highest-risk Early Head Start families did not benefit from the program in the same way that other families did.

Another model used to conceptualize multiple risks is an *additive risk* model, which proposes that each risk factor contributes independently to developmental outcomes. Research conducted according to an additive risk model examines the unique effects of multiple risk factors, providing an understanding of how contextual adversity translates into child adjustment difficulties (Ackerman et al., 1999), and it isolates qualitatively distinct sources of risk that are concealed when only

(continued)

Box 4.7. *(continued)*

the number of risk factors, rather than the specific nature of each risk, is considered (Jones, Forehand, Brody, & Armistead, 2002). Duncan and Brooks-Gunn (1997) demonstrated that family income significantly predicted children's academic achievement and ability, even after removing any predictive power associated with family risk factors that often go along with poverty. Likewise, Ackerman and colleagues (1999) found that although the 11 risk factors included in their study together were significantly associated with child behavior problems, parental alcohol–drug abuse was the only individual risk factor that accounted for a significant amount of unique variance.

Mediating Risk

At the beginning of this chapter, we puzzled over why families can look similar in their resources and the problems they face yet function differently. The answer may lie in less-obvious characteristics called *mediators* that are so important that, if they are not addressed, a great deal of energy can be invested in helping families achieve program outcomes without achieving success. Mediators are factors that come after a cause and result in a changed outcome. For example, EI programs are constructed to be mediators between family hardship and negative child outcomes. Without that intervention, positive outcomes will not happen.

Most strength-based infant and toddler enrichment programs are structured to mediate by providing what research tells us is important—such things as social support, positive structure and routine, parental self-esteem enhancement, parenting education, and collaborative relationships that build parents' sense of control. However, some families come to programs with characteristics that keep these powerful program-level mediators from working in the ways in which they were envisioned. Staff members need to work with each enrolled family to figure out what particular characteristics or circumstances may stand in the way of child or family well-being and progress. These challenging circumstances may include parental emotional distress, symptoms of mental illness, or severe levels of family conflict and violence. Once circumstances that present risks are identified, logical and reasonable strategies for changing these are identified. For example, studies of families have shown that parents with high levels of economic hardship can still be capable parents if their emotional distress is low (Conger & Donellan, 2007; McLoyd, Jayarante, Ceballo, & Borquez, 1994; Mistry, Biesanz, Taylor, Burchinal, & Cox, 2004). Thus, reaching out to families with high emotional distress and offering support (in ways that the families find truly supportive) will allow the program magic of strong, stimulating parenting (which cannot be done under high parental distress conditions) to work. In practical terms, programs can increase the positive effects of early education and intervention programs by focusing on factors that can keep a parent from thriving. Meeting a parent's mental health needs through referral for mental health services, and focusing on the parent–child relationship during home visits, will serve to support the parent's positive emotional states and supportive caregiving, which in turn will

Box 4.8. Mediator models

Mediator models assume that larger, distant ecological variables on child outcomes are mediated—or influenced—by proximal, or close, and personal process variables. For example, studies have suggested that mothers' positive emotionality and nurturing involvement in interactions with their children can moderate the impact of cumulative risk on children's problem behaviors (Ackerman et al., 1999). Burchinal, Roberts, Zeisel, Hennon, and Hooper (2006) investigated protective factors among African American children exposed to multiple risks. They found that children's language skills, parenting styles, and child care quality serve as protective factors that positively influence a child's acquisition of math skills, and they found a reduction in problem behaviors during the first 4 years of primary school.

support his or her child's general cognitive, language, and social-emotional development. Also, we reemphasize that, although a program should adopt a coherent general approach to providing services for children and families based upon evidence and ethics, services should also be tailored to address the particular and changing circumstances of individual children and families in order to promote successful outcomes.

PROGRAM SUPPORTS FOR ALL FAMILIES

As we mentioned earlier, programs that include children and families experiencing risk should deliberately incorporate the broad practices and program supports that will help those families successfully meet their infant or toddler's mental health needs. By striving to provide a range of services that address the individual child's ecology, programs can be successful with most families, leaving only a few families whose needs exceed the usual program scope and reach. Program administrators and staff should view families as persons experiencing difficult life circumstances rather than as "problem families." In addition, programs can begin to build capacity to serve these families by identifying whether it is the particular risk that the family presents, the sheer number of risks, the need to address a mediating factor, or a characteristic of the family that is preventing them from reaping the program benefits.

Our experience working hand in hand with Early Head Start programs to implement five different models of infant and toddler mental health intervention brought a few field-worthy messages home to us (Beeber et al., 2007). In this section, we share what we learned from programs and families.

Message 1: Direct service personnel require specialized training and consistent emotional support in order to be of help to high-risk families.

Most early childhood enrichment and intervention programs focus appropriately on the cognitive, social, and emotional development of the infant and toddler. However, the Early

Head Start infant and toddler mental health initiative emphasizes the essential partnership of child and caregiver and the important influence of parental mental health on the child's immediate and long-term development (Beeber et al., 2007). To meet parents' mental health needs, program staff must expand their skills to include recognition of parents' cues indicating that they are feeling distressed or are facing mental health issues. Program staff must show sensitivity to parents' readiness for discussion of their mental health, and staff must develop communication skills, self-reflection, and self-care skills that may not have been part of their child development training but are absolutely critical for mental health support to be effective. Programs must provide such training to staff as well as ongoing support mechanisms such as Reflective Supervision. Chapters 11 and 12 show exactly how programs can provide these kinds of training and support.

Message 2: Programs will be at different points in striving to meet the mental health needs of infants and toddlers in high-risk families, and no matter what the point of service development, leadership is critically important for program progress.

This topic is so complex that this book devotes Chapter 13 to program-level concerns. However, in our combined experience in addressing infant and toddler mental health across many programs, the role of the program leaders as the gatekeepers for successful implementation of infant and toddler mental health intervention is critical. Program leaders are usually in a position to recognize that certain families are more resource-intensive than others, or that families with certain characteristics drop out of the program. In general, these families also are at the highest risk for not meeting the mental health needs of their infant or toddler. It is often program administrators who make the critical call—either purposely or through benign neglect—as to whether families experiencing great challenges will drift away or whether the program will address those challenges in a broad and ecological way. The organizational developmental level, the degree to which the program adheres to quality indicators, and the access to mental health resources in the surrounding community will be strong determinants of the program's capacity to include families experiencing multiple risks.

Message 3: High-risk families who "fall by the wayside" frequently have characteristics that make them atypical for the program serving them.

Each program will need to engage in organizational-level self-reflection to identify what characteristics make certain families atypical for the program and to decide whether these families can be effectively served within the program's typical scope of service. If so, additional staff effort and training will pay off for both the program and the high-risk families. To help guide program self-reflection, we provide three profiles of atypical families that emerged from our combined work:

Profile A: Families in which a parent does not fit in with most of the other parents in the program

Large societal problems and trends such as addiction, crime, and extended military service have placed grandparents, distant relatives, and non-kin in parenting roles. In addition to struggling to meet the challenge of providing a secure emotional environment for a child in turmoil, these caregivers may be required to transform their own lives in order to accommodate their new role. In the following quotation, it is clear that one distant kin parent realizes that her life will never again be the same:

> I not only have the situation just trying to deal with raising a child that I feel like I'm too old to raise, but . . . I have no family support. I have very few friend-type supports because . . . my friends, they don't have no kids. In fact, one of my best friends . . . told me, "I can't wait till he goes back to his mother so we can get back to a normal life." And I'm thinking, "He's not going back to his mother." But she just doesn't grasp it, you know, and she just tells me every day that "your life will go back to the way that it used to be." I'm like, "It'll never go back to the way that it used to be."

If the caregiver's age or relationship to the child is not typical compared to other families in the program, the activities the program offers to support the majority of families may not be a good fit for a particular family, either in the type of support offered or the format. For example, a grandmother may not fit into a socialization group of young mothers, or a seasoned parent may fall into the role of giving more support than she receives. Her issues, such as age-related health concerns, may be different from those of other parents. Staff may not be equipped to assess these needs or may be unfamiliar with resources for older clients, leaving grandparents feeling isolated within the program. In another example, caregivers may not experience a good fit with programs because of differences in ethnic or cultural characteristics. Programs may have developed a particular comfort zone with parents and children of a particular ethnicity or economic status, whereas population changes and economic downturns bring in families that are different on these dimensions and require different skill sets and sensitivity from staff.

Profile B: Fathers who are single parents

Many programs that support the mental health of infants and toddlers are organized to serve single-parent, mother-headed families. Male staff and single-parent fathers may be a minority in those programs, leading to feelings of discomfort and isolation among fathers and male caregivers. The way in which fathers present their needs may also differ. One father expressed this by saying,

> I don't want to talk about my problems with staff; I need to reassure myself that I am strong and in control of things. . . . Talking about my problems leaves me feeling weak and less of a man. I need to know that my kids are safe and that the program is taking good care of them while I am out solving my problems on my own in my own way.

The family support staff person working with this particular father had expressed a sense of helplessness because he never asked for anything from her. With his permission, we shared this content with the staff person, who was surprised and relieved that she was serving him.

Profile C: Multiproblem families

Early childhood and intervention programs generally include family support in some fashion, even if the primary focus is the child. Often, programs become aware of families with multiple problems because those families do not seem to benefit from general program supports, and they frequently cannot meet basic program expectations. Some of our Early Head Start program partners who followed a 9-month enrollment schedule told us that by springtime, families with multiple problems were the ones who commanded most of their attention because they had not progressed according to staff and program expectations. Despite intensive team conferences to address family needs, these families were consuming staff attention and teetering on the edge of dismissal. Some families remained only because of the devotion and creative interventions by staff that kept them from dropping out of the program altogether. As one staff person described her work,

> I call them pretty much every day. If their kid doesn't come, I call. And usually they don't answer. So, I know where they live, so I usually drive by. And I make it a point to say, "Why wasn't your kid here? Why wasn't your kid here?" Because their kid will be dropped if they don't come a certain amount of days. So I keep on. I keep on. I do that on my own time.

In some instances, the additive approach of meeting one problem at a time will not work, because mediating issues such as chronic family stress, mental health issues, or severe parenting challenges need attention. The problems presented by a family will continue or repeat until the core issues are addressed. In the instance of the multi-problem family described, the staff person received additional training and support on how to make a mental health referral, the center director arranged a conference with the family, and the mental health coordinator assisted the family to a community mental health referral. Happily, the outcome was positive for the family, for the program and, most of all, for the toddler.

CONCLUSION

Psychologist James Garbarino (1990) has called the numerous, and relentless, difficult life circumstances so many young children and families in poverty experience "ecological conspiracies." These difficult life circumstances, especially when they accumulate in number, present real challenges to individual development—and to programs wishing to support optimal development.

The parent quoted earlier in this chapter as saying that her life "will never go back to the way that it used to be" recognizes something that may be difficult for programs to reckon with: dealing with challenging life circumstances is often an open-ended job. In time-limited programs that expect success according to a given timeline (often dictated by funding cycles rather than the inconvenient realities of human life), short-term successes may be small whereas overall risk conditions may remain large. For families experiencing chronically challenging circumstances such as a parent's mental health problems, childhood chronic illness, or intergenerational poverty, large changes in relatively short time periods may not be a reasonable expectation. Programs must focus on small but important daily goals and tasks and must take a long and broad view of development in the context of the greater human ecology.

In this chapter, we explored some of the guiding theories that are useful to programs in understanding, identifying, and trying to reduce or eliminate those ecological conspiracies, and mobilize and strengthen protective factors, in order to support children and families. We have recognized that an individual child's education and development cannot truly be addressed outside of the greater ecology of caregiving and family relationships and home and community circumstances in which the child grows.

However, addressing the multiple challenges families face is itself a challenge for programs. Some of these challenges cannot be easily remedied, and because change may be slow and problems may repeat, staff may share in a family's discouragement. Above all, the capacity of the program staff to engage families experiencing multiple risks is perhaps the greatest challenge. For it is through the establishment of these fundamental program–family relationships that children and families may come to benefit in large and small ways from the strength of program resources that support child and family mental health.

REFERENCES

Ackerman, B.E., Izard, C.E., Schoff, K., Youngstrom, E.A., & Kogos, J. (1999). Contextual risk, caregiver emotionality, and the problem behaviors of six- and seven-year-old children from economically disadvantaged families. *Child Development, 70,* 1415–1427.

Adams, C.D., Hillman, N., & Gaydos, G.R. (1994). Behavioral difficulties in toddlers: Impact of sociocultural and biological risk factors. *Journal of Clinical Child Psychology, 23,* 373–381.

Anderson Moore, K., Redd, Z., Burkhauser, M., Mbwana, K., & Collins, A. (2009). Children in poverty: Trends, consequences, and policy options. *Child Trends Research Brief, 2009–2011,* 1–12.

Beeber, L.S., Cooper, C., Van Noy, B.E., Schwartz, T.A., Blanchard, H.C., Canuso, R., et al. (2007). Flying under the radar: engagement and retention of depressed low-income mothers in a mental health intervention. *Advances in Nursing Science, 30*(3), 221–234.

Bronfenbrenner, U. (1979). *The ecology of human development: Experiments by nature and design.* Cambridge, MA: Harvard University Press.

Brooks-Gunn, J. (1990). Identifying the vulnerable young child. In D.E. Rogers & E. Ginzberg (Eds.), *Improving the life chances of children at risk* (pp. 104–124). Boulder, CO: Westview.

Brooks-Gunn, J., Klebanov, P.K., & Liaw, F. (1995). The learning, physical, and emotional environment of the home in the context of poverty: The Infant Health and Development Program. *Children and Youth Services Review, 17,* 251–276.

Burchinal, M., Roberts, J.E., Zeisel, S.A., Hennon, E.A., & Hooper, S. (2006). Social risk and protective child, parenting, and child care factors in early elementary school years. *Parenting: Science and Practice, 6,* 79–113.

Chau, M. (2009). *Low income children in the United States: National and state trend data.* New York: National Center for Children in Poverty, Mailman School of Public Health of Columbia University.

Child Welfare League of America, National Data Analysis System. (2003). *Special data tabulation of 2000 AFCARS and 2000 U.S. Census data (for foster care data).* Retrieved from http://ndas.cwla.org

Conger, R.D., & Donnellan, M.B. (2007). An interactionist perspective on the socioeconomic context of human development. *Annual Review of Psychology, 58,* 175–199.

Conger, R.D., Wallace, L.E., Sun, Y., Simons, R.L., McLoyd, V.C, & Brody, G.H. (2002). Economic pressure in African American families: Replication and extension of a family stress model. *Developmental Psychology, 38,* 179–193.

Duncan, G.J., & Brooks-Gunn, J. (1997). *Consequences of growing up poor.* New York: Russell Sage Foundation.

Duncan, G., Klebanov, P., & Brooks-Gunn, J. (1994). Economic deprivation and early-childhood development. *Child Development, 65,* 296–318.

Duncan, G.J., Yeung, W.J., Brooks-Gunn, J., & Smith, J.R. (1998). How much does childhood poverty affect the life chances of children? *American Sociological Review, 63,* 406–423.

Dunst, C.J., & Leet, H.E. (1986). *Family resource scale.* Brookline, MA: Brookline Books.

Dunst, C.J., & Leet, H.E. (1994). Measuring the adequacy of resources in households with young children. In C.J. Dunst, C.M. Trivette, & A.G. Deal (Eds.), *Supporting and strengthening families, Vol. 1. Methods, strategies, and practices.* Cambridge, MA: Brookline Books.

Early Head Start Research and Evaluation Project. (2003). *Research to practice: Depression in the lives of Early Head Start families* (Research Brief). Washington, DC: U.S. Department of Health and Human Services, Administration for Children and Families.

Edleson, J.L. (1999). The overlap between child maltreatment and woman battering. *Violence Against Women, 5*(2), 134–154.

Evans, G.W., & Wachs, T.D. (Eds.). (2010). *Chaos and its influence on children's development: An ecological perspective.* Washington, DC: American Psychological Association.

Friedman, S.L., & Wachs, T.D. (Eds.). (1999). *Measuring environment across the life span: Emerging methods and concepts.* Washington, DC: American Psychological Association.

Garbarino, J. (1990). The human ecology of early risk. In S.J. Meisels & J.P Shonkoff (Eds.), *Handbook of early childhood intervention.* Cambridge, United Kingdom: Cambridge University Press.

Gaudiosi, J.A. (2003). *Child maltreatment, 2003.* Washington, DC: U.S. Department of Health and Human Services, Administration for Children and Families.

Gore, S., & Eckenrode, J. (1996). Context and process in research on risk and resilience. In R. Haggerty, L.R. Sherrod, N. Garmezy, & M. Rutter (Eds.), *Stress, risk, and resilience in children and adolescents: Processes, mechanisms, and interventions* (pp. 19–63). Cambridge, United Kingdom: Cambridge University Press.

Gutman, L.M., Sameroff, A.S., & Eccles, J.S. (2002). The academic achievement of African American students during early adolescence: An examination of risk, promotive, and protective factors. *American Journal of Community Psychology, 30,* 376–399.

Halpern, D.F. (2000). Validity, fairness, and group differences: Tough questions for selection testing. *Psychology, Public Policy, and Law, 6,* 56–62.

Halpern, R. (1993). Poverty and infant development. In C.H. Zeanah, Jr. (Ed.), *Handbook of infant mental health* (pp. 73–86). New York: Guilford Press.

Hooper, S.R., Burchinal, M.R., Roberts, J.E., Zeisel, S., & Neebe, E.C. (1998). Social and family risk factors for infant development at one year: An application of the cumulative risk model. *Journal of Applied Developmental Psychology, 19,* 85–96.

Horton, C. (2003). *Protective factors literature review: Early care and education programs and the prevention of child abuse and neglect.* Strengthening Families Through Early Care and Education. Center for the Study of Social Policy. Retrieved from http://strengtheningfamilies.net/images/uploads/pdf_uploads/LiteratureReview.pdf

Individuals with Disabilities Education Act (IDEA) of 1990, PL 101-476, 20 U.S.C. §§ 1400 *et seq.*

Johnson, E.I., & Waldfogel, J. (2002). *Children of incarcerated parents: Cumulative risk and children's living arrangements* (JCPR Working Paper 306). Chicago: Joint Center for Poverty Research, Northwestern University and University of Chicago.

Jones, D., Forehand, R., Brody, G., & Armistead, L. (2002). Psychosocial adjustment of African American children in single-mother families: A test of three risk models. *Journal of Marriage and Family, 64,* 105–115.

Klerman, L. (1991). The health of poor children: Problems and programs. In A.C. Huston (Ed.), *Children in poverty* (pp. 79–104). New York: Cambridge University Press.

Langford, J. (n.d.). Introduction. In J. Langford, *Protective factors literature review: Early care and education programs and the prevention of child abuse and neglect.* Strengthening Families Through Early Care and Education. Center for the Study of Social Policy. Retrieved from http://strengtheningfamilies.net/images/uploads/pdf_uploads/LiteratureReview.pdf

Laucht, M., Esser, G., Baving, L., Gerhold, M., Hoesch, I., Ihle, W., et al. (2000). Behavioral sequelae of perinatal insults and early family adversity at 8 years of age. *Journal of the American Academy of Child and Adolescent Psychiatry, 39,* 1229–1237.

Levin, H.M. (1991). Educational acceleration for at-risk children. In A.C. Huston (Ed.), *Children in poverty* (pp. 222–240). New York: Cambridge University Press.

McLoyd, V.C. (1990). The impact of economic hardship on black families and children: Psychological distress, parenting, and socioemotional development. *Child Development, 61,* 311–346.

McLoyd, V.C. (1998). Socioeconomic disadvantage and child development. *American Psychologist, 53,* 185–204.

McLoyd, V., Jayarante, T., Ceballo, R., & Borquez, J. (1994). Unemployment and work interruption among African-American single mothers: Effects on parenting and adolescent socioemotional functioning. *Child Development, 65,* 562–589.

Mistry, R.S., Biesanz, J.C., Taylor, L.C., Burchinal, M., & Cox, M.J. (2004). Family income and its relation to preschool children's adjustment for families in the NICHD study of early child care. *Developmental Psychology, 40,* 727–745.

Mistry, R.S., Vandewater, E.A., Huston, A.C., & McLoyd, V.C. (2002). Economic well-being and children's social adjustment: The role of family process in an ethnically diverse low-income sample. *Child Development, 73,* 935–951.

National Center on Family Homelessness. (2003). *America's homeless children.* Newton, MA: Author.

National Household Survey on Drug Abuse. (2003). *Children living with substance-abusing or substance-dependent parents.* The NHSDA Report, June 2, pp. 1–3. Retrieved from http://oas.samhsa.gov/2k3/children/children.pdf

Popp, T., Spinrad, T., & Smith, C. (2008). The relation of cumulative demographic risk to mothers' responsivity and control: Examining the role of toddler temperament. *Infancy, 13,* 496–518.

Rutter, M. (1979). Protective factors in children's responses to stress and disadvantage. In M.W. Kent & J.E. Rolf (Eds.), *Primary prevention of psychopathology, Vol. 3. Social competence in children* (pp. 49–74). Hanover, NH: University Press of New England.

Sameroff, A.J., Bartko, W.T., Baldwin, A., Baldwin, C., & Seifer, R. (1998). Family and social influences on the development of child competence. In C. Feiring & M. Lewis (Eds.), *Families, risk and competence* (pp. 161–185). Mahwah, NJ: Lawrence Erlbaum.

Sameroff, A.J., & Chandler, M. (1975). Reproductive risk and the continuum of caretaking causality. In F. Horowitz, M. Hetherington, S. Scarr-Salapateck, & G. Siegel (Eds.), *Review of child development research* (Vol. 4, pp. 187–244). Chicago: Society for Research in Child Development.

Sameroff, A.J., & Fiese, B.H. (2000). Transactional regulation: The developmental ecology of early intervention. In J.P. Shonkoff & S.J. Meisels (Eds.), *Handbook of early childhood intervention.* New York: Cambridge University Press.

Sameroff, A.J., Seifer, R., Baldwin, A., & Baldwin, C. (1993). Stability of intelligence from preschool to adolescence: The influence of social and family risk factors. *Child Development, 64,* 80–97.

Sameroff, A.J., Seifer, R., Barocas, R., Zax, M., & Greenspan, S. (1987). IQ scores of 4-year-old children: Social-environmental risk factors. *Pediatrics, 79,* 343–350.

Seifer, R., Sameroff, A.J., Baldwin, C.P., & Baldwin, A. (1992). Child and family factors that ameliorate risk between 4 and 13 years of age. *Journal of the American Academy of Child and Adolescent Psychiatry, 31,* 893–903.

Singer, G.H.S. (2006). Meta-analysis of comparative studies of depression in mothers of children with and without developmental disabilities. *American Journal on Mental Retardation, 111*(3), 155–169.

Stanton-Chapman, T.L., Chapman, D.A., Kaiser, A.P., & Hancock, T.B. (2004). Cumulative risk and low income children's language development. *Topics in Early Childhood Special Education, 24,* 227–237.

Tjossem, T.D. (1976). Early intervention: Issues and approaches. In T.D. Tjossem (Ed.), *Intervention strategies for high risk infants and young children.* Baltimore: University Park Press.

U.S. Department of Health and Human Services, Administration for Children and Families. (2001). *National survey of child and adolescent well-being (NSCAW). One-Year Foster Care Report.* Washington, DC: Author.

U.S. Department of Health and Human Services, Administration for Children and Families. (2002). *Making a difference in the lives of infants and toddlers and their families: The impacts of Early Head Start.* Washington, DC: Author.

U.S. Department of Health and Human Services, Administration for Children and Families, Adoption and Foster Care Analysis and Reporting System. (2003). *Data submitted for FY 2003* (October 1, 2002 through September 30, 2003). Retrieved from http://www.acf.hhs.gov/programs/cb/stats_research/afcars/tar/report10.pdf

Vinovskis, M.A. (2005). *The birth of Head Start.* Chicago: University of Chicago Press.

Werner, E. (1990). Protective factors and individual resilience. In S.J. Meiseles & J.P Shonkoff (Eds.), *Handbook of early childhood intervention*. Cambridge, United Kingdom: Cambridge University Press.

Werner, E. (2004). Journeys from childhood to midlife: Risk, resilience, and recovery. *Pediatrics, 114,* 492.

Woodward, L.J., & Fergusson, D.M. (2002). Parent, child, and contextual predictors of childhood physical punishment. *Infant and Child Development, 11,* 213–235.

5

Exposure to Direct and Indirect Trauma

Meryl Yoches, Susan Janko Summers, Linda S. Beeber, Brenda Jones Harden, and Neena M. Malik

*E*ducators and caregivers in early childhood programs are on the front lines, helping children grow and develop in the context of an alarming increase in exposure to trauma among infants and toddlers. Some children experience catastrophic events such as natural disasters or singular violent acts. More often, however, young children are exposed to repeated or sustained, ongoing trauma in the form of violence in their families or communities (U.S. Department of Health and Human Services [DHHS], 2010). Trauma affects young children's development, behavior, and relationships—even during infancy (Schuder & Lyons-Ruth, 2004). For these children, early childhood programs are particularly important, because they can address many of the issues that traumatized children experience. Early childhood programs have the potential to help children and their families, not only in the short term, but also in terms of mitigating some of the long-term negative consequences of trauma exposure.

The first intimate relationships between infants and caregivers set the stage for health, growth, and development for the rest of a child's life (Bowlby, 1969, 1973). Because young children depend on their caregivers to meet their essential physical, psychological, and emotional needs, it is no surprise that the early relationships children have with caregivers also influence their experiences of trauma. A child's relationships with primary caregivers are central to how that child deals with exposure to trauma. Positive relationships with caregivers may help children deal constructively with their experiences, whereas negative relationships may make children's symptoms worse. Positive relationships with their caregivers in the home, at preschool, or in the community may help children immensely when coping with exposure to traumatic events (Scheeringa & Zeanah, 2001). Caregivers outside of the immediate family may be able to intervene early and refer children and families for mental health services in the aftermath of exposure, thereby helping to mediate the immediate effects of trauma and change for a better long-term trajectory of health, growth, and development (Lieberman & Van Horn, 2004; Osofsky, 2011).

UNDERSTANDING TRAUMA

Traumatic experiences in the lives of young children are unthinkable, and at the same time they are all too common. Although precise numbers are difficult to determine for the general population, an estimated 44,512 children younger than 3 years were exposed to trauma sometime during 2009. This represents about 33.4% of all children who were exposed to trauma during that year (DHHS, 2010). Children are more at risk for death or injury from violence exposure during the first 5 years of their lives than during any other time.

Although definitions of trauma vary, in general, *trauma* has been defined as "an event or events that involve actual or threatened death or serious injury to the child or others, or a threat to the psychological or physical integrity of the child or others" (ZERO TO THREE, 2005). Exposure to trauma can occur once or multiple times, and young children exposed to multiple traumatic events tend to experience worse outcomes than those exposed only once (Chu & Lieberman, 2010). In this chapter, we define trauma as exposure to community violence, family violence, and child maltreatment and neglect.

Box 5.1.   Definitions of trauma

What is *community violence?* (National Center for Children Exposed to Violence [NCCEV], 2006a)

- Violence outside the home, within the neighborhood
- Violence committed by people who are not known or related to witnesses
- Exposure to weapons, muggings, the sound of bullets, sexual assaults
- Contact with gangs and guns
- Being a victim of violence

What is *family violence?* (NCCEV, 2006b)

- Violence within the home
- Violence between family members

What is *child maltreatment?* (U.S. Department of Health and Human Services, 2009)

- Physical abuse, sexual abuse, emotional abuse, neglect
- *Physical abuse* includes nonaccidental acts that result in injury to a child
- *Neglect* includes absence of care by caregivers, failure to supervise young children, or failure to provide for the basic needs of children

Box 5.2. How many children are exposed to trauma?

- About 6% of children between ages 2 and 5 witnessed acts of violence in their communities in the past year; 9% witnessed acts of violence in their lifetime (Finkelhor, Turner, Ormrod, & Hamby, 2009).

- About 1% of children under 2 were exposed to a shooting in the past year (Finkelhor et al., 2009).

- Between 14% and 50% of children have been exposed to interpersonal violence (Litrownik, Newton, Hunter, English, & Everson, 2003).

- Almost 10% of children have seen one family member assault another (Finkelhor et al., 2009).

- About 20% of reported cases of family violence included an issue concerning a child, and in 12% of cases, a child placed the call to police to report the violent event (Margolin & Gordis, 2000).

- In the United States, a child is abused or neglected every 36 seconds; 40% of these children do not receive any help from authorities (U.S. Department of Heath and Human Services [DHHS], 2009).

- About 22% of proven cases of child abuse and neglect were in children younger than 1 year. Of these cases, almost 60% of children experienced neglect, 10% experienced physical abuse, less than 10% experienced sexual abuse, and less than 5% experienced psychological abuse (DHHS, 2009).

- About 1,760 children died from abuse and neglect in 2007, and 75% of those deaths were children younger than 4 years (DHHS, 2009).

- Almost 80% of abusers are parents. More than 90% are biological parents and more than 55% are women (DHHS, 2009).

- Children between birth and 1 year have a victimization rate of 21.9 per 1,000 children (DHHS, 2009).

- About 39% of victimizations occur in the first 30 days after birth. Of these, 87.7% occur during the first week of life (DHHS, 2009).

- Premature infants and those with disabilities are at greater risk for maltreatment than other young children (Sidebotham, Heron, & the ALSPAC Study Team, 2003).

In understanding the needs of children and their families, it may be helpful to view these families in the context of traumatic events and circumstances. By considering these contexts, those who work with children exposed to trauma may better understand what those children and their families have experienced psychologically, socially, and physically. If those who work with young children are able to better understand the circumstances that traumatized children typically experience, they will be better able to anticipate and provide appropriate help for children in crisis. This may include stopping repeated traumatic events, restoring a safe environment, and referring children and families for help in dealing with exposure to trauma (Harris, Lieberman, & Marans, 2007).

Trauma Symptoms in Young Children

Children exposed to traumatic events exhibit many of the same symptoms, regardless of the type of trauma they experience. In general, children exposed to trauma may show the following signs:

- "Reexperiencing" or playing out memories of the event in verbalization, play, or behavior
- Sleep problems such as trouble falling asleep and nightmares
- Eating problems such as overeating or finicky eating
- Regression in developmental functioning or "acting like a baby"
- Withdrawal, such as talking less, avoiding interactions, seeming less joyful
- Onset of new fears
- Aggressive outbursts or increased activity level
- Increased clinginess and/or separation anxiety
- Preoccupation with the traumatic event, such as bringing up the episode in ways that are repetitious, pressured, or uncontrollable
- Increased stress

For a more detailed list of the developmental consequences children may demonstrate according to the type of trauma they experience, see Table 5.1.

Resilience

Resilience is the ability to thrive, even in the face of challenges. Although many children exposed to violence develop symptoms related to the exposure, some children show resilience and fare well in the long run. Important factors in children's well-being following trauma include a positive relationship with a caring adult, access to a place where the child can be safe in their community, and the child's personality and temperament (Osofsky, 1999, 2011). Of these, the most important factor for young children is the presence of a sensitive adult who will help them psychologically process the traumatic event or circumstance. If children have one person in their lives to whom they can turn during times when they feel frightened and stressed, the symptoms discussed earlier will not be as severe. Therefore, early care providers have a unique opportunity to provide children with the sensitivity and care they need to mitigate negative consequences of exposure to traumatic events.

RELATIONSHIP ISSUES AROUND TRAUMA

Young children rely on their caregivers for most things. They rely on them for protection from harm, for reassurance during frightening events, for love and support, and to meet their basic needs for clothing, food, and shelter on a daily basis. When young children are directly traumatized, their caregivers may also secondarily experience trauma. Or, in violent households and communities, both caregiver and child may be exposed to

Table 5.1. Developmental consequences for children exposed to direct and indirect trauma

Community violence[a]	Family violence[b]	Child maltreatment[c]
Physical:	*Physical:*	*Physical:*
Bedwetting	Death and physical injury	Death and physical injury
Toileting problems	Sleep disruption	Shaken baby syndrome
Sleep disruption	Eating problems	Ocular damage
Eating problems	Failure to thrive	Brain damage
Compromised motor skills	Loss of developmental	Visual loss or blindness
Loss of developmental milestones	milestones	Compromised motor skills
		Failure to thrive
Cognitive:	*Cognitive:*	*Cognitive:*
Cognitive difficulties	Cognitive difficulties	Cognitive difficulties
Verbal or language impairments	Verbal or language impairments	Verbal or language impairments
Concentration problems	Developmental delay	Communication problems
Developmental delay	Later academic problems	Hyperactivity or attention-deficit/hyperactivity disorder
Later academic problems		
Socioemotional:	*Socioemotional:*	*Socioemotional:*
Posttraumatic stress disorder symptoms	Posttraumatic stress disorder symptoms	Posttraumatic stress disorder symptoms
Re-experiencing events	Hypervigilant	Externalizing problems
Avoiding location of events	Depression	Depression
Increased arousal	Anxiety	Aggression
Anxiety	Feelings of loss or sadness	Rule violation
Depression	Aggression	Self-blame
Clingy behavior or tantrums	Interpersonal relationship problems	Low self-esteem
Highly emotional	Poor attachment relationships	Dysregulation of stress system
Aggression	Fear of being alone	Insecure attachments
Irritability	Clingy	Less play
Emotional distress	Separation anxiety	Poor peer relations
Mistrust of adults	Anger toward parent	Reactive attachment disorder
Problems feeling safe		

[a]Harden and Koblinsky (1999).
[b]Harden and Koblinsky (1999).
[c]Goldman, Salus, Wolcott, and Kennedy (2003).

traumatic experiences. When this occurs, caregivers may become less effective in providing physical and emotional care for a child who has experienced trauma, because those caregivers may be less psychologically available as they deal with their own symptoms from trauma. Children with less psychologically present and effective caregivers may exhibit more trauma-related symptoms. Similarly, children who feel as though their parents are threatened tend to experience more symptoms, because they worry about their parents' safety in addition to processing the event (Scheeringa & Zeanah, 2001).

Ideally, the relationship between a caregiver and a child will be protective of the child in the face of trauma exposure. A caregiver's relationship with the child can have a moderating effect on the child and on his or her own functioning. If the parent reacts positively in the aftermath of trauma, there is an increased likelihood that the child may also react positively. Unfortunately, this relationship can also be reciprocal in a negative sense; a child who is having more difficulties with the experience of trauma may influence the caregiver's experience with trauma, and the caregiver in turn might exhibit more symptoms him- or herself. This can create a cycle whereby the child and caregiver influence each other continuously, unless adequate intervention is implemented (Scheeringa & Zeanah, 2001).

It is also important to remember that there is a very strong link between children's trauma symptoms and the amount of exposure a child has to traumatic events. It is imperative for early childhood staff to intervene early and offer help to a child or family if they know or suspect that the child or family has been exposed to violence—either in their home or their community. The longer and more often a child is exposed to violence, the worse off the child will be socially, emotionally, and psychologically in the long run. Therefore, intervention and support must be of sufficient duration to address both immediate needs and long-term developmental and relationship issues.

Trauma and Attachment

Children develop attachment relationships with their primary caregivers, most often their mother, during the first few months of life. Attachment is motivated by *biology*—the child's literal need to be in proximity (or physically close to) a caregiver in order to survive— and *psychology*—the child's emotional need to feel secure because a caregiver is physically available and emotionally responsive. In a securely attached relationship, both caregiver and child find satisfaction and enjoyment (Sroufe & Waters, 1977).

There are three kinds of behaviors seen among "securely attached" children (Wallin, 2007).

1. Children will seek out and attempt to maintain proximity (physical or visual closeness) with a caregiver who the child experiences as protective.

2. Children will use the caregiver as a safe, secure base from which to explore unfamiliar settings and experiences.

3. Children will return to the caregiver's presence as a safe haven from situations the child perceives as emotionally distressing or dangerous.

The concept of *attachment* represents a child's understanding that a primary caregiver is someone who provides love and support and will protect him or her from harm. Caregivers become a secure base from which children learn they can explore the world. Based on this relationship, infants create internal working models, or mental representations and expectations, whereby they learn to trust that their caregiver will protect them from harm or they learn that their caregiver is someone they cannot trust. This relationship lays the foundation for future relationships throughout one's life (Bowlby, 1969, 1973). (See Chapter 7 to learn more about the development of attachment and how it affects emotion regulation and Chapter 8 to learn more about how attachment theory may guide intervention.)

Infants between the ages of 12 and 18 months may be classified according to four attachment styles: secure, insecure-avoidant, insecure-resistant/ambivalent, and insecure-disorganized/disoriented (Ainsworth, Blehar, Waters, & Wall, 1978; Main & Soloman, 1986). A secure attachment has been shown to be positive for children's development as well as their functioning in future relationships. Children who are exposed to trauma may have difficulties developing and/or maintaining a secure attachment relationship for several reasons. Children develop insecure attachments when a caregiver is inconsistent—

Box 5.3. Reactive attachment disorder

What is reactive attachment disorder?

- Developmentally inappropriate social interactions with others before age 5 (American Psychiatric Association, 2000)
- Failure to initiate or respond in a developmentally appropriate way to social interactions
- Inhibited behavior, with hypervigilance or ambivalence to social interactions
- *Inhibited type:* Unable to form relationships with anyone
- *Disinhibited type:* Indiscriminant friendliness to anyone

How do children develop reactive attachment disorder?

- Result of child physical abuse, sexual abuse, or neglect (Hornor, 2008)
- Inconsistent and/or absent caregiving
- Parent drug use, alcohol abuse, mental illness
- Experience in foster care

How many children develop reactive attachment disorder?

- About 1% of the general population
- 38% of children in foster care, because of child abuse and neglect (Zeanah & Emde, 1994)

regardless of whether this inconsistency occurs because the caregiver is neglectful or because the caregiver is dealing with his or her own reaction to trauma. A child who repeatedly experiences this inconsistency may begin to believe that he or she is not worthy of care and protection from the caregiver (Ainsworth et al., 1978). If the caregiver is viewed by the child as threatening, as is the case when a caregiver is abusive, the child may develop an insecure-disorganized attachment, as he or she experiences time and again that the person who is supposed to protect is causing him or her harm (Hesse & Main, 2006; Main & Solomon, 1990). The attachment relationship that children have with their caregivers before a traumatic event also has an impact on a child's functioning after exposure. A child with an insecure attachment may be more vulnerable to the impact of trauma, because he or she does not have a person who provides a secure base and to whom he or she feels comfortable going to for comfort (Toth & Cicchetti, 1996). In extreme cases of abuse and neglect, some children may develop *reactive attachment disorder* (Hornor, 2008).

All children exposed to trauma, regardless of their attachment style, may not trust that their primary caregiver can protect them from harm. Likewise, children's attachment styles may change based on their traumatic experience and how their caregiver reacts following the trauma exposure. Caregivers who are preoccupied with traumatic experiences can become emotionally unavailable or perhaps even hostile to the child after the traumatic experience, and the child may consequently develop an insecure attachment to that caregiver (Schuder & Lyons-Ruth, 2004). However, even if a child has a secure attachment to their caregiver, the experience of trauma may damage that relationship. A child who previously felt as though he or she could go to the parent for protection and security may generalize the fear of being hurt in relationships to the parent and, at least temporarily, may experience the parent as no longer being a source of safety. Conversely, a caregiver who is unresponsive when the child is scared may actually make the child's symptoms of trauma exposure worse, because he or she is not providing comfort to the child.

Although many children exposed to chronic trauma develop insecure attachments, those who are able to securely attach to their caregiver, or are able to retain a secure attachment, may be protected from some of the symptoms of exposure to trauma. Secure attachments help children process and resolve their experiences. If the primary caregiver provides support to the child, the child may be buffered from some of the negative consequences of trauma exposure. In addition, because the caregiver and child influence each other's functioning after the trauma, it is essential to understand how both the parent and the child are functioning following the exposure to trauma (Chu & Lieberman, 2010).

IMPLICATIONS FOR PRACTICE

Because young children exposed to trauma are at risk for multiple developmental problems, early childhood programs can be a very important place to provide services that specifically target the needs of this vulnerable group. Programs should include child and adult victims, as well as perpetrators of violence when appropriate, and provide concrete and psychological services alike. This section describes how early childhood programs can approach early childhood trauma from multiple perspectives, employing multiple strategies, with the ultimate goal of improving outcomes for child victims of trauma.

Providers working directly with children and families who have been exposed to trauma can make sure that the child feels safe and that the child's basic needs are met, and they can refer families for psychological and social services to help them deal with the trauma. When legally mandated, programs must contact the appropriate authorities to make sure that repeated exposure to trauma is ended. The only way that a child will begin to recover from this exposure is for caregivers to make sure that the child is safe and avoids experiencing more traumatic events.

Screening to Identify Trauma

In order to identify children and families who have been exposed to trauma, it is essential that programs employ an effective, family-friendly screening procedure. For many children and families, especially those participating in home visiting programs, early education and intervention are based upon trusting and long-term relationships that continue through the first years of the child's life. In these circumstances, educators and home visitors often become aware of trauma, either because information is disclosed by a caregiver or the home visitor or classroom teacher is attuned to the child and observant of behavioral and developmental changes. Chapter 7 presents the fundamentals of interviewing caregivers. These skills are essential when talking with families dealing with trauma or families that early childhood professionals suspect are dealing with trauma.

Programs that serve particularly high-risk populations may wish to administer screening instruments more broadly. The sensitive nature of the questions included in screening instruments may require that screening protocols be administered after families have developed a beginning relationship with programs. Nevertheless, because violence can have such devastating consequences on families, screenings for high-risk populations should occur as soon after program enrollment as possible. Families completing the protocols should be clearly informed that the purpose of the screening is to identify resources and supports for children and families needing them, and they should be assured that all information will be kept private and confidential and shared only on a need-to-know basis.

In keeping with the purpose of screening, programs should be sure to anticipate and arrange in advance those resources likely to be needed by children and families. Ideally, mental health consultants or in-program mental health personnel should be immediately available to offer guidance to children and families, and sources for out-of-program resources should be contacted in advance and ready to receive referrals. In addition to mental health resources, programs should be sure to include child development specialists, given that developmental delays may result from trauma exposure and that child maltreatment appears to occur at higher rates among people with disabilities (DHHS, 1993).

A number of tools have been created to screen for violence exposure and trauma. Among the most commonly used are the Conflict Tactics Scales, which assess interadult and parent–child conflict and violence (Straus, 2007), and the Violence Exposure Scale (Fox & Leavitt, 1995), which assesses young children's exposure to home and community violence. Although these tools were initially developed for research purposes, programs with a clear purpose for using these tools may also administer them to gauge the level of trauma that children and families experience. These tools can be incorporated into ongoing assessment of the behavioral and developmental functioning and experiences of children and/or into family assessment and intervention plans (e.g., Early Head Start Family Partnership Agreements).

Most of these assessments are easy and quick to administer. However, the nature of the questions requires that staff be very sensitive to the range of responses that program participants may have to the questionnaire. For example, some parents may withdraw from the questions because they bring up traumatic memories that may be difficult to handle in the moment. Other parents may become emotionally distressed by the questions and exhibit emotions such as sadness or rage. Whatever the parental response, staff who administer such questionnaires must exude calm and gentle support, be willing to end the interview should it become too difficult for parents, and have a plan for follow-up care and support. Again, in anticipation that some caregivers or children may need immediate emotional support or psychological intervention, programs should have identified appropriate in-house supports, consultants, or referral sources for those needing these resources.

Programs should have identified procedures for when and how to make legally mandated reports to child protective services (CPS) should the need arise while maintaining constructive communication with and ongoing support for families. If families reveal that they have exposed their children to trauma, either directly or indirectly, early childhood program staff may be mandated to report the family to CPS in order to ensure the safety and well-being of the child. Although families often feel betrayed by such calls, if staff explain their rationale in an objective manner and maintain positive support for the family, reassuring caregivers that they can offer concrete support to help children and families make more healthy choices, the staff–family relationship can often be sustained and even strengthened.

Trauma Intervention

After trauma-exposed children and families have been identified, early childhood programs may begin to address the consequences of this exposure for individual children and parents. Children may or may not present with the behaviors described in Table 5.1. Nevertheless, they should receive intervention in every context of the early childhood program. For example, classroom teachers can carefully observe these children and provide opportunities for them to express their thoughts and emotions relative to the traumatic events through play and other activities. It is also recommended that programs call in mental health consultants to support the child in these activities, and that these activities take place in a setting that is private and feels safe and comfortable to the child. Children may need more intensive nurturance and scaffolding, or support, during regular classroom and caregiving routines such as toileting, eating, and playing with peers. Teachers should be aware that tasks that are challenging for all young children—such as managing transitions in the classroom, separating from caregivers, and responding to frustrating experiences—may be particularly difficult for trauma-exposed children. Responding with even more warmth, patience, sensitivity, and structure will be necessary for these children. Because of the overwhelming evidence that young children may be protected from the negative consequences of trauma by their caregivers, teachers have an important role to play in maintaining a close, intimate relationship with trauma-exposed children. Finally, classroom and other program staff, such as home visitors, should engage in activities to promote child development across domains so that this vulnerable group of children can continue to receive normative developmental experiences. (See Chapter 2 to learn more about supporting children exhibiting emotional dysregulation, aggressive behavior, and internalizing and externalizing behavior. See also Chapter 8 and Chapter 10 to learn additional ways of incorporating mental health expertise into educational practice.)

The consequences of trauma exposure for young children should be addressed in the context of the family as well. Promoting positive relationships between children and their families is paramount. In the case of family violence, a victimized spouse should be supported to address his or her own trauma and to parent and respond to his or her children in the best manner possible. In the case of child maltreatment, early childhood staff can deliver parent–child interaction intervention with a goal of reducing child abuse and neglect. Early childhood practitioners can also assist parents in coping with the consequences of community violence while placing primary importance on physically and psychologically protecting their children from violent experience. Home visitors and family support staff can help parents who have been exposed to violence develop safety plans that incorporate concrete strategies to meet their children's needs for physical and emotional safety as well as addressing their own needs. For example, parents who are going to domestic violence shelters can make sure to carry their children's favorite toys with them so that the children will have something that reminds them of the positive parts of their lives. Family support staff can also work on parent–child interaction activities that promote child development so that young children can have normative experiences as well as trauma-focused intervention.

Staff training and supervision about trauma and its effect on young children and their families are necessary if staff is to provide appropriate support to affected families. Didactic training sessions can address staff needs for information about the various consequences of trauma exposure and the multiple strategies that are used to intervene with families and children. It is important to note that experiential training and supervision can help staff recognize signs of domestic violence and child maltreatment, as well as behaviors that reflect posttraumatic stress. Staff should have access to program protocols—or specific plans for treatment—that guide their work with trauma-exposed families, including strategies for maintaining the safety of children, parents, and staff members; procedures for involving other agencies such as police and child welfare; and mechanisms for intervening with perpetrators. Administrative support for staff, such as providing educational materials and targeted training opportunities, can help programs promote child development, enhance parent–child interactions, and communicate productively with children and families.

Even with training and supervision, most staff members in early childhood programs do not have the expertise to intervene with families that have experienced trauma. Thus, collaboration with other professionals and programs serving these families is crucial. Some early childhood programs (including Early Head Start) include in-program or external mental health consultation as a regular component of family services. (See Chapter 10 to learn more about mental health consultation in early childhood programs.) Appropriately trained mental health consultants can provide brief psychotherapeutic intervention to children and adults who are the victims of violence. Evidence-based treatment approaches that address posttraumatic stress reactions in young children are available (Lieberman & Van Horn, 2004; Osofsky, 2011). For very young children, these approaches often target the parent–child dyad as a means to promote caregiving that is responsive and sensitive to the unique needs of traumatized infants and toddlers and that addresses physiologic and emotional dysregulation.

Similarly, mental health consultation may be used to engage the perpetrators of trauma. Although the evidence on treatment of perpetrators of family violence shows that there are significant challenges associated with improving the behaviors of this population (Edleson & Malik, 2008; Gewirtz & Edleson, 2007), mental health consultants can utilize approaches that have been studied. Evidence-based interventions for the perpetrators of child abuse tend to focus on cognitive-behavioral strategies to address impulse and emotion control while instilling appropriate parental expectations and using techniques that support parents in managing their child's behavior (Azar & Wolfe, 2006; Swensen & Chaffin, 2006).

Beyond obtaining treatment for trauma-affected children and families, it is important that early childhood professionals establish linkages with other community resources that serve this population. For example, informal relationships and formalized memoranda of understanding should be developed with domestic violence shelters, child protection agencies, police precincts, and neighborhood child abuse prevention centers.

These organizations typically have more experience with intrafamilial and extrafamilial violence, and they have devised protocols to help victims and perpetrators. They can assist early childhood programs to support the safety of trauma-exposed families and potentially reduce the incidence of violence that children and families experience. Linking families with programs and services that target children as well as families—such as domestic violence shelters that include children or workers who serve youth in their police precincts—could go far to promote the well-being of children exposed to trauma.

TRAUMA INTERVENTION APPROACHES

Although young children exposed to trauma are at risk for developmental problems, families and communities can do many things to mitigate this risk. The most important thing is to make sure that children and families are safe. As we have noted, when beginning treatment it is also important to make sure the focus is on both the child and the primary caregiver. Because young children are so dependent on their caregivers, and because an effective and sensitive caregiver is so important for a child's development, it is imperative that treatment for young children exposed to trauma includes the primary caregiver and focuses on the relationship between the child and that adult (Lieberman & Van Horn, 2004; Osofsky, 2011).

In addition, it is important for a child's treatment program to communicate with their child care or early education program. There may be certain routines that occur during care that might evoke responses from children that can only be understood if the caregivers at the child care setting are aware of the exposure to trauma. By working together, both the treatment program and child care or early education program will be able to support the child as he or she goes through the healing process (Lieberman & Van Horn, 2004; Osofsky, 2011).

Interventions that Focus on Relationships

Because relationships with primary caregivers are essential to a child's development, and because caregivers' symptoms and functioning can so profoundly affect a child's ability to cope with trauma, it is important to immediately attend to caregivers' symptoms in addition to attending to the child's symptoms. As Scheeringa and Zeanah pointed out,

> The most powerful potential change agent for children's development is their relationship with their primary caregiver; . . . making strategic changes in the nature of the primary caregiving relationship represents the best opportunity for making changes in the behavior and symptomology of the young child who is far less likely to respond to individually directed treatments. (2001, p. 811)

Chapters 8, 9, and 10 of this text describe approaches to intervention that support children's social and emotional development in home and classroom settings, parent–child interactions, and parent and caregiver mental health. In this chapter, we describe circumstances that may require programs to supplement these intervention approaches with more focused interventions that specifically address trauma. These more focused interventions require a level of specialized skill and expertise that is only sometimes available in early childhood education settings. In cases where in-program expertise is unavailable, programs should work closely and collaboratively with qualified people and programs in their community. We present three approaches to intervention that focus on relationships between children and caregivers that may be added to early childhood education and intervention, either within a program or as an out-of-program resource, depending on the availability of skilled therapists: child–parent psychotherapy, individual child psychotherapy, and the Circle of Security. In programs where relevant training and supervision are available, integrating any of these approaches into a given program can be transformative.

Child–Parent Psychotherapy

As discussed earlier, a child's relationship and attachment to his or her primary caregiver is central to healthy development regardless of the exposure to trauma. For children who have experienced trauma, this relationship is especially important because of the role caregivers have in mediating trauma and promoting positive developmental outcomes. Therefore, children exposed to trauma should be treated in terms of repairing the attachment relationship between the child and primary caregiver. Child–parent psychotherapy has been described as

> A relationship-based treatment approach for infants, toddlers, and preschoolers who are experiencing mental health problems or whose relationships with the parent is negatively affected as a result of parental factors such as mental illness, child constitutional characteristics that interfere with the formation of secure attachment, and/or discordant temperamental styles between the parent and child. (Lieberman, 2004, pp. 97–98)

Child–parent psychotherapy has also been used to improve the parent–child relationship after a traumatic event. This treatment helps address both the parent and child's individual symptoms, and it also helps in repairing the attachment relationship between the pair. Child–parent psychotherapy has the strongest research base for interventions designed for traumatized preschool-aged children and is effective in improving children's symptoms and their relationships with their primary caregivers (Chu & Lieberman, 2010).

Individual Child Psychotherapy

Although it is usually important to involve the parent and the child in psychotherapy together, sometimes this may not be possible. If the parent or caregiver's reaction to the traumatic event is so severe that he or she will not be able to focus on the child's treatment, individual psychotherapy for the child might be a viable option. This may also be appropriate if the child feels fear or confusion about divulging what happened during the trauma or if the child feels protective of the parent. Parents or caregivers would still be involved in this type of treatment, but individual child psychotherapy would focus more on the child and would include collateral sessions with the parent or caregiver to support the adult's ability to respond to the child's developmental needs (Lieberman & Van Horn, 2004).

Circle of Security   The Circle of Security program is an attachment-theory-driven intervention program. The intervention is designed to change insecure attachments into secure attachments. First, a trained psychotherapist assesses child–parent attachment by carefully observing interactions using a standardized procedure. Immediately following this observation, the caregiver is interviewed using the Circle of Security Interview (Hoffman, Marvin, Cooper, & Powell, 2006). This instrument was created to assess the caregiver's internal working models of attachment, focusing both on the adult's history with his or her own caregivers and the current relationship with the child. The material from the child–parent observation is then used to create short videos showing moments of missed connection, often including those typical of insecurity or disorganization. The intervention was originally designed as a group model with about eight caregivers meeting weekly for 26 weeks. The model has also been used in individual therapy or with couples. During the sessions, a psychotherapist explains attachment theory and then uses videotapes of the participants' interactions to help the caregiver gain insight into ways to improve the relationship. The group model has been shown to be effective in promoting secure attachment in at-risk children (Hoffman et al., 2006).

CHALLENGES IN PROVIDING TRAUMA INTERVENTION IN EARLY CHILDHOOD SETTINGS

This chapter touches upon several topics that may prove challenging to educators as they work with families to address incidents of trauma. In this section, we present some helpful strategies to address those challenges, including building and retaining close, collaborative relationships with parents and caregivers; discussing sensitive subjects; addressing one's own emotions while working with traumatized children and families; and the protracted time that complex problems may take to address.

Building and Maintaining Close and Collaborative Relationships

In their chapter on treating parent–infant relationships in the context of child maltreatment, Larrieu and Zeanah (2004) pointed out that parents who maltreat often have personal histories and circumstances that also present risks to their children's development. The authors describe the prevalence of poverty, unemployment, limited formal education, personal histories of abuse, substance abuse, mental health disorders, limited emotional support, involvement in violent relationships, and violent neighborhoods.

Larrieu and Zeanah also pointed out that parents who maltreat

> Often have had poor experiences with authority figures and believe that they have no one to whom they can turn for support or assistance. Given the low expectations and poor level of trust with which these parents enter treatment, our role as sensitive and empathic guides to change becomes paramount. (2004, p. 244)

However, providing guidance to parents is not a role or responsibility that early childhood educators always know how to do or will readily accept. One home visitor who struggled to incorporate infant mental health into her early education program reminded us that "I'm not a mental health worker. I'm a toddler teacher" (Summers, Funk, Twombly, Waddell, & Squires, 2007).

How can early childhood educators engage families who have difficulty keeping appointments, have trouble maintaining attention with their children or with home visitors, and lack positive experience engaging in trusting relationships with school programs? Also, how can early educators keep themselves engaged when families appear disinterested or displeased, or just take longer to "get better" than anticipated?

One way to begin is to make sure that services are comprehensive, flexible, responsive, and tailored to the individual needs, strengths, and interests of each family (Egeland & Erickson, 2004; Larrieu & Zeanah, 2004; Schorr, 1988). As we have noted, human development is situated in complex social, community, and economic contexts. Efforts to make positive change in one area must logically link to efforts that support that change—such as reducing risk factors, strengthening supportive relationships, and ensuring that basic human needs are met. An intervention focused upon reducing the effects of trauma will likely meet with greater success if family priorities are addressed in tandem with treatment. This kind of approach is described in detail in Chapter 4.

It is also important to attend to parents' and caregivers' emotional experiences (Weatherston, 2000). Weatherston explained that the infant mental health specialist's ability "to recognize, hold and tolerate the emotions expressed by both infant and parent offers a context in which a parent may openly talk about the infant's care" (p. 7). Although it is outside an educator's professional boundary to assume the role of therapist when working with children and families, it is appropriate and important to provide a safe space for families to express emotions that relate to their child and to parenting. The key to providing this space and building a trusting relationship in which parents may express how they think and feel about their children, as emphasized in Chapter 7, is active listening.

As parents and caregivers share their private thoughts and feelings, program staff must be vigilant in honoring their privacy. When traumatic events occur, an educator's real need to discuss these events in order to obtain guidance or to debrief must not turn into agency gossip. To safeguard family privacy, information should be shared with others only on a need-to-know basis. In other words, if someone in the agency needs information to make a treatment decision, to supervise, or to consult, then it is appropriate to share. An educator's legitimate need to talk about his or her own feelings should be addressed through reflective supervision and consultation.

Discussing Difficult Topics

The openness to parents' emotions and the active listening so important in establishing relationships with families and providing effective intervention are not always easy. We heard this frequently from home visitors during our interviews with infant mental health partner programs. One home visitor told us, "It's challenging sometimes to bring up to a family, 'I have concerns about your mental health and your emotional well-being' . . . because I don't have the background, or skills, or training to support them if I open that door" (Summers et al., 2007).

Even experienced early childhood educators are not always certain how to respond in emotionally complex situations. One home visitor shared that, at times, she found herself feeling "inept." When asked how she responded in this situation, she told us,

> Well, the worse-case scenario is, I feel really bad, and I get really hard on myself
> for that, and kick myself, and feel responsible. . . . Then there have been times that
> I've had to admit, "Whoops. I'm not doing that right. I'm not understanding it."
> And trying to always to go back to, "Okay, who am I? What am I feeling right now?"
> And use that. And that seems to help. . . . The idea is to keep it in a neutral place.

The self-questioning that occurs in difficult situations is an expected part of an early childhood educator's work. When educators have the benefit of an experienced and supportive guide, self-questioning can be channeled into constructive change, as described in detail in Chapters 10 and 11. See also Chapter 9 for more about the importance of self-awareness of one's values and attitudes when intervening with families.

Educators in our research shared the importance of receiving practical guidance from supervisors and consultants, especially in how to talk with parents about difficult subjects. One home visitor described how an infant mental health consultant helped keep a family connected with their program during a time when child maltreatment was occurring in the home:

> [The infant mental health consultant] was able to help me out with some issues the
> family was going through. I had to make a [child protective services] call. . . . How
> to approach it in a way . . . because I had built such a relationship with the parent,
> and because she had told me a lot of confidential information, and because then
> you had to get other people involved. The [infant mental health consultant] came
> through and said, "You know, let's get this, and let's do this, and say this," and she
> just pretty much wrote it down with me, gave me these tools. And then the mother
> later came back and thanked me. Which I thought, oh no, she's going to pull the
> kids out. And she didn't.

In the home visitor's words, the infant mental health consultant provided "support for me when I needed to speak with the parent, saying the right words at the right time." Another home visitor described how reflective supervision helped her practice: "It works because you get this feedback, additional ways on how to approach a situation. The right words." When educators find themselves needing to confront difficult issues while maintaining caring communication and their relationship with a family, trained supervisors and infant mental health consultants can share concrete ways to accomplish these tasks while supporting them through the process.

Feelings About What Happened

Gilkerson, in an important article on reflective supervision, expresses her belief that "the greatest challenge in infant-family work across all settings is the emotional experience of the work" (2004, p. 426). Osofsky echoes these concerns, stating that professionals on the "front lines" working with high-risk children and families "may continually be exposed to trauma for which they rarely received support, help, or even someone to talk to about the intense feelings that often accompany trauma exposure" (2004, p. 327).

At times, distressing emotions cannot be readily addressed during a single session with a supervisor. Burnout, secondary stress, and compassion fatigue may occur and should be addressed through ongoing social and organizational supports. Without this support, educators and intervention staff may continue to feel isolated and overwhelmed, and children and families may experience little progress (Osofsky, 2004). An experienced home visitor described compassion fatigue in her early intervention program:

> We are doing a lot of caring for other people, and at times we're just not caring enough for ourselves, and we put aside . . . our own needs. And we begin to tire. And some of us are doing that and showing lack of sleep, feeling overwhelmed, and not thinking that we're doing a good enough job.

This home visitor is fortunate in that her program provides periodic retreats that include activities designed to help staff deal with compassion fatigue. Chapter 12 presents specific strategies to address staff mental health needs.

Treatment Over Time

Maintaining relationships and intervention focus over time may present ongoing challenges for early childhood educators working with traumatized children and families. Educators and programs striving to obtain focused goals in the midst of challenging situations may bring closure to work before problems are solved, thereby limiting success or terminating therapeutic work prematurely (Osofsky, 2004). When programs impose artificial timelines unrealistic for the challenges children and families are experiencing, positive outcomes may be compromised and program staff may become discouraged (Janko, 1994). In a child maltreatment program, an interventionist talked about the difficulty of meeting goals over time:

> "It's the up and down," explained the interventionist. "When I first started, I'd see families going through the program and they would be doing really well. I would think, 'This is really working. The parent is succeeding, and the goals are being achieved, and moreover, there is a relationship developing with the child and there is responsiveness on the parent's part.' Then in 6 months, 8 months, or a year later, they're back again with the same problems and sometimes worse." (Janko, 1994, p. 116)

The complex risks described in Chapter 4 indicate that while programs may address some problems and issues according to a specified timeline, problems may also resurface as risks continue, life circumstances change, and a child's developmental status or behavior changes. The recurrence of problems or the emergence of other problems does not necessarily indicate failure; rather, it is something we might anticipate given the complexity of the problems we seek to address.

It is important to realize that organizational time divided into school years or numbers of home visits will not always match human time. There is a need for flexibility, as previously noted, as well as a need to recognize small but important indicators of progress. A home visitor working with an infant mental health consultant describes how the consultant helped a family "get to the point where they can make the choice" to use mental health services—an important goal in itself:

> [The family] is teetering, but they have gotten some help. They've made some healthier choices, and they've gotten help with some of the children's mental health issues. So there is pro and con going on, but I have to say they're in forward motion.

They're not just stuck. And they were very much stuck for a while, but I see there's forward motion.

In working with children and families, program staff must find ways to recognize these real and meaningful differences from the family's point of view as well as from their own expertise—no matter how seemingly small the change.

CONCLUSION

When trauma occurs, it may be situated in the relationship between child and caregiver, as in child maltreatment. It may be situated in the family context, as in family violence. Or it may be situated in more generalized community violence. Whatever the source and context of trauma, the way to healing is situated in the child–caregiver relationship. When the child–caregiver relationship is healthy, the child feels safe from harm, develops a secure sense of self, and feels free to explore the world from a secure base, to learn about it and from it. Supporting and repairing relationships that are compromised by trauma can mediate both initial risks to the child's safety and development as well as the long-term risks to the child's development and psychological well-being. Support of the child–caregiver relationship requires that programs work closely and collaboratively with caregivers, with children, with caregivers and children together, and, when warranted, with mental health therapists and consultants who can provide targeted treatment while supporting the work of educators. For some children and families experiencing chronically challenging circumstances, support requires a long-term commitment from programs. When early education programs form close relationships with children and families during this pivotal time of life, great rewards are possible.

REFERENCES

Ainsworth, M.D.S., Blehar, M.C., Waters, E., & Wall, S. (1978). *Patterns of attachment: A psychological study of the strange situation.* Hillsdale, NJ: Erlbaum.

American Psychiatric Association. (2000). *Diagnostic and statistical manual of mental disorders* (4th ed., text revision). Washington, DC: Author.

Azar, S., & Wolfe, D. (2006). Child physical abuse and neglect. In E. Mash & R. Barkley (Eds.), *Treatment of childhood disorders* (3rd ed.). New York: Guilford Press.

Bowlby, J. (1969). *Attachment and loss: Vol. 1. Attachment.* New York: Basic Books.

Bowlby, J. (1973). *Attachment and loss: Vol. 2. Separation anxiety and anger.* New York: Basic Books.

Chu, A.T., & Lieberman, A.F. (2010). Clinical implications of traumatic stress from birth to age five. *Annual Review of Clinical Psychology, 6,* 469–494.

Edleson, J., & Malik, N. (2008). Collaborating for family safety: Results from the Greenbook multisite evaluation. *Journal of Interpersonal Violence, 23*(7), 871–875.

Egeland, B., & Erickson, M.F. (2004). Lessons from STEEP™: Linking theory, research, and practice for the well-being of infants and parents. In A.J. Sameroff, S.C. McDonough, & K.L. Rosenblum (Eds.), *Treating parent-infant relationship problems.* New York: Guilford Press.

Finkelhor, D., Turner, H.A., Ormrod, R.K., & Hamby, S.L. (2009). Violence, crime, and exposure in a national sample of children and youth. *Pediatrics, 124*(5), 1411–1423.

Fox, N.A., & Leavitt, L.A. (1995). *The Violence Exposure Scale for Children-VEX.* College Park, MD: University of Maryland, Department of Human Development.

Gewirtz, A., & Edleson, J. (2007). Young children's exposure to intimate partner violence: Towards a developmental risk and resilience framework for research and intervention. *Journal of Family Violence, 22*(3), 151–163.

Gilkerson, L. (2004). Irving B. Harris Distinguished Lecture: Reflective supervision in infant-family programs: Adding clinical process to nonclinical settings. *Infant Mental Health Journal, 25*(4), 424–439.

Goldman, J., Salus, M.K., Wolcott, D., & Kennedy, K.Y. (2003). *A coordinated response to child abuse and neglect: The foundation for practice.* Washington, DC: U.S. Department of Heath and Human Services, Office on Child Abuse and Neglect.

Harden, B.J., & Koblinsky, S.A. (1999). Double exposure: Children affected by family and community violence. In R.L. Hampton (Ed.), *Family violence: Prevention and treatment* (pp. 66–102). Thousand Oaks, CA: Sage.

Harris, W.W., Lieberman, A.F., & Marans, S. (2007). In the best interests of society. *Journal of Child Psychology and Psychiatry, 48,* 392–411.

Hesse, E., & Main, M. (2006). Frightened, threatening, and dissociative parental behavior in low-risk samples: Description, discussion, and interpretations. *Development and Psychopathology, 18,* 309–343.

Hoffman, K.T., Marvin, R.S., Cooper, G., & Powell, B. (2006). Changing toddlers' and preschoolers' attachment classifications: The Circle of Security Intervention. *Journal of Counseling and Clinical Psychology, 24,* 1017–1026.

Hornor, G. (2008). Reactive attachment disorder. *Journal of Pediatric Health Care, 22,* 234–240.

Janko, S. (1994). *Vulnerable children, vulnerable families: The social construction of child abuse.* New York: Teachers College Press.

Larrieu, J.A., & Zeanah, C.H. (2004). Treating parent-infant relationships in the context of maltreatment: An integrated systems approach. In A.J. Sameroff, S.C. McDonough, & K.L. Rosenblum (Eds.), *Treating parent-infant relationship problems: Strategies for intervention.* New York: Guilford Press.

Lieberman, A.F. (2004). Child-parent psychotherapy: A relationship-based approach to the treatment of mental health disorders in infancy and early childhood. In A.J. Sameroff, S.C. McDonough, & K.L. Rosenblum (Eds.), *Treating parent-infant relationship problems: Strategies for intervention.* New York: Guilford Press.

Lieberman, A.F., & Van Horn, P. (2004). Assessment and treatment of young children exposed to traumatic events. In J.D. Osofsky (Ed.), *Young children and trauma: Intervention and treatment.* New York: Guilford Press.

Litrownik, A.J., Newton, R., Hunter, W.M., English, D., & Everson, M.D. (2003). Exposure to family violence in young at-risk children: A longitudinal look at the effects of victimization and witnessed physical and psychological aggression. *Journal of Family Violence, 18*(1), 59–73.

Main, M., & Solomon, J. (1986). Discovery of an insecure disoriented attachment pattern: Procedures, findings and implications for the classification of behavior. In T. Brazelton & M. Youngman (Eds.), *Affective development in infancy.* Norwood, NJ: Ablex.

Main, M., & Solomon, J. (1990). *Procedures for identifying infants as disorganized/disoriented during the Ainsworth strange situation.* Chicago: University of Chicago Press.

Margolin, G., & Gordis, E.B. (2000). The effects of family and community violence on children. *Annual Review of Psychology, 51,* 445–479.

National Center for Children Exposed to Violence. (2006a). *Community violence.* Retrieved from: http://www.nccev.org/violence/community.html

National Center for Children Exposed to Violence. (2006b). *Domestic violence.* Retrieved from: http://www.nccev.org/violence/domestic.html

Osofsky, J.D. (1999). The impact of violence on children. *The Future of Children, 9*(3), 33–49.

Osofsky, J.D. (2004). Perspectives on work with traumatized young children: How to deal with the feelings emerging from trauma work. In J.D. Osofsky (Ed.), *Young children and trauma: Intervention and treatment.* New York: Guilford Press.

Osofsky, J.D. (Ed.). (2011). *Clinical work with traumatized young children.* New York: Guilford Press.

Scheeringa, M.S., Salloum, A., Arnberger, R.A., Weems, C.F., Amaya-Jackson, L., & Cohen, J. (2007). Feasibility and effectiveness of cognitive-behavioral therapy for posttraumatic stress disorder in pre-school children: Two case reports. *Journal of Traumatic Stress, 20*(4), 631–636.

Scheeringa, M.S., & Zeanah, C.H. (2001). A relational perspective on PTSD in early childhood. *Journal of Traumatic Stress, 14,* 799–815.

Schorr, L.B. (1988). *Within our reach: Breaking the cycle of disadvantage.* New York: Doubleday.

Schuder, M., & Lyons-Ruth, K. (2004). "Hidden trauma" in infancy: Attachment, fearful arousal, and early dysfunction of the stress response system. In J.D. Osofsky (Ed.), *Young children and trauma: Intervention and treatment.* New York: Guilford Press.

Sidebotham, P.D., Heron, J., & the ALSPAC Study Team. (2003). Child maltreatment in the "children of the nineties": The role of the child. *Child Abuse & Neglect, 27,* 337–352.

Sroufe, L.A., & Waters, E. (1977). Attachment as an organizational construct. *Child Development, 48,* 1184–1199.

Straus, M.A. (2007). Conflict Tactics Scales. In N.A. Jackson (Ed.), *Encyclopedia of domestic violence.* New York: Routledge, Taylor & Francis Group.

Summers, S.J, Funk, K., Twombly, L., Waddell, M., & Squires, J. (2007). The explication of a mentor model, videotaping, and reflective supervision in support of infant mental health. *Infant Mental Health Journal, 28*(2), 216–236.

Swensen, C., & Chaffin, M. (2006). Beyond psychotherapy: Treating abused children by changing their social ecology. *Aggression and Violent Behavior, 11*(2), 120–137.

Toth, S.L., & Cicchetti, D. (1996). Patterns of relatedness and depressive symptomatology in maltreated children. *Journal of Consulting and Clinical Psychology, 64,* 32–41.

U.S. Department of Health and Human Services, Administration for Children and Families. (2009). *Child maltreatment 2007.* Washington, DC: U.S. Government Printing Office.

U.S. Department of Health and Human Services, Administration for Children and Families. (2010). *Child maltreatment 2009.* Retrieved October 2010, from http://www.acf.hhs.gov/programs/cb/stats _research/index.htm#can.

U.S. Department of Health and Human Services, National Center on Child Abuse and Neglect. (1993). *A report on the maltreatment of children with disabilities.* Washington, DC: Author.

Wallin, D.J. (2007). *Attachment in psychotherapy.* New York: Guilford Press.

Weatherston, D. (2000, October/November). The infant mental health specialist. *Zero to Three,* 3–10.

Zeanah, C.H., & Emde, R.N. (1994). Attachment disorders in infancy. In M. Rutter, L. Hersov, & E. Taylor (Eds.), *Child and adolescent psychiatry: Modern approaches.* Oxford, United Kingdom: Blackwell.

ZERO TO THREE, National Center for Infants, Toddlers, and Families. (2005). *Diagnostic classification of mental health and developmental disorders of infancy and early childhood, revised (DC:0-3R).* Washington, DC: ZERO TO THREE.

6

Assessing Young Children's
Social and Emotional Development

Jane Squires

*R*apid growth, expansion of skills, and a foundation for social-emotional compe-tence are hallmarks of the first 3 years of life. However, by age 3, some pre-school children are already "left behind" by their same-age peers. These children may suffer from social and emotional difficulties, and frequently these problems will be the primary cause of academic and behavioral difficulties (Hemmeter, Ostrosky, & Fox, 2006).

Previous chapters of this book noted that the psychological, biological, and social contexts surrounding a child greatly influence that child's social and emotional devel-opment. Trauma, severe or chronic medical conditions, household instability including frequent moves, and parents with symptoms of depression are some primary conditions identified as contributing to early social-emotional difficulties. How then can these dif-ficult circumstances be identified early on as they occur in the lives of very young chil-dren? How can social-emotional competence be evaluated in infants and toddlers, given that they have only limited communication skills? How can early childhood professionals sensitively and respectfully approach parents when they want to conduct assessments? What are the best tests and procedures to assess early social-emotional competence?

This chapter addresses ways to assess young children's social-emotional skills in the context of a linked system model. The key markers of a *linked system model* include clearly identifying the purposes and processes for assessment; conducting assessments in social contexts important to the child's development and necessary for interpreting assessment results; and using assessment results to provide essential information for designing, monitoring, and improving education and intervention. Before describing a linked system approach to assessment, I look again at the nature of early social and emotional development. Then I explore how a linked system approach is well suited to a sometimes challenging task.

EARLY SOCIAL AND EMOTIONAL DEVELOPMENT

Earlier chapters discussed characteristics of early social and emotional development. These characteristics are important to keep in mind when selecting and using assessment tools and procedures.

First, social-emotional development is inherently reciprocal and relational. Social and emotional development cannot be understood outside of a child's first relationships with caregivers. This relational nature of social-emotional development requires that early childhood professionals hear directly from parents and caregivers about their child, and the reciprocity inherent in social-emotional development requires observing children in caregiving and other social contexts. (At times, the reciprocal and relational nature of development may also require assessing parent–child relationships. Approaches to assessing caregiving are addressed in Chapter 7.)

Second, social-emotional development influences and is influenced by other developmental domains—that is, areas of related developmental skills. For example, a child who experiences chronically stressful situations and accompanying brain chemistry and neurological changes will likely also experience secondary cognitive differences or delays. A child with a shy or difficult temperament may withdraw in new situations, making all areas of development difficult to assess. Or a child with motor or sensory delays or disabilities may have difficulty interacting with others in conventional ways, which may make his or her social skills appear delayed despite a desire and intention to interact with other children and adults. Assessment tools and procedures must look at a child holistically and help educators and interventionists understand connections among skills within and across developmental domains.

Third, social-emotional development is subtle and not always easily or clearly represented by discrete social behaviors. For example, a child's ability to adapt to care and play routines, to self-regulate during changes in routines, to adapt easily to new situations, to exhibit curiosity and explore freely, or to persist in problem solving and repairing social breakdowns may be more difficult to observe than a child's positive interactive play with other children. However, these are all important markers of social-emotional development. Assessment of these markers requires a coherent framework that situates observed skills in a comprehensive developmental context and identifies strategies that support educators in interpreting social-emotional states and behavior.

A linked system approach is well suited to the challenging tasks of getting to know an infant or toddler in the context of relationships, important social settings, and related developmental domains, and these tasks in turn are prerequisite to designing meaningful and effective education and intervention programs.

THE LINKED SYSTEM MODEL

The linked system model of assessment and intervention was first proposed by Diane Bricker (1989) as ideal for assessing young children's development in early childhood education and intervention settings. Prior to this model, early education and intervention programs often used a checklist of skills that yielded a numerical score of items passed or failed. These checklists contained skills that were not developmentally sequenced, were not always appropriate as educational goals, and at times were stated in negative, critical terms. The checklists were rarely supported by sound psychometric data that assured users of their reliability or validity. Educators and interventionists were left with a numerical score indicating that a given child compared either favorably or unfavorably with his or her same-age peers. The numerical score did not help teachers, home visitors, or interventionists understand how the child's skills differed in different settings or with different people, how the "failed" items on the checklist fit into models of development for skill areas (e.g., language, social relationships, cognition), and what to work on today or in the future in order to help the child.

In contrast, a linked system model identifies processes and procedures that conceptually and practically link assessment, intervention, and evaluation activities. In other words, in a linked system model, assessment processes and procedures make sense according to current knowledge of child development, and they are practical and useful to both families and educators. In particular, a linked system uses the information acquired during social-emotional assessment to develop education, intervention, or treatment goals. These treatment goals, in turn, guide the selection of education or intervention content and strategies. Evaluation of progress made by children and families is in turn linked to intervention goals and is congruent with assessment procedures (Bricker, 1989; Pretti-Frontczak & Bricker, 2004).

The linked system is composed of five distinct but related processes, as shown in Figure 6.1: screening, assessment, goal development, intervention, and ongoing evaluation. Screening assessment should be relevant to diagnostic assessment by identifying which children need further examination. Diagnostic assessment should in turn relate to programmatic assessment by identifying which children need program placement and intervention. Programmatic assessment should be directly relevant to goal development for the child and family. In turn, goal development should guide and relate to the content and strategies of education and intervention efforts. Finally, the evaluation process helps determine the effectiveness of the previous assessments, goal development, and intervention processes. The strength of a linked system framework is that it supports the design

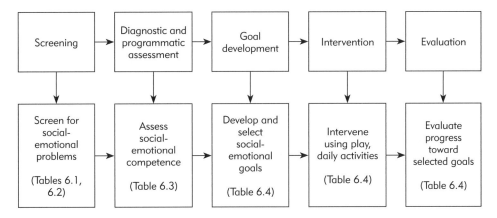

Figure 6.1. The five processes in the linked system approach.

and evaluation of meaningful educational interventions that improve social-emotional competence in young children and their families in real-life settings—home and community as well as programs and schools (Squires & Bricker, 2007).

To really understand a linked system approach to assessing social and emotional development, it is important to have a clear understanding of each of the five processes, their purposes, their strengths, and their limitations. Only by understanding them thoroughly can programs use them appropriately and effectively to support children and families.

Screening

Screening is a brief, formal evaluation of developmental skills intended to identify those children with potential problems who should be referred for a more in-depth diagnostic or programmatic assessment (Squires, Bricker, & Twombly, 2002). Screening instruments usually have a limited number of items representing important skill groups or developmental traits, are easy to administer, and sort children into two categories: those whose development appears typical or normal, and those who may have some developmental problems or delays and should be seen for a further assessment. Social-emotional screening assessments answer the question, *Is there a possible problem related to social or emotional development or skills?*

Why should early education programs screen when there is only the possibility of a problem? Educators too often fail to recognize or acknowledge social and emotional problems among infants and toddlers, or neglect to address those problems when they do recognize them. Numerous scholars and researchers, as well as a survey study by the National Alliance for the Mentally Ill (2000), indicate that physicians and medical personnel frequently also fail to identify even serious mental health problems among children. The younger the child, the more likely mental health problems will be overlooked (Stancin & Palermo, 1997; Wildman, Kinsman, Logue, Dickey, & Smucker, 1997).

Empirical evidence supports the need for ongoing screening of young children's social-emotional and developmental skills, conducted at repeated intervals, in order to identify problems as soon as they are apparent and to implement interventions at the earliest time possible (American Academy of Pediatrics, 2002, 2006; Squires & Bricker, 2009). By screening all young children and identifying delays early on, many problems are prevented before they become ingrained behavioral patterns (Severson, Walker, Hope-Doolittle, Kratochwill, & Gresham, 2007; Walker et al., 1998). Universal screening (i.e., screening for every child)—conducted in pediatric offices, child care settings, preschool classes, home child care programs, home visiting programs, child abuse prevention and treatment programs, and other community settings—is highly recommended. Simple screening tools, often completed by parents, can be administered at minimal cost and with the valuable input of parents and caregivers. Screening tests and processes also have the added advantage of offering a joint focus for parents or caregivers and educators or health care providers to discuss the child's development, and for professionals to offer anticipatory guidance about the child's development.

Screening tests should be quick and easy to administer, attractive to children, and culturally sensitive (i.e., a test should not identify children in error because of cultural differences, and administration and sharing of test results should occur in a culturally relevant way), and screening tests should have evidence as to their accuracy (i.e., the content of test items should be valid and measure what the test says it is measuring, and when the test is administered by different people, it should yield reliable or consistent results). It is important to screen early and periodically during a child's early years, because developmental changes occur so rapidly. It is also important to remember that community referral sources should be designated before screening begins, to ensure that families are referred for needed further services once potential delays or problems are identified through the screening process. Selected social-emotional screening tests for preschool children are summarized in Table 6.1.

In addition to child-focused measures, screening parents and caregivers for problems that may impinge upon healthy development is an important facet in the early identification of social-emotional problems. Parental depression, harsh parenting practices, and compromised parent–child interactions are examples of parent-focused factors that may impinge upon healthy child interactions. (Chapters 2 through 5 describe child, caregiver, and family interactions that may influence child social-emotional development. Chapter 7 describes approaches to assessing caregiving relationships, and Chapters 8 through 10 present education and intervention approaches to improving interactions between caregivers and children.)

Selected screening tools for caregivers are summarized in Table 6.2. As when using child-focused screening tests, it is important to remember that community referral sources should be identified before beginning administration of caregiver-focused screening tests. For example, screening for depression in mothers of young children may yield close to one third of mothers living in poverty with self-reported clinical symptoms (Hamre & Pianta, 2004; Knitzer, Theberge, & Johnson, 2008). Therefore, community mental health counseling centers and early childhood mental health specialists should be contacted and their availability for accepting referrals confirmed. Many programs, such as Early Head Start, employ mental health specialists who may be able to serve those families with mental health concerns. In other instances, community agencies such as mental health and counseling centers may be the referral of choice.

As the first step or process of the linked system, screening yields one of three outcomes: 1) social-emotional status is typical, 2) social-emotional status is at risk and further assessment is needed, and 3) social-emotional status is questionable. As shown in Figure 6.1, those children and families needing further assessment can be referred to a developmental, behavioral, or mental health specialist for an in-depth assessment to determine eligibility for mental health or early intervention (EI) services. Children and their caregivers whose social-emotional status is near the cutoff scores, indicating potential delays, may be referred for further assessment if parents and professionals think more assistance and supports are needed, or their status may be monitored at frequent intervals to make sure their social-emotional development is proceeding on track. Prevention activities targeting social, emotional, and behavioral needs should be shared with caregivers and teachers. Consistent use of natural consequences for undesired behaviors, arrangement of physical and social environments to encourage positive and skillful social behavior, and activities to promote social-emotional regulation such as deep breathing in and out and counting to 10 before responding are some examples of such prevention activities.

Table 6.1. Screening tools

Name	Author and copyright year	Age range	Administration	Psychometric data
Ages & Stages Questionnaires®: Social-Emotional (ASQ:SE)	J. Squires, D. Bricker, and E. Twombly (2002)	3–66 months	10–15 minutes, parent	Normative sample of 3,000 test–retest validity data; sensitivity: .78; specificity: .95
Behavioral Assessment of Baby's Emotional and Social Style (BABES)	K.M. Finello and M.K. Poulsen (1996)	Birth–36 months	10 minutes, parent	Limited; under development
Brief Infant-Toddler Social and Emotional Assessment (BITSEA)	A. Carter and M. Briggs-Gowan (2006)	12–36 months	Parent, child care provider	Normative sample of 600, not geographically distributed; test–retest: .80–.92; interrater: .64–78
Conners Rating Scales–Revised (CRS-R)	C.K. Conners (1997)	3–17 years	10 minutes; parent, teacher	Sample size: 8,000; multicultural
Devereux Early Childhood Assessment for Infants and Toddlers (DECA-I/T)	Devereux Foundation (2007)	Birth–3 years	10 minutes; trained testers	Normative sample of 2,143, geographically distributed; interrater: .47–.64; test–retest: .83–.98; internal consistency: .79–.94; small validity sample
Devereux Early Childhood Assessment (DECA)	Devereux Foundation (1998)	2–5 years	10 minutes; trained testers	Normative sample of 2,000; interrater: .59–.77; test–retest: .55–.94; sensitivity: 69
Early Screening Project (ESP)	H.M. Walker, H.H. Severson, and E. Feil (1995)	3–5 years	Stage 1: 1 hour; Stage 2: 1 hour; Stage 3: 40 minutes; teacher, counselor, parent	Normative sample of 2,853; test–retest: .77; interrater: .87; sensitivity: .80; specificity: .94; concurrent validity: .72

Instrument	Author(s)	Age range	Administration	Notes
Eyberg Child Behavior Inventory (ECBI)	S. Eyberg and D. Pincus (1999)	2–16 years	10 minutes; parent	Test–retest: .75–.86; interrater: .79–.86; sensitivity: .80; specificity: .86
Functional Emotional Assessment Scale (FEAS)	S. Greenspan, G. Degangi, and S. Wieder (2001)	7 months–4 years	15–20 minutes; professional	Norms not nationally representative; interrater: > .80
Greenspan Social-Emotional Growth Chart	S. Greenspan (2004)	0–42 months	10 minutes; family or caregiver	Reliability: .83–.94, depending on age band
Infant/Toddler Symptom Checklist	G. DeGangi, S. Poisson, R. Sickel, and A.S. Wiener (1995)	7–30 months	10 minutes; parent	Normative sample of 94% white; limited validity studies; sensitivity: .78; specificity: .84
Parenting Stress Index, Short Form (PSI-SF)	R.R. Abidin (1995)	Birth–12 years	20–30 minutes; parent	Small sample; test–retest: .84
Preschool and Kindergarten Behavioral Scales–Second Edition (PKBS-2).	K. Merrell (2002)	3–6 years	8–12 minutes; parent and teacher	Test–retest: .62–.87; interrater: .36–.63
Social Skills Rating System (SSRS)	F.M. Gresham and S.N. Elliot (1990)	3–18 years	15–25 minutes; parent and teacher	Normative sample of 4,000, stratified; test–retest: .65–.93
Temperament and Atypical Behavior Scale (TABS) Screener	S.J. Bagnato, J.T. Neisworth, J. Salvia, and F.M. Hunt (1999)	11–71 months	5 minutes; parent, professional	Reliability: .42–.64; sensitivity: .60
Vineland Social-Emotional Early Childhood Scales (SEEC)	S. Sparrow, D. Cicchetti, and D. Balla (2005)	Birth–5 years and 11 months	15–20 minutes; professional	Based on 1984 data

Table 6.2. Caregiver screening tools

Name	Author and copyright year	Age range	Administration	Psychometric data
Center for Epidemiological Studies Depression Scale (CES-D)	L.S. Radloff (1977)	Adult	20 questions	High internal consistency, adequate test–retest reliability; good agreement with other self-report measures
Family Environment Scale (FES)	R.H. Moos and B. Moos (1994)	Parent/adult	Rating on 4-point scale; assesses multiple dimensions of family environment; can select subtests	Acceptable internal consistency
Family Life Impairment Scale (FLIS)	M. Briggs-Gowan, A. Carter, J. Bosson-Heenan, A. Guyer, and S. Horwitz (2006)	Adult	6 items	Acceptable
Parenting Stress Index, Short Form (PSI-SF)	R.R. Abidin (1995)	Adult, for children birth–12 years	20–30 minutes	Small sample; test–retest: .84

Diagnostic or Eligibility Assessment

If a screening test suggests potential delays or problems in social-emotional development, the next step is to determine the nature of the problem and to match the child and family with appropriate services. This next step, diagnostic or eligibility assessment, answers two questions: What is the nature of the social-emotional problem or delay, and is the child or family eligible for specialized intervention or counseling services?

Diagnostic assessments are standardized, norm-referenced tests that are more in depth and detailed than screening tests. Diagnostic assessments yield information about a child's social and emotional development as compared with same age peers. Diagnostic assessments usually require specialized training to administer and interpret, and they typically take 1 or more hours to administer. Like screening tests, diagnostic assessments should have psychometric evidence to support their validity and reliability, be culturally sensitive, be based on a current normative sample, and have clear administration and interpretation guidelines. Diagnostic or eligibility assessments include "general intelligence" tests such as the Bayley Scales of Infant and Toddler Development, Third Edition (Bayley, 2005) and the Battelle Developmental Inventory, Second Edition (Newborg, 2005) that have a social-emotional domain, and they include targeted tests that focus specifically on social-emotional competence, such as the Infant-Toddler Social and Emotional Assessment (Carter & Briggs-Gowan, 2006), Child Behavior Checklist for ages 1½–5 (Achenbach & Rescorla, 2000) and Temperament and Atypical Behavior Scale (TABS) (Bagnato, Neisworth, Salvia, & Hunt, 1999). Selected social-emotional diagnostic assessments are summarized in Table 6.3. Ideally, both screening and diagnostic processes will entail a shared process between families, early childhood programs, and EI or early childhood special education programs.

Programmatic or Intervention Assessment

Following screening and diagnosis or eligibility testing, programmatic assessment is the next process in a linked system model. Programmatic assessment answers the question, *What are the child's current skills related to the program curriculum?*

Programmatic assessments are criterion-referenced, meaning that they measure a child's (or caregiver's) performance relative to a stated standard or developmental objective. This is in contrast to norm-referenced, diagnostic assessments that focus on skills with sound psychometric properties but that have little or no utility, or usefulness, for designing teaching and learning goals in natural contexts such as home visits or child care and early education settings (Bagnato, Neisworth, & Munson, 1997). For each criterion-referenced item on a programmatic assessment, there are specified criteria describing what a child needs to do to show he or she has acquired a particular skill. Criterion-referenced tests used in early childhood settings are most often *curriculum based* or *curriculum embedded*. This means that each criterion-referenced item can be used as a learning objective and that it fits within a developmentally sequenced curriculum that shows the range of skills the child has acquired and what skills should come next (Bagnato et al., 1997). As with screening and diagnostic assessment, the process of administering a criterion-referenced assessment and choosing goals and intervention approaches will be shared between the families and program personnel.

Table 6.3. Social-emotional assessment tools

Name	Author and copyright year	Age range	Administration	Psychometric data
Infant-Toddler Social and Emotional Assessment (ITSEA)	A. Carter and M. Briggs-Gowan (2006)	12–36 months	25–30 minutes	Strong reliability (.59–.84); moderate-strong validity
Child Behavior Checklist, 1.5–5	T.M. Achenbach (1992)	1.5–5 years	15–30 minutes	Externalizing and internalizing scores; strong reliability and validity
Child Behavior Checklist, 4–18	T. Achenbach (1991)	4–18 years	15–30 minutes	Externalizing and internalizing scores; strong reliability and validity
Social Skills Improvement System (formerly Social Skills Rating System)	F. Gresham and S. Elliott (2008)	3–18 years	Parent and teacher forms; 10–25 minutes	High reliability: internal consistency and test–retest; moderate concurrent validity
Vineland Social-Emotional Early Childhood Scales (taken from Vineland Adaptive Behavior Scales)	S. Sparrow, D. Cicchetti, and D. Balla (2005)	Birth–5 years and 11 months	20–30 minutes	High reliability: .80–.97; validity not available

From Squires, J., Bricker, D., & Twombly, L. (2002). *Ages & Stages Questionnaires®: Social-Emotional (ASQ:SE*, pp. 10–11). Baltimore: Paul H. Brookes Publishing Co.; adapted by permission.

Most curriculum-based measures contain items that are functional; that is, they focus on behaviors that enhance children's daily living skills and independence. "Initiates communication with peer," "quiets to familiar voice," and "responds to others in distress or need" are examples of items from the Assessment, Evaluation, and Programming System for Infants and Young Children (AEPS®), Second Edition (Bricker, 2002), a curriculum-based assessment for young children from birth to 6 years.

The specified criterion for the item "initiates communication with peer" reads, "Child initiates communication by directing gestures, signs, vocalizations, and/or verbalizations toward peer (e.g., child points and says to peer, "See that"; child pats his or her pocket and says to peer, "I have money")" (Bricker, 2002, p. 117). We know from observing a child in reference to this assessment item that the child wishes to engage a peer in order to make social contact and that he or she uses *joint referencing*, or shared perspective, by pointing and talking about something in their shared environment.

Items are also sequenced in a developmental order, with easier items appearing first and then increasing in difficulty. Items under the AEPS goal, "Initiates and maintains interaction with peer," become progressively more advanced: "1.1 Initiates social behavior toward peer"; "1.2 Responds appropriately to peer's social behavior"; "1.3 Plays near one or two peers"; "1.4 Observes peers"; "1.5 Entertains self by playing appropriately with toys" (Bricker, 2002). By observing and assessing a young child's current skills related to the curricular items, a current level of functioning and starting point for intervention can be easily designated. Examples of comprehensive early childhood curriculum-based measures include the Creative Curriculum (Dodge & Colker, 1992); HighScope Preschool Curriculum (HighScope Staff, 1992); AEPS (Bricker, 2002); and the Carolina Curriculum for Infants and Toddlers with Special Needs (CCITSN), Second Edition (Johnson-Martin, Attermeier, & Hacker, 2004a) and the Carolina Curriculum for Preschoolers with Special Needs (CCPSN), Third Edition (Johnson-Martin, Attermeier, & Hacker, 2004b).

Curriculum-based measures with a focus on social-emotional assessment are summarized in Table 6.4. Published measures with established validity and reliability provide a more effective and more targeted teaching approach. Children's social and emotional needs can be identified through an assessment process, followed by development of curricular activities focused on addressing these specific needs and supporting social, emotional, and related development.

Goal Development

After a curriculum-based measure has been administered to a child, results can be used to develop social-emotional goals for the child and/or the family. By reviewing the results and soliciting caregiver input, intervention goals can be identified that are functional and useful for the child and family. These goals can be prioritized, with the caregiver identifying which goals are most important as intervention priorities, usually no more than two or three so that they remain manageable for children and caregivers.

As shown in Figure 6.2, the assessment, goal development, intervention, and evaluation processes are all generated and linked through the use of a curriculum-based measure. That is, by assessing a child with the curriculum-based assessment, the interventionist can identify the skills a child uses regularly and robustly, as well as goals and objectives

Table 6.4. Selected general early childhood social-emotional curricula and assessments

Curriculum/assessment name	Description
Active Learning Series, D. Cryer, T. Harms, and B. Bourland (1988); ordering information: Dale Seymour Publications, Kaplan (http://www.kaplanco.com), (800) 334-2014	• Based on the Early Childhood Environment Rating Scales–Revised (ECERS-R) • Series of seven curriculum guides • More than 300 age-appropriate activities for listening and talking, activities for social growth, and suggestions for physical development and creative learning • Activities designed to help children "develop their minds and bodies in a safe and healthy environment" • Written for teachers of infants, toddlers, and children ages 2–5 years; separate guide for children with disabilities • Materials, required time, number of children, indoor or outdoor locations specified for each activity
Al's Pals: Kids Making Healthy Choices, J. Dubas, K. Bodisch Lynch, J. Gallano, S. Geller, and D. Hunt (1998); ordering information: Wingspan, LLC, http://www.wingspanworks.com, (804) 967-9002	• Includes 46 lesson manuals, puppets, audiotapes or CD-ROMs, parent letters, songbooks, school-to-home message pads, and a puppet house • Teacher training component as well as resiliency-based curriculum • Psychometric data supporting decreasing problem behavior using trained teachers • For preschool children ages 4–5 years
Assessment, Evaluation, and Programming System for Infants and Young Children (AEPS®), Second Edition, D. Bricker (Ed.) (2002); curriculum for birth–3 years; curriculum for 3–6 years; ordering information: Paul H. Brookes Publishing Co., http://www.brookespublishing.com, (800) 638-3775	• Curriculum component of comprehensive curriculum-based assessment • Psychometric data supporting the system • Designed for children with disabilities but also appropriate for at-risk population • Directly linked to assessment or evaluation and family participation components • Developmentally sequenced activities that move from simple to more advanced skills • Based on ecological and transactional theory
Beautiful Beginnings: A Developmental Curriculum for Infants and Toddlers, H. Raikes and J. Whitmer (2006); ordering information: Paul H. Brookes Publishing Co., http://www.brookespublishing.com, (800) 638-3775	• Curriculum divided into six age ranges between birth and age 3 • Includes more than 350 activities and forms for photocopying • Builds on children's natural strengths and interests • Fosters development in eight key areas, including communication, gross motor, fine motor, intellectual, discovery, social, self-help, and pretend • Low-cost activities that are easily implemented in Head Start and child care centers and homes • Includes forms for tracking progress and stickers to celebrate accomplished goals • Includes CD-ROM with all forms and activities
The Carolina Curriculum for Infants and Toddlers with Special Needs (CCITSN), Third Edition; The Carolina Curriculum for Preschoolers with Special Needs (CCPSN), Second Edition; N. Johnson-Martin, S. Attermeier, and B. Hacker (2004b); ordering information: Paul H. Brookes Publishing Co., http://www.brookespublishing.com, (800) 638-3775	• Curriculum component of comprehensive curriculum-based assessment • Curricula items that follow the same format: Title, Objective, Materials Needed • Teaching procedures • Integration strategies • Sensorimotor adaptations • Functional activities targeted • Specific information on disabilities • Adaptations for hearing, motor, and visual impairments

Curriculum/assessment name	Description
	• Designed for children with disabilities
	• Directly linked to assessment or evaluation component
	• Divided into 22 logical teaching sequences covering five developmental domains, including social adaptation
	• Reliability, validity, and program efficacy data
	• Classroom tips for effective teaching
Center on the Social and Emotional Foundations for Early Learning, Vanderbilt University, Department of Special Education; available for download: http://www.vanderbilt.edu/csefel/training.html	• Training materials and "What Works" briefs for promoting social and emotional competence in infants, toddlers, and preschool children
	• Practical strategies that include tools and resources for preschool teachers and caregivers
	• Parent training modules and family tools
Creating Teaching Tools for Young Children with Challenging Behavior (TTYL), R. Lentini, B.J. Vaughn, and L. Fox (2005); early intervention positive behavior support; ordering information: Division of Applied Research and Educational Support; available for download: http://challengingbehavior.fmhi.usf.edu/tools.html	• Materials designed to be used by educators of young children, higher education personnel, and in-service training personnel who support programs for young children
	• CD-ROM (that may be copied) includes user's manual, tips sheets, and reproducible forms necessary to gather information prior to strategy selection and implementation of supports
Creative Curriculum for Infants and Toddlers, A. Dombro, L. Colker, and D. Dodge (2001); teaching strategies; ordering information: Delmar Thomson Learning, http://www.teachingstrategies.com, (800) 637-3652	• Research-based preschool curriculum model based on Piaget's theories of child development
	• Focus on 10 interest areas or activities in the environment (i.e., blocks, house corner, table, toys, art, sand, water, library corner, music, movement, cooking, computers, and the outdoors)
Creative Curriculum for Early Childhood, D. Dodge and L. Colker (1992); teaching strategies; ordering information: Delmar Thomson Learning, http://www.teachingstrategies.com, (800) 637-3652	• Helps teachers understand how to work with children at different developmental levels to promote learning
	• Guides teachers in adapting the environment to make it more challenging
	• Includes a parent component
	• Infant curriculum, including
	o Comprehensive framework for planning and implementing quality activities
	o Focus on building social relationships
	o Emphasis on what children learn during the first 3 years
	o Experiences to achieve learning goals
	o Staff and parents' guidelines for reaching goals
	• Preschool (Fourth Edition) curriculum components
	o How children develop and learn
	o The learning environment
	o What children learn
	o The teacher's role
	o The family's role
Devereux Early Childhood Assessment (DECA), Devereux Foundation (1998); ordering information: http://www.devereuxearlychildhood.org, (866) TRAIN-US	• Strengths-based system designed to promote resilience in children ages 2–5
	• Includes assessment, family partnerships, and follow-up efforts that respond to children's individual characteristics and acknowledge the role of families
	• Classroom focus
	• Emphasis on social and emotional well-being

(continued)

Table 6.4.   *(continued)*

Curriculum/assessment name	Description
	• Encourages partnerships between teachers and families
	• Recommends classroom strategies that fit within an early childhood program
	• Supports effective collaboration between home and school
	• Stresses the importance of being a data-driven early care and education professional
Hawaii Early Learning Profile (HELP) for Infants and Toddlers Assessment and Curriculum Guide, Vort Corporation (1995); ordering information: http://www.vort.com, (650) 322-8282	• Curriculum component of comprehensive curriculum-based assessment
	• Focuses on children's strengths as well as needs
	• Provides adaptations for assessing and teaching each skill
Hawaii Early Learning Profile (HELP) for Preschoolers Assessment and Curriculum Guide, Vort Corporation (1995); ordering information: http://www.vort.com, (650) 322-8282	• Provides clearly written intervention plans, activities
	• Offers an easy-to-follow developmental sequence
	• HELP at Home (birth–3): Includes parent handouts, curriculum resources
	• HELP for Preschoolers: Activities at Home, including parent handouts and curriculum resources
High Reach Learning, S. Mayberry and K. Kelley (n.d.); ordering information: http://www.highreach.com, (800) 729-9988	• Learning materials for 3–12 months, 12–24 months, 2+ years, 3+ years, older 3s/4+ years, and pre-K/4+
	• Theme-based curriculum with child-initiated plus teacher-initiated and teacher-facilitated learning opportunities
	• Activities designed to promote development of the whole child
	• All support teaching tools and activities built in
	• Materials included for children and families to strengthen the school-to-home connection
	• Addresses social, emotional, cognitive, and physical domains
HighScope, HighScope Educational Research Foundation (2007); ordering information: http://www.highscope.org, (734) 485-2000	• Curriculum component of comprehensive curriculum-based assessment
	• Curricula focus on constructionist Piagetian activities for early childhood settings
	• Small- and large-group instructional activities
	• Children seen as active learners in classroom settings with rich materials
	• Adult role: challenge, support, and extend children's learning in social/academic development
The Ounce Scale, S. Meisels, A.L. Dombro, D.B. Marsden, D. Weston, and A. Jewkes (2003); ordering information: Pearson Early Learning, http://www.pearsonearly learning.com, (800) 552-2259	• For infants/toddlers ages birth–42 months
	• Observational assessment tool that transforms developmental information into guidelines for intervention
	• Focus on observation of children's functional behaviors by both parents and service providers
	• Children's performance measured within everyday routines and activities
	• Three components:
	◦ Observation Record: For observing and documenting behaviors
	◦ Family Album: For parents to record developmental observations
	◦ Developmental Profile: To evaluate developmental progress over time

Curriculum/assessment name	Description
Pathways to Competence for Young Children: A Parenting Program, S. Landy and E. Thompson (2006); ordering information: Paul H. Brookes Publishing Co., http://www.brookespublishing.com, (800) 638-3775	• Ten-step program to teach parents how to foster children's social-emotional development in nine key areas • Demonstrates strategies on helping parents manage children's difficult behaviors • Provides information on attachment, emotion regulation, and temperament • Includes group discussions, lesson, activities and exercises, and role-play scenarios • Looks at how a parent or caregiver's upbringing influences how they parent today • Includes flexible program for various group sizes and types • Includes CD-ROM with more than 140 handouts • Contains numerous components for preschool classroom teachers for improving social-emotional competence and providing positive behavior supports • Provides a user's manual and teaching tool kit, including forms for developing a positive behavior support classroom, such as tips for establishing buddy system, teacher tools, turtle technique, scripted story tips, feeling vocabulary tips, home kit, supporting articles • Includes downloadable CD-ROM with complete materials, manual
Social-Emotional Intervention for At-Risk 4-Year-Olds, S. Denham and R. Burton (1996); *Journal of School Psychology, 34*(3), 225–245; see also Denham, S. and Burton, R. (2003). *Social Emotional Prevention and Intervention Programming for Preschoolers*. New York: Springer Publishing, http://www.springer.com	• Relationship building through floor time • Didactic lessons in regulating emotions • 32 week intervention, 4 days per week • Empirical evidence to support increased peer and social skills and reduced negative emotion

From Squires, J., & Bricker, D. (2007). *An activity-based approach to developing young children's social and emotional competence* (pp. 247–250). Baltimore: Paul H. Brookes Publishing Co.; adapted by permission.

that target skills the child has not yet mastered. The curriculum component will provide steps for teaching or intervening on these goals, and ongoing evaluation can occur by conducting probes or spot checks on the child's acquisition of the target skills and how the child is progressing through the series of curricular steps.

Intervention

After goals have been identified and prioritized, the curriculum portion of the curriculum-based measure will assist educators in identifying intervention steps to follow in order to support the child or family in achieving priority goals. The curriculum portion of the assessment will also provide suggestions for materials and activities for education and intervention. In naturalistic or play-based approaches, daily routines and activities provide opportunities for practicing identified goals throughout the child's day. Multiple and varied opportunities should be provided for children and caregivers to practice or acquire targeted skills.

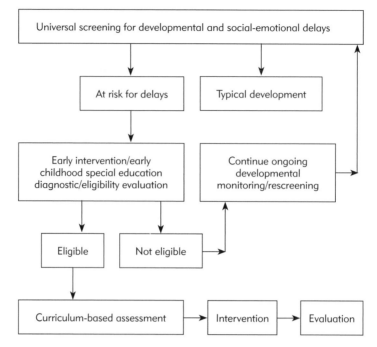

Figure 6.2. Universal screening and assessment in a linked systems model. (From Squires, J., & Bricker, D. [2007]. *An activity-based approach to developing young children's social and emotional competence* [pp. 43, 118]. Baltimore: Paul H. Brookes Publishing Co.; adapted by permission.)

For example, if a toddler has goals related to self-regulation including self-soothing, opportunities for practice may be provided throughout the day during diapering, naptime, mealtimes, and bedtime. In another example, if the toddler shows discomfort or displeasure while sitting in his or her high chair waiting for lunch, he or she can be asked to label the discomfort: "What's the matter? Are you hungry?" When the toddler calms down and begins to eat, he or she can receive more of the lunch foods and specific praise.

With multiple and varied opportunities throughout the day, needed skills can be mastered and the next item on the curriculum sequence can be targeted and practiced.

Evaluation

The fifth and final process in the linked system approach is evaluation. Evaluation requires professionals and caregivers to gather comparative data at selected time intervals so that judgments can be made about the effectiveness of the intervention. Two types of evaluation are necessary for effective intervention: 1) ongoing monitoring of progress toward individual child and family goals (usually selected from the curriculum-based assessment), and 2) assessment of the overall program impact on participating children and families.

Progress may be monitored daily, weekly, or monthly—depending upon the skill in question and the child's age and rate of growth—to determine if intervention strategies are providing appropriate and sufficient learning opportunities to support the child's or caregiver's attainment of target skills. Assessing overall program impact requires data gathering for quarterly and annual evaluation, which is often more global than when monitoring individual child or family progress. Examples of evaluation activities include determining caregiver satisfaction, staff effectiveness, and children's and caregivers' overall acquisition of targeted curricular goals. When using a curriculum-based assessment, ongoing systematic data collection to monitor progress toward long-range goals should provide an effective and efficient method for evaluation of child or family progress.

Consistent evaluation is also essential in order to determine if the screening, assessment, goal development, and intervention processes are being conducted effectively. If a child or family is not making progress toward targeted goals, it is necessary to review the previous processes in the linked system to determine what type of modification needs to be made for improved outcomes. Goals may have been selected that are too difficult for the child or too easy. The curriculum-based assessment may need to be readministered and alternative goals targeted. Modifications to goals or intervention strategies may also need to be made, with smaller or modified steps determined that can be attained by the child and family. Or "ecological conspiracies" such as those identified in Chapter 5 may be competing with interventions, requiring programs to address these before they can realistically and effectively work on goals that support caregiving and child development.

INCLUDING FAMILIES IN THE ASSESSMENT PROCESS

Based on decades of research, there is no doubt that parents and primary caregivers are the essential partners for their infants and young children. The early influence of caregivers affects the way an infant's brain will develop and function far into the future. Also, a child's early experience within important caregiving environments will exert immediate and long-term effects on learning, behavior, and physical and mental health (Fox, Levitt, & Nelson, 2010; Shonkoff, 2010). Therefore, when early childhood professionals assess children's social and emotional behavior, they must carefully consider caregivers and caregiving contexts.

First and foremost, including caregivers in assessment processes honors their essential role in their child's life. By including families, program staff gain opportunities to understand caregivers' concerns and perspectives. Although important with all families, this is particularly important in order to decrease the cultural distance and minimize misunderstandings that may occur when families' cultural backgrounds, perspectives, and belief systems differ from programs and staff. Including families also increases the accuracy of the assessment information gathered, helping staff to understand how a child may behave differently in different physical and social contexts. In addition, including families in the assessment process provides naturally occurring opportunities to offer information, guidance, and support—and to show caregivers the respect and delight staff feel for their children.

To include caregivers when screening infants and toddlers, an instrument that includes a parallel parent form can be used, allowing caregivers to share their observations and expertise with staff as they share theirs with them. When assessing infants and toddlers in order to identify education and intervention goals and strategies, staff might ask parents about the best places and times to observe, what toys and activities the child prefers, and what people the child prefers. In this way, staff observations are more likely to be easy for the child and family and to yield more accurate information. Staff observations are also likely to provide information about the environment that influences child behavior and development.

Specific information about communication with families is included in Chapter 7. I reiterate here the importance of open, active, and respectful listening and of clear communication with families about exactly what staff would like to do during the assessment process (and when and how), why these activities are important in supporting the child's development, and how staff will use the information they gather. Staff also must be sensitive that some parents will equate "testing" with painful experiences they had in school—experiences that were accompanied by judgments and, perhaps, self-punishing thoughts. It is very important to distinguish assessment in early childhood and intervention settings for the purpose of supporting child development with school testing that ranks and compares children. It is also important to reassure parents and caregivers that all information gathered during assessment is private and will never be shared without their permission—and then to keep that promise and honor a child's and family's privacy by sharing sensitive information only on a need-to-know basis, with family permission.

LINKED SYSTEM AND PREVENTION MODELS

The linked system framework can be viewed as the overarching context for a continuum of prevention activities aimed at improving social-emotional competence in young children and families. A hierarchy of service options and stages has been represented as part of a prevention model, or prevention pyramid (Fox, Dunlap, Hemmeter, Joseph, & Strain, 2003; Horner, Sugai, Todd, & Lewis-Palmer, 2005; Squires, 2010). This hierarchy begins with a broad base of prevention activities and moves to progressively more specialized and targeted interventions, based on the outcomes of the assessment performed at each of the levels or tiers, as shown in Figure 6.3.

INTERVENTION

In the first prevention tier, universal prevention activities can be guided by screening assessments, which are conducted to see if a child or family has potential social-emotional problems and should be referred for a more in-depth evaluation as described earlier (Squires et al., 2002). Through universal screening, many social-emotional problems are prevented before they become ingrained in young children's social-emotional behavioral patterns (Walker et al., 2007).

In addition to universal screening, Tier 1 includes the provision of structured, supportive environments for groups of children and families experiencing risk factors and/ or showing early signs of problem behaviors or delayed social-emotional competence. Examples of supportive activities include program designs that meet standards of high-quality early education such as developmentally and culturally appropriate activities; positive and explicit guidance to children about classroom expectations and rules; and activities that maximize child engagement and learning in home, child care, and classroom settings (Benedict, Horner, & Squires, 2007). Developmental and behavioral screenings can be conducted in order to identify those children and families that are not benefiting or being maximally served in Tier 1 environments.

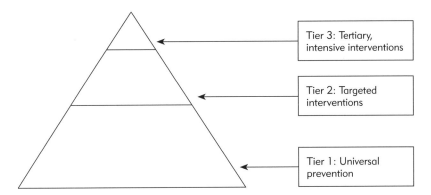

Figure 6.3. Prevention pyramid for preventing social-emotional delays in young children. (From Squires, J., & Bricker, D. [2007]. *An activity-based approach to developing young children's social and emotional competence* [p. 19]. Baltimore: Paul H. Brookes Publishing Co.; adapted by permission.)

Tier 2 includes secondary prevention activities for those children and families that need more targeted and explicit interventions. The assessment processes used in Tier 2 include curriculum-based assessments and interventions focused on high-risk groups, such as the Dinosaur Program (Webster-Stratton, 1997) and the Devereux Early Childhood Assessment Program (Benedict, Horner, & Squires, 2007; Devereux Foundation, 1998, 2007).

Finally, Tier 3 or tertiary interventions represent the top of the pyramid, the most intensive and in-depth assessment and intervention services for those children and families with clear and persistent signs of social and emotional problems. In addition to standardized diagnostic assessments, function-based assessments (O'Neil et al., 1997) and special education, and focused mental health assessments and services are included in Tier 3 activities.

RESPONSE TO INTERVENTION

The response to intervention (RTI) model for preschool children has recently been paired with the pyramid approach to describe a continuous and data-based process for delivering effective social-emotional assessment and intervention (Fox, Carta, Strain, Dunlap, & Hemmeter, 2009). RTI prescribes a systematic decision making process expressly designed for three purposes. First, the model promotes early and effective responses to children's learning and behavioral difficulties; second, it provides children with a level of instructional intensity matched to their level of need; and third, the model employs a data-based method for evaluating the effectiveness of instructional approaches (Fox et al., 2009). RTI follows the three-tier model of primary, secondary, and tertiary prevention using universal screening, continuous progress monitoring, a continuum of evidence-based interventions, data-based decision making and problem solving, and measurement of the fidelity of implementation (Fox et al., 2009). A critical component underlying the three tiers and RTI are clear rules for making instruction and program decisions that are based on child performance, allowing educators to determine when a child or family needs to receive less or more intensive services (Sugai, 2008). Timely screening, ongoing progress monitoring, and data-based decisions are used so that effective interventions can be provided to children and families who are not responding to less intensive interventions

(Sugai, 2008). Assessment provides the mechanism for determining when and how children are in need of more intensive interventions.

An RTI system specifically developed for preschool children, Recognition and Response (Coleman, Buysse, & Neitzel, 2006), relies on systematic, informal assessments by parents and teachers to recognize critical early warning signs and respond in ways that positively affect a child's early learning success. An intervention hierarchy; screening, assessment, and progress monitoring; research-based curriculum, instruction, and focused interventions; and a collaborative problem-solving process for decision making are the four essential components of the early childhood Recognition and Response model (Coleman et al., 2006).

SUMMARY OF SOCIAL AND EMOTIONAL ASSESSMENT

The processes of screening, diagnostic assessment, programmatic assessment, and evaluation appear at first to be technical and cumbersome. Assessment is too often something educators have to do but want to "get it over with" so they can get on to the business of teaching. However, screening and diagnostic or eligibility assessment are critically important in early education settings in order to make certain that children and caregivers are prevented from unnecessary suffering for lack of identifying their needs and qualifying them for services. In addition, programmatic assessment and evaluation are critically important in order to make certain that limited and valuable monetary, temporal, and human resources are used in ways that make real and meaningful differences in the lives of children and families.

Several things are worth noting here by way of encouraging early childhood and intervention staff to acquire the skills necessary to assess social and emotional development, to identify appropriate and high-priority goals and objectives, and to design effective learning strategies and environments. Programmatic assessment processes take place in the context of the warm social relationships the staff establishes with a child and family and in the context of play and caregiving routines during home visits and program-based activities. A well-designed assessment instrument will provide the necessary structure and guidelines that allow a staff member to observe in these important contexts, making it minimally obtrusive to families, enjoyable for children, and—it is hoped—pleasurable and edifying for the staff member. Also, because this process enables combining staff knowledge and expertise in early development with observation in important social contexts, the administration of the test will lend itself to continued monitoring of the child's development, the child–caregiver relationship, and the extent to which the staff and program are effectively supporting these in order to always be responsive to the rapid changes that are hallmarks of early social-emotional development.

ESSENTIAL RESOURCES

Accurate assessment and effective intervention for social and emotional development are highly dependent on a deep knowledge of typical social and emotional development. Further, social and emotional behaviors are only interpretable in context—including cultural contexts. Assessment and intervention skills take years to acquire, and educators new to the field of infant mental health feel that they lack the skills they need to accomplish these important tasks. To help professionals grow and deepen their skills in assessment, I recommend the following excellent resources.

An Activity-Based Approach to Developing Young Children's Social Emotional Competence. (2007). By Jane Squires, Ph.D., & Diane Bricker, Ph.D. Baltimore: Paul H. Brookes Publishing Co.

This guidebook by the authors of the Ages & Stages Questionnaires® gives non–mental-health professionals practical ways of identifying concerns and improving young children's social-emotional health.

Pathways to Competence: Encouraging Healthy Social and Emotional Development in Young Children (2nd ed.). (2009). By Sarah Landy, Ph.D. Baltimore: Paul H. Brookes Publishing Co.

This is an essential text for early childhood educators. It provides a comprehensive guide to addressing every facet of social-emotional development, working skillfully with children and families, and improving parents' interactions with their children.

Skilled Dialogue: Strategies for Responding to Cultural Diversity in Early Childhood. By Isaura Barrera, Ph.D., & Robert M. Corso, Ph.D., with Dianne Macpherson, M.S.W., C.I.S.W. (2003). Baltimore: Paul H. Brookes Publishing Co.

This book presents a field-tested model designed to support respectful, reciprocal, and responsive interaction that honors cultural beliefs and values among educators and interventionists in order to improve their relationships with the children and families they serve and better address developmental and educational goals.

The Baby Human 2. (2009). Directed by Eileen Thalenberg.

This DVD from an award-winning Discovery Channel series incorporates recent research on social and emotional development and presents findings in a visually beautiful, accessible, and compelling way.

Interventions for Children with or at Risk for Emotional and Behavioral Disorders. By Kathleen L. Lane, Ph.D., Frank M. Gresham, Ph.D., and Tam E. O'Shaughnessy, Ph.D. (2002). Boston: Allyn & Bacon.

Focused primarily on preschool and early elementary students, this book provides comprehensive information on how to educate and intervene with children with emotional and behavioral disorders. Early screening and detection; intervention in classroom settings; academic and instructional issues; and reading, math, and writing strategies for preschool children are included. Teaching social skills and strategies for students with internalizing behavior disorders are also described

Emotional and Behavioral Problems of Young Children: Effective Interventions in the Preschool and Kindergarten Years. By Gretchen A. Gimpel, Ph.D., & Melissa L. Holland, Ph.D. (2003). New York: Guilford Press.

An overview is provided of interventions that have been found effective or appear promising for use with young children. Suggestions are summarized for interventions with children with externalizing problems (e.g., attention-deficit/hyperactivity disorder, oppositional defiant disorder), internalizing problems (e.g., separation anxiety), autism, and pervasive developmental disorders. Handouts and worksheets, such as Frequently Asked Questions About Time-Out for parents and Self Assessment of Anxiety for children, are included and may be photocopied.

The Emotional Development of Young Children: Building an Emotion-Centered Curriculum (2nd ed.). By Marilou Hyson. (2004). New York: Teachers College Press.

Research-based strategies to promote healthy emotional development in young children are described in this book. Chapters focus on creating a secure emotional environment, helping children understand emotions, modeling genuine emotions, recognizing and honoring children's expressive styles, and uniting learning with positive emotions. Activity suggestions related to the Head Start child outcomes framework as well as examples of model programs and curricula are included in appendices.

Emotional Connections: How Relationships Guide Early Learning. By Perry McArthur Butterfield, Carole A. Martin, & Arleen Pratt Prairie. (2004). Washington, DC: ZERO TO THREE Press.

This book is a training resource for child care providers and early childhood educators serving the birth-to-3 population. Scenarios are included to teach basic concepts related to developing responsive relationships in early childhood settings. Although specific activities are not included, information on the importance of emotional connections and developing relationship-building skills is given.

How to Promote Children's Social and Emotional Competence. By Carolyn Webster-Stratton. (1999). Thousand Oaks, CA: Paul Chapman.

Designed primarily for teachers of children ages 4–8 years, the book gives suggestions on enhancing children's educational and emotional needs. A variety of classroom management strategies are given, as well as practical scripts, games, activities, role plays, and teaching plans to use with children with behavioral and social-emotional concerns.

REFERENCES

Abidin, R.R. (1995). *The parenting stress index professional manual.* Odessa, FL: Psychological Assessment Resources.

Achenbach, T. (1991). *Manual for the Child Behavior Checklist/4–18.* Burlington: University of Vermont, Department of Psychiatry.

Achenbach, T.M. (1992). *Manual for the Child Behavior Checklist/2–3 and 1992 profile.* Burlington, VT: University Associates in Psychiatry.

Achenbach, T., & Rescorla, L. (2000). *Manual for the Achenbach system of empirically based assessment preschool forms and profiles.* Burlington, VT: University of Vermont, Department of Psychiatry.

American Academy of Pediatrics. (2002). Identifying infants and young children with developmental disorders in the medical home: An algorithm for developmental surveillance and screening. *Pediatrics, 118*(1), 405–420.

American Academy of Pediatrics. (2006). Identifying infants and young children with developmental disorders in the medical home: An algorithm for developmental surveillance and screening. *Pediatrics, 118,* 405–420.

Bagnato, S., Neisworth, J., & Munson, S. (1997). *LINKing assessment and early intervention: An authentic curriculum-based approach.* Baltimore: Paul H. Brookes Publishing Co.

Bagnato, S., Neisworth, J., Salvia, J., & Hunt, F. (1999). *Manual for the Temperament and Atypical Behavior Scale: Early childhood indicators of developmental dysfunction.* Baltimore: Paul H. Brookes Publishing Co.

Bayley, N. (2005). *Bayley Scales of Infant and Toddler Development* (3rd ed.). San Antonio, TX: The Psychological Corporation.

Benedict, E., Horner, R., & Squires, J. (2007). Assessment and implementation of positive behavior support in preschools. *Topics in Early Childhood Special Education, 27*(3), 174–192.

Bricker, D. (1989). *Early intervention for at-risk and handicapped infants, toddlers and preschool children.* Palo Alto, CA: VORT.

Bricker, D. (Ed.). (2002). *Assessment, Evaluation, and Programming System for Infants and Young Children (AEPS®): Administration guides* (2nd ed., Vols. 1–4). Baltimore: Paul H. Brookes Publishing Co.

Briggs-Gowan, M., Carter, A., Bosson-Heenan, J., Guyer, A., & Horwitz, S. (2006). Are infant-toddler social-emotional and behavioral problems transient? *Journal of the American Academy of Child and Adolescent Psychiatry, 45,* 849–858.

Carter, A., & Briggs-Gowan, M. (2006). *ITSEA Infant-Toddler Social and Emotional Assessment.* San Antonio, TX: Pearson.

Coleman, M., Buysse, V., & Neitzel, J. (2006). *Recognition and response: An early intervening system for young children at risk for learning disabilities: Full report.* Chapel Hill, NC: University of North Carolina at Chapel Hill, FPG Child Development Institute.

Conners, C.K. (1997). *Conners Rating Scales–revised technical manual.* North Tonawanda, NY: Multi-Health Systems.

Cryer, D., Harms, T., & Bourland, B. (1988). *Active learning series.* Menlo Park, CA: Addison-Wesley.

DeGangi, G., Poisson, S., Sickel, R., & Wiener, A.S. (1995). *Infant/Toddler Symptom Checklist.* San Antonio, TX: Pearson Clinical Assessment.

Denham, S., & Burton, R. (1996). Social-emotional intervention for at-risk 4-year-olds. *Journal of School Psychology, 34*(3), 225–245.

Denham, S., & Burton, R. (2003). *Social and emotional prevention and intervention programming for preschoolers.* New York: Kluwer-Plenum.

Devereux Foundation. (1998). *Devereux Early Childhood Assessment (DECA).* Lutz, FL: Psychological Assessment Resources.

Devereux Foundation. (2007). *Devereux Early Childhood Assessment for Infants and Toddlers (DECA-IT).* Lutz, FL: Psychological Assessment Resources.

Dodge, D., & Colker, L. (1992). *The Creative Curriculum for Early Childhood.* Washington, DC: Teaching Strategies.

Dombro, A., Colker, L., & Dodge, D. (2001). *Creative curriculum for infants and toddlers* (Rev. ed.). Washington, DC: Teaching Strategies Inc.

Dubas, J.S., Bodisch Lynch, K.B., Gallano, J., Geller, S., & Hunt, D. (1998). Preliminary evaluation of a resiliency-based preschool substance abuse and violence prevention project. *Journal of Drug Education, 28,* 235–255.

Eyberg, S., & Pincus, D. (1999). *Eyberg Child Behavior Inventory & Sutter-Eyberg Student Behavior Inventory–Revised.* Odessa, FL: Psychological Assessment Resources.

Finello, K.M., & Poulsen, M.K. (1996). The behavior assessment of baby's emotional and social style (babes): A new screening tool for clinical use. *Infant Behavior and Development, 19*(1), 453.

Fox, L., Carta, J., Strain, P., Dunlap, G., & Hemmeter, M. (2009). *Response to intervention and the pyramid model.* Tampa, FL: University of South Florida, Technical Assistance Center on Social Emotional Intervention for Young Children.

Fox, L., Dunlap, G., Hemmeter, M., Joseph, G., & Strain, P. (2003). The teaching pyramid: A model supporting social competence and preventing challenging behavior in young children. *Young Children, 58*(4), 48–52.

Fox, S., Levitt, P., & Nelson, C.A. (2010). How the timing and quality of early experiences influence the development of brain architecture. *Child Development, 81*(1), 28–40.

Greenspan, S.I. (2004). *Greenspan social-emotional growth chart.* San Antonio, TX: Pearson. Retrieved October 24, 2008, from http://pearsonassess.com/HAIWEB/Cultures/en-us/Productdetail.htm?Pid =015-8280-229&Mode=summary

Greenspan, S., Degangi, G., & Wieder, S. (2001). *The Functional Emotional Assessment Scale (FEAS) for infancy and early childhood: Clinical and research applications* (2nd ed.). Bethesda, MD: Interdisciplinary Council on Developmental and Learning Disorders.

Gresham, F., & Elliott, S. (1990). *Social Skills Rating System manual.* Circle Pines, MN: American Guidance Service.

Gresham, F., & Elliott, S. (2008). *Social Skills Improvement System.* Circle Pines, MN: American Guidance Service.

Hamre, B., & Pianta, R. (2004). Nonfamilial caregiver self-reported depression: Prevalence and associations with caregiver behavior in child care settings. *Early Childhood Research Quarterly, 19,* 297–318.

Hemmeter, M., Ostrosky, M., & Fox, L. (2006). Social and emotional foundation for early learning: A conceptual model for intervention. *School Psychology Review, 35,* 583–601.

HighScope Staff. (1992). *HighScope child observation record: For ages 2–6.* Ypsilanti, MI: HighScope Press.

HighScope Staff. (2007). *HighScope step-by-step lesson plans for first 30 days.* Ypsilanti, MI: HighScope Press.

Horner, R., Sugai, G., Todd, A., & Lewis-Palmer, T. (2005). School-wide positive behavior support: An alternative approach to discipline in schools. In L. Bambara & L. Kern (Eds.), *Individualized supports for students with problem behavior: Designing positive behavior plans* (pp. 359–390). New York: Guilford Press.

Johnson-Martin, N., Attermeier, S., & Hacker, B. (2004a). *The Carolina Curriculum for Infants and Toddlers with Special Needs (CCITSN)* (3rd ed.). Baltimore: Paul H. Brookes Publishing Co.

Johnson-Martin, N., Attermeier, S., & Hacker, B. (2004b). *The Carolina Curriculum for Preschoolers with Special Needs (CCPSN)* (2nd ed.). Baltimore: Paul H. Brookes Publishing Co.

Knitzer, J., Theberge, S., & Johnson, K. (2008). *Reducing maternal depression and its impact on children: Toward a responsive early childhood policy framework.* New York: Columbia University, National Center for Children in Poverty.

Landy, S., & Thompson, E. (2006). *Pathways to competence for young children: A parenting program.* Baltimore: Paul H. Brookes Publishing Co.

Lentini, R., Vaughn, B.J., & Fox, L. (2005). *Teaching tools for young children with challenging behavior.* Tampa, FL: University of South Florida.

Mayberry, S., & Kelley, K. (n.d.). *E-LAP assessment and evaluation.* Charlotte, NC: HighReach Learning.

Meisels, S., Dombro, A.L., Marsden, D.B., Weston, D., & Jewkes, A. (2003). *The Ounce Scale: An Observational Assessment for Infants, Toddlers, and Families.* New York: Pearson Early Learning.

Merrell, K. (2002). *Preschool and Kindergarten Behavior Scales (PKBS).* Austin, TX: PRO-ED.

Moos, R., & Moos, B. (1994). *Family Environment Scale manual: Development, applications, research* (3rd ed.). Palo Alto, CA: Consulting Psychologist Press.

National Alliance for the Mentally Ill. (2000). *Families on the brink—Executive summary: The impact of ignoring children with serious mental illness.* Retrieved October 30, 2000, from http://www.nami .org/youth/brink3/html

Newborg, J. (2005). *Battelle Developmental Inventory* (2nd ed.). Itasca, IL: Riverside.

O'Neil, R., Horner, R., Albin, R., Sprague, J., Storey, K., & Newton, J. (1997). *Functional assessment and program development for problem behavior: A practical handbook.* Pacific Grove, CA: Brooks/ Cole.

Pretti-Frontczak, K., & Bricker, D. (2004). *An activity-based approach to early intervention* (3rd ed.). Baltimore: Paul H. Brookes Publishing Co.

Radloff, L.S. (1977). *Center for epidemiologic studies depression scale.* Retrieved June 7, 2011, from http://apm.sagepub.com/content/1/3/385.short?rss=1&ssource=mfr

Raikes, H., & Whitmer, J. (2006). *Beautiful beginnings: A developmental curriculum for infants and toddlers.* Baltimore, MD: Paul H. Brookes Publishing Co.

Severson, H., Walker, H., Hope-Doolittle, J., Kratochwill, T., & Gresham, F. (2007). Proactive, early screening to detect behaviorally at-risk students: Issues, approaches, emerging innovations, and professional practices. *Journal of School Psychology, 45,* 193–223.

Shonkoff, J.P. (2010). Building a new biodevelopmental framework to guide the future of early childhood policy. *Child Development, 8*(1), 357–367.

Sparrow S., Cicchetti D., & Balla D. (2005). *Vineland Adaptive Behavior Scales–II* (Survey Form). Circle Pines, MN: American Guidance Service.

Squires, J. (2010). Designing and implementing effective preschool programs: A linked systems approach for social emotional early learning. In M. Shinn & H. Walker (Eds.), *A three tier approach to prevention of behavior problems* (pp. 293–312). Bethesda, MD: National Association of School Psychologists.

Squires, J., & Bricker, D. (2007). *An activity-based approach to developing young children's social and emotional competence.* Baltimore: Paul H. Brookes Publishing Co.

Squires, J., & Bricker, D. (2009). *Ages & Stages Questionnaires®: A parent-completed child monitoring system* (3rd ed.). Baltimore: Paul H. Brookes Publishing Co.

Squires, J., Bricker, D., & Twombly, L. (2002). *Ages & Stages Questionnaires®: Social-Emotional (ASQ:SE).* Baltimore: Paul H. Brookes Publishing Co.

Stancin, T., & Palermo, T. (1997). A review of behavioral screening practices in pediatric settings: Do they pass the test? *Journal of Developmental and Behavioral Pediatrics, 18*(3), 183–193.

Sugai, G. (2008, March). *Sustaining change: RTI and SWPBS.* [PowerPoint slides]. Retrieved June 7, 2011, from http://www.pbis.org/common/pbisresources

Vort Corporation. (1995). *Hawaii Early Learning Profile (HELP).* Palo Alto, CA: Vort Corporation.

Walker, H., Kavanagh, K., Stiller, B., Golly, A., Severson, H., & Feil, E. (1998). First steps: An early intervention approach for preventing school antisocial behavior. *Journal of Emotional and Behavioral Disorders, 6*(2), 66–80.

Walker, H.M., Severson, H.H., & Feil, E.G. (1995). *Early screening project: A proven child-find process.* Longmont, CO: Sopris West.

Webster-Stratton, C. (1997). Early intervention for families of preschool children with conduct problems. In M.J. Guralnick (Ed.), *The effectiveness of early intervention* (pp. 429–454). Baltimore: Paul H. Brookes Publishing Co.

Wildman, B., Kinsman, A., Logue, E., Dickey, D., & Smucker, W. (1997). Presentation and management of childhood psychosocial problems. *The Journal of Family Practice, 44,* 77–84.

7

Assessing Primary Caregiver Relationships

Neil W. Boris and Timothy F. Page

*H*ave you ever noticed what happens when an infant of a few months of age is brought into a room of adults? When the infant is alert and awake, if given a chance, strangers will stop conversations with each other to talk to the infant. Most adults will smile widely, raise their eyebrows, and begin to speak to the infant in a predictable way. They will exaggerate vowel sounds, elongate words, and adapt a new rhythm of speech that matches their exaggerated facial expressions. Though the infant may at first look puzzled, very soon he or she will be engaged in a rhythmic conversation with a complete stranger!

So what is going on here? It may sound strange, but the question of why adults are attracted to infants is something that researchers have been studying for some time. As discussed in other chapters, and as a matter of intuitive knowledge, the answer to this question has to do with the child–caregiver relationship. This relationship has a greater and more pervasive influence on a child's development than all other influencing factors. Before we look at ways to assess child–caregiver relationships as part of the work in providing infant mental health services, we will attempt to explain some important characteristics of child–caregiver relationships by answering that important question, *What is going on here?*

It is a certainty that whoever got first crack at having a conversation with the infant would perceive the infant to be cute. In fact, it is a pretty good bet they might even say so: "Ooohh, aren't you cute! Look at you smiling." What defines *cute* is actually quite predictable. The infant's round face and disproportionately large eyes, for instance, are universally rated by adults as pleasing, though recent research suggests that relative attraction to infants' faces may be regulated by many factors, including sex hormones. For instance, when adults were shown computer-simulated pictures of infants' faces that were subtly manipulated to change "cuteness factors" (e.g., disproportionately large eyes), premenopausal women and women taking oral contraceptives (which change levels of estrogen and progesterone in the body) were more sensitive to the shifts in the infant's face than men or postmenopausal women (Sprengelmeyer et al., 2009). This study and other studies make it clear that our perceptions about infants, and even our actions toward infants, are tied to our biology.

What about the way adults talk to infants? It turns out that the acoustic qualities of adult speech when talking to infants are quite similar across cultures. No matter what language an adult speaks, no matter where he or she is from, the way adults talk to infants (those long vowel sounds, that sing-song quality) will be quite similar. That is true whether the adults speak Chinese or Hebrew! In fact, researchers have named this peculiar (and universal) form of speech *motherese* and are now delving into how even very small cultural differences in the way infants are talked to and played with in various parts of the world make a difference in language development (Keller, Otto, Lamm, Yovsi, & Kärtner, 2008).

EARLY ATTACHMENT: KEY PRINCIPLES

Why are adults attracted to infants? Furthermore, why do they speak to them in a predictable fashion? From an evolutionary perspective, humans, like all species, have a vested interest in protecting their young and preserving their genes. Humans are not the only species that has visually attractive infants. For human infants, of course, it is quite critical to be cute: They cannot move without assistance or eat without help, so they would perish if others did not take care of them. However, what function does motherese serve? As it turns out, the infant is hardly a passive participant in conversations with adults. There is growing evidence that infants are calmed by this speech and that this likely contributes to such maternal speech being genetically passed along over many generations (Falk, 2004). In other words, human caregivers and infants have evolved together such that, across cultures, caregivers use speech that calms infants. Of course, a careful observer of the interaction between the infant and the adult would appreciate that the infant actively contributes to the rhythm of the conversation.

Put simply, humans are social beings, and we are born that way. We are not alone, of course: Social interaction is an important quality of other species as well. Animal research on early experiences conducted during the middle part of last century gave rise to a comprehensive theory on how and why human infants "attach" to their caregivers (van der Horst, Leroy, & van der Veer, 2008). Attachment theory has, in turn, become a cornerstone for much of the research on the social capacities of infants (Karen, 1994). The word *attachment* has been used in many ways since British psychiatrist John Bowlby wrote his highly influential books on attachment and early social development in the 1960s (Bowlby, 1973, 1982). The main thrust of Bowlby's argument was that humans have an inborn "attachment system," shaped by the forces of evolution. This attachment system is operative throughout life—adults are attracted to infants because we all have inborn attachment systems that have been selected for over many generations. The human attachment system is a biological-behavioral system, and the behaviors that can be observed in the conversations between adults and infants are, in effect, being driven by this biological-behavioral system.

Box 7.1.   Infants' early imitation

Infants were once thought to arrive in the world as passive beings, waiting for the world to shape them. Based on a large body of research, it is now known that instead they arrive with remarkable abilities to perceive, learn, form mental representations, and interact in ways that powerfully shape their cargivers. One research study that powerfully demonstrates this is Andrew Meltzoff and Keith Moore's 1977 work on infants' early imitation. In this study, Meltzoff and Moore found that newborns between 12 and 21 days could imitate a range of facial and manual gestures. Further, Meltzoff and Moore learned that infant imitation was specific (e.g., when imitating tongue protrusion, the infant imitated with the tongue), that infants recognized being imitated, and that they could correct their imitative actions. The implication is that infants can link their own behaviors with gestures they see others perform (Meltzoff & Moore, 1977).

Since that early study, researchers have tried to understand why infants demonstrate imitation, how imitation develops, and why it matters (Meltzoff & Moore, 1999). According to Meltzoff and Moore, imitation, and imitative interactive games between infants and caregivers, serve social and communication development by allowing infants to distinguish among individuals and to verify their identity. Imitation skills change over time, and the way 14-month-old children imitate is developmentally different from that of infants. In Meltzoff and Moore's words, "Fourteen-month-olds seem to recognize the interaction as a 'matching game,' and gleefully test whether they are being copied, by abruptly changing acts while staring at the adult to see what he will do" (Meltzoff & Moore, 1999, p. 153). At 18 months, children observing an adult who tries but fails to perform an act on an object will no longer imitate exactly what they see the adult doing but will imitate what the adult attempted to do. This shows us that the child holds an internal representation of others, allowing the child to see people in terms of their intentions, rather than just their behavior.

This information is important to early educators and interventionists, because it reminds us that with every interaction infants and young children engage in with others, they are building an internal theory about themselves, others, and the world, and that they will carry this internal theory with them as they grow and develop.

If the age of the infant brought into the room of adults were changed, then the pattern of interactions might change as well. With an infant 10 months of age, the adults are still likely to engage quickly, but there is a good chance that the infant will show protest and reach for his or her caregiver instead of happily being passed around a room full of strangers. Ten-month-olds will have developed a very clear preference for a small group of consistent caregivers. Their protest signals both brain maturation and cumulative experience. There is, in other words, a developmental sequence of attachment behavior in early childhood, and this sequence is summarized in Table 7.1.

One of Bowlby's great insights was that infants' varying experiences in attachment relationships shape their behavior with each caregiver. In other words, young children develop specific patterns of attachment with different caregivers. This makes sense when you consider how socially perceptive even very young infants are. By the time an infant

Table 7.1. Developmental phases of attachment

Phase of attachment	Birth to 2 months	2–7 months	7–12 months	12–18 months	18 months and beyond
	Limited discrimination	Discrimination with limited preference	Preferred attachment	Secure base	Goal-corrected partnership
Characteristics	Physical attributes of babyishness attracts caregivers, but infant expressions of preference are limited to olfactory and auditory realm and require experimental conditions to demonstrate	Differentiates among different interactive partners and may seem more comfortable with primary caregiver but willing to interact readily with other social partners	Clearly expressed preference for a small number of caregiving adults; separation protest and stranger wariness appear	Use of the attachment figure as a secure base from which to venture out confidently and explore the world and a safe haven to which to return in times of danger; proximity to caregiver promotes internal feeling of security in infant	Cooperation with caregiver despite conflicting goals and to balance autonomous functioning with reliance on caregiver for help when needed; verbal relatedness important, including attention to emotional integration and fluency of discourse

From Boris, N.W., Aoki, Y., & Zeanah, C.H. (1999). The development of infant-parent attachment: Considerations for assessment, *Infants & Young Children, 11*, 1–10; reprinted by permission.

has spent a year interacting with a particular caregiver, there have been thousands upon thousands of interactions—a personal history of social exchanges that characterize the caregiver–child relationship. Attachment theory has highlighted the critical importance of sensitive and responsive parenting for developing a child's acquisition of trust and confidence in the availability of protective caregivers when needed (Ainsworth, 1979). As children move into the phase of *discriminated attachment* at about 7 months, they organize approach and signaling behavior. What follows is a predictable sequence of interactive behavior unique to a specified caregiver, with the immediate purpose of gaining physical proximity to the caregiver in distressing circumstances (e.g., when the child feels frightened, hungry, sick, or injured; Bowlby, 1982). When the child is not distressed, a complimentary behavioral system, the *exploratory system,* is activated, which enables the child to develop mastery skills and autonomy by exploring immediate surroundings and learning about the wider physical and social world. Attachment and exploratory behavioral systems thus operate in close synchrony. In circumstances free of distressing stimuli, children instinctively seek to explore their surroundings. When distressed, however, attachment instincts are activated, prompting the child to seek physical proximity—or physical closeness—to a specific caregiver. This caregiver is known through the child's experience to be stronger and protective, with resources to offer to address the child's distress (Bowlby, 1982).

Also about this time, between 6 and 18 months, a child begins to develop the ability to match his or her mental state with that of the caregiver through *joint attention* to an object or a third person (Bretherton, 1991). Sometime between 11 to 18 months, when a child signals to her caregiver and the caregiver misinterprets the signal, the child is able to revise and repair his or her communication in order to get the response he or she wants. For example, when a mother offers food to her 1-year-old, the infant at first looks above and beyond the food, and when the mother persists in offering the food, the infant bounces in the high chair, pushes the food away, and looks at the mother. The mother asks, "Want some?" and the child withdraws. The mother asks, "No?" and the child bounces in the high chair and shakes his or her head, "No" (Golinkoff, 1986, p. 460). Both of these early skills show that a child is beginning to develop a primitive representation that there is oneself, and there are others, and it is important that others understand one's communicative intentions. Also, it is equally important that caregivers accurately read and sensitively respond to their child's early attempts to communicate. It has been said that perhaps the most important thing infants learn from these early attempts at communication is that "their signals work and that caregivers are available and willing to respond" (Erikson & Kurz-Reimer, 1999, p. 65).

As the child matures through toddlerhood into the preschool years, the complexity of interactions with the caregiver grows. Bowlby argued that as children develop increasing interest in independence and autonomy, caregivers and children must enter into "goal-corrected partnership." The goal of getting a 3-year-old to clean up toys, for instance, often involves a series of negotiations between parent and child. How each partner engages the other is influenced by their history together and the ideas, or mental representations, they hold about one another. One can imagine that a caregiver who is not firm in giving commands and instead uses bribes and begging to get compliance is likely to struggle in getting the child to reach the clean-up goal. On the other hand, a caregiver who is harsh or threatening may have early success in getting compliance, only to have the child either become anxious or withdrawn over time, or become defiant and aggressive.

Table 7.2.   Relationship domains

Parent	Child
Warmth/empathy/nurturance	Security/trust
Provision of comfort	Comfort seeking
Protection	Vigilance
Play	Play
Teaching	Learning/mastery/curiosity
Structure/instrument care/routines	Self-regulation/routines
Limit-setting/discipline	Self-control

From Zeanah, C. (Ed.). (2009). *Handbook of infant mental health* (3rd ed.). New York: Guilford Press; adapted from Sameroff, A., & Emde, R. (1989). *Relationship disturbances in early childhood.* New York: Basic Books; copyright ©1992 Arnold Sameroff. Reprinted by permission of Basic Books, a member of the Perseus Book Group.

One useful way to think about the complexity of relationships is to consider the domains that make up each evolving relationship. Table 7.2 lists these domains and links parent capacity to the child's needs. From the provision of warmth and empathy to the use of play to socialize the child, or the use of discipline to improve self-control, parent–child interactions form the foundation for early social and emotional development. In fact, another topic of intense research interest in developmental psychology has to do with the child's development of the capacity to regulate emotions, a task clearly related to early parent–child attachment.

ATTACHMENT AND EMOTION REGULATION

Bowlby (1973) also proposed that, beginning in infancy, the development of the attachment system reflects—is indeed founded upon—a system of mutual regulation of affective states—that is, emotional states or moods. A sensitive and responsive caregiver accurately interprets the infant's expressions of distress and effectively soothes him or her. Through the experience of having a caregiver sensitively respond in a contingent fashion—that is, in a way that relates to the infant's behavior and emotional state—the infant learns how to self-regulate. Infants who are able to self-regulate can manage feelings of distress with increasing independence and self-direction. Self-regulation is an accomplishment that is strongly influenced by the experience of consistent, predictable caregiver support. Self-regulatory capacities, in turn, become a key developmental foundation that enables the growing child to effectively engage in mutually satisfying social relationships, focus on and engage in school activities, delay gratification when required, engage in problem-solving strategies, and even manage adversity. Research in recent years suggests that the root of children's capacities for self-regulation of affect and behavior lies in well-functioning attachment relationships, where children experience emotional security through the consistent presence of a nurturing and protective caregiver (Weinfield, Sroufe, Egeland, & Carlson, 2008).

Advances in clinical intervention with young children—that is, focused intervention that addresses affective states and child–caregiver relationships—have been shaped by attachment theory over the last 30 years. Instead of viewing challenging behavior solely as "a problem with the child," most clinicians who work in early childhood understand children's behavior through assessing key relationships. Therefore, to effectively address concerning behaviors—for example, disruptive behavior, poor peer relationships, social withdrawal, or anxiety—interventions should be directed toward strengthening attachment relationships (Guttmann-Steinmetz & Crowell, 2006). The most effective approach to behavior management in parenting, consistent with modern developmental science, therefore is likely to lie in assisting parents to learn how to better provide for their children's needs for emotional security, and not simply how to be more effective disciplinarians. (To understand how focused intervention with a mental health professional differs from the broader, more general work of early childhood educators and interventionists, see Chapter 1 for a distinction between promotion, prevention, and treatment.)

A first step in working with parents is to understand how they think about their child and his or her behaviors. The ways that parents perceive their children is important to assess, as this may color how they approach their child in the moment and may influence how open they are to trying new ways to meet the child's needs. How does one find out how a parent perceives their child? The answer is deceptively simple: One only has to listen. Although listening to caregivers sounds easy, for many programs, parent–teacher conferences can end up more like lectures than occasions during which parents freely share their experiences and perspectives and feel truly heard. As noted in Chapter 2, many child care program staff feel uncomfortable in talking with a parent about stress or depression. Yet, if staff want to understand a child's behavior and identify families who may need referral for mental health intervention, they will need to reserve time and build communication skills so that the parent can feel supported and be heard.

WHEN BEHAVIOR CONCERNS YOU:
BE EMPATHIC, ORGANIZE A MEETING, AND LISTEN FIRST

Empathy—the ability to understand or identify with another's feelings or situation—is the starting point with stressed parents, because stressed parents rarely open up unless they have reason to trust. Empathy is the foundation for building connections with stressed parents. In effect, before early childhood professionals prepare to listen to a parent, they have to find inside themselves a way to be calm, welcoming, and open. When a child has been biting peers, overturning tables, or refusing to follow directions, tapping into a well of empathy can be challenging indeed. It is natural, in fact, for professionals to find themselves blaming parents in such situations. The thing about parenting stress, though, is that as soon as a stressed person senses a professional's exasperation, the chances that they will "put up their guard" skyrockets.

So a professional entering a meeting with a parent about his or her child's problematic behavior must find empathy and bring it to the meeting. A first consideration is being sure that such a meeting is set up in a way that promotes success. As educators, we have all experienced hallway meetings with parents that felt uncomfortable. Planning an appropriate place and time for a meeting about a child's difficult behavior is essential. Often, it is necessary to plan a meeting with a stressed parent well in advance. Whether the first discussion happens by phone or at pick-up or drop-off, it is also necessary to think through how the meeting should be framed. Not many parents are pleased to hear, "Your son is behaving badly and we need to meet about this!" Choosing words carefully is the first step to connecting with the parent. A more appropriate way of framing a meeting might be, "I'd like to sit down with you to talk about Byron's progress at our program. Meeting together will be a chance to review how he's doing. I'd like to talk about everything from his interests to his behavior, and I really want to hear your thoughts about Byron's development." This invitation clearly conveys why the staff member wishes to meet, what parents can expect, and that their thoughts are valued. Once a meeting time has been set, it can be useful to tell a parent to expect a reminder call. Inviting parents to bring someone else who is close to the child is often helpful, because if parents hear something in the meeting that elicits feelings of stress, they may spend the rest of the meeting processing what they heard and will be unable to hear or discuss anything else. A close and concerned other may be able to hear, offer support to the parent, and share valuable knowledge about the child.

Once the meeting is set and confirmed, the staff member's thoughts should turn to how to get off to a good start. It may be surprising to know, for example, that pharmaceutical companies have their sales representatives go through hours of training, emphasizing things like how to greet a prospective client warmly. In fact, videotaped role playing of greeting the client—usually a busy doctor—and engaging him or her in conversation is pored over in slow motion. The goal is to train sales representatives to make a good first impression. First impressions make for strong connections, and strong connections mean money for pharmaceutical companies. For child care programs, strong connections mean something equally important: engaged caregivers who will stay with the program.

Once the staff member greets the caregiver warmly, just as he or she did in setting up the meeting, the staff member should choose words carefully to start the meeting. Staff should be alert to the use of professional terminology, or jargon, making sure they clearly understand what professional terms mean so that when they must use them, they can explain them to others. This is particularly important when communicating with families who may not share staff members' cultural perspective. It is important to remember that communication must be reciprocal—staff members are obliged to discuss their point of view and the reasons behind it, and also to try to understand and value the point of view of others.

There are three principles to remember in framing the meeting: 1) say something positive about the parent or child first, 2) let the parent take the first shot at setting the agenda, and 3) shift into listening mode. Starting with something positive is important, because a significant portion of stressed parents have had repeated experiences of rejection or abuse. For some, the pattern of abuse goes back to childhood. One interesting finding from research on children who have been abused is that a large proportion of these children develop something that developmental psychologists came to label *hostile attribution bias* (Dodge, Price, Bachorowski, & Newman, 1990). Such children regard even neutral facial expressions as hostile; it is as if their experiences have programmed their brains to expect to be attacked. Starting with something genuine and positive helps skirt the hostile attribution bias by giving the parent a sense that they are not about to be "called out." This does not mean being false or obsequious. The staff member's job is not to avoid the child's negative behavior. Rather, he or she needs to firm up the alliance with the parents and trust that they will come around to talking about negative behaviors if given the chance. In order for staff to get to their concerns, as strange as it sounds, they need to switch into listening mode!

Many people consider listening to be nothing more than hearing someone say something. The kind of listening that is needed in working with stressed parents, however, is called *active listening*. Active listening is a term that encompasses more than hearing what is said. In fact, active listening involves understanding another person's perspec-

Table 7.3. Communicating through active listening

Communication components	Communication skills
Inviting dialogue	Asking open-ended questions that allow caregivers to define what is important from their perspective instead of relying on close-ended questions
Promoting shared understanding	Paraphrasing to acknowledge, clarifying, and checking accuracy
Discovering feelings	Acknowledging feelings expressed, eliciting feelings, identifying feelings not expressed
Moving the dialogue forward	Summarizing and synthesizing information, prioritizing

From Boris, N.W., & Grabert, J.C. (2009). Where do I begin? In S.S. Heller & L. Gilkerson, *A practical guide to reflective supervision.* Washington, DC: ZERO TO THREE Press; reprinted by permission.

tive through what has been termed *empathic inquiry*. Active listening is made up of the following: 1) inviting dialogue through the use of questions, 2) promoting shared understanding by paraphrasing, 3) discovering feelings, and 4) moving dialogue forward by summarizing and prioritizing (Boris & Grabert, 2009; Grabert, 2009). These same components, summarized in Table 7.3, can guide connections with parents. Furthermore, for those to whom the concept of active listening is new, it is worthwhile to read more about it.

Active listening involves the eyes as much as the ears. It is no secret that all humans communicate nonverbally, and yet because nonverbal signals are processed without thinking about them, during times when we are stressed we are sometimes less attuned to nonverbal signs. Actively attending to nonverbal signals is important when meeting with stressed parents; as noted in Table 7.3, discovering feelings is one key component of active listening. Often, feelings are expressed in nonverbal ways first, so keeping eyes and ears open is an essential skill.

Of course, building active listening skills needs to be complemented by knowing what to listen for. It is easy to think of examples of parents who talk with pride and joy about their children, and also of parents who seem to express anger, frustration, and dismay. As active listening skills are applied, it is important to listen for how parental stress and parents' personal histories may have shaped the parents' attitudes toward their child. Research makes it clear that attachment relationships are strongly influenced by parents' perceptions about their children. In fact, Bowlby's original writings on attachment theory included discussion of what he called *internal working models* (Bowlby, 1973). Bowlby posited something quite profound:

> Each individual builds working models of the world and of himself in it, with the aid of which he perceives events, forecasts the future, and constructs his plans. In the working models of the world that anyone builds a key feature is his notion of who his attachment figures are, where they may be found, and how they may be expected to respond. Similarly, in the working model of the self that anyone builds a key feature is his notion of how acceptable or unacceptable he himself is in the eyes of his attachment figures. (Bowlby, 1973, p. 203)

What Bowlby is saying is that every person carries around a set of expectations and emotions about relationships that were shaped primarily by their past experiences with those who raised them. Without even thinking about it, each of us is influenced in how we relate to others by these past formative experiences and by current ongoing relationships. When early childhood professionals encounter parents who are punitive or rejecting, who seem stressed or distant, who are angry or dismissive, they need to remember that their own past experiences are an important factor in shaping their behavior. If they are to help the parents connect in a different way with the child, staff members will need to understand them without judgment. One key thing to understand is how the parents perceive their child and how stress may affect those perceptions.

This understanding cannot occur unless staff members are impartial listeners. Psychologist David Wallin (2007) offered sage advice for early childhood professionals about mindfully maintaining a fresh and open attitude with families so that they do not impose their own perspective at the cost of not really being able to hear another's perspective. If they are not impartial in their interactions with parents, not only will parents feel they have not been heard or seen, but the staff members will be in danger of not really seeing or understanding them.

THE POWER OF POSITIVE (AND NEGATIVE) THINKING

A first challenge in assisting parents to provide for their children's needs for emotional security is to remove barriers to appreciating these needs in the first place: Often parents are so stressed by their child's behavior that they become overwhelmed. As noted in Chapter 3, maternal depression is one important barrier to appreciating a child's needs. Furthermore, parents may experience external stresses that make even typical child behavior feel frustrating. In fact, there is good evidence that high levels of parenting stress affect key aspects of parenting behavior, from simply paying attention to the child's signals to disciplining the child (Raikes & Thompson, 2005). As parents struggle with stress at the same time that the child is struggling to regulate his or her emotions, the development of disruptive behavior or social withdrawal may follow (Bayer, Hiscock, Ukoumunne, Price, & Wake, 2008). Many things predict parenting stress, of course, and research makes it clear that each specific stressor (e.g., low family income) is less important than the effects of multiple stressors of varying types on the parent's functioning (Saisto, Salmela-Aro, Nurmi, & Halmesmaki, 2008). One key sign that parental stress is affecting the developing relationship is the development of what have been called *negative parental attributions* (Miller, 1995). In fact, negative parental attributions may be the final common pathway for how stress, depression, and negative life events affect parent–child relationships. Figure 7.1 captures the pathway between parent stress and child behavior.

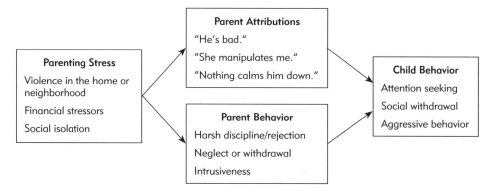

Figure 7.1. A model for how parenting stress links to child behavior.

Parents who form negative attributions about their child will experience challenging child behavior as stable rather than transient, as spurred by internal forces rather than external events, and to be a global response rather than one that is specific to a particular event or situation (Dix, Ruble, Grusec, & Nixon, 1986; Scott & Dadds, 2009). Such parents are likely to express that the child's behavior is designed to upset the parent and is therefore intentional. The child may be said to take after a family member who is particularly disliked and/or may be labeled "bad" or "manipulative." Evidence that the child's behavior is influenced by positive interactions will be selectively ignored (Dadds, Mullins, McAllister, & Atkinson, 2003). Parents who form negative attributions about their children typically are experiencing stress. Parenting, which is challenging for everyone, has become a "no-win" situation for parents who have developed fixed negative attributions about their child. A first step in getting negative attributions out on the table is using active listening skills to start conversations with parents about what their child's behavior means to them.

Engaging parents to explore and examine their attributions of their children is one way that early intervention (EI) programs can leverage attachment theory for more effective education and intervention outcomes. Because the way early childhood professionals label children influences the way they think about and treat children, it is important to help parents reframe how they see and describe their child. Just observing a child with a parent during a home visit or classroom activity and sharing with the parent a different perspective and new words to describe the child's behavior can be helpful. For example, an "out of control" child may be seen as a "spirited" child. A "stubborn" child may be seen as a child who is "independent and knows her own mind." A "crybaby" child may be seen as a child with "great sensitivity to himself and to others."

In the next section, we review other important ways in which attachment can and should influence EI programs.

USING ATTACHMENT
THEORY IN EARLY INTERVENTION

EI programs have long used attachment principles to shape their programs. Because each person is influenced by his or her internal working models and the biological-behavioral attachment system is literally a part of us, it makes sense to think that attachment is in some way infused into each program. Nevertheless, it can be revolutionary to think about ways to look at the structure and function of EI programs using attachment as a framework. A good beginning is simply recognizing that warmth, empathy, and nurturance builds security and trust in children (see Table 7.1) and then engaging all levels of staff to think about ways to make a warm and inviting setting for the child.

Because attachment research makes it clear that continuity of relationships in early childhood are particularly important, programs that strive to keep children with the same care provider for longer periods of time rather than frequently shifting children to new classrooms and care providers serve the young child's attachment needs by decreasing the number of disruptions in caregiving. Disruptions in important relationships have been shown to be difficult for young children, and keeping children younger than age 4 with the providers they are most familiar with is a sound investment (Hinshaw-Fuselier, Heller, Parton, Robinson, & Boris, 2007). Just planning transitions by introducing children to their new care provider in stages will ease transitions and serve the child's need for predictability.

Assessing Caregiver–Child Relationships

Programs with home visiting components have the opportunity to assess parent–child relationships in the home. Home visitors regularly have a chance to see parent–child interactions in the moment. It can be very helpful to systematically organize one's observations of parent–child interactions, and the Attachment Q-set is a useful tool for doing so (Waters, 1987). The Attachment Q-set is available on the Internet at no cost and is made of 90 discrete behaviors, many of which are derived from studies of attachment security. The rationale for each item is also available so that home visitors can understand how each of the behaviors that make up the Q-set relates to attachment security. Though the Attachment Q-set is an important research instrument, and for that purpose requires some training (van IJzendoorn, Vereijken, Bakermans-Kranenburg, & Marianne, 2004), it is also useful as a training tool and can give home visitors a sense of the kinds of behaviors that are most important. Measures like the Attachment Q-set are typically used in research studies by having a pair of individuals compare their ratings of behaviors. Though there is added cost to having home visitors work in pairs, the experience of rating behaviors together and comparing impressions is valuable.

Another instrument that is supported by strong psychometric data for reliability and validity and has been shown to be effective in supporting positive parent–child interactions in the context of home visits is the Nursing Child Assessment Satellite Training scales (NCAST; Kelly, Buehlman, & Caldwell, 2000; Sumner & Spietz, 1994). The NCAST allows educators and home visitors to systematically look at parents' sensitivity to their child's cues, parents' response to their child's distress, how parents foster their child's social and emotional growth, how parents foster their child's cognitive growth, the clarity of a child's communicative cues, and how responsive the child is to her parent or caregiver. The NCAST also allows home visitors to assess the amount and quality of a parent's contingent behavior in relation to the child. The NCAST requires programs to purchase the instrument and invest in staff training time, but for those programs working with families at risk for or experiencing serious relationship problems (e.g., parents of children experiencing significant biological or environmental risk, families involved with child protective services), these investments can make positive and meaningful differences in parent–child relationships and in a child's development over time.

Another promising instrument for observing child–caregiver interactions—with strong psychometric data supporting its reliability, validity, and cultural sensitivity—is the Parenting Interactions with Children: Checklist of Observations Linked to Outcomes (PICCOLO; Roggman, Cook, Innocenti, Jump Norman, & Christiansen, 2009). The PICCOLO measures positive parenting behaviors—including affection, responsiveness, encouragement, and teaching—with children ages 1 through 3 years. These behaviors have been shown to predict positive outcomes in children's school readiness and cognitive, language, and social development.

Checklists that rate relationships (as opposed to psychometrically sound observational instruments)—although tempting, because they are easy to administer—are, unfortunately, of little use. Attachment is a complex process, and the irony is that the parents who struggle most with attachment rarely see the problem as one that exists between them and the child. Instead, as described in the section on parental attributions, one hallmark of relationship disturbances is a parent who sees his or her young child as incorrigible or manipulative. More often than not, the same parent has trouble appreciating his or her own struggles in providing warmth and nurturance or setting limits for that child. However, when the EI team senses that parental negative attributions are combined with disruptive behavior, further assessment can be helpful. Table 7.2 can be a guide to looking at the child and his or her caregiver across domains, providing a systematic way to think about caregiver–child and family relationships. Much more is gained from looking at a child's behavior and listening to a parent talk about that child than handing the parent some kind of attachment checklist—not that any valid checklists exist! Of course, once the team has identified relationship concerns, it is helpful to first go into active listening mode and engage the parent or caregiver in dialogue about concerns. Once the parent or caregiver is engaged and concerns have been aired in an empathic way, then screening for depression or family violence should also be considered (see Chapter 4). Documenting developmental status is also helpful (see Chapter 6).

Working with Mental Health Consultants

Many EI programs have already engaged community partners, especially well-regarded therapists in the area, so that referrals for children with developmental delays can be made. It can be difficult to find therapists trained in infant and early childhood mental health intervention, though many states have such referral networks listed on the Internet. Given the central importance of attachment developmentally, more such therapists are being trained each year, and specialized programs and training opportunities have mushroomed. A key source in the United States for training is the organization ZERO TO THREE, which has a useful web site with links to helpful training tools (http://www .zerotothree.org). It is important to recognize the extent and limitations of one's own professional training and expertise. When a professional recognizes that he or she cannot competently or ethically serve a child and family, this is to his or her credit. It is very important to recognize the limits of our expertise and find the support children and families— and at times programs—need.

SUMMARY

Our understanding and assessment of qualities of infant–caregiver relationships should begin with an appreciation for some of the important biologically inherited characteristics shared by all humans. Our evolution as a species has promoted the selection of many characteristics that increase our likelihood of survival, including behaviors such as how we respond to an infant's cuteness and the way we use voice tone and rhythm to calm infants. Of great importance along these lines is the way we form emotional bonds, as infants, to those responsible for our care and protection. As children mature, we can expect to see their abilities to engage in increasingly complex relationships attain increasingly higher organization and sophistication. Among the great developmental accomplishments associated with these relational capacities, lasting a lifetime, are the capacities for self-regulation, an individual's abilities to cope with and regulate the internal states and be-havior affected by changes in stress-related demands encountered in the social world.

In our work in the helping professions, our abilities to make positive connections with parents—and children—will involve many of the interpersonal skills we want to encourage in the parents themselves. These include qualities such as sensitively under-standing their points of view, listening well, showing sincere appreciation for positive behavior, and following their lead in addressing concerns, instead of only pushing our expectations and agenda. The negative mind-sets that we often see in troubled parent–child relationships, and the hostile attributions parents may impart to their children, should also be a lesson to those of us in the helping professions to maintain an open-mindedness and willingness to learn, as opposed to moving too quickly to judgment.

Finally, some standardized assessment tools can be used to help guide our assess-ments, especially our observations of parents. The bottom line here, though, is about our abilities to perceive accurately, to see and hear well, what our parents communicate to their children and to us. As we improve our sensitivity and responsiveness to our parents' realities, we provide an opportunity for them to be truly understood, and experience sup-port in the process. This sort of mutual understanding may, in turn, become the basis for our productive collaboration.

REFERENCES

Ainsworth, M.D.S. (1979). Infant-mother attachment. *American Psychologist, 34*(10), 932–937.

Bayer, J.K., Hiscock, H., Ukoumunne, O.C., Price, A., & Wake, M. (2008). Early childhood etiology of mental health problems: A longitudinal population-based study. *Journal of Child Psychology and Psychiatry, 49*(11), 1166–1174.

Boris, N.W., & Grabert, J.C. (2009). How do I introduce reflective supervision to my program? In S.S. Heller & L. Gilkerson, *A practical guide to reflective supervision* (pp. 41–60). Washington, DC: ZERO TO THREE Press.

Bowlby, J. (1973). *Attachment and loss: Vol. 2. Separation anxiety and anger.* New York: Basic Books.

Bowlby, J. (1982). *Attachment and loss: Vol. 1. Attachment* (2nd ed.). New York: Basic Books.

Bretherton, I. (1991). Intentional communication and the development of an understanding of mind. In D. Frye & C. Moore (Eds.), *Children's theories of mind: Mental states and social understanding.* Hillsdale, NJ: Lawrence Erlbaum.

Dadds, M.R., Mullins, M.J., McAllister, R.A., & Atkinson, E. (2003). Attributions, affect, and behavior in abuse-risk mothers: A laboratory study. *Child Abuse and Neglect, 27*, 21–45.

Dix, T., Ruble, D.N., Grusec, J.E., & Nixon, S. (1986). Social cognition in parents: Inferential and af-fective reactions to children of three age levels. *Child Development, 57*(4), 879–894.

Dodge, K.A., Price, J.M., Bachorowski, J., & Newman, J.P. (1990). Hostile attributional biases in se-verely aggressive adolescents. *Journal of Abnormal Psychology, 99*(4), 385–392.

Erickson, M.F., & Kurz-Reimer, K. (1999). Identifying and building on parenting strengths. In M.F. Erickson & K. Kurz-Reimer, *Infants, toddlers, and families: A framework for support and intervention* (pp. 53–87). New York: Guilford Press.

Falk, D. (2004). Prelinguistic evolution in early hominids: Whence motherese? *Behavioral and Brain Sciences, 27*(4), 491–503.

Golinkoff, R.M. (1986). "I beg your pardon?": The preverbal negotiation of failed messages. *Child Language, 13*, 455–476.

Grabert, J. (2009). Integrating early childhood mental health into early intervention services. *Zero to Three, 29*(6), 13–17.

Guttmann-Steinmetz, S., & Crowell. J.A. (2006). Attachment and externalizing disorders: A developmental psychopathology perspective. *Journal of the American Academy of Child and Adolescent Psychiatry, 45*(4), 440–451.

Hinshaw-Fuselier, S., Heller, S.S., Parton, V.T., Robinson, L., & Boris, N.W. (2007). Trauma and attachment: The case for disrupted attachment disorder. In J. Osofsky (Ed.), *Young children and trauma* (pp. 47–68). New York: Guilford.

Karen, R. (1994). *Becoming attached: First relationships and how they shape our capacity to love.* New York: Oxford University Press.

Keller, H., Otto, H., Lamm, B., Yovsi, R.D., & Kärtner, J. (2008). The timing of verbal/vocal communications between mothers and their infants: A longitudinal cross-cultural comparison. *Infant Behavior and Development, 31*(2), 217–226.

Kelly, J., Buehlman, K., & Caldwell, K. (2000). Training personnel to promote quality parent-child interaction in families who are homeless. *Topics in Early Childhood Special Education, 20*(3), 174–185.

Meltzoff, A.N., & Moore, M.K. (1977). Explaining facial imitation: A theoretical model. *Early Development and Parenting, 6,* 179–192.

Meltzoff, A.N., & Moore, M.K. (1999). Resolving the debate about early imitation. In A. Slater & D. Muir (Eds.), *The Blackwell reader in developmental psychology.* Oxford: Blackwell.

Miller, S.A. (1995). Parents' attributions for their children's behavior. *Child Development, 66*(6), 1557–1584.

Raikes, H.A., & Thompson, R.A. (2005). Links between risk and attachment security: Models of influence. *Applied Developmental Psychology, 26,* 440–455.

Roggman, L.A., Cook, G.A., Innocenti, M.S., Jump Norman, V., & Christiansen, K. (2009). *PICCOLO (Parenting Interactions with Children: Checklist of Observations Linked to Outcomes).* Logan, UT: Utah State University.

Saisto, T., Salmela-Aro, K., Nurmi, J.E., & Halmesmaki, E. (2008). Longitudinal study on the predictors of parental stress in mothers and fathers of toddlers. *Journal of Psychosomatic Obstetrics and Gynaecology, 29*(3), 213–222.

Scott, S., & Dadds, M.R. (2009). Practitioner review: When parent training doesn't work: Theory-driven clinical strategies. *Journal of Child Psychology and Psychiatry. 50*(12), 1441–1450.

Sprengelmeyer, R., Perrett, D.I., Fagan, E.C., Cornwell, R.E., Lobmaier, J.S., Sprengelmeyer, A., et al. (2009). The cutest little baby face: A hormonal link to sensitivity to cuteness in infant faces. *Psychological Science, 20*(2), 149–154.

Sumner, G., & Spietz, A. (1994). *NCAST caregiver/parent-child interaction teaching manual.* Seattle: University of Washington, School of Nursing, NCAST Publications.

van der Horst, F.C., Leroy, H.A., & van der Veer, R. (2008). "When strangers meet": John Bowlby and Harry Harlow on attachment behavior. *Integrative Psychological & Behavioral Science, 42*(4), 370–388.

van IJzendoorn, M.H., Vereijken, C.M., Bakermans-Kranenburg, M.J., & Marianne, J. (2004). Assessing attachment security with the attachment Q-sort: Meta-analytic evidence for the validity of the observer AQS. *Child Development, 75*(4), 1188–1213.

Wallin, D.J. (2007). *Attachment in psychotherapy.* New York: Guilford Press.

Waters, E. (1987). *Attachment Q-set (Version 3).* Retrieved June 7, 2011, from http://www.psychology .sunysb.edu/attachment/measures/content/aqs_items.pdf

Weinfield, N.S., Sroufe, L.A., Egeland B., & Carlson, E. (2008). Individual differences in infant-caregiver attachment: Conceptual and empirical aspects of security. In J. Cassidy & P.R. Shaver (Eds.), *Handbook of attachment: Theory, research, and clinical applications* (2nd ed., pp. 78–101). New York: Guilford Press.

II

Supporting Infant Mental Health

Intervention Strategies and Organizational Supports

Susan Janko Summers

*J*ust as change must begin with individual practice that is intentional and informed, it must also be integrated into systemwide intervention approaches that are supported by organizations through professional development, supervision and evaluation. This section of *Understanding Early Childhood Mental Health: A Practical Guide for Professionals* describes important parallel processes of supporting education and intervention staff as they plan and deliver supportive interventions for children and families.

Jones Harden and Duchene in Chapter 8 present strategies for promoting infant mental health through intervention with children and their caregivers. Beeber and Canuso in Chapter 9 provide practical ways for practitioners, who are trained to work primarily with children, to include caregivers in their professional practice. In Chapter 10, Heller, Boothe, Keyes, and Malik present various models of infant mental health consultation to early childhood classrooms as a way to meet child and family needs that extend beyond the scope and expertise of traditional early childhood programs. Heller, in Chapter 11, describes approaches to reflective supervision as an essential component of professional development and support, and in Chapter 12 Denmark and Jones Harden expand the notion of professional development and support in their chapter on ways to meet the mental health needs of staff working under conditions of elevated stress. In Chapter 13, White and Jones Harden describe how organizational culture, climate, and commitment work together to make infant mental health a viable and effective part of early childhood education. In Chapter 14, Summers describes ways to incorporate program evaluation into daily practice to make sure individual and organizational efforts to support infant mental health are effective.

Although the chapters in *Understanding Early Childhood Mental Health* cover individual topics of importance, the authors believe that chapters are also complementary and will result in more effective practice when considered as a whole. We sincerely hope you gain skill and confidence in promoting infant mental health during your daily practice with children and families, and we hope your work is wholeheartedly supported by your colleagues and organization and that it results in beneficial changes, small and large, in children and families.

8

Promoting Infant Mental
Health in Early Childhood Programs

Intervening with Parent–Child Dyads

Brenda Jones Harden and Melissa Duchene

$\mathcal{T}$he phrase *infant mental health* conjures up many images that seem at odds with early childhood professionals' vision of optimal infant and toddler functioning. For example, we may associate the phrase with psychopathology (i.e., mental illness) in very young children, which stands in contrast with our inclination to focus on promoting core developmental processes in infants, such as emotion expression and regulation (Cicchetti, Ackerman, & Izard, 1995; Denham, Bassett, & Wyatt, 2007). In terms of infant mental health treatment, we may regard this as a traditional psychotherapeutic approach that is inappropriate for very young children. For example, we know that preverbal infants and toddlers just developing language use cannot avail themselves of therapies that rely on language and its cognitive underpinnings as the primary modality. We also understand that toddlers who have not developed symbolic play skills may not benefit from play-based therapies that are often used with preschool children. Further, we recognize that infants cannot benefit from cognitive-behavioral approaches that have been found to be so effective with older children, given infants' high levels of emotional arousal that is not yet modulated by thought.

Just as the field of early childhood has expanded over the last few decades, the conceptualization of infant mental health has matured. For example, Zeanah (2009) reminds us that the phrase *infant mental health* refers to the child's social-emotional functioning as well as the intervention approach that is designed to promote the child's psychological well-being. In *Supporting Children's Mental Health,* key concepts of infant mental health were identified, including the following: "Through relationships with parents and other caregivers, infants and toddlers learn what people expect of them and what they can expect of other people" (U.S. Department of Health and Human Services, 2000, p. 10). Based on these notions, the primary goal of infant mental health intervention has evolved to include fostering relationships between infants or toddlers and their caregivers as both a primary focus for intervention and a means for intervention.

Thus, the intervention mechanism through which infant mental health, as psychological well-being, is best addressed is one that incorporates the caregivers of these young children. These caregivers may be the child's parents, or may be grandparents, foster parents, or other persons primarily responsible for providing concrete and affective care to the child. The infant mental health interventions may address parental mental health specifically (see Chapter 9) or may be geared to support early childhood educators and child care providers (see Chapter 10). In this chapter, we examine mental health approaches that target the caregiver–infant dyad. First, we provide a conceptualization of infant mental health from a dyadic perspective, with an emphasis on preventing psychopathology in infants and toddlers. Then, we explore infant–parent psychotherapy, parent–child interaction therapy, and interaction guidance as exemplars of these types of dyadic approaches. In addition, we examine parent education interventions that address child well-being, specifically infant mental health. We conclude with a discussion of how early childhood programs can integrate such interventions into their ongoing services.

AN INFANT MENTAL HEALTH CONCEPTUAL FRAMEWORK

It can be argued that the sine qua non, or most essential goal, of infant mental intervention is to promote secure attachments between infants and their caregivers. Many studies suggest that early attachment experiences are important contributors to later child outcomes (Berlin, Cassidy, & Appleyard, 2008; Sroufe, Carlson, Levy, & Egeland, 1999) and document the benefits of attachment-oriented interventions (Berlin, Zeanah, & Lieberman, 2008).

Specifically, a developing child needs warm, supportive, and responsive parents in order to establish a secure attachment relationship with his or her caregivers (Bowlby, 1982). Parents' responses to their children's signals are likely to determine the quality of the parent–child relationship. When children are in need, they seek out their caregivers and expect them to attend to their needs. If the caregiver is usually unresponsive, then the child may begin to perceive the social world as unsupportive and harsh, which may influence the quality of the child's later relationships. (See Chapter 7 to learn more about attachment relationships.)

The infant–caregiver relationship has been viewed as being so powerful that it can shape children's development of the concept of self (Stern & Elias, 2007), guide how children behave in other relationships contemporaneously and throughout their lifetime (Berlin, Cassidy, et al., 2008; Bowlby, 1982; Main, Kaplan, & Cassidy, 1985), and determine a child's overall mental health (Lieberman & Zeanah, 1999). Parent behaviors, in the context of their interactions with their children, have a major influence on child outcomes. For example, a balance of parental warmth and restrictiveness in child rearing is strongly related to child outcomes, such as prosocial behaviors (Hastings, McShane, Parker, & Ladha, 2007). Child behaviors can also influence the quality of the parent–child relationships. For example, children at risk for a number of negative developmental outcomes may be too demanding for some parents, which may render the parent at increased risk for stress (Baker-Ericzén, Brookman-Frazee, & Stahmer, 2005). Parents with elevated levels of stress may have more negative perceptions of their children, which may influence child outcomes, such as an increase in the number of behavior problems (Renk, Roddenberry, Oliveros, & Sieger, 2007).

Infant mental health interventions are grounded in the theoretical and research propositions described earlier. Specifically, they are designed to improve parenting behaviors and parent–infant interaction, as well as infant development and mental health. To accomplish these goals, infant mental health intervention is best situated in a prevention framework that is informed by knowledge of early child development. From this perspective, infant mental health programs can achieve positive child outcomes if they address the multiple risk and protective factors that children and families may experience (Cicchetti & Hinshaw, 2002). (See also Chapter 4.) Thus, practitioners must address the individual mental health needs of the child and the parent, as well as the more systemic concrete, psychological, social, and relational needs of the family.

Typically, infant mental health approaches include intervention at all these levels, depending on child and family needs, over the course of the intervention. As Weatherston (1995) stated, infant mental health interventions should include developmental guidance (i.e., increasing parental knowledge of infant developmental processes and milestones), emotional support to the parent (e.g., empathy and nurturance, referral to mental health treatment), and concrete services (e.g., obtaining infant health care, securing Special Supplemental Nutrition Program for Women, Infants, and Children vouchers). Most important, infant mental health interventions target the dyad, facilitating more positive caregiver–infant relationships and interactions. In this way, parents and caregivers can become more emotionally available, more contingently responsive, and more nurturing to their own children. With the support of the infant mental health practitioner, caregivers may also increase their attention to other aspects of infant functioning such as the child's need for comfort during times of distress, for a language-rich environment, for interaction with novel objects and experiences, and for opportunities to explore their environment.

Multiple strategies have been used within infant mental health approaches. Observation and assessment of the parent–child relationship and interaction are primary intervention mechanisms, which should be conducted at the initiation of the intervention and on an ongoing basis. The notion of parallel process (i.e., nurturing the parent or caregiver so he or she can nurture the child) is critical here as well, given the centrality of the relationships at multiple levels, including the parent-practitioner relationship. In addition, as Selma Fraiberg and colleagues proposed in their groundbreaking paper "Ghosts in the Nursery," dyadic infant mental health interventions link the parents' own experiences receiving early care with the caregiving they currently provide to their infants (Fraiberg, Adelson, & Shapiro, 1975). They also provide developmental guidance through coaching or more explicit parenting education within the context of the parent–infant interaction. Strategies derived from these early theories remain a part of most infant mental health approaches, exemplars of which are described in the following section.

EXEMPLARS OF INFANT MENTAL HEALTH APPROACHES

There are multiple infant mental health models being conducted across the country, many of which target parent–child dyads (see Table 8.1 for sources for major infant mental

Table 8.1.   Program manual and curriculum resources

Interaction guidance intervention	Sameroff, A.J., McDonough, S.C., and Rosenblum, K.L. (2005). *Treating parent–infant relationship problems: Strategies for intervention* (pp. 1–304). New York: Guilford Press.
Nurturing Parenting program	Bavolek, S.J. (1999). *Nurturing parenting: Teaching empathy, self-worth and discipline to school-age children* (4th ed.). Park City, UT: Family Development Resources. Can be found at http://www.nurturingparenting.com/npp/index.php
Parent–child interaction therapy	Urquiza, A.J., and McNeil, C.B. (1996). Parent–child interaction therapy: An intensive dyadic intervention for physically abusive families. *Child Maltreatment, 1*(2), 132–141. Available at http://www.pcittraining.tv/pdf/1996cm.pdf
Parent–child psychotherapy	Lieberman, A., and Van Horn, P. (2005). *Don't hit my mommy! A manual for child–parent psychotherapy with young witnesses of family violence.* Washington, DC: Zero to Three.
The Incredible Years	Webster-Stratton, C., and Reid, M. (2010). The Incredible Years, parents, teachers and children training series: A multifaceted treatment approach for young children with conduct problems. In A.E. Kazdin and J.R. Weisz (Eds.), *Evidence-based psycho-therapies for children and adolescents* (pp. 224–240). New York: Guilford Press. Available at http://www.incredibleyears.com/library/paper.asp?nMode=1&nLibraryID=430

health models). Such models are grounded in the infant mental health framework described earlier, which focuses on enhancing the relationship between parents or caregivers and children. These models include child–parent psychotherapy, parent–child interaction therapy, and parent–child interaction guidance, each of which is described in the following sections. Also discussed are parenting interventions, which are designed to improve parents' skills at promoting their children's development and well-being. Interventions explicitly designed to address parental mental health are covered in Chapter 9.

Child–Parent Psychotherapy

Child–parent psychotherapy is a relationship-based therapeutic approach with a goal of restoring the emotional bond between the parent and child (Lieberman & Van Horn, 2008). After engaging in child–parent psychotherapy, parents are expected to be equipped with the necessary tools for establishing a positive quality relationship with their children that is based on mutuality and respect. Child–parent psychotherapy originated in the work of Selma Fraiberg (1980), who advocated focusing on the parents' own early childhood experiences and how these experiences shape parents' perceptions of their children. To attain a positive parent–child relationship, parents' own childhood experiences or "ghosts in the nursery" had to be addressed, specifically their unresolved problems that affect the way they view and interact with their children (Lieberman & Van Horn, 2005). In addition, parental beliefs, attributes, and emotions may influence parental practices, which in turn influence children's behavior (Hastings et al., 2007). For example, a depressed parent may perceive his or her crying child as being ill-tempered and as a result may react by employing some type of discipline. A nondepressed parent, however, may perceive his or her child's cry as a way of expressing some kind of need and may be more responsive and sensitive in nature. Thus, child–parent psychotherapy is designed to ad-

Box 8.1. Tenets of child–parent psychotherapy

- The goal of child–parent psychotherapy is to reflect with parents on their inter-actions with their children, their perceptions of their children, and their own experiences as children.
- Interactions within the parent–child relationship can shape child behavior.
- Parent characteristics can influence child outcomes, and child characteristics can influence parent outcomes and parenting practices.
- Parents' early caregiving experiences may be reflected in the ways in which they care for their own young children.

dress parents' unresolved issues from their own childhoods, as well as their beliefs and emotions relative to their children.

There is a growing evidence base about the effectiveness of child–parent psychotherapy. It has been found to reduce child maltreatment and improve parental positive response to toddlers who have been maltreated (Cicchetti, Rogosch, & Toth, 2006). Also, child–parent psychotherapy has been found to reduce maternal depressive symptoms and enhance the relationship between depressed mothers and their toddlers (Toth, Rogosch, & Cicchetti, 2006). In situations of intimate partner violence, it has been found to reduce behavior problems and trauma symptoms of exposed children, as well as to decrease maternal posttraumatic stress disorder symptoms (Lieberman, Van Horn, & Ippen, 2005). Thus, this model can address the fundamental relationship difficulties that may manifest in parent–child dyads, but it can also be used to address the infant mental health issues that emanate from other major family risk factors.

Parent–Child Interaction Therapy

Parent–child interaction therapy was initially designed as a parenting intervention for families in which there was a young child with a behavioral problem (Eyberg & Bussing, 2010). Despite its focus on child behavior problems, parent–child interaction therapy treats the parent and child as a cohesive unit (Finnelo, 2005). As such, the overall goal of this intervention is to strengthen the caregivers' relationships with their children. This therapeutic approach considers the parent's psychological well-being, the child's ability to seek comfort and a connection with the parent, and how the parent's or child's behavior in the dyad triggers the other to react.

Parent–child interaction therapy relies on concrete, skill-building strategies for improving parent–child relationships. Specifically, parent–child interaction therapy involves direct skill modeling, practice, and observation (Urquiza & McNeil, 1996). Further, parent–child interaction therapy interventionists coach parents while they interact with their children, using a one-way mirror and a wireless earphone worn by the parents. Parents are trained to praise their children's positive behavior and to refrain from directing

Box 8.2.   Tenets of parent–child interaction therapy

- The goal of parent–child interaction therapy is to improve parenting practices and child behavior as well as parent–child relationships.
- Parents are explicitly coached on ways to interact with their children.
- Positive interactions between the parent and child are highlighted.
- The focus is on skill-building in parents with regard to responsiveness and positive behavioral support.

their children's play (Dombrowski, Timmer, Blacker, & Urquiza, 2005). Further, the practitioner explicitly recognizes the strengths of the parent and child and highlights these positive interactional behaviors.

Parent–child interaction therapy has been found to be effective with several populations of young children and their families. A strong body of research has documented the effectiveness of parent–child interaction therapy when implemented with families of children with behavior problems. Specifically, parent–child interaction therapy has reduced young children's behavior problems, increased child compliance, enhanced parent–child interaction, and improved parental sensitivity, contingent praise, and other positive parenting behaviors (Eyberg & Bussing, 2010; Timmer, Urquiza, & Zebell, 2006). Timmer, Ware, Urquiza, and Zebell (2010) found that parent–child interaction therapy reduces behavior problems and parenting stress in families exposed to intimate partner violence. In their evaluation of parent–child interaction therapy with young children who were maltreated or at risk for maltreatment, Chaffin and Friedrich (2004) and Chaffin, Funderburk, Bard, Valle, and Gurwitch (2011) reported sequential improvements in the negative and disengaged parent behaviors in the parent–child interaction context, ultimately fewer abusive behaviors on the part of parents, and lower rates of child welfare recidivism (i.e., families becoming reinvolved with the child welfare system). Other outcomes of parent–child interaction therapy with maltreating populations include improved parent–child interactions, increased maternal sensitivity, reduced parental stress, and decreased child behavior problems (Thomas & Zimmer-Gembeck, 2011). Given its effectiveness with these high-risk populations, parent–child interaction therapy represents a preeminent model for incorporation into early childhood programs.

Interaction Guidance

Interaction guidance is a therapeutic treatment model that combines features of child–parent psychotherapy and parent–child interaction therapy. As such, it focuses on the infant–caregiver relationship and attempts to build parenting skills of program participants (McDonough, 2004). Unlike many therapeutic models, interaction guidance was designed to meet the needs of very high-risk families, including those from low socio-economic backgrounds who contend with poverty-associated challenges (McDonough,

Box 8.3.   Tenets of interaction guidance

- The goal of interaction guidance is to increase parents' awareness of their interactions with their children.
- Parents are trained to appropriately respond to children's behavior.
- Positive interactions between the parent and child are highlighted through videotape review.
- Interaction guidance intervention is specifically geared to address the needs of high-risk families.

2004). Practitioners who employ this approach videotape parents interacting with their children and provide feedback to parents while jointly viewing the videotape. Practitioners highlight parents' positive interactions with their children and facilitate their awareness of their children's behavior through interaction. In addition, parents are trained to appropriately respond to their children's behaviors and taught ways to better manage their children's problem behaviors. During parent–child interactions, factors such as parents' verbal comments and their ability to understand that people have beliefs, desires, and goals that are different from their own are assessed and addressed (Rosenblum, McDonough, Sameroff, & Muzik, 2008).

Because this interaction model is targeted to high-risk families, there is a focus on problems that may arise within these families. Interventionists attempt to address these problems in the context of the parent–child interaction as well. Although the research base for interaction guidance is not as extensive as it is for child–parent psychotherapy or parent–child interaction therapy, there is some evidence of its effectiveness with high-risk families. Thus, interaction guidance can be used as a model for enhancing parent–child interactions among the high-risk families who many early childhood programs serve.

Parent Education Models

Because parents are children's primary caregivers, many therapeutic interventions are aimed at improving parenting behaviors. As Weatherston (1995) asserted, providing developmental guidance should be an essential component of infant mental health programs. Both goals—improving parenting behaviors and providing developmental guidance—can be achieved through dyadic approaches, as described earlier, or through educational or skill-building interventions designed explicitly for parents. The potential for parent education programs to foster positive parenting skills and ultimately enhance children's developmental outcomes has been reviewed elsewhere (Barth, 2009; Kaminski, Valle, Filene, & Boyle, 2008). In the main, these reviews suggest that parent education programs can enhance child outcomes, with a strong corpus of evidence demonstrating benefits for children's social-emotional functioning. Further, such programs have the potential to improve parenting skills and parental mental health, which both have an impact on children's outcomes. For example, in their implementation and evaluation of a parent management training intervention, DeGarmo, Patterson, and Forgatch (2004) documented improved parenting skills as well as decreased parental depression, both of which were linked to more positive child behavioral outcomes. Reductions in parental depression tended to enhance parenting skills and children's behavior over time.

We propose that the strategic use of parent education interventions within the context of dyadic approaches can augment the effectiveness of such approaches. Although this combination of interventions exists in many programs for high-risk families of young children, the research base to support this combined approach is slim. There is evidence that parent training is much more effective if it is conducted using a "hands-on," experiential approach, with the professional coaching parents to improve their skills in the context of parent–child interaction (Kaminski et al., 2008). In the following paragraphs, we review parent education models and strategies that hold promise for being effective as a component of a dyadic infant mental health approach. We pay particular attention to parent education models that target the parent–child dyad.

Cognitive-behavioral approaches to improving parenting skills have been found to be particularly effective in regard to parent and child outcomes. For example, the Incredible Years program has been shown to benefit families of children at risk for behavioral problems (Webster-Stratton & Reid, 2010). The Incredible Years began as a treatment program that included children between the ages of 3 and 8. Children and their parents were provided social skills training in a group setting over a period of 10–12 sessions. Benefits of the Incredible Years included improvements in parent management skills, reductions in harsh parenting, increases in responsive parenting and stimulation of child's learning, and decreases in child behavior problems such as aggression (Brotman et al., 2005; Webster-Stratton & Reid, 2010). Notably, the Incredible Years has been implemented within a Head Start program and was found to be particularly beneficial for families that included children with significant behavior problems and parents who were highly critical (Reid, Webster-Stratton, & Baydar, 2004). More recently, the Incredible Years parents and babies and parents and toddlers programs were designed to strengthen positive, nurturing parenting skills among parents of children birth to 12 months and 1–3 years (see http://www.incredibleyears.com/program/parent.asp).

Box 8.4.   Tenets of parent intervention models

- The goals of parent intervention models are, globally, to improve parenting practices, but specific purposes vary by model.
- Improved parenting can enhance child development and parents' psychological well-being.
- Parent intervention can lead to better quality parent–child relationships.
- Parental skill-building interventions and those designed to address child behavior problems have been found to be particularly effective in enhancing parenting and parent–child relationships.

Many other parent intervention models and strategies have been shown to improve parents' interactions with their children. For example, Stephen Bavolek (1999) developed the Nurturing Parenting Program, with a version that focuses on children ages birth to 5 years. His program attempts to help parents have more appropriate expectations of their children, increase their empathy toward their children, and engage in more positive forms of discipline. In a program for substance-using mothers, Pajulo and colleagues (2011) worked to enhance mothers' positive connections to their children as a mechanism to reduce their substance dependency. It has also been documented that helping parents to express their emotions more effectively enhances their parenting skills (Kaminski et al., 2008).

INTEGRATING INFANT MENTAL HEALTH APPROACHES INTO EARLY CHILDHOOD INTERVENTIONS

The overarching goal of early childhood programs is to promote the optimal development of young children. With regard to infant mental health, a relationship-based approach is essential. Early Head Start and other early childhood programs can embrace this approach by integrating the models described in the previous section, in whole or in part, into their ongoing service provision. In addition, the principles and strategies that emanate from such models can be incorporated into the services that early childhood programs already provide.

Building on Infant Mental Health Principles and Strategies

As we have highlighted, a major goal of infant mental health interventions is to support healthy relationships, interactions, and attachment between parents and their young children. Thus, programs have to move beyond child-centered intervention (e.g., child care or child therapy) and parent-centered intervention (e.g., parent support or parent therapy) and create opportunities to focus on parent–child or caregiver–child dyads. Thus, during parent groups and home visits, practitioners should find opportunities to support parental emotional availability, foster parent responsiveness, promote parental emotional attunement, and enhance joint attention and involvement, as well as encourage affective expression, understanding, and sharing. Developmental guidance can easily occur during parent groups and home visits as well, in which parents are helped to understand the developmental progression of their children and to adjust their expectations to their children's developmental status.

Simultaneously, positive parenting can be promoted by practitioners' empathy with parents' vulnerability regarding parenting, connection with parents' desire to be good parents, and identification and reinforcement of positive parental behaviors, no matter how small. Another important strategy is to focus on coaching parents to build their skills in managing their children's behavior (including providing choices, praising good behavior, and using more positive disciplinary approaches such as teaching the correct behavior). Other skills that are essential to address for parents in their interactions with their children include parental emotional modulation and fostering the emotional regulation of their children, as well as engaging in safe parenting practices such as close supervision of their young children and maintaining a safe home environment (e.g., covering outlets, lowering water temperature, locking away poisons and medicines).

Six infant mental health principles for Early Head Start programs are identified in *Pathways to Prevention* (Early Head Start National Resource Center, 2004); two are particularly relevant to our discussion here. The first is to identify and share observations of strengths in the infants' and toddlers' relationships with their parents. The second is to listen to parents. Further, practitioners should always look for opportunities to affirm parents' special role and relationship with their children and help them find some joy in caring for their children. These two infant mental health principles are easily incorporated into the home visits, parent groups, and other parent–child activities that are conducted by early childhood programs. (See Chapter 7 to learn more about listening to and communicating with parents and caregivers.)

There are multiple mechanisms through which practitioners can coach parents to enhance their relationships with their young children. Parent groups and home visits can include naturalistic play interactions, in which parents and children use their own or easily created toys to engage in unstructured play. Parents can be encouraged to follow their children's lead in play and narrate the play scenes that the children create. Practitioners can also capitalize on caregiving routines that occur regularly in the families' daily lives, such as feeding, grooming, and diapering. Parents can be supported to engage in positive interactions with their children during these routines, in which they talk, smile, and touch their children. In addition, programs can organize parent–child activities to enhance parent–child interaction, such as infant massage, interactive songs, family dancing, and field trips to settings that allow for interaction.

Program Adaptations to Promote a Dyadic Infant Mental Health Approach

As Zeanah, Bailey, and Berry (2009) suggested, it is important to consider the systemic and logistic issues that affect how infant mental health interventions are integrated into early childhood programs. Similarly, the *Pathways to Prevention* report (Early Head Start National Resource Center, 2004) underscored the importance of management systems, human resources, and collaboration with mental health providers to the integration of such programs. Organizational adaptations necessary to establish solid infant mental health services are addressed in Chapter 13. Herein, we discuss more explicitly how ongoing services of early childhood programs can be adapted to have an infant mental health orientation.

As is typically done, programs should conduct a needs assessment relative to the families that are participants and include an emphasis on the mental health needs of children and families. Programs can develop specific dyadic interventions aimed at meeting the mental health needs manifested by program participants, such as those targeted to substance-using parents and their children (Pajulo et al., 2011), depressed parents and their children (Toth et al., 2006), or maltreating parents and their children (Cicchetti et al., 2006). Mental health consultants can assist programs in identifying, adapting, and implementing such interventions.

Further, programs should develop a "theory of change" (i.e., an explicit intervention strategy to achieve program goals) that builds on using an interactional approach to improve parent and child social-emotional outcomes. Specifically, parent mental health can be promoted through improving parent management skills, and infant social-emotional functioning can be enhanced through increasing parent responsiveness, both of which can be addressed in the context of parent–child interaction. Staff at all levels should be integrally involved in developing these theories of change and reflecting on the best strategies for using parent–child interactional interventions for the families the program serves.

In her early descriptions of infant mental health intervention, Fraiberg (1980) coined the term *kitchen therapy* and asserted that practitioners should intervene with parents and children in their homes. Thus, home visits, which have been found to be pivotal to parent change in a variety of early childhood programs (Barth, 2009; Jones Harden, Chazan-Cohen, Raikes, & Vogel, 2010), are a prime venue for delivering infant mental health services. An essential component of home visits should be parent–child interaction, through naturalistic play or caregiving routines as described earlier. Home visitors can observe the parent–child interaction as a way of identifying the relationship issues that need to be addressed for particular dyads. They can then coach parents to achieve the relationship goals identified in the context of parent–child interactional activities that are appropriate for individual families.

Parent and caregiver groups should move beyond didactic instruction sessions in which information is shared with caregivers about child development and positive parenting. Rather, these groups should include both caregivers and young children, and should incorporate activities that promote the growth of positive caregiver–child interactions (Barth, 2009; Webster-Stratton & Reid, 2010). Such activities should be those in which parents would feel safe engaging, such as interactive songs and stories. Instead of didactic parenting education sessions, parent groups could incorporate activities that facilitate parent knowledge and skills about child rearing in the context of caregiver–child interactions. For example, the meal that is typically a part of these sessions could be an opportunity for group leaders to coach parents on proper nutrition, bottle feeding, breast feeding, stimulating language, and being emotionally responsive to their young children.

Videotaping parent–child or caregiver–child interactions during either of these activities or venues allows for later examination of the interaction, in which the practitioner can coach the parent to improve their skills as parents in multiple ways (Barth, 2009; McDonough, 2004). Practitioners can identify the moments in the video in which parents exhibited positive parenting or when there was a particularly poignant interaction. They can show these sections to parents, providing praise for parent behavior and reflecting with the parent on the meaning of those behaviors for the infant. Programs can purchase inexpensive camcorders that can be easily transported to home visits or used during parent groups.

An important mechanism for integrating an infant mental health approach into early childhood programming relates to staff support (see Chapter 12). First, staff should be trained on the key features of an infant mental health approach and how they should be translated into their ongoing work with families and children. This might include didactic training from infant mental health experts, reading groups in which staff collectively read practitioner-oriented empirical or case material about infant mental health, and observation of practitioners who regularly provide infant mental health services. Initial training and subsequent "fidelity boosts" (i.e., boosting the degree to which they are carrying out interventions as intended) on a particular intervention is critical should the program decide to import a previously established model (e.g., Parent–Child Interaction Therapy, the Incredible Years).

Paraprofessional staff, who may not have an educational background that includes basic counseling and other family engagement skills, will need more intensive training that facilitates their understanding of the overlap and distinctions between infant mental health and other human service approaches. They will need ongoing training that allows them to translate their infant mental health knowledge to their practice (e.g., building their skills as interventionists) and that promotes basic professional mental health interventionist skills (e.g., maintaining boundaries with their families, recognizing parental mental health symptoms).

Finally, staff should always have an opportunity to reflect on their use of parent–child interaction. This can be achieved through reflective supervision and other staff support activities (see Chapters 10 and 11), as well as viewing videotapes of their interactions with parents. The same video-recorded sessions described above can prove valuable to the reflective supervision and mentoring process by providing a focus for education and support of staff acquiring new skills in working with caregiver–child dyads. Through these reflection activities, staff should address the fidelity of their infant mental health interventions and specifically the quantity and quality of their parent–child interaction activities. They should consider how they can ensure that parent–child interaction occurs in each home visit, particularly with families who present many risk factors. They should also carefully examine whether the interaction activities they have elected to use with families are leading to the relationship and social-emotional functioning enhancements that are expected. Further, through reflection, they can be helped to identify the "teachable moments" in their interactions with families that they can use to enhance the parent–child relationship.

Cultural Considerations

It is well documented that culture shapes parents' beliefs and their child-rearing practices, particularly in the early years (Ippen, 2009). A family's culture can determine how receptive a parent is to receiving assistance when they or their children have a potential mental health problem (Lieberman & Van Horn, 2008). Clinicians must be cognizant of their own cultural beliefs, especially when they are interacting with families who hold beliefs that are different from their own. A process useful in developing self-awareness of one's own cultural beliefs is *cultural auditing*. A cultural auditing model is presented in Chapter 11.

Finally, an intervention treatment will likely be more effective if it is grounded in the culture of the families who receive it (Coard, 2007). In this vein, dyadic approaches to infant mental health should parallel the parent–child interactive processes that occur in specific cultures (Lewis, 2000). It is essential that infant mental health providers learn from parents about their cultural values, beliefs, and practices, as they are the experts and best teachers about the nuances of parent–child interactional processes in their respective cultures (Coard, 2007; Lewis, 2000). For example, feeding young children has distinct cultural connotations, as in the sustainment of breastfeeding throughout the early childhood years in some groups. Dancing and other physical movement are also more prominent in some cultures, so parent–child interaction could build on these activities rather than the more sedentary interactions that occur during play. Safety practices that are taught in the context of parent–child interaction also have to be considered from a cultural perspective. For example, some cultural groups hold strong beliefs about early introduction of solids (e.g., cereal) and cosleeping, both of which have health and survival implications for infants. Finally, family cultural rituals (e.g., religious activities, parties, meals) can be used to promote more positive parent–child interaction (Fiese et al., 2002).

CONCLUSION

Infant mental health has been defined as the social-emotional functioning of the very young child and the interventions that support such functioning. Because infants' functioning is inextricably tied to the functioning of their caregivers, infant mental health must be considered from the perspective of the infants' relationship with their caregivers. Therefore, infant mental health interventions should target the parent–child dyad and have a goal of enhancing dyadic interactions. Early Head Start and similar early childhood programs are prime venues for the delivery of such infant mental health interventions.

One mechanism for delivering these infant mental health services is through the incorporation of established interventions, such as child–parent psychotherapy, parent–child interaction therapy, interaction guidance, and parent education models. Another mechanism is to adapt ongoing services, such as home visits and parents groups, to include infant mental health strategies. Practitioners can use play, caregiving routines, and family rituals to coach parents to increase their responsiveness and attunement, to improve their parenting skills (e.g., discipline), and generally to enhance their affective nurturance to their children.

As Zeanah (2007) observed, the integration of infant mental health principles into Early Head Start and similar programs marks a revolutionary milestone for the early childhood and mental health fields. However, he argues that "the glass is half-full," and we have substantially more work to do to ensure that young children's mental health needs are met. The careful integration of infant mental health programs, principles, and strategies into Early Head Start and other early childhood programs can move the programs closer to the promise of achieving optimal developmental outcomes of very young children from impoverished and other high-risk backgrounds.

REFERENCES

Baker-Ericzén, M., Brookman-Frazee, L., & Stahmer, A. (2005). Stress levels and adaptability in parents of toddlers with and without autism spectrum disorders. *Research and Practice for Persons with Severe Disabilities, 30*(4), 194–204.

Barth, R.P. (2009). Preventing child abuse and neglect with parent training: Evidence and opportunities. *The Future of Children, 19*(2), 95–118.

Bavolek, S.J. (1999). *Nurturing parenting: Teaching empathy, self-worth and discipline to school-age children* (4th ed.). Park City, UT: Family Development Resources.

Berlin, L., Cassidy, J., & Appleyard, K. (2008). The influence of early attachments on other relationships. In J. Cassidy & P. Shaver (Eds.), *Handbook of attachment: Theory, research, and clinical applications* (2nd ed., pp. 333–347). New York: Guilford Press.

Berlin, L., Zeanah, C., & Lieberman, A.F. (2008). Prevention and intervention programs for supporting early attachment security. In J. Cassidy & P.R. Shaver (Eds.), *Handbook of attachment: Theory, research, and clinical applications* (2nd ed., pp. 745–761). New York: Guilford Press.

Bowlby, J. (1982). *Attachment and loss: Vol. 1. Attachment* (2nd ed.). New York: Basic Books.

Brotman, L., Gouley, K., Chesir-Teran, D., Dennis, T., Klein, R.G., & Shrout, P. (2005). Prevention for preschoolers at high risk for conduct problems: Immediate outcomes on parenting practices and child social competence. *Journal of Clinical Child and Adolescent Psychology, 34*(4), 724–734.

Chaffin, M., & Friedrich, B. (2004). Evidence-based treatments in child abuse and neglect. *Children and Youth Services Review, 26*(11), 1097–1113.

Chaffin, M., Funderburk, B., Bard, D., Valle, L., & Gurwitch, R. (2011). A combined motivation and parent–child interaction therapy package reduces child welfare recidivism in a randomized dismantling field trial. *Journal of Consulting and Clinical Psychology, 79*(1), 84–95.

Cicchetti, D., Ackerman, B.P., & Izard, C.E. (1995). Emotions and emotion regulation in developmental psychopathology. *Development and Psychopathology, 7*(1), 1–10.

Cicchetti, D., & Hinshaw, S.P. (Eds.). (2002). Prevention and intervention science: Contributions to developmental theory. *Development and Psychopathology, 14*, 667–981.

Cicchetti, D., Rogosch, F.A., & Toth, S.L. (2006). Fostering secure attachment in infants in maltreating families through preventive interventions. *Development and Psychopathology, 18*(3), 623–649.

Coard, S. (2007). Considering culturally relevant parenting practices in intervention development and adaptation: A randomized controlled trial of the Black Parenting Strengths and Strategies (BPSS) program. *Counseling Psychologist, 35*(6), 797–820.

DeGarmo, D.S., Patterson, G.R., & Forgatch, M.S. (2004). How do outcomes in a specified parent training intervention maintain or wane over time? *Prevention Science, 5*(2), 73–89.

Denham, S.A., Bassett, H.H., & Wyatt, T. (2007). The socialization of emotional competence. In J.E. Grusec & P.D. Hastings (Eds.), *Handbook of socialization: Theory and research* (pp. 614–637). New York: Guilford Press.

Dombrowski, S.C., Timmer, S.G., Blacker, D.M., & Urquiza, A.J. (2005). A positive behavioural intervention for toddlers: Parent-child attunement therapy. *Child Abuse Review, 14*(2), 132–151.

Early Head Start National Resource Center. (2004). *Pathways to prevention.* Washington, DC: Author.

Eyberg, S.M., & Bussing, R. (2010). Parent-child interaction therapy for preschool children with conduct problems. In R. Murrihy, A. Kidman, & T. Ollendick (Eds.), *Clinical handbook of assessing and treating conduct problems in youth* (pp. 139–162). New York: Springer.

Fiese, B.H., Tomocho, T.J., Douglas, M., Josephs, K., Poltrock, S., & Baker, T. (2002). A review of 50 years of research on naturally occurring family routines and rituals: Cause for celebration? *Journal of Family Psychology, 16*, 381–390.

Finello, K. (Ed.). (2005). *The handbook of training and practice in infant and preschool mental health.* San Francisco: Jossey-Bass.

Fraiberg, S. (1980). *Clinical studies in infant mental health: The first year of life.* New York: Basic Books.

Fraiberg, S., Adelson, E., & Shapiro, V. (1975). Ghosts in the nursery. *Journal of the American Academy of Child Psychiatry, 14*, 387–421.

Hastings, P., McShane, K., Parker, R., & Ladha, F. (2007). Ready to make nice: Parental socialization of young sons' and daughters' prosocial behaviors with peers. *Journal of Genetic Psychology, 168*, 177–200.

Ippen, C. (2009). The sociocultural context of infant mental health. In C. Zeanah (Ed.), *Handbook of infant mental health* (3rd ed., pp. 104–119). New York: Guilford Press.

Jones Harden, B., Chazan-Cohen, R., Raikes, H., & Vogel, C. (2010). *Early Head Start home visitation: The role of implementation in bolstering program effects.* Manuscript submitted for publication.

Kaminski, J., Valle, L., Filene, J., & Boyle, C. (2008). A meta-analytic review of components associated with parent training program effectiveness. *Journal of Abnormal Child Psychology, 36*(4), 567–589.

Lewis, M. (2000). The cultural context of infant mental health: The developmental niche of infant-caregiver relationships. In C. Zeanah (Ed.), *Handbook of infant mental health* (2nd ed., pp. 91–107). New York: Guilford Press.

Lieberman, A., & Van Horn, P. (2005). *Don't hit my mommy!: A manual for child–parent psychotherapy with young witnesses of family violence*. Washington, DC: Zero to Three.

Lieberman, A.F., & Van Horn, P. (2008). *Psychotherapy with infants and young children: Repairing the effects of stress and trauma on early attachment*. New York: Guilford Press.

Lieberman, A., Van Horn, P., & Ippen, C. (2005). Toward evidence-based treatment: Child-parent psychotherapy with preschoolers exposed to marital violence. *Journal of the American Academy of Child and Adolescent Psychiatry, 44*(12), 1241–1248.

Lieberman, A., & Zeanah, C. (1999). Contributions of attachment theory to infant-parent psychotherapy and other interventions with infants and young children. In J. Cassidy & P. Shaver (Eds.), *Handbook of attachment* (pp. 555–574). New York: Guilford Press.

Main, M., Kaplan, N., & Cassidy, J. (1985). Security in infancy, childhood, and adulthood: A move to the level of representation. *Monographs of the Society for Research in Child Development, 50*(1–2), 66–104.

McDonough, S.C. (2004). Interaction guidance: Promoting and nurturing the caregiving relationship. In A. Sameroff, S. McDonough, & K. Rosenblum (Eds.), *Treating parent-infant relationship problems: Strategies for intervention* (pp. 79–96). New York: Guilford Press.

Pajulo, M., Pyykkönen, N., Kalland, M., Sinkkonen, J., Helenius, H., & Punamäki, R. (2011). Substance abusing mothers in residential treatment with their babies: Postnatal psychiatric symptomatology and its association with mother–child relationship and later need for child protection actions. *Nordic Journal of Psychiatry, 65*(1), 65–73.

Reid, M., Webster-Stratton, C., & Baydar, N. (2004). Halting the development of conduct problems in Head Start children: The effects of parent training. *Journal of Clinical Child and Adolescent Psychology, 33*(2), 279–291.

Renk, K., Roddenberry, A., Oliveros, A., & Sieger, K. (2007). The relationship of maternal characteristics and perceptions of children to children's emotional and behavioral problems. *Child & Family Behavior Therapy, 29*, 37–57.

Rosenblum, K., McDonough, S., Sameroff, A., & Muzik, M. (2008). Reflection in thought and action: Maternal parenting reflectivity predicts mind-minded comments and interactive behavior. *Infant Mental Health Journal, 29*(4), 362–376.

Sameroff, A.J., McDonough, S.C., & Rosenblum, K.L. (2005). *Treating parent–infant relationship problems: Strategies for intervention* (pp. 1–304). New York: Guilford Press.

Sroufe, L.A., Carlson, E., Levy, A., & Egeland, B. (1999). Implications of attachment theory for developmental psychopathology. *Development and Psychopathology, 11*, 1–13.

Stern, R., & Elias, M.J. (2007). Emotionally intelligent parenting. In R. Bar-On, J.G. Maree, & M. Elias (Eds.), *Educating people to be emotionally intelligent* (pp. 37–48). Westport, CT: Praeger/Greenwood.

Thomas, R., & Zimmer-Gembeck, M. (2011). Accumulating evidence for parent–child interaction therapy in the prevention of child maltreatment. *Child Development, 82*(1), 177–192.

Timmer, S.G., Urquiza, A.J., & Zebell, N. (2006). Challenging foster caregiver-maltreated child relationships: The effectiveness of parent-child interaction therapy. *Children and Youth Services Review, 28*(1), 1–19.

Timmer, S.G., Ware, L.M., Urquiza, A.J., & Zebell, N.M. (2010). The effectiveness of parent–child interaction therapy for victims of interparental violence. *Violence and Victims, 25*(4), 486–503.

Toth, S.L., Rogosch, F.A., & Cicchetti, D. (2006). The efficacy of toddler-parent psychotherapy to reorganize attachment in the young offspring of mothers with major depressive disorder: A randomized preventive trial. *Journal of Consulting and Clinical Psychology, 74*(6), 1006–1016.

Urquiza, A.J., & McNeil, C. (1996). Parent–child interaction therapy: An intensive dyadic intervention for physically abusive families. *Child Maltreatment, 1*(2), 134–144.

U.S. Department of Health and Human Services, Administration for Children and Families. (2000). *Supporting children's mental health*. Washington, DC: Author.

Weatherston, D. (1995). She does love me, doesn't she? *Zero to Three, 15*(4), 6–10.

Webster-Stratton, C., & Reid, M.J. (2010). The Incredible Years parents, teachers and children training series: A multifaceted treatment approach for young children with conduct problems. In A.E. Kazdin

& J.R. Weisz (Eds.), *Evidence-based psychotherapies for children and adolescents* (pp. 224–240). New York: Guilford Press.

Zeanah, C.H. (2007). Infant mental health and Early Head Start: The glass is half full. *Infant Mental Health Journal, 28*(2), 252–254.

Zeanah, C. (Ed.). (2009). *Handbook of infant mental health* (3rd ed.). New York: Guilford Press.

Zeanah, P.D., Bailey, L.O., & Berry, S. (2009). Infant mental health and the "real world"—Opportunities for interface and impact. *Child and Adolescent Psychiatric Clinics of North America, 18*(3), 773–787.

Intervening with Parents

Linda S. Beeber and Regina Canuso

*Y*ou came into this business because you love children and now you are working with parents. As a skilled early childhood provider, you appreciate the central role that parents and families play in the mental health of infants and toddlers. However, your education and training may not have prepared you to work with adults or older adults (e.g., a custodial grandparent), especially if this person has mental health needs that go beyond the support and parenting guidance you give to all parents. Furthermore, the public still views mental health and mental disorders as mysterious, stigmatized, and secret. Hence, parents may not be forthcoming in sharing their troubles with you, and you may not feel comfortable bringing up the topic with them. You may even think that helping a parent with mental health needs can only be done by a mental health professional. This chapter will help you reach out to parents and offer them mental health care directly through targeted approaches and indirectly through the regular program activities.

UNHELPFUL ASSUMPTIONS AND HELPFUL PRINCIPLES

As adults, we arrive at our place in life with years of informal training in how to think about others. These are assumptions, and may be beliefs that were handed down from our parents and teachers, expectations that we have of others based on values, or conclusions that we have drawn from our experiences. Sometimes, our assumptions are helpful. For example, previous experience helps us make quick decisions (e.g., "I think I can ask that person for help") or solve a new problem. Our values help us know how to behave when the rules are not clear. Sometimes, however, we can make unhelpful assumptions that lead us astray. This is especially true about the assumptions we might make about parents and ourselves. Let's look at some unhelpful ones.

Parents cause their children's problems. When we see an infant or toddler in pain, our natural response is to blame the person in charge, usually the parent. There is no question that parents are the adult members of the parent–child emotional system, and by virtue of that, bear ultimate responsibility for the child. However, the assumption that the parent causes the child's problems gives the parent too much power and, at the same time, takes power away from them. Parents and children inherit the same family history and share the same social and community context. To see the child as a product of bad parenting disconnects parents from their own history of being parented and the huge forces that now affect them and their child. Likewise, assuming that the parent and child are victims of their history and context removes their incredible power to bend, flex, grow, and change for the better.

Early childhood professionals know what is best. Over and over, we are reminded that the parents know what is best for their child. However, it is difficult to put aside our own beliefs and values about how children thrive or the new knowledge we acquire about the kinds of parenting behaviors that are best for infant and toddler development. We approach a parent with the best intentions of placing him or her in charge, yet we struggle to keep our own opinions in the background. At the same time, we see parents behaving in ways that we believe are not good for the child. Often, these parental behaviors trigger strong feelings in us that come to the surface in heated discussions with our fellow providers or during reflective supervision. It is clear that all child care providers must intervene when a parent is placing the child in danger. However, many parents' behaviors fall short of endangering their child but still contradict what we believe to be good parenting. At these moments, it becomes very easy to step in and exert our authority.

Parents should look to early childhood professionals as experts on problems with the child. Parents approach us for help with problems they are having with their infant or toddler's feeding, soothing, energy level, or social behavior. It is natural for us to focus on those problems, to offer advice about how to fix them, and even model ways that the parent should behave. A slower route is to establish from the start that the parent is the expert, take the role of guide and coach, draw out their strengths, and help them shape the behaviors that will stop the problem with the child. The assumption that we can do it better or that they cannot solve the problem undermines the parent's competence. Modeling behavior can be especially difficult for parents with mental health issues. If the parent's sense of self-efficacy and self-esteem is low, to see an accomplished staff person soothe their child or set a limit may add evidence to their sense of incompetence. If parents construct their own solution, it is much more likely that they will carry it out consistently with the child. As long as their solution fits the general principle of helping the child, it will be effective, even if we believe it is not as wonderful as the one we might have showed them.

When we work with parents with mental health issues, several principles can be helpful as major guideposts.

Begin where the parent is, not where you want them to be. Several practical steps can help put this into practice. First, invest energy in the parent before attempting to intervene. This will not necessarily take a long time, but may mean scheduling an extra home visit or extending the length of your standard intake appointment. The time will be well spent, because it will allow you to see strengths as well as problem areas, identify resources around the parent (e.g., kin, community, needs that may qualify him or her for services), and help the parent establish enough initial trust in you to promote honesty. Second, invest energy in reflecting on your own limitations and strengths and your experiences of being parented and being a parent. The more you accept yourself, the more you will be able to accept parents where they are when you begin the work with them.

Lose the skirmish, win the battle. An Early Head Start program colleague told us,

> What keeps me up at night is my worry about the child we lose from the program. . . . The harder we pushed her [mother], the more it became a battle. By spring, she was avoiding us by having other people drop [the child] off at the center. Then she pulled [the child] out of the program. We never talked about it, but I think each of us worries about that child to this day.

Often, the issues that parents bring to providers become the target of intervention, not because they the most important, but because they trigger the strongest feelings in providers. Multiple skirmishes around these provocative issues, which may or may not be the most important ones, can undermine the establishment of trust and rapport with the parent. Ultimately, your relationship with the parent is essential to the well-being of the child, especially if you can only reach the child through continued enrollment in your program, as the following story from an Early Head Start program conveys.

> The [child] kept showing up in his unwashed clothes from the day before and everyone was pushing me to call in the mother [and make a report to child protective services]. I said, "No, I am going to go out of the way to greet her and be real positive with her about getting the child to the Center. . . . [The child] is still in the program, and he comes with clean clothes now. . . ."

It is not unusual for a depressed parent to be unable to comply with program requirements. Depression robs parents of motivation and the ability to organize themselves. If missed appointments and failure to complete paperwork lead to dismissal, opportunities to intervene with both the parent and the child are lost. Giving the parent more support while completing the requirements (avoiding the skirmish) may pay off with long-term retention of both parent and child in the program (winning the battle).

Honor your feelings about your own upbringing and parenting problems. Human behavior is influenced by issues that we keep out of our awareness. Acknowledging your own feelings about the way you were reared, as well as your own struggles as a parent, will deepen your ability to empathize with parents' struggles. The process of acknowledging these issues is best done with an appropriate colleague and, ideally, in an ongoing reflective supervision relationship. (See Chapter 11 to learn about the reflective supervision process.)

Balance your assessment of parents to include shortcomings and treasures. No parent is without potential. No parent is without areas in need of growth. Usually, our perceptions of a parent as "perfect" or "perfectly awful" are influenced by unhelpful assumptions or feelings of our own that are not acknowledged. Both extremes will become problematic over time. The "perfect" parent can become unwilling to let us down by acknowledging problems; the "perfectly awful" parent will sense our hopelessness and withdraw as well.

MENTAL HEALTH RISKS AND
PARENT–CHILD CHARACTERISTICS

Parents' characteristics increase or decrease the risk for developing mental health issues. These include their access to economic resources, where they are in the lifespan, their physical health, and their capacity to gain access to high-quality social support. The way these factors come together can increase or decrease parents' or caregivers' risk of developing symptoms of mental illness or their functioning with existing mental health issues.

Economic Resources

Many early childhood programs target children whose parents earn incomes that are at or below official poverty levels. More than half of these parents are working full time (Knitzer, 2007). Other parents whose income may look adequate are in a position in which being hospitalized or losing the car will pitch the family into economic hardship. The number of families on the edge of severe economic hardship grows exponentially during an economic recession. In 2011, a family of four required an income twice that of the poverty level to meet basic needs; a parent earning three times the minimum hourly wage would need to hold two full-time jobs to reach this income level (Knitzer, 2007). A tangled web of stressors comes with economic hardship, and these stressors are closely related. Thus, a single stressful issue can rapidly turn into a catastrophe. For example, a parent depends on an affordable but unreliable car; the car will not start, the parent is late for work (again), gets fired, and cannot pay the cell phone bill or the rent; eviction is right around the corner. In addition, most parents have a third job—caring for children and maintaining the home. In many households, this is accomplished without the timesaving advantages of a dishwasher or in-home washer and dryer. All of these factors add up to chronic exhaustion, persistent stress, and constant reminders of inadequacy—a recipe for the development of depression, anxiety, and other mental disorders in the parent and behavioral issues in the child (Feder et al., 2009; Seguin, Xu, Gauvin, Zunzunegui, Potvin, & Frohlich, 2005; Tucker-Drob, Rhemtulla, Harden, Turkheimer, & Fask, 2011). Money is not everything, but it is very important.

Not every low-income parent with economic hardship develops symptoms of a mental health disorder. Many parents recognize trouble, analyze problems, take preparatory steps, plan strategies, rehearse them, and act when faced with stressful issues (Yoshikawa, Rosman, & Hsueh, 2001). As a result of successfully solving problems, these parents develop stronger self-efficacy (belief that they can control their lives) and take more positive risks. Programs that serve children often reach out to parents and help them develop these qualities through parent education and work experiences.

The Fit of Lifespan Development with Parenting Roles

Much attention has focused on the characteristics of adolescent parents, particularly those characteristics that interfere with parenting (Black, Papas, Hussey, Dubowitz, et al., 2002; Black, Papas, Hussey, Hunter, et al., 2002; Percy & McIntyre, 2001). We know less about kin who step into parenting roles, older foster parents, or fathers who become sole

Box 9.1. Does money talk when it comes to parent–child mental health?

An unplanned mental health experiment shed some light on how important money is to parent and child mental health (Costello, Compton, Keeler, & Angold, 2003). Halfway through an 8-year study of 1,420 rural children (25% American Indian, 75% Caucasian) ages 9–13 years at intake, a casino opened on an Indian reservation that gave every American Indian family an income supplement. This increase moved 14% of study families out of poverty, while 53% remained poor, and 32% were never poor. Prior to the opening of the casino, children in the low-income families had more conduct and oppositional defiant disorders compared with the children whose families were never low income. After the casino opened, these disorders in the ex-low-income children fell to the levels of the never-low-income children. However, symptoms of depression and anxiety in the children were not affected by the rapid change in income. Non-Indian children whose families moved out of poverty during the same period showed similar patterns. The authors speculated that the increased income relieved parents of a major stressor that may have allowed them to become more involved with the children, manifesting as a sharp reduction in behavioral problems. The study suggests that lifting some of the stressors from low-income parents may have immediate benefit for their children.

parents. Stepping into a parenting role may not fit well with the parent's age-appropriate developmental needs. Mental health can suffer as a result. The most obvious example is the grandparent who steps in to take care of an infant or toddler because the parent is out of commission. This may happen unexpectedly due to the illness or death of the parent or the institutionalization of the parent due to mental illness, substance abuse, or criminal activity. As a grandmother said so clearly,

> That's probably my biggest problem, feelings of inadequacy. How am I gonna do this? I'll be 70 years old when he turns 20. How will that be? . . . He's not gonna have parents he can depend on to help him with his kids because I'm either gonna be too old or dead by the time he has children . . . but then there is nobody else. It's me or foster care.

Developmentally, grandparents or older foster parents will usually be in a different place in the course of their life development than younger parents; hence, they will have unique needs that are not addressed in early childhood programs. The grandparent may be downsizing financially in preparation for retirement, experiencing reduced vigor and health, or coping with guilt and grief over the loss of their child (the parent). If not addressed, these issues can generate mental health issues. The social needs of older custodial kin may also be in jeopardy. Their friends will most likely have launched their children or be in more typical grandparent roles:

> One of my best friends . . . told me, "I can't wait till he goes back to his mother so we can get back to a normal life." And I'm thinking, "He's not going back to his mother." But she just doesn't grasp it, you know, and she just tells me every day

that "your life will go back to the way that it used to be." I'm like, "It'll never go back to the way that it used to be." I don't think you really understand unless you're in that situation . . . what it's like. So they [friends] tend to avoid you. They just sort of drift away. You don't get invited out to dinner. You don't get asked, you know, people don't come by your house anymore. I definitely started becoming isolated.

Isolation may be an issue for any parent who is not typical for the population served by the program, because it is difficult for them to find other parents or caregivers like themselves. Atypical and nonkin parents may feel uncomfortable in socialization activities promoted by the program, because they are not the biological parent. Although early childhood programs have made great strides in reaching out to fathers through programming and male staff with targeted activities to meet their needs, cultural child-rearing practices may still prevent fathers from feeling comfortable participating in parent activities. At a site that served Latino families, the staff coordinator (a male) successfully involved fathers by offering topics that interested them, such as electrical engineering, toy making, and home construction projects. During these activities, the coordinator wove in topics relevant to fathering. This coordinator told us, "When they realized how important they are to their children, they came back to the group."

In groups attended by atypical parents, we have observed grandmothers taking on the role of adviser to younger parents rather than asking for help with their own needs, and adolescents withdrawing from groups where they were treated as children by older mothers. Where possible, specialized groups can be offered if there are sufficient numbers of parents; otherwise, these parents may need additional individualized attention to prevent the development of mental health issues.

Physical Health

Good physical health contributes to mental health. A long-lasting illness or series of illnesses can weaken resistance and make mild symptoms of depression or anxiety worse. The medicines used to treat physical health problems can also have side effects that mimic or worsen the symptoms of mental disorders. Program approaches that teach parents how to help their family eat well, regulate sleep, exercise, and relax can have a powerful impact on the mental health of the parent by promoting general wellness.

Social Support

The social support that people receive through their interpersonal relationships is one of the most consistent positive forces for mental health. A parent who has close relationships that are low in conflict and provide material help, good information, advice, and emotional support is more strongly protected from depression, anxiety, and other stress-related mental health problems (Balaji et al., 2007). Strong social support also protects infants and toddlers by enriching the environment and relieving some of the demands on the parent. Parents who are geographically or socially isolated or who are working so much of the time that they cannot take time to develop relationships struggle to develop adequate social support.

Characteristics of infants and toddlers can also raise the risk of parental mental health problems. These include the fit of the child's temperament with the parent's (e.g., a highly active child with a quiet, passive parent), the resemblance of a child to a former partner, and unanticipated complications with the child's birth and disabilities (Singer et al., 2003). It is interesting to note that these qualities are not highly stressful to parents unless they are accompanied by other pressures, such as economic hardship (Singer, 2006).

OPPORTUNITIES FOR PARENT INTERVENTION: APPROACHES TO HELP PARENTS

As a provider, you can reach out to parents in many different ways, including using your relationship with them, calling on other program resources, and linking them to help in the broader community. You will feel more confident if you define your role, responsibilities, the extent of your authority, and the lines of communication you will use. These definitions help you provide direct and indirect support for parents' mental health needs.

Defining Roles and Margins of Authority

The recipe for success in helping parents strengthen their mental health is not complicated, but it does require that an early childhood program be organized and fully staffed, and have a working relationship with mental health professionals. To address parents' and caregivers' mental health needs, programs should form a formal relationship with a mental health professional. In some programs, a mental health professional is part of the program structure; in others, a consultation and referral relationship has been established between the program and a community mental health resource. In addition, the margins of authority need to be understood by each person in the program. Margins of authority are the boundaries defining the work that belongs to each person, where their authority to act ends, and who needs to be involved at that point. Clarifying margins of authority takes away much of the fear and uncertainty that staff feel when they are working with a parent who has mental health needs. To define the margins of authority, it is helpful to discuss a specific situation with a parent or caregiver and have each staff person define what actions they have the authority to carry out alone, and when they need to involve others. In the discussion, it is really helpful to talk about parent behaviors that are important, and about who within the agency needs to know if staff members observe these behaviors. After discussing what actions are possible and which people in the program should be involved in a response, it is helpful to write a protocol that defines each step and identifies who is responsible for particular actions. Reflective supervision or regular team meetings are excellent structures for these discussions.

Here is an example of this process of establishing a margin of authority and developing a response protocol. Suppose there is a parent whose depression is preventing her from meeting minimum program requirements. The regular educational team—including the family's home visitor, the staff supervisor, and the infant–toddler teacher who sees the child 2 days a week—meet to discuss their observations and concerns about this parent. The first decision the team must make is whether and how to change usual protocols in order to accommodate this parent. The direct care staff (in this case, the home visitor) is expected to have the most time-intensive and intimate relationship with the parent. The home visitor is responsible for knowing how the parent is doing and maintaining regular contact. The home visitor has the authority to carry out the activities defined by the program (e.g., parenting guidance, emotional support, child enrichment, referrals to typical resources). These program activities are carried out with all parents, but with a parent who has mental health needs, the home visitor has the authority to make changes in these activities as needed to accommodate the parent. The home visitor has a regular route of communication to update supervisory staff. The program team has also, in advance, defined signals, parental behaviors, and situations that exceed the home visitor's margin of authority and will need specific mental health intervention. If the home visitor observes these indicators in the parent, the home visitor follows a communication pathway that usually involves relaying information about parent behaviors or challenging situations to a designated supervisor. Reporting this information triggers a response that may involve an internal team, a program-designated mental health professional, or a community mental health resource.

If an early childhood program appreciates the instrumental nature of each person's contribution, strives for continuous communication among staff, and creates support for staff at every level, high-quality support for a parent with mental health needs can be accomplished. Honest and efficient communication among helpers is essential, and mutual support must be part of the recipe. The outcome will be better mental health for the infant or toddler.

The next section discusses the direct and indirect ways in which an early childhood program can intervene to support parents' mental health needs.

Direct Mental Health–Focused Intervention

Mental health–focused care for parents includes screening for mental health issues, referring parents to treatment, and supporting parents and caregivers not yet ready to accept treatment.

Screening for Mental Health Issues
Putting a screening structure in place is one of the most powerful interventions that a program can employ to address parent mental health issues. A program can either screen for general mental health issues or a specific issue that is known to influence infant and toddler mental health. Depression is one of the most important mental health problems, because it is prevalent in mothers, has been linked to delayed outcomes in infants and toddlers, and can be treated effectively with a variety of approaches (Knitzer, Theberge, & Johnson, 2008; see Chapter 3 to learn more about the relationship between caregiver depression and child development). However, programs located in communities where substance use problems or trauma are prevalent would be wise to screen for substance use or abuse and posttraumatic stress disorder or anxiety disorders as well (Woolhouse, Brown, Krastev, Perlen, & Gunn, 2009). Critical to the screening process is determining when screening should be performed, deciding what instrument or questions will be used, and defining to whom the screening results will go and what will be done with positive screening results. Figure 9.1

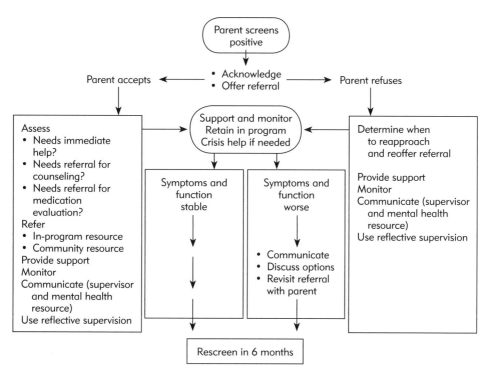

Figure 9.1. Flow chart for working with parents with mental health needs.

indicates how this could be determined and shows the decision tree that might be used to follow parents who accept and those who refuse help.

It is helpful to consider a screening schedule, instrument selection, and screening questions when building a structure for screening in an early education program.

- *When should screening occur?* Intake is an ideal time if all parents are to be screened. Screening all parents allows a program to weigh parents' needs against the program resources and make wiser decisions about resource use. For example, parents with mild levels of distress may benefit from the educational and social activities in the program and will require informal monitoring and encouragement to attend. Parents who have more severe distress or who screen as positive for depression or substance use may accept a referral to a community mental health resource. These parents will need formal follow-up, monitoring, and rescreening. A third group of parents who are distressed or screen positive and are not willing to accept a referral will need more intensive program resources to support and retain them in the program. Although parents may feel uncomfortable talking about mental health issues on their first encounter with the program, the screening procedure can be introduced as an educative approach: "parent mental health affects the child and we take it seriously and screen all parents." The advantage here is that the parent with concerns is not singled out. Even if a parent is not comfortable revealing mental health concerns or refuses to answer questions on a screening questionnaire honestly, the subject has been broached. More important, program staff have relayed how much the program values mental health and have opened a door that may allow a parent to ask for help later on.

Ongoing screening can either be performed annually or whenever a parent or family experiences a major change or event. The annual plan is less likely to allow a parent to be missed but is more labor-intensive. However, if a very short screener is used, it can be done without an enormous outlay of staff time. Programs that have successfully used change or event-related screenings have tied them to pregnancy, birth, death of a family member, major crisis (e.g., relocation, job loss, injury), or shift in a relationship (e.g., separation, divorce). Screening during pregnancy is crucial. New evidence shows that depression affects the developing fetus. Discovering that a mother is struggling with depression allows her to get help before the infant is born, when many mothers have a sense of hope and are motivated to make changes.

A third approach may be to screen parents at the same time that the child is given developmental and health evaluations. Program provider can use the opportunity to emphasize to parents how central their mental health is to the child's.

- *What screening tools should be used?* As noted above, the questionnaire chosen depends on the target mental health issue. Most screening questionnaires are self-reports, meaning that the person answers the questions themselves with paper and pencil rather than being questioned during a person-to-person interview. For programs serving parents with limited English language skills, having a questionnaire that is written in the parent's or caregiver's native language is preferable to having a staff person translate the questions. The parent's reading ability is an important issue, and for parents who are beginning readers, the questions may have to be read aloud by a staff person. Table 9.1 presents several self-reports that have been used with parents in early childhood programs. Most of these are available in several languages and are appropriate for beginning readers. Two of these, the Beck Depression Inventory and the Edinburgh Postnatal Depression Scale (Beck, Rial, & Rickels, 1974; Cox, Holden, & Sagovsky, 1987), ask about suicidal thoughts. These self-reports may not be appropriate for use at intake but may be used later when parents have a trusting relationship with staff.

- *What questions should be asked?* Instead of questionnaires, some programs have chosen to use a few questions in the intake form that address the most commonly occurring problems. For example, a three-question screening for depression can be used. The first two questions are, "During the past month, have you often been bothered by feeling down, depressed, or hopeless?" and "During the last month have you often been bothered by little interest or pleasure in doing things?" (Arroll, Goodyear-Smith, Kerse, Fishman, & Gunn, 2005; U.S. Preventative Services Task Force, 2002). These questions plus a third one, "Do you want help for these feelings?" were initially tested in health care clinics and have shown enough effectiveness to be part of the U.S. Preventative Services Task Force recommendations for adult depression screening (U.S. Preventative Services Task Force, 2002). Extensive testing of this procedure showed that merely asking the first two questions reduced depression prevalence by 6%, probably as a result of people becoming more aware of their mood states and taking steps to help themselves (Pignone, Gaynes, Lohr, Rushton, & Mulrow, 2003). The third question has been helpful in identifying parents who are ready to receive help and for whom an immediate referral is appropriate. By accomplishing this at intake or each year, the program staff can support parents who are getting help and direct other efforts toward parents who are not yet ready. (To learn more about communicating with parents and caregivers, see Chapter 7.)

Table 9.1. Brief screening questionnaires for distress, depressive symptoms, anxiety, alcohol and substance use, and exposure to violence or trauma

Type of screening questionnaire	Multiple languages
General psychological distress	
Kessler Psychological Distress Scale (K10; Kessler et al., 2002)	
Depressive symptoms	
Center for Epidemiological Studies Depression Scale (CES-D; Radloff, 1977)	x
Patient Health Questionnaire (PHQ-2; PHQ-9; Kroenke, Spitzer, & Williams, 2001)	x
General Health Questionnaire (GHQ; Goldberg & Hillier, 1979)	x
Beck Depression Inventory (BDI; BDI-II; Beck, Rial, & Rickels, 1974)	x
Edinburgh Postnatal Depression Scale (EPDS; Cox, Holden, & Sagovsky, 1987)	x
Anxiety	
Inventory of Depression and Anxiety Symptoms (IDAS; Watson et al., 2007)	
Generalized Anxiety Disorder Assessment (GAD-7; Spitzer, Kroenke, Williams, & Lowe, 2006)	
Beck Anxiety Inventory (BAI; Beck, Epstein, Brown, & Steer, 1988)	x
Alcohol and substance use	
CRAFFT Screen for Substance Abuse (Kessler et al., 2002)	x
Exposure to violence or trauma	
Impact of Event Scale (IES; Horowitz, Wilner, & Alvarez, 1979)	

Referring Parents for Treatment

Mental health treatment is a big step for many parents to take. Despite our best efforts, mental health treatment carries a stigma, and parents will usually have fears about seeking treatment (Rusch, Kanter, Manos, & Weeks, 2008). In addition, many states have limited budgets for mental health and are focusing state-supported treatment on the most severe mental illnesses. This leaves the resources for parents who need support and counseling for less severe mental illnesses out of the equation. There are three important steps that a program can take to create a referral system for parents.

A first step is to create relationships with community resources for treatment and support. A program can begin by contacting local chapters of national mental health organizations such as Mental Health America (http://www.nmha.org) or National Alliance on Mental Illness (htttp://www.nami.org). These organizations provide information about treatment resources and mental health support groups that parents can attend. Local psychotherapy practices and publicly funded clinics may have reduced fees for low-income parents and may be willing to accept referrals. Community organizations and faith-based groups may sponsor therapy and support groups for specific needs such as grief or domestic violence. Nearby universities with professional training programs may be seeking clients and provide free or low-cost therapy. Ideally, the program sets into place a formal agreement with a mental health provider to streamline referrals from the program. At the very least, every program should have a current list of treatment resources that is maintained by program personnel or consultants who have the authority to refer parents. The list should include providers who speak the languages spoken by parents in the program (Ruiz, 2007).

A second step is to provide education about mental health for parents. Local mental health professionals are often willing to come and speak with parents. Mental health associations maintain a list of people who are recovering from mental illness, addiction, or other issues who will come and speak with parents. The program can sponsor activities during national mental health awareness weeks. All of these are ways to educate parents and demystify mental health.

The third step is the most important and requires that the program staff have a trusting relationship with the parent. This step—broaching the topic and helping the parent accept a referral for help—may be the biggest hurdle for staff. Specialized training devoted to the "how to's" usually is needed to help staff feel confident. The training should include the following components:

- *Preparing for the conversation.* Staff can plan when and where to have a relatively private conversation with a parent about mental health needs. The conversation could take place in a regular conference or home visit, or spontaneously during times when the parent connects with staff (e.g., drop-off or pick-up at the child care center). Staff members need to practice how to start the conversation with broad openers (e.g., "I notice that you have been looking stressed out lately. Would you like to talk for a few minutes?"). Then staff need to identify what their next step will be and define their "margin of authority."

- *Communicating the results.* Staff must be clear on whom to inform about the results of the conversation with the parent and what to document.

- *Following up.* Staff should be clear about what steps will be taken to evaluate the outcome of the conversation. Follow-up should include ongoing support if the parent decides not to accept a referral. Parents may require several invitations before they decide to get help, and the program staff will need to remain supportive and nonjudgmental. Some parents will never take a referral; for them, the program may be the only mental health intervention they receive.

In-Program Mental Health Care   Some programs provide access to a mental health professional (psychiatric nurse, social worker, psychologist, or counselor) or specialized parenting approaches such as parent–child psychotherapy (Cicchetti, Toth, & Rogosch, 1999; Toth, Rogosch, Manly, & Cicchetti, 2006), attachment enhancement (Nylen, Moran, Franklin, & O'Hara, 2006) or parent training (Gross, Fogg, & Tucker, 1995). These are described in Chapters 5 and 8.

Support and Monitoring for Parents Who Decline Mental Health Care   Parents who refuse to accept a referral or in-program mental health care are often the most vulnerable parents in the program and the most challenging to educators. The following set of practical approaches can help staff support a parent who may have obvious mental health needs but who is not accepting help. For that parent, the program benefits may be as much as he or she can accept, and the parent will benefit from them.

- Do everything to *keep the child in your program—the parent will benefit*. A parent who is depressed is likely not to do what is expected. It would be very easy to dismiss the family from the program. It may take all your skill to negotiate ways for the parent and child to remain in the program.

- *Reach out.* No matter how you do it, the message will be delivered. If it is genuine, the parent will hear that. Ask yourself why you are reaching out to this parent. Be sure you are secure in your motivation (not to rescue a parent!).

- *Keep trying.* Timing is everything! All the right strategies will not work if the parent is not ready. If it did not work this time, it might next time.

- *Be patient.* Accept the parent as is. Do not try to wrestle the parent away from the symptoms, "cheer up" the parent, talk the parent out of fears, or minimize stressful issues.

- *Be consistent in your behavior.* Do not take over because you are frustrated at the parent's slow progress. Be nurturing, but do not do anything for a parent that he or she can do. This will undermine the parent's sense of self-efficacy.

- *Stay sensitive to a parent's symptoms that get in the way of doing even simple tasks.* Ease up on the work you do with them. Focus on being present instead of on accomplishing your goal.

- *Keep things simple.* Do not talk down to parents and caregivers, but pare down to the bare essentials the message you wish to give.

- *Repeat material.* Write it down on cards where the parent can see it.

- *Give reminders.* This can be in the form of gently checking in during regular home visits or contacts, or follow-up questions that check on previously shared information.

- *Emphasize at least one strength the parent has every time you are with him or her.*

- *Only emphasize one strength.* Do not overpraise; too much praise may produce too much pressure to "keep up the good work."

- *Break big goals into small ones.* Support the parent in taking one "baby step" at a time. Prevent parents from setting themselves up for failure by setting impossible goals. Acknowledge progress, never praise progress.

- *Keep reasonable expectations for performance and your optimism and belief in parents and caregivers high.*

- *Stay watchful for worsening symptoms or signs of crisis,* such as a parent's sudden shift from being very depressed to having unusually high energy. A recent string of uncharacteristic absences need to be followed up.

- *Invest in the parent but not his or her improvement.* Do not link the parent's recovery to your skill. This is a recipe for failure.

- *Balance your load* with parents who vary in their need for intervention and support. Have periodic celebrations with other staff about successes with parents and families.

- *Guard yourself:* your energy, health, and mental health (see Chapter 12).

Indirect Mental Health–Focused Intervention

Data from the Early Head Start evaluation project showed that depressed mothers recovered over time if they remained in the program (U.S. Department of Health and Human Services, 2006). Program support is a powerful intervention, even if a parent does not accept treatment for the symptoms and impairments that come with mental health issues. A thriving infant or toddler is the primary goal of early childhood programs. For a parent who is depressed, watching the positive growth and development of their child is a daily antidepressant. Over time, the positive efforts of the program to improve the child's ability to communicate, regulate emotions, behave appropriately in social situations, and show affection contradict the hopelessness and self-depreciation that depressed parents feel.

Regular Progress Evaluations   Most programs include a periodic progress review in which parents have a precious moment of self-reflection and goal setting. If mental health screening is included, the parent can reflect on those issues, and a reluctant parent will have several opportunities to acknowledge troubles and ask for help. The inclusion of mental health screening and assessment in the regular progress review takes the mystery and stigma out of mental health issues.

Support Through Transitions

Most programs provide help for parents during difficult transitions such as an unplanned pregnancy, relocation, loss, or a shift in health. As noted earlier, these are excellent points at which to screen for or assess for mental health issues.

Parenting Education   As noted in the introduction to this chapter, parenting brings parents' own issues about being parented to the surface. When programs are offered to parents that help them stimulate and provide security for their infant or toddler, the parent can reflect on his or her own experiences, understand the impact, and adopt more productive behaviors. For example, we have observed that parents who had experienced physical abuse as children frequently had trouble setting limits on the high activity of their toddlers. As one mother said, "All I know to do is to hit, so I don't do anything at all." These parents benefit greatly from learning and practicing other options. In the process of becoming gentler and more compassionate toward their child, a parent can begin to heal from an abused past.

A factor that is critical in engaging parents is the degree to which staff members are sensitive to variations in parenting and skilled at understanding what the parent is trying to accomplish. For example, one African American mother of toddler twin sons anticipated that as her sons entered adolescence, they would be targeted as shoplifters. She said, "My boys will be watched in every store they enter; from the start, they have to learn to keep their hands visible, quiet, and not pick up anything." This mother had a clear working model of what she needed to teach her sons to avoid being arrested in the future. Her sense of the discrimination and racial profiling they would face came from her own experience as an African American woman in her community. Her working model was

Box 9.2. How parents try to teach survival skills to their vulnerable children

Mothers living in dangerous environments and mothers who prepare their children to survive discrimination use different parenting strategies when they perceive their children to be vulnerable (Burton, 1997; Jarrett, 1997). These strategies include segregating the family from others in the neighborhood, confining children to the home, restricting children from interacting with neighbors, monitoring children closely, imposing behavioral restrictions, and providing chaperones for children (Belle, 1982; Belle & Doucet, 2003; Furstenberg, 1993; Jarrett, 1997, 1994; Jarrett & Burton, 1999). In several studies, ethnic minority mothers who had boys explained that certain parenting behaviors they exhibited, such as spanking, limitations on exploration, or harsh-sounding reprimands, were done to control behaviors that they thought would endanger the child (Beeber, Perreira, & Schwartz, 2008). Parental negative control has not been found to have detrimental effects on the development of ethnic minority children when it is combined with parental warmth (Yoos, Kitzman, Olds, & Overacker, 1995). Indeed, high levels of negative control combined with parental warmth, also termed *no nonsense parenting*, have been associated with more optimal outcomes in rural African American children (Brody & Flor, 1998). These studies demonstrate the impact of parents' perceptions of their child's vulnerabilities on parenting behaviors.

translated into a parenting practice of slapping the toddlers' hands whenever they reached out to explore a new object, a practice that contradicted most guidance on developmental stimulation. Our work with this mother centered on helping her talk about the painful experiences she had encountered as a child, ultimately reaching a compromise in which she would allow free exploration in safe settings and restrain it in stores. When her experience-based fears were acknowledged and honored, the mother felt supported. After discussing her options, she reached the decision that, as the twins matured, she could teach them to recognize situations in which it was safe to explore and others in which they needed to control exploration. Understanding the parent's working model helped her feel validated, not violated, and supported her and her toddlers' mental health needs.

Peer Support Through Program Activities
We noted earlier that social isolation is a cause and effect in mental health issues. By providing and requiring parents to attend program activities, staff can make note of parents who are struggling with loneliness and who might need support to remain in a group activity. The benefits to parents are huge in helping them share issues, get advice and practical help, and experience the strengths they can give to others.

Respite Care
A secure child care program is a huge support to parents. Parents who are not ready to acknowledge mental health issues may benefit from having to do less child care. When respite is combined with parenting education, the parent–child experience can be a quality one for both. In this instance, less is more.

Box 9.3. Management levels according to key symptoms and behaviors of parents with a mental health crisis

TRIPLE ALERT: *Immediate assessment, possible hospitalization, treatment, and continuous monitoring, especially when with the child*

- Thoughts are mostly about depression or self-harm that may include harming the child
- Suicidal ideas present with a plan and/or a method
- Excessive activity or high energy without productivity
- Hears voices or has beliefs that are out of the ordinary
- Not able to function (e.g., remaining in bed all day, inability to care for the child)
- Not able to sleep or eat for several days
- Unusual ideas about the child (e.g., possessed, in need of divine protection)

WATCHFUL WAITING: *Prompt assessment by a mental health professional; frequent monitoring with family or others in constant contact*

- Sad all the time, most of the day, every day; cannot get out of the mood
- Highly energetic and scattered, but able to stay focused with help from others
- Focused on other thoughts; short attention span; cannot concentrate; cannot make decisions
- Continuous crying
- Irritated with others and noise (especially crying or whining by the child)
- Explodes with anger
- Regular work and care of child is poor but is able to carry out some care
- Sleep is poor, but can get some; eating is poor, but is able to eat

NURTURE: *Treatment, intensive services, and close contact by phone*

- Sad, but can get out of the mood
- Scattered thoughts, but able to focus on tasks for short periods; child care does not suffer
- Bursts of energy; able to stay focused without help from others
- Pleasure in things absent most of the day, every day; little interest in activities
- Irritated by others
- Critical of self; calls attention to deficits; repeats the same process with the child
- Withdraws from others; stays to self
- Sleep, eating, sexual desire, energy level are all down but not totally disrupted
- Cooperating in treatment and taking prescribed medication

Improvement of Overall Health   Many programs include general health and nutrition education, provide food pantries and free farm produce to families, and encourage regular health care for the family. These supports help parents who have or are at risk for mental health issues by promoting general wellness.

MENTAL HEALTH CRISES IN PARENTS

We have heard frequently from early childhood education staff that their worst fear is that opening up the issue of their mental health with parents will either make them worse or cause them to fall apart. Educators also report not knowing what to do in the case of a crisis with a parent. This final section of the chapter provides some guidance about these situations. The most important reminder: the parent is living with his or her issues every day. Your thoughtful invitation to talk cannot put anything in front of the parent that is not already there. In fact, the invitation to talk and the expression of your concern for parents is healing, not harming. When a parent is experiencing severe distress or mental-health-related symptoms, it is important to have some guidelines for action.

Critical to the safe management of a parent's crisis is the support of the program and the presence of staff with whom they have a trusting relationship. When all the key factors are in place—a strong program, compassionate staff, and a trusting parent—the outcomes will be in favor of better mental health for parent and child.

CONCLUSION

We have explored the crucial role that early childhood providers can take with parents and caregivers to strengthen their mental health through general ways that early childhood programs provide enrichment, and through specific approaches that are designed to reach parents who are depressed or under pressure. A parent's mental health is so central to whether their infant or toddler thrives that we forget the other societal costs of compromised mental health in families of young children. Each parent we help changes the course of a family and offers hope that our youngest citizens will be positive contributors to our world. Each parent we engage in mental health care becomes a warrior against stigma and an ambassador for positive mental health practices.

REFERENCES

Arroll, B., Goodyear-Smith, F., Kerse, N., Fishman, T., & Gunn, J. (2005). Effect of the addition of a "help" question to two screening questions on specificity for diagnosis of depression in general practice: Diagnostic validity study. *British Medical Journal, 331*(7521), 884.

Balaji, A.B., Claussen, A.H., Smith, D.C., Visser, S.N., Morales, M.J., & Perou, R. (2007). Social support networks and maternal mental health and well-being. *Journal of Women's Health, 16*(10), 1386–1396.

Beck, A.T., Epstein, N., Brown, G., & Steer, R.A. (1988). An inventory for measuring clinical anxiety: Psychometric properties. *Journal of Consulting and Clinical Psychology, 56*(6), 893–897.

Beck, A.T., Rial, W.Y., & Rickels, K. (1974). Short form of depression inventory: Cross-validation. *Psychological Reports, 34*(3), 1184–1186.

Beeber, L.S., Perreira, K.M., & Schwartz, T. (2008). Supporting the mental health of mothers raising children in poverty: How do we target them for intervention studies? *Annals of the New York Academy of Sciences, 1136,* 86–100.

Belle, D. (1982). *Lives in stress: Women and depression.* Beverly Hills, CA: Sage.

Belle, D., & Doucet, J. (2003). Poverty, inequality, and discrimination as sources of depression among US women. *Psychology of Women Quarterly, 27,* 101–113.

Black, M.M., Papas, M.A., Hussey, J.M., Dubowitz, H., Kotch, J.B., & Starr, R.H., Jr. (2002). Behavior problems among preschool children born to adolescent mothers: Effects of maternal depression and perceptions of partner relationships. *Journal of Clinical Child and Adolescent Psychology, 31*(1), 16–26.

Black, M.M., Papas, M.A., Hussey, J.M., Hunter, W., Dubowitz, H., Kotch, J.B., et al. (2002). Behavior and development of preschool children born to adolescent mothers: Risk and 3-generation households. *Pediatrics, 109*(4), 573–580.

Brody, G.H., & Flor, D.L. (1998). Maternal resources, parenting practices, and child competence in rural, single-parent African American families. *Child Development, 69*(3), 803–816.

Burton, L. (1997). Ethnography and the meaning of adolescence in high-risk neighborhoods. *Ethos, 25*(2), 208–217.

Cicchetti, D., Toth, S.L., & Rogosch, F.A. (1999). The efficacy of toddler-parent psychotherapy to increase attachment security in offspring of depressed mothers. *Attachment and Human Development, 1*(1), 34–66.

Costello, E.J., Compton, S.N., Keeler, G., & Angold, A. (2003). Relationships between poverty and psychopathology: A natural experiment. *JAMA: The Journal of the American Medical Association, 290*(15), 2023–2029.

Cox, J.L., Holden, J.M., & Sagovsky, R. (1987). Detection of postnatal depression. Development of the 10-item Edinburgh postnatal depression scale. *British Journal of Psychiatry, 150,* 782–786.

Feder, A., Alonso, A., Tang, M., Liriano, W., Warner, V., Pilowsky, D., et al. (2009). Children of low-income depressed mothers: Psychiatric disorders and social adjustment. *Depression and Anxiety, 26*(6), 513–520.

Furstenberg, F.F. (1993). *How families manage risk and opportunity in dangerous neighborhoods.* Newbury Park, CA: Sage.

Goldberg, D.P., & Hillier, V.F. (1979). A scaled version of the general health questionnaire. *Psychological Medicine, 9*(1), 139–145.

Gross, D., Fogg, L., & Tucker, S. (1995). The efficacy of parent training for promoting positive parent-toddler relationships. *Research in Nursing and Health, 18*(6), 489–499.

Horowitz, M., Wilner, N., & Alvarez, W. (1979). Impact of event scale: A measure of subjective stress. *Psychosomatic Medicine, 41*(3), 209–218.

Jarrett, R. (1994). Living poor: Life among single parent, African American women. *Social Problems, 41,* 30–49.

Jarrett, R. (1997). African American family and parenting strategies in impoverished neighborhoods. *Qualitative Sociology, 20*(2), 275–288.

Jarrett, R., & Burton, L. (1999). Dynamic dimensions of family structure in low-income African American families: Emergent themes in qualitative research. *Journal of Comparative Family Studies, 30*(2), 177–187.

Kessler, R.C., Andrews, G., Colpe, L.J., Hiripi, E., Mroczek, D.K., Normand, S.L., et al. (2002). Short screening scales to monitor population prevalences and trends in non-specific psychological distress. *Psychological Medicine, 32*(6), 959–976.

Knitzer, J. (January 24, 2007). Hearing on economic and societal costs of poverty. Retrieved July 2, 2010, from http://www.nccp.org/publications/pub_705.html

Knitzer, J., Theberge, S., & Johnson, K. (2008). *Reduce maternal depression and its impact on young children: Toward a responsive early childhood policy framework.* New York: National Center for Children in Poverty.

Kroenke, K., Spitzer, R.L., & Williams, J.B. (2001). The PHQ-9: Validity of a brief depression severity measure. *Journal of General Internal Medicine, 16*(9), 606–613.

Nylen, K.J., Moran, T.E., Franklin, C.L., & O'Hara, M.W. (2006). Maternal depression: A review of relevant treatment approaches for mothers and infants. *Infant Mental Health Journal, 27*(4), 327–343.

Percy, M.S., & McIntyre, L. (2001). Using Touchpoints to promote parental self-competence in low-income, minority, pregnant, and parenting teen mothers. *Journal of Pediatric Nursing, 16*(3), 180–186.

Pignone, M., Gaynes, B., Lohr, K., Rushton, J., & Mulrow, C. (2003). Screening for depression in adults. *Annals of Internal Medicine, 138*(9), 767–768.

Radloff, L.S. (1977). The CES-D scale: A self-report depression scale for research in the general population *Applied Psychological Measurement, 1*, 285–401.

Ruiz, P. (2007). Spanish, English, and mental health services. *American Journal of Psychiatry, 164*(8), 1133–1135.

Rusch, L.C., Kanter, J.W., Manos, R.C., & Weeks, C.E. (2008). Depression stigma in a predominantly low income African American sample with elevated depressive symptoms. *Journal of Nervous and Mental Disease, 196*(12), 919–922.

Seguin, L., Xu, Q., Gauvin, L., Zunzunegui, M.V., Potvin, L., & Frohlich, K.L. (2005). Understanding the dimensions of socioeconomic status that influence toddlers' health: Unique impact of lack of money for basic needs in Quebec's birth cohort. *Journal of Epidemiology and Community Health, 59*(1), 42–48.

Singer, G.H. (2006). Meta-analysis of comparative studies of depression in mothers of children with and without developmental disabilities. *American Journal of Mental Retardation, 111*(3), 155–169.

Singer, L.T., Fulton, S., Davillier, M., Koshy, D., Salvator, A., & Baley, J.E. (2003). Effects of infant risk status and maternal psychological distress on maternal-infant interactions during the first year of life. *Journal of Developmental and Behavioral Pediatrics, 24*(4), 233–241.

Spitzer, R.L., Kroenke, K., Williams, J.B., & Lowe, B. (2006). A brief measure for assessing generalized anxiety disorder: The GAD-7. *Archives of Internal Medicine, 166*(10), 1092–1097.

Toth, S.L., Rogosch, F.A., Manly, J.T., & Cicchetti, D. (2006). The efficacy of toddler-parent psychotherapy to reorganize attachment in the young offspring of mothers with major depressive disorder: A randomized preventive trial. *Journal of Consulting and Clinical Psychology, 74*(6), 1006–1016.

Tucker-Drob, E.M., Rhemtulla, M., Harden, K.P., Turkheimer, E., & Fask, D. (2011). Emergence of a Gene *X* socioeconomic status interaction on infant mental ability between 10 months and 2 years. *Psychological Science, 22*(1), 125–133.

U.S. Department of Health and Human Services, Administration for Children and Families. (2006). *Research to practice: Depression in the lives of Early Head Start families.* Washington, DC: Author.

U.S. Preventative Services Task Force (2002). Screening for depression: Recommendations from the U.S. Preventative Services Task Force. *Annals of Internal Medicine, 136*(10), 156.

Watson, D., O'Hara, M.W., Simms, L.J., Kotov, R., Chmielewski, M., McDade-Montez, E.A., et al. (2007). Development and validation of the inventory of depression and anxiety symptoms (IDAS). *Psychological Assessment, 19*(3), 253–268.

Woolhouse, H., Brown, S., Krastev, A., Perlen, S., & Gunn, J. (2009). Seeking help for anxiety and depression after childbirth: Results of the Maternal Health Study. *Archives of Women's Mental Health, 12*(2), 75–83.

Yoos, H.L., Kitzman, H., Olds, D.L., & Overacker, I. (1995). Child rearing beliefs in the African-American community: Implications for culturally competent pediatric care. *Journal of Pediatric Nursing, 10*(6), 343–353.

Yoshikawa, H., Rosman, E.A., & Hsueh, J. (2001). Variation in teenage mothers' experiences of child care and other components of welfare reform: Selection processes and developmental consequences. *Child Development, 72*(1), 299–317.

10

Infant Mental Health
Consultation in Early Childhood Classrooms

Sherryl Scott Heller, Allison B. Boothe, Angela Walter Keyes, and Neena M. Malik

One of the most rewarding parts of this work is hearing directors and teachers tell me that something new they tried went well or worked. Forming relationships with so many individuals and having the opportunity to treat them like professionals. I appreciate the appreciation they give me for talking to them as individuals who make a real difference in our community.

—Mental health consultant in an early childhood education program

n the United States today, the majority of children younger than 5 spend most of their weekdays in out-of-home care while their parents work, look for work, or attend educational or vocational training. Of children ages 3 and younger, 79% are cared for outside of their homes, in center-based programs or family child care homes (Lombardi, 2003). The number of children in child care under the age of 5 has doubled over the past 30 years. The number of hours spent in child care settings has also increased over the years, so that most children under age 3 spend more than 35 hours a week in care outside of their homes (National Institute of Child Health and Human Development, Early Child Care Research Network, 2001). Moreover, the children who spend the most time in child care typically are from the most disadvantaged backgrounds. Child care can be a very positive experience, but for vulnerable children, there may be some challenges.

With the large number of children in child care, it is no surprise that child care providers reported seeing increasing numbers of children with special needs (Cohen &

Kaufmann, 2000) and children affected by at least one socioeconomic stressor (e.g., single-parent home, poverty, or domestic violence) that puts them at risk for adverse social, emotional, and cognitive outcomes (Raver & Knitzer, 2002). Not only are disruptive and challenging behaviors occurring at higher frequency, they are also occurring among children at younger ages. Child care providers are often unprepared for the level and intensity of problems exhibited by even very young children in their care. These providers often feel ill-equipped to manage challenging behaviors or address social and emotional problems.

Children exhibiting challenging behaviors are at an increased risk of being expelled from child care programs. In the most comprehensive national study on preschool expulsion rates, it was demonstrated that preschoolers are expelled at higher rates than school-age children from kindergarten through 12th grade (Gilliam, 2005). The single best way to reduce these high rates of preschool expulsion, researchers discovered, was by making sure that their teachers had access to a mental health consultant with specialized expertise in the social-emotional development of young children (Gilliam, 2005).

EARLY CHILDHOOD MENTAL HEALTH CONSULTATION

Staff scream at children in an effort to manage behaviors. Staff bring children with challenging behaviors to the director to "fix," because the teacher does not have the skills, knowledge or patience to work with the child.

—MENTAL HEALTH CONSULTANT DESCRIBING CHILD CARE DIRECTORS' CONCERNS

In response to the increase in problematic behavior exhibited by preschool children, many states are turning to early childhood mental health consultation as a strategy to promote positive and supportive classroom environments. In a recent report on early childhood mental health consultation in early childhood education settings, a national survey found that of the 35 states and territories that responded, 83% (29 states) indicated that this service was available in their state, and the remaining 17% (6 states) indicated that their state or territory was working on implementing it (Duran et al., 2009).

The goal of early childhood mental health consultation is to improve the ability of child care staff, families, programs, and systems "to prevent, identify, treat, and reduce the impact of mental health problems among children from birth to age six and their families" (Cohen & Kaufmann, 2000, p. 4). To meet this goal, mental health consultation to child care centers is typically implemented in the following ways: child-centered consultation, program-centered consultation, or a combination of both.

Child-centered consultation focuses on the needs of a specific child in the classroom. The goal of child-centered consultation is to reduce the impact of a particular child's challenging behavior within the classroom setting and help staff engage with the child in ways that improve the child's behavior. The consultant works with the child's teacher and other staff to develop strategies and techniques that support the child's positive development (Green, Everhart, Gordon, & Garcia-Gettman, 2006). Consultation may include screening, assessment, or referrals. Typically, the consultant observes the child in the classroom and gathers information from a variety of sources, including the child's parent or guardian and classroom teacher, to determine how to intervene to better support that child's development. The consultant then works with the teacher and parent to design and implement behavioral management strategies. Consultants may also suggest a referral to a specialist, such as a speech-language therapist or community mental health professional, in order to address other related needs. It is important to note that parental consent must be expressly obtained before embarking on consultation with an individual child.

Program-centered consultation is broader in scope and focuses on the child care program as a whole. The consultation aims to determine how factors specific to a child care program affect the social and emotional development of the children enrolled there. The consultant may be asked to assist with concerns about social interactions with a specific teacher or among a group of children, or perhaps with the way classroom time and activities influence child behavior, or how the center is structured physically and organizationally to support infant mental health. The primary goal is to improve the overall quality of the program (Alkon, Ramler, & McLennan, 2003) by developing the capacity of the staff to work with children with challenging behavior (Green et al., 2006). Most early childhood mental health consultation programs use a combination of child-centered and program-centered approaches.

THE MENTAL HEALTH CONSULTANT

I was initially concerned about how the teachers would receive me . . . but for the most part they have been very receptive to having me in their classroom. I think it helps that I am willing to get my hands dirty.

—Mental health consultant in Quality Start

A mental health consultant can be an invaluable resource for supporting child care teachers in developing and maintaining classroom environments that promote social and emotional development. This is critical because preschool children who develop appropriate social skills and good emotion regulation are better prepared for elementary school and more likely to succeed throughout the school years (Bowman, Donovan, & Bums, 2000; Shonkoff & Philips, 2000). Moreover, social and emotional competence have been associated with more positive peer and teacher relationships (LaFreniere & Sroufe, 1985) and less aggressive behavior (Denham et al., 2002; Lemerise & Arsenio, 2000). Having access to an early childhood mental health consultant helps early childhood educators identify problem behaviors earlier, and gives the child care teacher and consultant the opportunity and the skills to address children's challenging behavior before serious problems or expulsion occur.

Johnston and Brinamen (2006) suggest that a competent mental health consultant should have an understanding of the principles underlying not only mental health, but also early childhood education and child development. Moreover, consultants should be familiar with practical aspects of group care and its impact on children's development, and should be able to make a clear distinction between consultation for and treatment of mental health. Consultants must also work to become familiar with the context and culture of each setting in which they practice, as the development of relationships with program staff is among the first and most important elements of their work. Early childhood mental health consultants work closely with teachers on site to serve as a resource and support for providers as they foster and enhance children's early development. Consultants must actively encourage staff to consider the role they play in the lives of the children in their care, especially how their actions contribute to the development of children's social competence and emotion regulation (Cohen & Kaufmann, 2000). The increase in the quality of care that can be supported through an early childhood mental health consultation program makes this an optimal tool for enhancing the child care environment and overall child development.

Increasing teachers' understanding of children and how best to foster healthy development improves not only basic care, but also teachers' feelings of competence in their role as caregivers (Alkon et al., 2003). Therefore, consultation should focus on recognizing and enhancing existing skills, increasing knowledge, and addressing needs of teachers as well as providing support in managing the challenging behaviors of specific children. The kinds of skills and knowledge teachers possess vary greatly from teacher to teacher, in a field that includes first-time child care workers learning their skills on the job as well as teachers with graduate degrees and specialized knowledge and expertise. A consultant discovers each teacher's needs through careful observation and discussion with that teacher about his or her experiences and concerns. Areas that need to be enhanced may range from how in-class transitions are handled to the teacher's tone of voice to working with a child with autism or attention deficit disorder.

The consultant enters into a partnership with the center as a whole and with the individuals within the center, which enables the consultant to join the teachers at whatever level they may be functioning and support them in creating an environment that nurtures the healthy development of the children in their care. It is through building a nonjudgmental relationship and recognizing each teacher as the expert on the children in her classroom that teachers feel comfortable enough to work with and accept the consultant and the consultative process. Once a level of comfort, trust, and mutual respect is reached, teachers can safely acknowledge areas in need of improvement, while also taking pride in the work they do and ownership of the responsibility to seek and maintain ways to improve their own program and professional growth.

During infant mental health consultation, the consultant strives to respect and empathize with the teacher while motivating the teacher to improve the level or type of social-emotional support she provides to the child. The consultant accomplishes this goal through a combination of strategies and chooses these according to the particular circumstances of people and programs. When, where, how, and which strategic tools are used may differ at any given center on any given day. These strategies and tools include classroom observations, in-class modeling, didactic group meetings, meetings with teachers, meetings with families, meetings with home visitors, designing specific interventions for challenging child behaviors (with parents' consent), parent education seminars, and referrals to outside agencies (e.g., speech and language evaluation, individual or family therapy, behavioral intervention in the home).

One of the key elements to successful infant mental health implementation is the consultant's ability to listen. Early childhood providers are tremendously dedicated to their work but frequently do not have the training to understand mental health issues in young children. Therefore, they may feel responsible for the problems exhibited by the children in their classes. They may feel underprepared for the tasks of governing and teaching the youngsters in their classrooms, while they also have deep reservoirs of caring, affection, and a sense of culpability if things are going wrong. An outside consultant can alleviate stress significantly by engaging in careful, supportive listening, which elicits both teacher strengths and concerns. The consultant should take a cooperative, collaborative stance and bring mental health expertise to the partnership while acknowledging the expertise of the teacher—who knows, cares for, and works hard for the children every day. In this way, the consultant learns what he or she needs to know in order to respect and empathize with the teacher and successfully collaborate with him or her.

INFANT MENTAL HEALTH CONSULTATION SERVICES

She was very professional and at the same time her friendly ways made her a part of our school family. The children and parents trusted her not only as a consultant but also as a person who really cares.

—Teacher after participating in infant mental health consultation

Although infant mental health consultation varies in terms of its focus on the overall child care program, on individual children, or a combined approach, six general activities are typically used across approaches (Duran et al., 2009):

- Information gathering
- Individualized service plan (ISP) development
- ISP implementation
- Early childhood education provider and/or family education
- Early childhood education provider and/or family emotional support
- Linkages to services outside of consultation

Across early infant mental health consultation programs, consultants engage in these six steps collaboratively with the centers and families they serve. We discuss each of these activities and provide examples from our own work with early childhood programs using infant mental health consultation to illustrate the process (the names of people, places, and early education programs have been changed to protect the privacy of those involved).

A discussion of mental health consultation activities within a center cannot begin without a word about the relationship foundation that must be created, either before the consultant engages in these activities or simultaneously while proceeding through these steps. Central to the consultative work is the consultant's understanding of the multiple relationships already occurring within a center and the relationships that will be formed and potentially altered when the consultant enters into the system (Johnston & Brinamen, 2006). Green and colleagues (2006) found that it was the quality of the consultant–staff relationship that contributed to the effectiveness of early childhood education mental health consultation.

A mental health consultant cannot underestimate the importance of relationship building with the caregivers and families with whom he or she will work. A consultant's relationships with center staff can be seen as a catalyst for any change that may occur

(Duran et al., 2009). It is hoped that by forming and modeling a nonjudgmental relationship and partnership with teachers, teachers will in turn form positive partnerships with the parents of children in their care. To date, research has found that teachers reported having experienced a positive and helpful relationship with mental health consultants (Green et al., 2006; Heller et al., 2011). Furthermore, Green and colleagues have found that teacher report of a positive relationship with the consultant is related to numerous outcome variables. (Later in this chapter, we discuss program and professional characteristics that are positively influenced by mental health consultation.)

The consultant engenders positive relationships through his or her "way of being" or his or her consultative stance (Johnston & Brinamen, 2006, p. 15). Central to the consultative stance is avoiding the role of outside expert or teacher and instead collaborating with center staff in thinking creatively about solutions to situations and behaviors that occur in a center (Johnston & Brinamen, 2006). The consultant strives to conduct him- or herself in the manner of a partner, to be seen as a partner who holds expertise in infant and early childhood mental health and who is open to and respectful of the expertise that already exists within the center. The consultant is focused on both collaborating with center staff and supporting the healthy growth and development of all individuals within the center's sphere of influence. The consultant must actively work to maintain this stance as he or she collaboratively works with educational staff on center dilemmas, as outlined in the following steps.

Information Gathering

It is always nice to have a fresh pair of eyes to see things that I may have missed . . . just to see the same situation in a different perspective . . . the idea that all situations have a solution. You just have to figure it out!

—Teacher after participating in infant mental health consultation

Consultative work must be guided by a thorough assessment. The information-gathering phase can take several different forms, including in-classroom observations of particular children or of the overall classroom; interviews with early childhood education providers; interviews with parents; and completion of standardized instruments for individual consultation, such as the Ages & Stages Questionnaires®: Social-Emotional (ASQ:SE; Squires, Bricker, & Twombly, 2002) or, for classroom-wide consultation, the Infant/Toddler Environment Rating Scale–Revised or Early Childhood Environment Rating Scale–Revised (ECERS-R; Harms, Clifford, & Cryer, 1998, 2006) or the Classroom Assessment Scoring System™ (CLASS™; Pianta, La Paro, & Hamre, 2008). Any combination of these sources can assist a consultant in providing joint focus and understanding that facilitates working together with early childhood educators and families to develop a plan acceptable to all involved. In their review of four agencies providing mental health consultation to child care centers, Alkon and colleagues (2003) found that 98% of teachers and directors working with a consultant reported that observing children in their classroom was the most common consultant activity. In addition, teachers and directors listed the following as common consultant activities, all of which are typically part of the information-gathering phase of consultation: director consultation, individual teacher consultation, and meeting with families (Alkon et al., 2003).

When working with an individual child, parent permission is needed before initiating the assessment process, though work with an individual child may come on the heels of having completed a full classroom observation. Some consultation models may include a home visit for a child-centered consultation to obtain more in-depth information about an individual child and his or her family. Although home visitation as a component of the assessment process is seen as beneficial, many programs do not incorporate home visitation into their consultation services (Duran et al., 2009). Although Duran and colleagues do not elaborate on why programs do not make use of home visiting, we suspect cost, time, and staff comfort level and training are contributing factors.

In our work, consultants typically spend a majority of their time observing and modeling in the classroom. This time serves multiple purposes. The consultant can gather information about the overall functioning of the classroom and/or can observe children who have been identified as having challenging behaviors while establishing and strengthening a relationship with the teacher. Consultants have reported that this classroom time is invaluable to their work, and is one of the best ways to establish a relationship built on mutual expertise with teachers. It is also a time when consultants can actively assist teachers in classrooms, if needed or welcomed, and actively demonstrate a collaborative stance with teachers.

The following examples illustrate how a mental health consultant is invited into a program and begins her work supporting teachers and programs in their work.

When Judy, mental health consultant for Little Learning Center, first began consultation with the center, she was asked to visit the classroom for 2-year-olds, the "Ducks." Martha was the Ducks teacher. The director stated that there were several children in the classroom she thought may need child-centered consultation. Judy spent the majority of her first day at the center talking with Martha, then observing the classroom and children as they functioned as a whole. From her initial observation, Judy was able to begin to formulate how she could best support Martha in creating a classroom environment that would support all of the 2-year-olds.

In conversation with Martha, Judy learned that Martha was the third teacher in 3 months for the Duck class and that Martha felt overwhelmed in her role as the sole caregiver in the room. Martha was a recent high school graduate who had no previous experience working in a child care center. She loved children but was beginning to doubt her ability to continue as the Duck teacher. After hearing Martha's concerns and observing the classroom, Judy discussed and clarified her consultative role with the director and conveyed her wish to spend time supporting Martha by establishing a working relationship with her that would parallel the relationship that Martha could then develop with her class. Judy surmised that, although there may be a need for a child-centered consultation for one or two of the children in the room, several of the challenging behaviors would calm as the children learned what to expect from their routine and their caregiver on any given day.

Individualized Service Plan Development

Once the consultant has collected sufficient information, he or she moves into ISP development (Duran et al., 2009). In a child-focused consultation, collaboration among early childhood education providers, parents, and the consultant is the key to successfully determining intervention strategies. The consultant may assist the early childhood education provider in designing a behavior plan for the classroom and may make similar suggestions for parents to use at home. Some early childhood mental health consultation programs provide individualized direct services to children (Duran et al., 2009), which may include one-on-one psychotherapy or therapeutic playgroups. Otherwise, the consultant may refer the family to professionals in the community for further evaluation and/or treatment. Referrals are often made to Medicaid Part C evaluators or providers, to local infant or child mental health agencies, to speech and language evaluators, and to other auxiliary interventions that may be important to the child's overall development (Duran et al., 2009; Heller et al., 2011). An ISP may also be developed for a classroom as part of program consultation, as demonstrated in the following example.

Judy noticed that Martha's class had a loose schedule throughout the day and that the Ducks did not appear to always know what was coming next. Judy asked Martha if she thought it would be helpful for her and the Ducks to be able to see what activity was coming up next each day. Judy used an adult's calendar as an analogy for the importance of being able to have a visual reminder of what the plans are for the day. Together, Judy and Martha worked on creating a visual schedule for the classroom, which included pictures of typical activities such as lunch, nap, and drop-off or pick-up attached to a poster board with Velcro. Martha was able to use the schedule to assist with transitions each day and to help the children understand when the schedule was modified from day to day (e.g., if rain prevented them from going to the playground one day). As the Ducks began to know what to expect and what was expected each day and were able to anticipate transitions, some of the challenging behaviors that had been occurring lessened. Martha enjoyed her success with this visual aid so much that she began to think aloud with Judy about visual methods of positively reinforcing the Ducks when they engaged in good behaviors.

Individualized Service Plan Implementation

I had a challenging child in my class, and [the consultant] and I worked together to find solutions to help him. She was very encouraging to me. She taught me to praise good behavior and other children will follow.

—Teacher after participating in infant mental health consultation

Consultants actively work with early childhood education providers to assist with implementing the ISP. They may model in the classroom, provide in-person or telephone coaching to providers and/or parents, and participate in team meetings with referral sources (Duran et al., 2009; Heller et al., 2011). Seventy-five percent of teachers surveyed in one study reported that their consultant modeled behavior management techniques in their classroom (Alkon et al., 2003), illustrating the usefulness of this method of ISP implementation. Modeling allows the consultant to build rapport with the children, reinforce the partnership nature of the work, and demonstrate how to apply techniques in action.

Judy and Martha regularly spent time together in the Duck classroom thinking about and working on ways to implement consistency for the children. As Martha began to follow a more consistent schedule, praised positive behavior, and consistently interacted with the children in her classroom, challenging behaviors were markedly decreased.

One child, Emile, continued to have difficulties despite positive classroom changes. Together with the director, Martha and Judy decided to approach Emile's parents about a child-centered consultation. Judy met with Emile's parents, and after informing them about her role in the program and gaining consent, she interviewed them and Martha about Emile, conducted specific observations of Emile in the classroom, and worked with Emile's parents and Martha on specific methods of interacting with Emile.

Early Childhood Education Provider and/or Family Education

I have gained the ability to sit back and think about and try to figure out what the child needs with my other team members. It is a kind of skill I wouldn't have had if I hadn't worked with a mental health person.

—Teacher commenting in a focus group about her participation in mental health consultation (Alkon et al., 2003, p. 97)

In addition to ISP planning and implementation, several mental health consultation programs have a training component for early childhood education providers, families, or both as an integral part of the program (Duran et al., 2009; Heller et al., 2011). Our program provides continuing education credits for teachers attending on-site didactic training sessions. On-site training that is set up to accommodate a center's schedule helps to build rapport and also motivates teachers and directors to find the time to attend. Trainings cover a variety of topics related to healthy social-emotional development in children, such as working with families, managing challenging child behavior, or addressing teacher stress. (The Center on the Social and Emotional Foundations for Early Learning's web site [http://csefel.vanderbilt.edu] and the Center for Early Childhood Mental Health Consultation's web site [ECMHC; http://ecmhc.org] are good resources for consultation training modules.)

Parent training may occur informally as part of ISP implementation, with a plan specific to that individual family and child (Duran et al., 2009). Parent training may also be tailored to meet the needs of a center's parent base (Heller et al., 2011). Possible topics may include, for example, developmentally appropriate caregiving activities, child development through the first 5 years, or navigating the transition to kindergarten. Of teachers surveyed by Alkon and colleagues (2003), 70% reported participating in mental health consultant-led trainings, and 55% of programs reported that trainings were available for parents.

Judy provided trainings to all of the teachers at Little Learning Center on building relationships with young children and maintaining supportive environments for young children. The interactive group format of the trainings allowed Martha to hear from more experienced teachers on how they had coped with challenging behaviors in their classrooms, and it gave her the opportunity to share what she had already implemented in her room that had worked. This group time helped Martha to feel supported by her fellow teachers and recognize that she was developing her own expertise in working with 2-year-olds.

Early Childhood Education Provider and Family Emotional Support

How do we feel? Frustrated, stressed, sometimes scared, powerless.

—Teacher commenting in a focus group about her work in early childhood education
(Alkon et al., 2003, p. 97)

Although emotional support to parents and providers may be the activity most difficult to quantify, this service is easily one of the most valuable aspects of a mental health consultation program. Early childhood education providers, often overwhelmed with responsibility and stressors, can call upon their mental health consultant for support, which in turn may help to reduce stress levels. In fact, having access to a mental health consultant has been shown to reduce stress and burnout among early childhood education providers (Alkon et al., 2003). Duran and colleagues (2009) noted that early childhood education providers and families appreciated being able to "have someone to turn to who would validate their frustration and affirm that the difficulties they encountered were not due to lack of ability or hard work" (Duran et al., 2009, p. 76). Mental health consultation support has also been linked to teacher reports of increases in job satisfaction and decreases in teacher turnover (Alkon et al., 2003), both of which can strengthen teacher–child relationships. Mental health consultants can help ensure their support is available and accessible by adhering to a regular and predictable consultation schedule, being sure to check in with all staff when at the center, and creating a way to have private meetings when needed, and if possible, arranging mutually agreeable ways for staff to contact them about urgent questions and problems.

Martha found that, although at first she had been somewhat reluctant to have a stranger in her classroom, she now looked forward to Judy's visits. Not only did Judy think with her about possible strategies to try in the classroom, she also listened to Martha when she just needed to talk about a difficult day.

Linkages to Other Services

She listened to the children and families and communicated well with them. She also . . . made them aware of the many services available without making them feel like bad parents.

—Teacher after participating in infant mental health consultation

A common activity for mental health consultants is making referrals for the early childhood education providers, children, and families they serve. Early childhood education providers have reported that they value the link that mental health consultation can provide between supportive services, such as family support agencies, and early intervention services, such as occupational therapy or speech and language therapy (Alkon et al., 2003). In our home state of Louisiana, mental health consultants have as one of their primary referral sources Early Childhood Supports and Services, which provides evaluation and treatment services to children from birth through 5 years and their families. Many states have similar state-funded, free-of-charge early intervention evaluation services available for children from birth through 5 years. A mental health consultant may make a referral for early intervention services and be included as part of the evaluation or treatment team. Some mental health consultation programs provide direct services such as therapeutic playgroups or direct therapy for a child, family member, and/or early childhood education provider; however, these services are not as typical as the others discussed here (Alkon et al., 2003; Duran et al., 2009).

After gathering initial information from Emile's parents and observing Emile in the classroom, Judy facilitated a referral to a local early childhood mental health agency that could support Emile's family and work more closely with them in their home. As a consultant, Judy was able to support Emile's parents as they began to work with evaluators and interventionists. Judy attended team meetings to offer information related to Emile's behaviors in the classroom and to offer emotional support to his parents as they learned to navigate the new system.

Although Emile continued to be a child who would need more attention than some other children in his classroom, with Judy's support, Martha and Emile's parents were able to recognize his strengths and work together to support his growth and development. To her surprise, when the center director asked Martha if she would consider keeping Emile in her classroom for an additional time period instead of moving him to the next class with his classmates, Martha agreed wholeheartedly. She realized the importance for Emile and his parents of maintaining relationship consistency and found herself looking forward to continuing to be one of the supports in Emile's life. In addition, she knew she could count on Judy's support in the months to come.

CHALLENGES TO EARLY
CHILDHOOD MENTAL HEALTH CONSULTATION

[I'm] coming to terms with the fact that as I leave a center, all of the problems will not be solved. This work is daunting in that we have the ability to make things different for so many children, but the changes that we can assist centers to make may be small.

     —Infant mental health consultant describing some of the challenges of her work

Despite the obvious benefits of consultation, challenges often arise. A major challenge in providing ECMHC results from confusion regarding what a consultant does or does not do (Duran et al., 2009). Many times, teachers are unsure about the role of the consultant, believing that the consultant is able to provide more traditional direct therapeutic services to children and families rather than the broad support and guidance that typically constitute consultation. Consultants may arrive at a program with one task in mind only to find they must address other related issues in order to accomplish that task. For example, consultants tell us that supervisory staff may lack knowledge and experience with mental health issues and may require training and support in order to provide competent and confident supervision that is consistent with what consultants are encouraging and teaching. In programs organized in layers that do not facilitate open communication and understanding among administrators, supervisors, and direct-service staff, consultants may find themselves needing to communicate across levels to clarify goals, roles, responsibilities, and expectations. It is also important that the administration (i.e., owner, director, and assistant director) not only understands the purpose of consultation but also is willing to commit necessary resources to the consultation, such as time for staff to meet with the consultant, space for the consultant to meet with staff and parents, and support from director and assistant director to make and maintain positive changes.

Another challenge involves the rate and depth of change that occurs in centers in terms of classroom practices as well as teachers' and children's behavior. Change is often a process that occurs over time and requires skill and patience to initiate and maintain. Consultants must focus on supporting teachers as they implement new practices and guide them as they assist children in adapting to these changes. Once changes have been implemented, it is important that consultants and teachers temper their expectations and notice the small successes that often occur over the course of the consultation relationship; this is the final challenge of consultation.

RESEARCH FINDINGS ON EARLY CHILDHOOD
EDUCATION MENTAL HEALTH CONSULTATION

"If I decide to incorporate early education mental health consultation, what is in it for my center?" That question can best be answered by turning to the research literature on early childhood education mental health consultation to child care centers. As mentioned earlier in this chapter, early childhood education mental health consultation may be program-focused, child-focused, or a combination of the two. Current research tends to focus on outcomes at three levels: teacher, child, or classroom level. The consultant focuses on all three levels, as each is believed to influence the ultimate goal: to increase

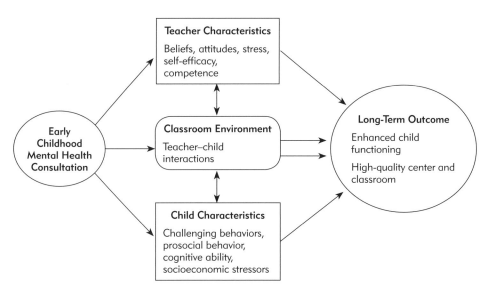

Figure 10.1. Model of change representing the proposed impact of early childhood mental health consultation on child outcome.

children's social and emotional competence. The diagram in Figure 10.1 represents the model of change we believe leads to positive child outcomes. Unfortunately, published research on mental health consultation to child care programs has been very limited; this is typically due to short-term funding for the services and a lack of financial support for systematic evaluations (Brennan, Bradley, Allen, & Perry, 2008). This section reviews what we do know about mental health consultation in early childhood settings based upon the current findings from reported studies. See Table 10.1 for a brief summary of research findings to date.

Teacher Outcomes

Early childhood education mental health consultation strives to enhance staff and especially teacher capacity, particularly in the area of social-emotional development of children. Changes in staff capacity can be examined by measuring staff behavior (especially

Table 10.1. Impact of early childhood mental health counseling at a glance

Child	Teacher	Classroom
Decrease in expulsion rates or risk for expulsion	Increase in self-efficacy	Increase in positive interactions
Decrease in externalizing behaviors	Increase in sense of competence[a]	Decrease in negative interactions
Decrease in internalizing behaviors	Decrease in job-related stress[a]	Increase in teacher sensitivity[a]
Increase in social skills	Reduction in staff turnover	Increase in teacher's classroom management skills[a]

[a]There are mixed results for this variable in that at least one study did not find this effect. However, if the majority of studies found a result, it is listed here.

interactions with the children in the classroom), staff level of knowledge, and/or staff attitudes or beliefs. Specifically, studies have examined teachers' feelings of effectiveness, stress experienced by teachers, and teacher competence.

Teachers' Feelings of Effectiveness   Teacher self-efficacy has been a primary focus of research on the impact of early childhood education mental health consultation. Self-efficacy refers to a teacher's belief that he or she has the skills needed to bring about a desired outcome—in this instance, supporting children's social-emotional development and addressing challenging behaviors. Research in primary and secondary education settings has found that teachers with high levels of self-efficacy have a more positive impact on child development and exhibit better teaching skills than teachers with low levels of self-efficacy. Extrapolating from research findings of primary and secondary school teachers, one would expect high teacher self-efficacy to have a positive impact on teacher behavior and, in turn, child outcomes. Teacher self-efficacy therefore may be an important target of intervention in child care and early education settings.

To date, two published studies have examined change in self-efficacy over the course of consultation. Both studies found that teacher self-efficacy increased over the time of the intervention (Alkon et al., 2003; Heller et al., 2011). Heller and colleagues identified two factors of teacher self-efficacy in early childhood teachers: personal teaching efficacy and teacher influence (Heller et al., in press). *Personal teaching efficacy* is a teacher's belief that he or she has the ability to make a positive difference in children's lives (e.g., "If I keep trying, I can find some way to reach even the most challenging children"). *Teacher influence* reflects a teacher's sense of powerlessness or hopelessness about her ability to influence children's development (e.g., "As a caregiver I can't really do much, because the way a child develops depends mostly on what goes on at home"). The items on the Teacher Influence Scale (Heller et al., in press) are reverse-scored so that a higher score indicates a belief that the teacher can influence child development regardless of external factors. It is interesting to note that, not only did both scales of teacher self-efficacy increase over the time of the intervention, but analysis also found that teachers maintained the increase in personal teaching efficacy that occurred during the intervention for 6 months after the intervention, and teachers continued to increase their sense of teacher influence even after the intervention had concluded (Heller et al., in press).

Teacher Stress   Job-related stress is defined as "discomforting reactions to the demands of the position and the lack of control the teacher feels over her work" (Brennan et al., 2008, p. 1011). Researchers have found that teachers report feeling less stressed and programs report higher levels of staff wellness after participation in early childhood education mental health consultation (Brennan et al., 2008; Green et al., 2006). In addition, lower levels of burnout and staff turnover have been documented after early childhood education mental health consultation (Brennan et al., 2008). We must also note that one study did not find a difference between teachers in the intervention and control group in reported level of stress at the end of the consultation (Gilliam, 2007). Clearly this is an area where further research is needed, as stress levels can affect teacher behavior within the classroom as well as with colleagues within programs and, in turn, the social and working environment of the entire center.

The majority of studies that examined teacher stress found that teachers who participated in early childhood education mental health consultation reported a decrease in stress, a perceived decrease in burnout, and a more positive perspective on continuing a career in early childhood education (Brennan et al., 2008). As with many of the other outcome variables associated with an early childhood education mental health consultation model, consultations of longer durations were associated with lower staff turnover (Alkon et al., 2003).

Teacher Competence   Teacher competence encompasses a wide variety of behaviors, including classroom management abilities and knowledge, instructional skills and knowledge, and knowledge of and ability to support child development. Mental health consultation would be expected to affect competence behaviors that involve interacting with children and parents, supporting children's social-emotional development, and managing children's behavior—especially challenging behaviors. To date, three published studies have reported on teacher competence. Two published studies (Alkon et al., 2003; Heller et al., 2011) reported positive changes in teacher report of competence. In addition, Brennan and colleagues' (2008) literature review of the early childhood mental health consultation literature reported that six of the unpublished research reports they reviewed found an increase in teacher competence across the time in which mental health consultation occurred.

Teacher–Child Classroom Interactions   Research has demonstrated that the best way to support healthy development or to change children's challenging behavior is through high-quality relationships, specifically those essential relationships for infants and young children—the teacher–child and/or parent–child relationship (Bowman et al., 2000; Curby et al., 2009; Mashburn et al., 2008; Pianta et al., 2008; Rimm-Kaufman, Curby, Grimm, Brock, & Nathanson, 2009). Research has demonstrated that preschool classrooms with higher-quality interpersonal interactions show larger academic and developmental gains at the end of the year as compared to classrooms with lesser-quality interpersonal interactions, and these early gains continue into kindergarten (Howe et al., 2008).

Two reliable and valid outcomes measures are frequently used to assess changes in classroom interactional quality: CLASS (Pianta, La Paro, & Hamre, 2008) and ECERS-R (Harms, Clifford, & Cryer, 1998). The two studies that have used the CLASS to assess change in the classroom found changes in teacher sensitivity, positive climate, negative climate, and classroom management (Heller et al., in press; Raver et al., 2008). A third study, using the ECERS-R, did not find changes over time or between the intervention and comparison group (Gilliam, 2007). One possible reason for the difference in findings is the shorter duration of Gilliam's early childhood education mental health consultation model compared with that of the other two studies (Heller et al., in press; Raver et al., 2008). These contradictory findings may also be due to the measures used to assess the classrooms. The ECERS-R is more global than the CLASS in that it assesses important indicators of child care quality beyond teacher–child interactions, whereas the CLASS focuses specifically on teacher–child interactions and thus gives a more in-depth assessment of interaction quality and emotional climate within the classroom. Researchers in early childhood education mental health consultation are looking at ways to use the ECERS-R as an outcome tool. One group has created a social-emotional subscale from items on the ECERS-R (A. Keyes, personal communication, March 2007), and another group has had some success with a factor analysis using ECERS-R items (Beers & Dickstein, 2010).

Child Outcomes

The goal of early childhood education mental health consultation is to enhance staff and especially teacher capacity, particularly in the area of social-emotional development of children. The underlying purpose of this goal is to improve children's social-emotional development and level of school readiness. Changes in child development can be examined by assessing child behavior such as externalizing and internalizing behavior, social skills, and even cognitive development.

Externalizing and Internalizing Behavior   Two types of challenging behaviors are typically reported by caregivers and teachers and are studied by researchers: *externalizing* (e.g., hyperactivity, aggression, impulsivity) and *internalizing* (e.g., fearful, sad, withdrawn). Whereas typically developing children can exhibit any of these behaviors, it is considered detrimental when the intensity or frequency of any of these behaviors impedes the child's social, emotional, and/or academic development. Unfortunately, as highlighted earlier in this chapter, without intervention, challenging behaviors often lead to a child's expulsion from school or negative relationships with teachers and peers, which carry with them considerable risk for later difficulties. (See Chapter 2 for more about internalizing and externalizing behaviors.)

Overall, research has found that early childhood mental health consultation decreases the occurrence of externalizing behavior as measured by teacher report and child observation (Perry, Allen, Brennan, & Bradley, 2010; Perry, Dunne et al., 2008; Raver et al., 2008). This finding is true for both child-focused and program-focused programs. With regard to internalizing behaviors, results have been mixed, with some studies reporting a decrease in behaviors and others reporting no significant change (Perry et al., 2010; Gilliam, 2007; Raver et al., 2008). It is interesting to note that Raver and colleagues (2008) found a decrease of internalizing behaviors according to teacher and parent report but not according to observational data. It is also noteworthy that decreases in child externalizing and internalizing behaviors were linked to consultant attributes such as a positive consultant–teacher relationship or more frequent consultant visits (Green et al., 2006), thus supporting the idea that the consultant–teacher relationship serves as a catalyst for change within a center.

Social Skills   Social-emotional development "refers to children's growing ability to experience, regulate, and express emotions; form close and secure interpersonal relationships; explore the environment and learn" (Parlakian, 2003, p. 2). Social-emotional competence (e.g., friendliness, good language skills, persistence at challenging tasks) has been linked not only to success in kindergarten but also to elementary school

success and even to accomplishments in adulthood (McClelland et al., 2007; McClelland, Morrison, & Holmes, 2000; Parlakian, 2003; Peth-Pierce, 2000). Unfortunately, many students start kindergarten with limited social-emotional competence, especially those children from impoverished backgrounds. Up to 46% of kindergarten teachers reported that more than half of their students have problems in one or more of the areas of social-emotional development, including following directions, individual work, group work, social skills, and immaturity (Rimm-Kaufman, Pianta, & Cox, 2000). This means that teachers are distracted from a focus on learning and educational plans so important during kindergarten, as they spend disproportionate amount of time responding to negative behaviors related to inadequate social and emotional skills (Fox, Dunlap, Hemmerte, Joseph, & Strain, 2003).

In a review of the literature, Perry and colleagues (2010) reported that the majority of studies assessing social and emotional development showed an improvement in development among children in programs using early childhood mental health consultation. Similar to the findings regarding child externalizing and internalizing behaviors, improvements in social and emotional behaviors were linked to consultant attributes such as a positive consultant–teacher relationship or more frequent consultant visits (Green et al., 2006).

Expulsion   One of the many negative outcomes of challenging behavior is an increased risk that even very young children will be expelled from early education and child care settings. In a national study including data from 40 states, it was demonstrated that child care expulsion rates (1 in every 36 children) exceeded the rates of expulsion in preschool (1 in every 149 children) as well as expulsion rates among children in kindergarten through 12th grade (1 in every 476 children) (Gilliam, 2005). Furthermore, centers with access to a mental health consultant reported lower rates of expulsion compared with centers that did not have access to a mental health consultant (Gilliam & Shahar, 2006). Another study (Perry, Dunne, et al., 2008) examining the impact of early childhood mental health consultation on children at risk for expulsion found that 75% of the children at risk for expulsion were retained in their current setting if the center had access to early childhood mental health consultation. The study also reported that early childhood mental health consultation affected the behaviors that put children at risk for expulsion. Specifically, for the children who participated in programs using early childhood mental health consultation, teachers reported a decrease in children's challenging behaviors and an increase in their prosocial skills.

CONCLUSION

Although the research so far on early childhood education mental health consultation is promising, it is important to keep in mind that much of the research is in the early stages. Most of what practitioners know about the importance of early childhood education mental health consultation comes from the staff of centers, the families they work with, and the behavior of the children themselves. What practitioners also know, which is a parallel with what we know about child development, is that early childhood education mental health consultation is at its best when good relationships are developed. Just as in early childhood, development has to occur in the context of a supportive, respectful, and nurturing environment. One of the most important roles of a consultant is to be a catalyst, supporter, and participant in the ongoing, dynamic process of finding the best in every adult who cares for children, and the best in every child for whom teachers give their time, their energy, and their considerable care. Clearly we are still at the beginning of understanding when and how mental health consultation works in early education and intervention settings. As we continue to learn how early childhood mental health consultation works, we can optimize our work in supporting children's social and emotional health.

REFERENCES

Alkon, A., Ramler, M., & MacLennan, K. (2003). Evaluation of mental health consultation in child care centers. *Early Childhood Education Journal, 31*(2), 91–99.

Beers, M., & Dickstein, S. (2010, December). *The integration of early childhood mental health consultation into pediatric primary care.* Paper presented at the meeting of ZERO TO THREE: 25th National Training Institute, Phoenix, AZ.

Bowman, B., Donovan, M., & Bums, S. (Eds.). (2000). *Eager to team: Educating our preschoolers.* Washington, DC: National Academy Press.

Brennan, E.M., Bradley, J.R., Allen, M.D., & Perry, D.F. (2008). The evidence base for mental health consultation in early childhood settings: Research synthesis addressing staff and program outcomes. *Early Education and Development, 19*(6), 982–1022.

Cohen, E., & Kaufmann, R. (2000). *Early childhood mental health consultation.* Washington, DC: U.S. Department of Health and Human Services, Substance Abuse and Mental Health Services Administration.

Curby, T.W., LoCasale-Crouch, J. Konold, T.R., Pianta, R.C., Howes, C., et al. (2009). The relations of observed pre-K classroom quality profiles to children's achievement and social competence. *Early Education and Development, 20*(2), 346–372.

Denham, S.A., Caverly, S., Schmidt, M., Blair, K., DeMulder, E., Caal, S., et al. (2002). Preschool understanding of emotions: Contributions to classroom anger and aggression. *Journal of Child Psychology and Psychiatry, 43*(7), 901–916.

Duran, F., Hepburn, K., Irvine, M., Kaufmann, R., Anthony, B., Horen, N., et al. (2009). *What works?: A study of effective early childhood mental health consultation programs.* Washington, DC: Georgetown University, Center for Child and Human Development.

Fox, L., Dunlap, G., Hemmerte, M.L., Joseph, G.E., & Strain, P.S. (2003). The teaching pyramid: A model for supporting social competence and preventing challenging behavior in young children. *Young Children, 58,* 48–53.

Gilliam, W.S. (2005). *Pre-kindergarteners left behind: Expulsion rates in state pre-kindergarten systems.* New Haven, CT: Yale University, Child Study Center.

Gilliam, W.S. (2007). *Early childhood consultation partnership: Results of a random-controlled evaluation. Final report and executive summary.* New Haven, CT: Yale University, Child Study Center.

Gilliam, W.S., & Shahar, G. (2006). Preschool and child care expulsion and suspension: Rates and predictors in one state. *Infants and Young Children, 19*(3), 228–245.

Green, B.L., Everhart, M., Gordon, L., & Garcia-Gettman, M. (2006). Characteristics of effective mental health consultation in early childhood settings: Multi-level analysis of a national survey. *Topics in Early Childhood Special Education, 26*(3), 142–152.

Harms, T., Clifford, R.M., & Cryer, D. (1998). *Early Childhood Environment Rating Scale–Revised.* New York: Teachers College Press.

Harms, T., Clifford, R.M., & Cryer, D. (2006). *Infant/Toddler Environment Rating Scale–Revised.* New York: Teachers College Press.

Heller, S.S., Keyes, A.W., Boothe, A.B., Nagle, G., Vaughn, K., Sidell, M., et al. (2011). Evaluating the impact of mental health consultation on early childhood teachers' efficacy and competence. *Infant Mental Health Journal 32,*143–164.

Heller, S.S., Rice, J., Sidell, M., Vaughn, K., Boothe, A.B., Keyes, A.W., et al. (in press). Mental health consultation and teacher interaction. *Early Education and Development.*

Howes, C., Burchinal, M., Pianta, R.C., Bryant, D., Early, D., Clifford, R., et al. (2008). Ready to learn? Children's pre-academic achievement in pre-kindergarten programs. *Early Childhood Research Quarterly, 23,* 27–50.

Johnston, K., & Brinamen, C. (2006). *Mental health consultation to child care: Transforming relationships with directors, staff and families.* Washington, DC: ZERO TO THREE Press.

LaFreniere, P.J., & Sroufe, L.A. (1985). Profiles of peer competence: Interrelations among measures, influence of social ecology, and relation to attachment history. *Developmental Psychology, 21,* 56–69.

Lemerise, E.A., & Arsenio, W.F. (2000). An integrated model of emotion processes and cognition in social information processing. *Child Development, 71,* 107–118.

Lombardi, J. (2003). *Time to care: Redesigning child care to promote education, support families and build communities.* Phildelphia: Temple University Press.

Mashburn, A.J., Pianta, R.C., Hamre, B.K., Downer, J.T., Barbarin, O. A., Bryant, D., et al. (2008). Measures of classroom quality in prekindergarten and development of academic, language, and social skills. *Child Development, 79* (3), 732–749.

McClelland, M.M., Cameron, C.E., Connor, C.M., Faris, C.L., Jewkes, A.M., & Morrison, F.J. (2007). Links between behavioral regulation and preschoolers literacy, vocabulary, and math skills. *Developmental Psychology, 43*(4), 947–959.

McClelland, M.M., Morrison, F.J., & Holmes, D.H. (2000). Children at-risk for early academic problems: The role of learning-related social skills. *Early Childhood Research Quarterly, 15,* 307–329.

National Institute of Child Health and Human Development, Early Child Care Research Network. (2001). Before Head Start: Income and ethnicity, family characteristics, child care experiences, and child development. *Early Education and Development, 12*(4), 545–576.

Parlakian, R. (2003). *Before the ABCs: Promoting school readiness in infants and toddlers.* Washington, DC: ZERO TO THREE.

Perry, D.F., Allen, M.D., Brennan, E.M., & Bradley, J.R. (2010). The evidence base for mental health consultation in early childhood settings: A research synthesis addressing children's behavioral outcomes. *Early Education & Development, 21,* 795–824.

Perry, D.F., Dunne, M.C., McFadden, L., &Campbell, D. (2008). Reducing the risk for preschool expulsion: Mental health consultation for young children with challenging behavior. *Journal of Child and Family Studies, 17,* 44–54.

Peth-Pierce, R. (2000). *A good beginning: Sending America's children to school with the social and emotional competence they need to succeed.* Bethesda, MD: The Child Mental Health Foundations and Agency Network [FAN] Monograph.

Pianta, R.C., La Paro, K.M., & Hamre, B.K. (2008). *Classroom Assessment Scoring System™ (CLASS™) manual, pre-K.* Baltimore: Paul H. Brookes Publishing Co.

Raver, C.C, Jones, S.M., Li-Grining, C.P., Metzger, M., Champion, K.M., & Sardin, L. (2008). Improving preschool classroom processes: Preliminary findings from a randomized trial implemented in Head Start settings. *Early Childhood Research Quarterly, 23,* 10–26.

Raver, C., & Knitzer, J. (2002). *Ready to enter: What research tells policymakers about strategies to promote social and emotional school readiness among three- and four-year-old children.* New York: Columbia University, National Center for Children in Poverty.

Rimm-Kaufman, S.E., Curby, T.W., Grimm, K.J., Nathanson, L., & Brock, L.L. (2009). The contribution of children's self-regulation and classroom quality to children's adaptive behaviors in the kindergarten classroom. *Developmental Psychology, 45*(4), 958–972.

Rimm-Kaufman, S.E., Pianta, R., & Cox, M. (2000). Teachers' judgments of problems in the transition to kindergarten. *Early Childhood Research Quarterly, 15,* 147–166.

Shonkoff, J.P., & Philips, D.A. (Eds.). (2000). *From neurons to neighborhoods: The science of early childhood development.* Washington, DC: National Academy Press.

Squires, J., Bricker, D., & Twombly, E. (2002). *Ages & Stages Questionnaires®: Social-Emotional (ASQ:SE). A parent-completed, child-monitoring system for social-emotional behaviors.* Baltimore: Paul H. Brookes Publishing Co.

11

Reflective Supervision

Sherryl Scott Heller

How you are is as important as what you do.

—Jeree Pawl and Maria St. John (1998)

As is clear from Section I of this book and as we know from our own work as early childhood educators and interventionists, early childhood education and intervention require addressing challenges at multiple levels. Educators and interventionists must address children's developmental and behavioral challenges, but they cannot effectively do this without also supporting caregivers and families and confronting the difficult life circumstances that contribute to the child's development and behavior—challenges such as maternal depression, intractable poverty, and family and community violence. Because infant mental health is a profession that is, in ways, in its own infancy, some professionals beginning to incorporate it in their practice may not feel adequately prepared for the task. Others, despite appropriate training and experience, find the human emotions inherent in infant mental health work troubling. In response to the challenge of supporting staff so that they may in turn address these complex and varying issues and circumstances, programs increasingly turn to reflective practice and supervision. More and more, early intervention agencies—from child care centers to human service agencies to neonatal intensive care units—are incorporating reflective practice and/or reflective supervision in their organizational structure (Gilkerson, 2004; Gilkerson & Taylor, 2005; Heller, Jazefowicz, Redmond, & Weinstock, 2004; Norman-Murch, 2005). Reflective practice and supervision are tools that programs can use to build staff capacity to meet challenges, to improve the kinds and levels of support the program offers to staff, and to thoughtfully and caringly enhance the services the program provides to children and families.

REFLECTIVE PRACTICE

Within the field of early intervention there is a growing recognition that the caregiver–interventionist relationship can either enhance or weaken service delivery. In order to support interventionists in developing beneficial relationships with caregivers, programs have begun to use reflective practice. *Reflective practice* is a process of carefully considering the qualities and characteristics of one's ideas and/or actions that goes beyond the simple application of professional knowledge (Schon, 1987). It is a process of thinking about what you think and what you do. Reflective practice integrates a set of ideas or sensibilities within a particular body of knowledge (e.g., nursing, mental health, or child care) that guide how we, as educators and interventionists, do our work (Pawl, St. John, & Pekarsky, 1999). Regardless of the particular professional discipline, past ZERO TO THREE board president Jeree Pawl contended, there are several overarching ideas or sensibilities that form a "crucial interpersonal center" of the work of interventionists, and the consideration of these overarching ideas is central to the work of reflective practice (2000). (See Table 11.1 for a list and description of these ideas.)

Working with infants and their caregivers in natural caregiving settings, holding the client and/or family in mind at all times, responding to behaviors and events while maintaining professional practice: These form the core and essential tenets of reflective practice, but they are professional skills that take some effort to develop. Reflective supervision is one method used to support professionals' efforts to intervene with families while remaining connected to the interpersonal center of intervention work.

DEFINING REFLECTIVE SUPERVISION

What is *reflective supervision?* In order to define it, we must first examine each word, *reflection* and *supervision,* separately. *Reflection* has been described as a mental action for learning:

- The mindful consideration of one's actions (Tremmel, 1993)
- "A process through which patterns of behavior become clear and insights dawn" (Gilkerson & Shahmoon-Shanok, 2000, p. 39)
- "A reconstructing experience, the end of which is the identification of a new possibility for action" (Beam, O'Brien, & Neal, 2010, p. 132)

In contrast, *supervision* has been described as a relationship for learning

- "In which strengths are emphasized and vulnerabilities partnered" (Costa, 1999)
- That "allows workers to feel that they are not alone and that they can count on the support of others to help them determine the course of their work" (Costa, 2005)
- That is "a dialogue of thinking and doing which allows one to become more skillful" (Schon, 1987, p. 83)

Table 11.1. Core sensibilities of reflective work in the field of early childhood intervention

Trust the caregiver	Interventionists must hold genuine trust in the parent's investment in the well-being of his or her child. It is the interventionist's challenge to be the holder of hope and to communicate this belief in the possibilities to the parent.
Mutual clarity	The interventionist needs to establish joint and shared goals with the family or client. This requires the interventionist to work with the family toward a mutual understanding of why the interventionist is there, and above all, to find ways to understand the parent's perspectives and goals—even when these seem inappropriate or out of reach.
Hearing and representing *all* voices	Often it is the infant's voice the interventionist is representing; however, the interventionist needs to be committed to hearing and representing any voices that are muffled, not heard, or misheard.
Hypotheses, not truth	The interventionist's professional knowledge can only be a hypothesis, at best, when applied to a particular family or infant. It is essential that the interventionist convey the understanding that the client has all the information needed. When this is conveyed in a genuine manner, clients are then able to recognize that they are partners in the intervention process—not the recipients or ones being judged.
Maintaining an appropriate role	Boundaries serve to maintain and contain the relationship in an appropriate context. In early intervention work, boundaries often need to be flexible or able to shift. It is essential that the interventionist maintain a clear sense of his or her role *and* that the client feels that he or she is being "worked with" and not "done to."
Knowledge, beliefs, biases, and meanings	The interventionist must be aware of and in tune with his or her own beliefs, values, and biases. Equally important, the interventionist needs to recognize the client's beliefs and values—and be respectful of differences (or sameness). The interventionist's own willingness to embrace the client's sense of meaningfulness allows the interventionist to be curious and leads to understanding.
Inclusive interaction	Pawl defines *inclusive interaction* as "the capacity to continue to embrace and hold *all* of those with whom we are involved together at a particular time" (as cited in Weston, 2005, p. 347). This includes the interventionist recognizing how his or her "use of self" impacts the client.

Sources: Pawl (2000) and Weston (2005).

When combined, these two respective definitions of reflective and supervision may be described as "a relationship that aims at creating a climate in which both the client and the helper's needs are being considered, so that the effectiveness of the intervention is being optimized" (Costa, 2006, p. 124). Reflective supervision establishes a partnership in which the supervisee never feels alone; is not overwhelmed by fear or uncertainty; feels safe to express fears, uncertainties, thoughts, feelings, and reactions; and learns more about him- or herself, the client, co-workers or colleagues, and the work.

In the following example from research with partner early education programs, Melinda, a highly trained and very experienced home visitor, talks about a home visit she had with a family headed by two parents, both of whom had developmental disabilities.

There were "a number of borderline safety/health/neglect issues," Melinda told us. This particular home visit, Melinda said,

> Was one of the most chaotic home visits—chaotic home situations—I've ever entered in and tried to do a home visit. People were coming in and out. There was someone literally passed out on the couch, asleep from partying the night before. There was an argument going on with one parent and some friends. . . . it was just chaos beyond belief. And here is this little boy, with identified special needs.

Melinda told us that, after the home visit, when she met for reflective supervision, she

> Really just needed to talk about how I felt walking out of there. The noise, the chaos, the confusion, the needs of the child, and what was happening with that in the midst of all this. And how I felt about it personally. I felt sad for this little boy. I felt like this was an everyday occurrence; that this wasn't necessarily really an unusual thing for him to see. So his level, how he came to adjust to all this chaos, where it really, still for me, made me feel like I wanted to get out. I wanted to flee the situation.
>
> But it was really great that [my supervisor] and I talked. . . . It was very therapeutic. . . . And when you face situations like that, you have to be able to go into the next home and give your attention to what's going on there. And [my supervisor's] help . . . really helped me to do that. . . . I know I was able to go on the next home visit because of meeting and talking to [my supervisor].

This example illustrates the importance of dealing with the emotions inherent in such difficult circumstances so that one is able to then focus on identifying intervention issues and strategies.

Often an interventionist feels uncomfortable with not having the answer to a problem or situation confronting him or her. Simultaneously, the interventionist must be adept at thinking on his or her feet while holding all parties and their relationships in mind. He or she must also be able to maintain a multitude of tools and resources to be used at any given moment—a difficult task in itself. Many times, it is the process of being held and nurtured by an interventionist that leads to a caregiver's self-discovery and positive change, rather than a simple, single remedy (supplied by the interventionist) to the caregiver's problem. This process of holding and nurturing, rather than rushing in to fix things, means there are no set road maps or rules to follow. It means an interventionist has to become comfortable with possibilities rather than absolutes. It is through the safety of a reflective supervisory relationship that an interventionist is able to reflect honestly on his or her work and how thoughts, feelings, and behaviors influence that work as it occurs over time. The reflective supervisory relationship supports the interventionist in focusing not only on what one does, but how one does it. As Pawl and St. John (1998) so succinctly state, "How you are is as important as what you do when working with infants, toddlers and their families."

Relationships take time to establish and maintain. In addition, change, even very important developmental and clinical changes, may be difficult to realize—or even recognize—in the short term. Reflective supervision helps the supervisee to realize that change occurs in "human time," which often is not in sync with "institutional time," and that he or she must work to reconcile the two timeframes. Reflective practice and supervision are key mechanisms to support and maintain motivation and commitment required for both families and staff along the way. In other words, reflective supervision helps staff, who in turn help families—not only to keep going, but also to feel good about the progress they are accomplishing together.

WHY REFLECTIVE SUPERVISION?

One way to answer a *why* question is to ask the counter question, *why not?* Or, what happens without reflective supervision? The result of inadequate (or no) supervision "may not be starvation but rather failure to thrive. Responsible staff can get by, but they won't grow" (Fenichel & Eggbeer, 1992, p. 22). Whereas many agencies do manage without reflective supervision, adding reflective supervision to your program allows your program to function more smoothly and in turn enhances the services your agency provides. As one of our program partner's director put it, "I cannot believe I thought scheduling time would be the biggest problem . . . now I speed to the phone because I value that one hour so much." Without reflective supervision, staff members describe a sense of chaos or panic within their agency and describe themselves as floundering or feeling insecure with regard to their work—sometimes to the point of looking for another job (Fenichel & Eggbeer, 1992).

Reflective supervision allows practitioners to "debrief experiences, develop skills in clinical reasoning and identify best practices" (Tanner, as cited in Beam, O'Brien, & Neal, 2010, p. 137). In addition, it has been argued that reflective supervision can help reduce staff turnover, burnout, and secondary trauma (Beam et al. 2010; Costa, 2005; Gilkerson & Cochran, 2005). Numerous processes that occur during reflective supervision help providers and interventionists draw insights and acquire knowledge that can enhance the effectiveness of their work with a client. Several of these processes are briefly described in this section.

Relationships that Support Learning

Relationships are a central part of human existence. It has been well documented in studies of infant–caregiver attachment that children who have a secure relationship with their mother and/or father are more comfortable exploring the world, more trusting of the world, and have a more positive developmental trajectory (including cognitive, social, and emotional domains) than children who do not experience secure caregiver relationships (see Thompson, 2008, for a comprehensive review). Research has also demonstrated that children who have positive relationships with their early childhood teacher(s) exhibit a more positive developmental trajectory compared with children who do not experience high-quality relationships (Birch & Ladd, 1997; Buyse, Verschueren, Doumen, Van Damme, & Maes, 2008; Howes, Matheson, & Hamilton, 1994; Howes & Smith, 1995; Pianta, Nimetz, & Bennet, 1997). It is within the context of these relationships that children feel safe enough to engage in the exploration of their physical and cognitive worlds that fuels optimal growth and development.

Early childhood interventionists recognize the importance of larger social context as well as the powerful influence of immediate relationships on child and adult development. One of the main pathways through which the early childhood professional intervenes is that of relationships. Relationship-based, preventive intervention includes a focus on the importance of parent–child interaction, recognition that the staff–family relationship influences the caregiver–child relationship (as a parallel process), and the intervention-ist's intentional use of self as an instrument of positive change (Heffron, 2000). The field recognizes that one relationship influences multiple relationships; therefore, when an interventionist focuses on a single relationship, he or she simultaneously influences re-lationships at several levels (Emde, 2001; Heffron, 2000; Weston, Ivins, Heffron, & Sweet, 1997).

The following example illustrates how even one relationship (among the many that are part of an early education center) can influence the center's social climate and the greater educational and therapeutic environment, and how reflective supervision can work to support the health of that relationship and, consequently, the health of the program.

Sarah had been a mental health consultant to child care centers for several years. Her program's model focused on enhancing teacher capacity in supporting children's healthy social–emotional development and working with children exhibiting challeng-ing behaviors. She had been consulting at 1-2-3 Childcare for a couple of months. The center was owned by Ann and directed by her daughter Jane. Ann also owned a second center where she was the director. Although Ann had a great deal of confi-dence in her daughter's abilities to direct, she was also very attached to the center. 1-2-3 Childcare was Ann's first center and she saw it as her "baby." Ann would often stop by to visit the teachers and staff and make "helpful" suggestions ranging from how to set up a classroom to managing parents to policy issues. Often this was done when Jane was not present. Jane saw this behavior as undermining her authority and as a sign that her mother really did not believe in Jane's abilities to direct the center. Jane and Ann were estranged for a period of time, prior to Jane taking over the cen-ter. Their relationship was still tenuous; the two misinterpreted each other's motives yet would not discuss with each other these interpretations or any of their other rela-tionship issues. The stress in their relationship affected the entire center, including preventing them from focusing their energy and time on improving the quality of the classroom interactions.

In her role as mental health consultant to the center, Sarah recognized that until Jane and Ann addressed some of their relationship issues, the center would have limited success in increasing its level of quality. Due to the positive relationship she had established with Jane and Ann, Sarah was able to share her observations with both of them. A short while after Sarah and Ann had shared their observations, Ann attended a staff meeting and told her staff,

> I realize that my visits here may not have been in the best interest of the center. I know the center is in good hands with my daughter as the director and I have complete confidence in her. I plan to continue my visits here, as you all and this center are important parts of my life and I enjoy coming here. However, I will be here in the role of visitor only, not administrator. Any comments, questions, or issues you have must go through Jane.

Later that day, when Sarah was meeting with Jane and her staff, they discussed Ann's comments. One teacher looked at Jane and said, "It is as if you were both doing double duty. We had two directors. Now we only have one. It will make things much better here now."

PAYING ATTENTION TO AFFECT

Relationships depend upon feelings, and feelings drive action.

—T. NORMAN-MURCH (2005, P. 310)

Affect, consisting of a person's thoughts, feelings, and emotions, is a critical part of learning and development. Affect helps people to organize, classify, and give meaning to our world. We often respond to our affect before consciously and deliberatively considering a situation. For example, think of a person walking into a new and unfamiliar place, entering and smelling freshly baked bread (or another comfort food from childhood). Often that smell alone brings back positive memories, and the person responds by relaxing and feeling comfortable in this new setting. This can occur so instantaneously that the person may not even be aware of it. Using an affective response to judge a situation can serve as a survival mechanism. Taking the time to think about a situation at a cognitive level may mean injury or death, whereas processing a situation as dangerous at an affective level happens more quickly and, to some degree, unconsciously. As another example, think of a person walking down a dark, quiet street. Automatically that person becomes more alert and wary, perhaps even reaching into a pocket or purse for keys so as to be able to enter his or her car or house more quickly, guarding the person's safety.

In those situations when people respond to their affect at an unconscious level, they may be behaving or evaluating a situation in a way that is counterproductive. One example a colleague of mine, Gerry Costa, uses is that of going on a home visit. Picture yourself having had a long and stressful day. You have one final home visit before you can go home. This is a visit you have been putting off, as it is with a client who has been resistant to your attempts to build rapport. In addition, the neighborhood is not the safest of places. You park and slowly walk up to the door. You hear loud music coming from the building. You knock, but there is no response. Then you knock again, but not as vigorously, while thinking to yourself (somewhat hopefully) that perhaps no one is home. No answer, so you sigh and also begin to feel more hopeful that no one is home—even though the loud music would indicate otherwise. You tap on the door one final time. With no answer, you turn and briskly walk back to your car and call it a day.

How did you feel walking up the walkway? How did you feel at the second knock? What about as you were returning to your car? How do you think your affect would have impacted the session if the client had answered the door? Do you think your affective response is something other home visitors have felt before?

Reflective supervision allows providers not only to process these kinds of questions in a safe, calm environment, but also to consider ways to improve or adapt a situation and move forward with a client or case in a way that serves the best interests of the child and family. By attending to our own emotional state before going into a situation with a client, and monitoring shifts in our emotional state while with a client, we are able to become aware of how those affective states may be impacting the situation. Acknowledging and discussing our feelings during reflective supervision sessions does not mean that we have to disclose them to the client or even act upon them. Reflective supervision allows us to pay attention to our feelings and use them in ways that can benefit the client.

REFLECTIVE SUPERVISION SUPPORTS USE OF SELF-REFLECTION AND SELF-AWARENESS

Often, a provider's feelings about a client or the client's situation can be related to his or her own personal history (i.e., experiences, values, and beliefs), current emotional state or stress level (which maybe unrelated to the client's situation), and professional strengths and challenges. Reflective supervision not only allows providers to become more aware of these variables, it also helps them to contemplate and consider how to respond to them in ways that increase professional capacity and competence as a provider. With this increase in competence comes an increase in confidence and satisfaction in our work.

Many professionals in the field of early intervention are nurturers and are drawn to the profession to take care of others—a trait that can be a double-edged sword. Nurturers tend to be fixers. If something is not going right, they jump in and attempt to fix it. Unfortunately, this is not the best way to support many of the populations early interventionists find themselves caring for. As one Early Head Start director would tell her staff, "We do *with* our families, not *to* our families." Providers can easily be drawn into "doing for" a

---

Box 11.1.   B.E.T.H.

B.E.T.H. is a strategy used to help individuals examine their own affect and responses in the moment they occur. This four-step approach stems directly from cognitive therapy. It is a technique that enables the management of one's own emotions in stressful situations so that one can respond appropriately rather than impulsively.

One way to introduce the strategy to non-mental-health professionals is, "B.E.T.H. is a great friend to have when things get stressful. If you practice calling on her, she will start appearing in your thoughts more and more automatically with time."

B.	**B**elly breath:	Take a slow, deep abdominal breath.
E.	**E**motions:	Take a look at your emotions by asking, *What am I feeling right now?*
T.	**T**houghts:	Take a look at your thoughts by asking, *What negative thoughts am I having right now?*
H.	**H**elpful response:	Ask yourself, *What is a more helpful response?*

From Feldman, D. (1999). *The handbook of emotionally intelligent leadership: Inspiring others to achieve results.* Paonia, CO: Leadership Solutions Press; adapted by permission.

family, especially when a young child is involved. This often prevents the family from gaining needed skills and a corresponding sense of self-empowerment. Reflective supervision allows providers to slow down, take a breath, and think about why they are responding the way there are, and how (or whether) the response merely decreases the immediate discomfort one feels in the face of a problem or if it benefits the client in the long term. It also allows the provider to consider alternative actions and how clients may receive those actions.

One area of professional competence that can be enhanced through self-reflection is that of cultural competence. It is through the ongoing process of enhanced self-awareness focused in reflective supervision that an interventionist gains insight into how she or he perceives and responds to clients from diverse cultural backgrounds. Addressing one's own—often unconscious—biases or preconceived notions, especially in the area of cultural diversity, can be especially challenging. Often our cultural biases are so ingrained, we are unaware of their existence. Furthermore, we may struggle to acknowledge them, because it is considered socially unacceptable to judge anyone based on their race, ethnicity, social or economic background, or abilities. Thus there are often many defensive walls that must be removed in order to allow an honest examination of this area. Reflective supervision provides the opportunity to create a safe environment where this kind of self-examination can be supported and used to enhance the capacity to work with families. One approach that can be used to examine cultural perceptions is cultural auditing.

Cultural auditing is a process that allows an interventionist to examine his or her actions and thoughts in regard to a client's culture and cultural identity and then take steps to optimize his or her effectiveness when working with clients of differing cultural backgrounds (Collins, Arthur, & Wong-Wylie, 2010). Collins and colleagues (2010) presented a 13-step cultural auditing model to guide self-reflection. The detailed probes and questions include reflection on the influence of culture in

- Establishing initial rapport: What are my initial reactions to this client? How might gender dynamics and differences between my client and me in age, sexual orientation, ethnicity, or range of ability affect this relationship?

- Potential influences of broader social, economic, and political systems on the client's presenting concern: How might the client's presenting problems be affected by family, cultural subgroup, community, and larger social systems? How do the specific experiences of racism, sexism, heterosexism, ageism, ableism, and other forms of oppression affect the client's view of self and others?

- Links between the client's experience and the provider's continued competency development: What feedback has the client provided about the working alliance, the intervention process, and the outcomes of intervention? What attitudes, knowledge, and skills might I need to develop to work more effectively with a similar client in the future?

REFLECTIVE SUPERVISION FACILITATES
PROBLEM SOLVING AND ENHANCES PERSPECTIVE TAKING

Reflective supervision also provides a venue for individuals to contemplate various responses to situations or client needs. Reflective supervision provides individuals with the opportunity to slow down and sort through various options that facilitate problem solving. For individuals new to the field, having an invested and experienced individual (a reflective supervisor) to ask helpful and focused questions, or to wonder aloud about different responses, is an indispensable part of reflective supervision.

For some individuals, especially those with limited exposure to situations (e.g., college, training in mental health) that require critical thinking skills, the ability to take others' perspectives, resolve conflict, or work toward shared decision making can be an area of challenge. For those acquiring these new skills, individual supervision can be intimidating, and it may be advisable to have group supervision wherein less skilled individuals can be exposed to the problem-solving process by observing colleagues who are more skilled at critical thinking. Group supervision is also helpful to individuals new to the field when more experienced individuals also make up a part of the group. This allows the less experienced colleagues to benefit from the other group members' experiences, as illustrated by the following example.

Tanya had just started working as a mental health consultant to early education programs. She had been a clinician in private practice for several years and was just returning to the work force after taking off a couple of years to work as a stay-at-home mom. Tanya had a caseload of six centers and had been working in the centers for about 1 month, visiting each center every other week. She had begun to feel frustrated, because she felt like she was not making any progress in her centers. Tanya participated in a monthly group conference call with three other consultants (John, Meredith, and Erin). During one group call, John, one of the more experienced consultants, asked Tanya how it was going. Tanya replied hesitantly, "Okay, I guess."

John: Oh?

Tanya: Well the centers seem to like me and glad to have me there.

John: Uh-huh, and . . .

Tanya: It is just that I feel like I am not doing anything. I mean, don't get me wrong, I love going to the centers and hanging out with the staff and children. But I feel like I am just hanging out and not working.

Meredith: Oh, I remember that feeling! I was so worried in the beginning. Believe me, you are doing something. You are building trust! Without that, the staff will not confide in you, and you will make little progress.

Tanya: That is what my reflective supervisor said, but I thought she was just being nice. [Group members laugh.]

Erin: It takes time, but before you know it, they will be coming to you with all kinds of questions and issues. Or you will sense when you can push a little more and ask questions or make suggestions. You just need to trust the process a bit.

Tanya: Wow, that makes me feel better. I thought I was doing something wrong! Oh, and I have another question . . .

THREE KEY PRINCIPLES OF REFLECTIVE SUPERVISION

There are three major elements that are central to the success of reflective supervision: reflection, collaboration, and regularity (Fenichel, 1992). The first term, *reflection,* speaks to the process or purpose of the session, as described in the definitions of *reflection* listed at the start of this chapter. In brief, reflection involves taking the time to wonder what an experience, interaction, or event really means, and what it tells one about the client and about oneself. (Although reflection does involve exploring experiences, feelings, and thoughts directly connected with one's work, and managing stress related to work, reflection is *not* therapy and should not be treated as such. When reflective supervision begins to focus primarily on a supervisee's life events, struggles, or negative emotions—and not simply on how those things affect the supervisee's work—the supervisee should be referred to a clinician or therapist.) Reflection allows us to use our thoughts and feelings to identify the response that best meets the family's needs for self-sufficiency, growth, and development.

The second term, *collaboration,* speaks to the tone of the supervisory relationship. In a reflective supervisory relationship, the supervisor and supervisee partner in a joint dialogue. A joint, collaborative dialogue is one that consists of open, two-way conversation. In addition, to be productive a collaborative dialogue must be characterized by trust and safety (i.e., issues can be discussed confidentially and without fear of judgment or ridicule). Collaboration within reflective supervision involves genuine curiosity and active listening, especially on the part of the supervisor. For a reflective supervisory relationship to be truly collaborative, the supervisee and supervisor must share responsibility and control of power. However, this does not exempt the supervisor from setting limits or exercising authority when necessary. (See Bertacchi & Gilkerson, 2009, for a discussion on managing the role of reflective and administrative supervision within a reflective supervision model.)

Regularity stresses the need for continuous support in order to maintain and enhance personal relationships and also the important resulting insights and skills. Regularity means scheduling reflective supervision sessions on a reliable schedule for a sufficient amount of time. In addition, the time should be protected from interruption, cancellation, rescheduling, or procrastination. It is vital for a supervisee to know when he or she will be meeting with the supervisor. This allows the supervisee to prepare for the meeting, for example, by reviewing his or her cases and deciding which one(s) to discuss. Sessions are more productive when the supervisor is aware of the case over time and the supervisee does not feel rushed or pressured to give information because it is not clear when he or she will be able to speak with the supervisor again. Although impromptu, informal reflective supervision sessions can be helpful; they should take place in addition to, and never replace, regularly scheduled reflective supervision meetings.

Active Listening

Active listening involves not only hearing what is said; it involves understanding another person's perspective. This is typically accomplished through *empathic inquiry,* supportive questioning that results in a mutual understanding of another's thoughts, feelings, and motives (Boris & Grabert, 2009). There are four elements of active listening that accomplish empathic inquiry: inviting dialogue, promoting shared understanding, discovering feelings, and moving the dialogue forward (Grabert, 2009).

The first element, *inviting dialogue,* encourages a supervisee to tell his or her story. The best way to invite dialogue is to ask single, open-ended questions and allow time for the supervisee to respond fully. It is important to avoid questions that lead to simple yes or no answers or brief responses.

Once the supervisee has had an opportunity to fully share his or her story, the next step is to *promote shared understanding*. Here paraphrasing is a good strategy for checking understanding and providing the supervisee opportunities to offer corrective information or clarification. In some instances, asking close-ended questions related to key issues, as well as to content the supervisee has shared during the session, is another good strategy. Promoting understanding is important, because it helps the supervisee recognize that the supervisor not only is interested in what he or she has to say, but also wants to be sure to understand the supervisee's perspective.

The third element, *discovering feelings,* acknowledges the importance of affect. Here the supervisor must be attuned to what is said as well as what is *not* said. The supervisor not only needs to acknowledge feelings readily expressed by the supervisee, but also needs to identify feelings that are not readily or easily expressed. A supervisee's affect may be communicated in body language, tone, or even by what is left unsaid. Reflecting back is one technique that can be used to help identify affect and create an opening to discuss those feelings and their impact on the intervention. For example, a supervisor could say, "You look puzzled by my response . . ." or "You have not said it, but I am wondering if it could be that you are nervous about . . ." or "Wow, it sounds like everyone is getting frustrated with. . . ." As stated earlier in this chapter, affect helps us to organize, classify, and give meaning to our world. We often respond to our affect before consciously and deliberatively considering a situation. Thus, first identifying affect, both our own and the client's, then considering its impact, is necessary to the success of any intervention. It is important to make certain that the supervisee understands that affect alone is neither good nor bad. Rather, it is what one does in response to that affect, consciously or unconsciously, that can positively or negatively impact the outcome of an intervention or the building of a relationship.

The final element of active listening is to *move the dialogue forward*. This allows for a sense of closure and also helps to keep the dialogue focused on the topic at hand. Moving dialogue forward involves summarizing and synthesizing information discussed and, in some cases, prioritizing issues or concerns. In this phase (which in actuality may occur at times throughout a reflective supervision session), it is important to allow space for the supervisee to provide clarification or corrective information. It is especially important that the supervisee is allowed the opportunity to decide the next course of action, if any, in regards to the intervention, client, or issue being discussed. It is important that this phase continues to be a dialogue between partners and not an administrative session in which the supervisor dictates to the supervisee. One strategy to support this is to phrase summaries in a manner that provides a supervisee the opportunity to disagree with or expand upon the supervisor's statements. For example, "So what it sounds like you are saying is. . . . Do you agree?" or "Hmm, so my understanding is. . . . Is that what you were thinking?"

Reflection, collaboration, regularity, and active listening are essential components of reflective supervision and reflective practice. However, it is important to remember that they are not sufficient in themselves to create an environment that supports professional growth and excellence through reflective practice.

Supervisor Experience and Training

The person in your program providing reflective supervision should have training and/or experience in the field of mental health and, if possible, infant mental health. Further, he or she should have training and/or experience in providing reflective supervision. Unfortunately, few early education and intervention programs specifically train their staff to provide reflective supervision. Rather, because the majority of infant mental health training programs use reflective supervision to train their interns, it is more likely that trainees or interns experience reflective supervision first-hand while receiving supervision. This being said, it is unlikely that an intervention program will have someone with the ideal qualifications to provide reflective supervision. In response to this limitation, many organizations using reflective supervision have gotten creative in developing a reflective supervision program that is both doable and useful. For example, some programs hire an outside consultant with the necessary qualifications, have the consultant train staff within the organization to provide reflective supervision, then provide reflective supervision to these newly trained individuals as they, in turn, begin providing reflective supervision to staff.

We have learned that reflective supervision is one of the most important tools a program may use to support staff members as they acquire the knowledge and skills necessary to implement relationship-based infant mental health services. As we have noted, supervisors must themselves possess some knowledge about infant mental health in order to practice reflective supervision. After all, supervisors must be able to recognize and understand what they observe in order to help others develop these same skills.

When programs first take on the complex task of incorporating infant mental health services, however, they typically have few if any staff members—at any organizational level—with the knowledge and skills necessary to implement services. Therefore, as my colleagues and I learned in our research with Early Head Start and early intervention program partners, mental health consultants need to think and work with programs in broader terms so that they may be successful in training and supporting supervisors to implement reflective supervision.

For example, one mental health consultant told my colleagues and me that the foundation for her work in consulting and in training supervisors was highly dependent on program administration. According to this consultant (who also served as an infant mental health mentor), program administrators must introduce the topics of infant mental health and reflective supervision to staff "in very positive ways" and administration must be consistent in offering necessary supports for a change in practice—administrators need to go beyond "just saying the words" and "walk the walk."

In addition, mental health consultants told us that, just as relationship-based work gives staff members the strength to face difficult situations, positive relationships are equally important for mental health consultants working to institute program change. When administrative support was absent or inadequate, infant mental health consultants became discouraged and found it difficult to muster the fortitude to persevere in helping to make fundamental program changes.

Mental health consultants talked about ways, once they had administrative support, to create a learning environment that indirectly supports reflective supervision. As noted earlier, reflective supervision in infant mental health programs requires that staff have content and clinical knowledge about infant mental health. Therefore, mental health consultants, in addition to providing direct training on reflective supervision, worked to promote general understanding and competence among all staff by addressing other content and skill areas. In terms of a general approach to promoting learning, consultants believed it was of the utmost importance that they could form and model good relationships themselves and that they had the willingness and ability to listen to others in order to learn what was important to them, and not make assumptions based solely on the consultant's own notions or the organization's agenda.

Further, mental health consultants identified the following strategies as helpful in creating an environment that was supportive of reflective supervision:

- Promote general knowledge and competence among intervention and supervisory staff in the area of infant mental health by locating and advocating for professional training opportunities.

- Bolster individual staff knowledge and skills by providing on-site training in key areas identified by individual interventionists and supervisors, such as skillful observation of parent–child interactions, recognizing professional boundaries, or parent–infant attachment.

- Create a resource center of books, newsletters, web sites, and information about infant mental health to which all staff has easy access.

- "Feed staff" by periodically sending out personal notes or making positive statements that recognize particularly good work a staff member has done in the area of infant mental health.

- Promote supervisor buy-in by showing them first-hand how reflective supervision can help them improve their professional skills and have a positive effect on their supervisees, and in turn, on families. Consultants describe this as a process of teaching and modeling, but much more feeling- and relationship-based and really going into things in more depth. This involves observing and reflecting as part of the reflective process, then observing and reflecting again upon the reflective process itself.

- Provide continued support to supervisors as they come to feel truly comfortable with reflective and supportive processes. Without this, mental health consultants tell us, supervisors will not move from providing regular case supervision to reflective supervision.

In each of these activities, the consultant, through his or her relationships with supervisors, home visitors, and administrators, is serving as a model of professionalism and a resource for information and support as program staff members become proficient. After all, a supervisor will need not only the specific training and skills to provide skillful reflective supervision, he or she will also need colleagues in the program who recognize the value of reflective supervision and who are willing and able to engage in it and support it. In other words, it is important to see reflective supervision in context, as an inseparable part of the greater complex of infant mental health services. See Table 11.2 for information on further readings about reflective supervision.

Table 11.2.   Readings on reflective supervision

Reflective supervision and practice in early intervention programs: Using a reflective supervision model in different settings

Costa, G. (2006). Mental health principles, practices, strategies, and dynamics pertinent to early intervention practitioners. In G.M. Foley & J.D. Hochman (Eds.), *Mental health in early intervention: Achieving unity in principles and practice* (pp. 113–138). Baltimore: Paul H. Brookes Publishing Co.	In this chapter, the author discusses integrating infant mental health into early intervention programs. Reflective practice (including reflective supervision) and relationship-based intervention are emphasized as two key concepts integral to infant mental health work.
Gilkerson, L. (2004). Irving B. Harris Distinguished Lecture. Reflective supervision in infant-family programs: Adding clinical process to nonclinical settings. *Infant Mental Health Journal, 25*(5) 424–439.	Implementation of reflective process in two settings: neonatal intensive care unit and early intervention program. Provides a brief description of reflective supervision and its usefulness in nonclinical settings that serve very young children. A brief outline and description of different parts of a reflective supervision session are provided.
Gilkerson, L., and Taylor, T. (2005). The role of reflective process in infusing relationship-based practice into an early intervention system. In K.M. Finello (Ed.), *The handbook of training and practice in infant and preschool mental health* (pp. 427–452). San Francisco: Jossey-Bass.	This chapter focuses on Illinois's statewide pilot of a relationship-based model for promoting social-emotional development in early intervention programs. Survey data collected from managers, service coordinators, and specialists on the impact of reflective supervision is presented.
Norman-Murch, T. (2005). Keeping our balance on a slippery slope: Training and supporting infant/family specialists within an organizational context. *Infants & Young Children, 18*(4), 308–322.	This article focuses on the ongoing implementation of reflective practice in a large nonprofit human services agency. Reflective leadership and supervision are briefly defined and described. The core reflective practice training content used for management as well as staff is outlined. Strategies for incorporating reflective practice throughout the organization from supervision to staffing meetings are presented.

Reflective supervision books: How-to guides

Fenichel, E. (1992). *Learning through supervision and mentorship to support the development of infants and toddlers and their families: A sourcebook.* Washington, DC: ZERO TO THREE Press.	This collection of 18 articles, also referred to as the "yellow book," was developed by a National Center for Clinical Infant Programs task force of leaders in the infant mental health field. This sourcebook was developed "to improve understanding of supervision and mentorship as crucial elements in the training of practitioners who work to support the development of infants, toddlers and their families" (Fenichel, p. 5).
Heffron, M.C., and Murch, T. (2010). *Reflective supervision and leadership in infant and early childhood programs.* Washington, DC: ZERO TO THREE Press.	This book was created to assist program leaders in incorporating reflective practice and reflective supervision into their programs. The book strives to provide information to support reflective practice in a wide variety of early intervention settings.
Heller, S.S., and Gilkerson, L. (2009). *A practical guide to reflective supervision.* Washington, DC: ZERO TO THREE Press.	This book was created to help program leaders and supervisors gain a better understanding of the purpose of reflective supervision as well as the nuts and bolts of providing reflective supervision.

(continued)

Table 11.2.   *(continued)*

Parlakian collection

Parlakian, R. (2001). *Look, listen, and learn: Reflective supervision and relationship-based work.* Washington, DC: ZERO TO THREE Press.

Parlakian, R., and Seibel, M.L. (2001). *Being in charge: Reflective leadership in infant/family programs.* Washington, DC: ZERO TO THREE Press.

Parlakian, R. (Ed.). (2002). *Reflective supervision in practice: Stories from the field.* Washington, DC: ZERO TO THREE Press.

This collection of resource books guides the reader through important aspects of reflective supervision. In *Look, Listen, and Learn*, the usefulness of reflective supervision in early intervention settings as well as implementation steps are provided. Parlakian's second book, *Being in Charge*, focuses on issues related to being a reflective program leader, such as how to encourage collegial work and how to learn from conflict. In the third book, *Reflective Supervision in Practice*, four infant–family programs that have implemented reflective supervision are highlighted. Key elements of the transition and the outcomes experienced are discussed. Tools designed to present reflective supervision to staff members are also presented.

CONCLUSION

In order to implement a successful reflective supervision program within an organization, it is important that time is committed to planning the implementation process and timeline. Gauging the organization's level of readiness and awareness or understanding of reflective practices and supervision is an important first step. For example, does the administration understand and support the implementation of reflective supervision? Is the administration willing to commit resources to reflective supervision? What is the staff's level of understanding about reflective supervision? Also, what are the staff's fears or concerns about reflective supervision? (To learn more about how organizations can support staff in their work and how to foster professional partnerships, see Chapters 13 and 14.)

In addition, decisions about how often reflective supervision should occur, who should participate, and whether it should it be mandatory need to be made. Heller and Gilkerson's *A Practical Guide to Reflective Supervision* (2009) provides valuable information on what to consider and how to implement a reflective supervision program (see Boris & Grabert, 2009; Heller, 2009) as well as information on how to lead reflective supervision meetings and handle issues such as relationship ruptures and managing the dual roles of reflective and administrative supervisor. The key in implementing reflective supervision within early childhood and intervention programs is to honor the main tenets of reflective practice: that is, to ensure that all parties are able to openly express their hopes and concerns regarding reflective supervision and its implementation, to ensure that they will be actively heard, and to trust that they can effect positive change within the organization.

REFERENCES

Beam, R.J., O'Brien, R.A., & Neal, M. (2010). Reflective practice enhances public health nurse implementation of nurse-family partnership. *Public Health Nursing, 27*(2), 131–139.

Bertacchi, J., & Gilkerson, L. (2009). How can administrative and reflective supervision be combined? In S.S. Heller & L. Gilkerson (Eds.), *A practical guide to reflective supervision* (pp. 25–40). Washington, DC: ZERO TO THREE Press.

Birch, S.H., & Ladd, G.W. (1997). The teacher-child relationship and children's early school adjustment. *Journal of School Psychology, 35*(1), 61–97.

Boris, N.W., & Grabert, J. (2009). How do I introduce reflective supervision to my program? In S. Heller & L. Gilkerson (Eds.), *A practical guide to reflective supervision* (pp. 41–62). Washington, DC: ZERO TO THREE Press.

Buyse, E., Verschueren, K., Doumen, S., Van Damme, J., & Maes, F. (2008). Classroom problem behavior and teacher-child relationships in kindergarten: The moderating role of classroom climate. *Journal of School Psychology, 46*, 367–391.

Collins, S., Arthur, N., & Wong-Wylie, G. (2010). Enhancing reflective practice in multicultural counseling through cultural auditing. *Journal of Counseling and Development, 88*(3), 340–347.

Costa, G. (1999). *Practices in reflective supervision.* Unpublished handout, Youth Consultation Services Institute for Infant and Preschool Mental Health.

Costa, G. (2005). *Reflective practices. Training resources.* Unpublished handout, Youth Consultation Services.

Costa, G. (Ed.). (2006). Mental health principles, practices, strategies, and dynamics pertinent to early intervention practitioners. In G.M. Foley & J.D. Hochman (Eds.), *Mental health in early intervention: Achieving unity in principles and practice* (pp. 113–138). Baltimore: Paul H. Brookes Publishing Co.

Emde, R. (2001 April/May). From neurons to neighborhoods: Implications for training. *ZERO TO THREE, 21,* 30–34.

Feldman, D. (1999). *The handbook of emotionally intelligent leadership: Inspiring others to achieve results.* Paonia, CO: Leadership Solutions Press.

Fenichel, E. (1992). *Learning through supervision and mentorship to support the development of infants and toddlers and their families: A sourcebook.* Washington, DC: ZERO TO THREE Press.

Fenichel, E., & Eggbeer, L. (1992). Overcoming obstacles to reflective supervision and mentorship. In E.S. Fenichel (Ed.), *Learning through supervision and mentorship to support the development of infants and toddlers and their families: A sourcebook* (pp 18–26). Washington, DC: ZERO TO THREE Press.

Gilkerson, L. (2004). Irving B. Harris Distinguished Lecture: Reflective supervision in infant family programs: Adding clinical process to nonclincial settings. *Infant Mental Health Journal, 25*(5), 424–439.

Gilkerson, L., & Cochran, C.K. (2005). Relationship based systems change: Illinois' model for promoting social-emotional development in Part C early intervention. *Infants & Young Children, 18*(4), 349–365.

Gilkerson, L., & Shahmoon-Shanok, R. (2000). Relationship for growth: Cultivating reflective practice in infant, toddler and preschool programs. In J. Osofsky & H. Fitzgerald (Eds.), *WAIMH Handbook of IMH: Volume 2. Early intervention, evaluation and assessment* (pp 33–79). New York: Wiley.

Gilkerson, L., & Taylor, T. (2005). The role of reflective process in infusing relationship-based practice into an early intervention system. In K.M. Finello (Ed.), *The handbook of training and practice in infant and preschool mental health* (pp. 427–452). San Francisco: Jossey-Bass.

Grabert, J. (2009). Intergrating early childhood mental health into early intervention services. *Zero to Three, 29*(6), 13–17.

Heffron, M.C. (2000). Clarifying concepts of infant mental health: Promotion, relationship-based preventive intervention, and treatment. *Infants & Young Children, 12*(4), 14–21.

Heffron, M.C., & Murch, T. (2010). *Reflective supervision and leadership in infant and early childhood programs.* Washington, DC: ZERO TO THREE Press.

Heller, S.S. (2009). How do I develop an implementation plan to begin reflective supervision in my program? In S.S. Heller & L. Gilkerson (Eds.), *A practical guide to reflective supervision* (pp. 25–40). Washington, DC: ZERO TO THREE Press.

Heller, S.S., & Gilkerson, L. (2009). *A practical guide to reflective supervision.* Washington, DC: ZERO TO THREE Press.

Heller, S.S., Jazefowicz, F., Redmond, R., & Weinstock, J. (2004). Starting where the program is: Three infant mental health consultants discuss reflective practice. *Zero to Three, 24*(6), 10–19.

Howes, C., Matheson, C.C., & Hamilton, C.E. (1994). Maternal, teacher, and child care history correlates of children's relationships with peers. *Child Development*, 65(1), 264–273.

Howes, C. & Smith, E.W. (1995). Relations among child care quality, teacher behavior, children's play
activities, emotional security, and cognitive activity in child care. *Early Childhood Research Quarterly*, 10(4), 381–404.

Norman-Murch, T. (2005). Keeping our balance on a slippery slope: Training and supporting infant/
family specialists within an organizational context. *Infants & Young Children*, 18(4), 308–322.

Parlakian, R. (2001). *Look, listen, and learn: Reflective supervision and relationship-based work.* Washington, DC: ZERO TO THREE Press.

Parlakian, R. (Ed.). (2002). *Reflective supervision in practice: Stories from the field.* Washington, DC:
ZERO TO THREE Press.

Parlakian, R., & Seibel, M.L. (2001). *Being in charge: Reflective leadership in infant/family programs.*
Washington, DC: ZERO TO THREE Press.

Pawl, J. (2000). The interpersonal center of the work we do. *Zero to Three, 20,* 5–7.

Pawl, J., & St. John, M. (1998). *How you are is as important as what you do in making a difference in
infants, toddlers and families.* Washington, DC: ZERO TO THREE: National Center for Infants Toddlers and Families.

Pawl, J.H., St. John, M., & Pekarsky, J.H. (1999). Training mental health and other professionals in
infant mental health: Conversations with trainees. In J. Osofsky & H. Fitzgerald (Eds.), *WAIMH handbook on infant mental health: Vol. 2. Early intervention, evaluation, and assessment* (pp. 379–402).
New York: John Wiley.

Pianta, R.C., Nimetz, S.L., & Bennet, E. (1997). Mother–child relationships, teacher–child relationships,
and school outcomes in preschool and kindergarten. *Early Childhood Research Quarterly, 12*(3),
263–280.

Schon, D.A. (1987). *Educating the reflective practitioner: Toward a new design for teaching and learning
in the professions.* San Francisco: Jossey-Bass.

Tanner, C.A. (2006). Thinking like a nurse: A research-based model of clinical judgment in nursing.
Journal of Nursing Education, 45(6), 204–211.

Thompson, R.A., (2008). Early attachment and later development: Familiar questions, new answers. In
J. Cassidy & P.R. Shaver (Eds.), *Handbook of attachment: Theory, research, and clinical applications*
(2nd ed., pp. 348–365). New York: Guilford Press.

Tremmel, R. (1993). Zen and the art of reflective practice in teacher education. *Havard Educational
Review, 63*(1), 434–458.

Weston, D. (2005). Training in infant mental health: Educating the reflective practitioner. *Infants &
Young Children, 18*(4), 337–348.

Weston, D.R., Ivins, B., Heffron, M., & Sweet, N. (1997). Formulating the centrality of relationships in
early intervention: An organizational perspective. *Infants & Young Children, 9,* 1–12.

12

Meeting the Mental Health Needs of Staff

Nicole Denmark and Brenda Jones Harden

Through our collective experience as teaching and home visiting staff in early childhood programs, we have become convinced of the value of focusing explicitly on staff mental health. We have observed teachers and home visitors struggle mightily to maintain their commitment and passion to providing young children and parents with the highest quality service they are capable of providing, while trying to cope with the challenges of working with families and organizations bereft of resources. In this chapter, we explore mental health issues that early childhood staff may present, and offer strategies for addressing these issues within their programs.

Two assumptions guide our discussion of mental health issues among program staff. The first relates to the notion of parallel process. *Parallel process* holds that the nurturance of young children is best achieved in a context in which their caregivers (parents, teachers, home visitors) are nurtured as well (Saul & Jones Harden, 2009). Staff members, like parents, need support to be able to reflect on their own feelings and behaviors and thus improve their work with families. The second assumption is that challenges in working with the high-risk children and families who are targeted by early childhood programs can compromise the mental health of program staff over time, especially in the absence of social and organizational supports (Figley, 1995).

Supporting mental health among early childhood staff is crucial to quality service delivery and the promotion of infant mental health. Qualities of center-based staff that support infant mental health, such as the ability to engage infants in sensitive interactions and the ability to create a warm classroom emotional climate, appear to be dampened by depression, chronic stress, and burnout (Gerber, Whitebook, & Weinstein, 2007; Hamre & Pianta, 2004; Hamre, Pianta, Downer, & Mashborn, 2007). Characteristics of home visitors deemed essential to engaging program participants, such as conscientiousness

Table 12.1.   Research on staff mental health needs in relation to service delivery

Mental health needs	Relevance to early childhood staff	Links to service delivery
Stress	Lack of clinical skills to help families cited as stressor; low wages for staff create financial stress; organizational challenges (e.g., overwhelming responsibility, low autonomy) create job stress	Job stress linked with expulsion of children from child care; higher wages linked with greater sensitivity in child care; lower caseloads linked with client engagement in home visiting
Depression	Early childhood staff have higher rates of depression than adults in other occupations	Depression linked with less sensitivity and responsiveness in caregivers; home visitor negative emotionality linked with less engagement of families
Trauma	Staff working with children and families who have experienced traumas may develop secondary traumatic stress; current stressors, past trauma, and coping skills affect how staff react to trauma	Secondary traumatic stress may lead to preoccupation, anxiety, and avoidance of families
Burnout	Emotional exhaustion and compassion fatigue from prolonged periods of stress	Burnout linked with less sensitivity in child care; burnout linked with less personal accomplishment in occupations in general
Physical effects of mental health issues	Short-term stress linked with greater susceptibility to illness; long-term stress linked with decreased cardiovascular health and early onset of age-related diseases	Illness and compromised health linked with absenteeism, lower job competence, and turnover

(Brookes, Summers, Thornburg, Ispa, & Lane, 2006), empathy (Wasik & Roberts, 1994), and clinical skill (LeCroy & Whitaker, 2005), may be masked by trauma and stress experienced on the job.

This chapter begins with a brief discussion of the importance of staff mental health for service delivery, and challenges to staff mental health in early childhood programs. Next, we describe specific mental health issues for early childhood staff, such as depression and trauma. We draw on research and our own experiences in partnerships with Early Head Start programs. Finally, we turn to strategies that can be used to minimize stressors and support the mental health of early childhood staff. A summary of the research is displayed in Table 12.1.

MENTAL HEALTH NEEDS AND CHALLENGES IN EARLY CHILDHOOD PROGRAMS

Work with high-risk families and their children can be stressful for early childhood educators and home visitors. Families may be dealing with multiple risk factors associated with poverty, and unfortunately, program staff is often ill-prepared to address these problems. In addition, economic realities and organizational challenges can be sources of personal stress for program staff. The following are some potential stressors for staff in early childhood programs.

- *Program staff often do not have the skills to address clinical problems of families and their infants.* Although home visiting staff typically report that they have received training on mental health needs of high-risk families, they also suggest they need more training on the skills and concrete steps needed to help families (Tandon, Mercer, Saylor, & Duggan, 2008). When interviewed, home visitors across multiple programs express a lack of confidence in their abilities to address clinical issues with families—such as lack of knowledge of how to begin these conversations and how to balance addressing these issues and helping families with more basic needs (Altman, 2008; LeCroy & Whitaker, 2005; Tandon et al., 2008). For a home visitor, feeling ineffective in addressing difficult family issues may be a chronic stressor. Center-based staff may receive even less training on addressing family risks and may feel less skilled in interacting with vulnerable parents experiencing difficult life circumstances. Further, it is likely that both center-based staff and home visitors serve children with disabilities or mental health problems. For example, over 20% of children in Early Head Start programs were referred for evaluation for special learning or physical or emotional needs (U.S. Department of Health and Human Services [DHHS], 2006). Particularly in center-based programs, teachers need special skills to meet the needs of these children as well as skills to balance this attention with attention paid to other children in the classroom (Howes & Ritchie, 2002). Such situations can be major stressors to early childhood education staff. (For further discussion of skills and knowledge relevant to working with high-risk populations, see Chapters 4 and 5.)

- *Success is not easily defined.* The promotion of mental health in infants and their families is a slow process within which "success" is hard to define (Chamberlain, 2008). The teacher who slowly works to form a trusting relationship with a child who has been maltreated may find that progress is slow, that there may be periods of "regression," and that the child may graduate to a different classroom before a healthy attachment relationship has been built (Howes & Ritchie, 2002). The home visitor may recognize postpartum depression and help a mother seek mental health services, but the mother may not follow through with these services (Jones Harden, Denmark, & Saul, 2010). Without definitions for job success or accomplishment, it may be easy for teachers and home visitors working with high-risk families to experience prolonged stress and a decreasing sense of self-efficacy over time (Chamberlain, 2008).

- *Program staff may receive low wages.* Compounding the stressors of the actual work with families and children, other factors related to their employment can create daily stress for child care staff and home visitors. National surveys have shown that child care and home visiting personnel receive near-poverty-level wages (Phillips, Howes, & Whitebook, 1991). In 2003, the median hourly wage for a lead teacher or pre-K teacher was $9.53 an hour (Brandon & Martinez-Beck, 2005). In 2007, home visitors in a typical Early Head Start program made $11.16 an hour (Gill, Greenberg, Moon, & Margraf, 2007). In many situations, then, early education staff may suffer from chronic financial insecurity, just like the families they serve.

- *Organizational demands create chronic stress.* Although varying from program to program, organizational settings within early childhood programs can create stress and hinder a personal sense of accomplishment. Home visitors often have excessive caseloads (Daro, McCurdy, Falconnier, & Stojanovic, 2003). Both center-based teachers and home visitors have an overwhelming amount of daily paperwork, with little time on the job to complete it. Organizations may place excessive demands on staff, while their staff lacks a sense of personal control over these tasks (Jones Harden, Denmark, & Saul, 2010). In many programs, major policy changes or new program partnerships are formed at the management level, with staff then responsible for "buying in" to the changes or collaborating with new partners (DHHS, 2006; Gill, Greenberg, & Vasquez, 2002). Working overtime hours, facing excessive demands, and feeling a lack of job control can lead to increased work stress and decreased job satisfaction (Jones, Flynn, & Kelloway, 1995) and ultimately burnout (Gill et al., 2002).

MENTAL HEALTH ISSUES
AMONG EARLY CHILDHOOD STAFF

Early childhood staff—especially those in intimate relationships with family members, such as home visitors—are not immune to the challenging circumstances that children and families experience. Some early childhood programs are purposely situated in high-risk neighborhoods and communities where they can be of most benefit to children and families. Just as exposure to noise, poverty, violence, and homelessness affects children and families, it also presents practical and emotional challenges to early childhood educators. Vulnerability to depression, exposure to trauma, increased burnout, and negative physical effects may be increased among staff in early childhood education and intervention programs.

Depression

Depressive disorders are mood disorders with combinations of symptoms that can impair an individual's ability to work, sleep, eat, and enjoy activities. Depression can often result from periods of prolonged stress and or traumatic life events (National Institute of Mental Health, 2007). Compared with full-time female workers in other categories of occupations, early childhood staff have the second-highest rates of experiencing a major depressive episode annually (13.3%), second only to females working in the food preparation and service industries (Substance and Mental Health Services Administration, 2007). A national survey of child care workers found that about 9.4% reported clinical levels of depressive symptoms (Hamre & Pianta, 2004). In addition, high levels of depressive symptoms and lower self-efficacy have been noted as contributing to more conflict in relationships among early childhood teachers and their students (Hamre et al., 2007). Further, teachers' emotional stability, hardiness, self-efficacy, and coping are vital personality traits related to their success in the classroom (Van Horn, Schaufeli, & Enzmann, 1999).

Although the literature is scant on the mental health of family support providers, surveys of home visitors have documented high rates of reported clinically significant levels of depressive symptoms (DHHS, 2006; Gill et al., 2007). Gill et al. (2007) found that Early Head Start home visitors reported increasing levels of emotional exhaustion over time, and about a fifth endorsed depressive symptoms above the clinical cutoff.

These high rates are alarming, given that depressive disorders can affect the ability to perform even basic duties, let alone the capacity to engage in the intense work of teaching or home visiting. Without treatment, early childhood staff suffering from depression are unlikely to be able to nurture the mental health of children or participating clients under their care. Signs of depression among early childhood staff may include the following:

- Decreased sensitivity and warmth with children, families, and co-workers
- Increased irritability with children, families, and coworkers
- A reduction in planning and follow-through
- Self-deprecating statements about oneself and one's work
- Problems making decisions
- Decreased empathetic responses to families' problems
- Reports of inability to sleep, or arriving to work late due to oversleeping
- Missing work
- Reports of persistent aches and pains

Trauma

Early childhood staff members who work with low-income families may be at greater risk for experiencing trauma than other early childhood professionals or workers in other occupations. Direct trauma can occur from witnessing a sudden, unexpected, and overwhelming event. Reactions to trauma include feelings of helplessness; anxiety; anger; occurrence of bad memories and dreams; and trouble with basic functioning such as sleeping, eating, and paying attention (Centers for Disease Control and Prevention, 2009). Trauma can also occur from prolonged exposure to stressful events. Early childhood staff may experience traumas such as being threatened, experiencing violence, and experiencing disasters or accidents with children under their care. Such trauma can occur in the classroom or on home visits.

Early childhood staff is also vulnerable to the experience of *secondary traumatic stress*. This stress emanates from exposure to traumatic work stressors such as interadult violence, child maltreatment, premature death, acute and chronic physical and mental illness, and poverty (DHHS, 2006; Lieberman & Van Horn, 2008). Home visitors' intense and intimate work with families who experience trauma may lead to the internalization of these experiences and trauma symptoms for staff themselves (Figley, 1995). The symptoms of secondary traumatic stress include reexperiencing clients' trauma, persistent arousal (or increase in emotional states) due to knowledge of clients' trauma, and attempts to avoid clients or reminders of clients' trauma. The experience of secondary traumatic stress can lead to emotional exhaustion, *compassion fatigue*—a decrease in feelings of empathy and compassion for families, at times accompanied by increased physical and emotional exhaustion (Figley, 1995)—and, ultimately, burnout (discussed in the next subsection).

Early childhood staff's reaction to trauma and/or their development of secondary traumatic stress will depend on their own histories of coping with stressful events as well as the current degree of stress in their home and work environments. With healthy coping mechanisms, social support, and a healthy lifestyle that prevents excessive stress, staff are likely to recover from trauma and to avoid experiencing secondary trauma (American Psychological Association, 2009). However, for many other staff members, trauma and secondary traumatic stress can lead to burnout and depression.

Burnout

One of the hazards of working in human services, such as in early childhood programs, is burnout. *Burnout* is a psychological response to prolonged, demanding interpersonal situations. Burnout is characterized by emotional exhaustion, depersonalization, and reduced personal accomplishment (Figley, 1995). Although understudied among early childhood staff, research with social workers has documented that burnout is more likely among those who work in stressful or unsupportive organizations, those with stressful personal lives, those with unrealistically high expectations, and those with a history of coping problems (Adams, Boscarino, & Figley, 2006).

Employee burnout is a severe problem that can undermine the effectiveness of any early childhood program. In the classroom, teachers experiencing burnout are less sensitive and more withdrawn with children (Phillips, Howes, & Whitebook, 1991). Burnout can also lead to employee turnover, especially among teachers with higher educational levels (Whitebook & Sakai, 2003). It has also been found that, among child welfare social workers, degree of burnout is also associated with job exit (DePanfilis & Zlotnik, 2008).

Turnover is notoriously high in early childhood programs. One national study documented that approximately half of the child care teaching force leaves every year (Phillips et al., 1991). The turnover rate for Early Head Start programs is notably lower but still high—20% annually for center-based staff and 24% for home visitors (DHHS, 2006). Occasional turnover may not be disruptive to the overall organization and families served. However, turnover often begets more turnover. When multiple employees leave, the remaining staff may be asked to take over their duties. This can increase stress and have a ripple effect on morale and mental health across the program.

Physical Effects of Mental Health Issues

In addition to impairing cognitive, emotional, and behavioral functioning, mental health problems affect staff physically and can lead to long-term health problems. Physical symptoms of stress or other mental health problems include the following (American Psychological Association, 2008):

- Headaches, muscle tension, neck or back pain
- Upset stomach
- Dry mouth
- Chest pains, rapid heartbeat
- Jitters
- Difficulty falling or staying asleep
- Fatigue

- Loss of appetite or overeating "comfort foods"
- Increased frequency of colds

Prolonged periods of stress can wreak havoc on the physical health of early childhood staff. Behaviors associated with stress, such as erratic eating and too little exercise, combined with the body's "fight or flight" response to stress, can lead to cardiovascular problems, increase the rate of aging and onset of age-related diseases (e.g., arthritis, cancers), and complicate the body's ability to recover from illness (American Psychological Association, 2008). These physical conditions affect an individual's quality of life. Furthermore, these physical ailments are related to service delivery. Across occupations, stress-related illness can lead to absenteeism, inability to perform job duties, and turnover (Schat, Kelloway, Kevin, & Desmarais, 2005).

STRATEGIES FOR PROMOTING THE MENTAL HEALTH OF STAFF

The psychological well-being of early childhood staff is integral to the promotion of infant mental health. We have seen that early childhood staff serving high-risk families may experience mental health problems such as personal and professional stress, depression, trauma, burnout, and physical effects of mental health problems. Challenges inherent in working with high-risk families, as well as organizational stressors, can leave staff vulnerable to such mental health problems.

Reflective supervision is a key strategy for fostering the psychological well-being of early childhood interventionists (see Chapter 11 of this volume). Through the reflective supervision process, supervisors can scaffold, or structure, staff members' learning in ways that support their learning to intervene in new and effective ways. In the privacy and safety offered through reflective supervision, staff members also receive emotional support and have the opportunity to reflect on the joys and challenges of their work. Beyond supervision, there are other mechanisms that may be utilized for promoting the mental health of early childhood staff—the "nurturing the nurturer" activities that can ward against staff stress and burnout. Brief descriptions of some of these strategies follow.

- *Workshops on stress management and self-care:* Staff development activities should include training on how to manage stress, such as meditation and coping techniques. There should be ongoing training on how to care for self, including setting limits, focusing on self-goals, taking time out to meet one's own needs, self-knowledge regarding stress levels, and giving psychological gifts to oneself (e.g., learning an avocation for restoration or enjoyment, or engaging in nonservice activities).

- *Activities for physical exercise and psychological healing:* On-the-job activities that promote physical and psychological well-being send important messages to staff about the importance of maintaining a healthy lifestyle. Examples of physical activities include lunchtime exercise groups, walks or runs for causes relevant to program participants, and healthy eating and exercising campaigns and competitions among staff. Activities explicitly directed to mental health might include self-help book clubs, lunchtime films about characters who engage in psychological healing, and "mental exercise" groups that focus on problem solving, goal setting, and self-care.

- *Mental health consultants:* Just as mental health consultants should be available for facilitating psychological services for children and families, they should be available for addressing staff concerns and experiences that could affect their work. The consultants could conduct staff mental health training, implement self-care groups, and individually meet with staff as necessary. There should be established mechanisms for referring staff to external mental health services if necessary. Obviously, staff mental health intervention has to be treated with the strictest confidentiality.

- *Safety protocols:* Programs that adhere to safety protocols show acknowledgment of the risks staff face and their worth to the program. Programs should establish protocols for managing crisis situations that may be unsafe for staff and families, such as when children or parents become out of control or violent. All classrooms should have in-house telephones and emergency buttons. For home visitors, there should be a system for knowing where staff are, accompanying home visitors to new families, and assigning teams to work in more dangerous communities and with more difficult families. Technological aids, such as cell phones and global positioning systems, go a long way to facilitating staff achievement of home visits but also provide a mechanism to ensure staff safety.

- *"Mental health days":* Creating a mechanism to provide staff with time off from the stress of direct work with children and families sends them a message about the importance of self-care and the willingness of the organization to promote their health. This can be accomplished through a formal leave policy or routine staff development days that focus on their mental health. In-house reflection meetings, visits to other programs, paperwork days, or self-care activities allow staff to perform work functions while being relieved from the stress of direct work with program participants.

- *Peer support:* Early childhood programs often underutilize this very important facet of staff support and development. Formal and informal mechanisms of peer support can be established in myriad ways, such as weekly conferences on children and families; staff buddies who can be consulted for questions regarding how to intervene with children and families as well as agency employment processes; staff clubs that may focus on physical exercise, books and films, psychological health, or shared interests; and staff cooperatives in which resources are shared.

- *Concrete staff validation:* Acknowledging staff effort and sharing examples of their expertise in supervision during staff meetings, in newsletters, and to funders demonstrates to staff that what they do is valued. It is often helpful to have a journal or box where staff can document their own or their peers' accomplishments, which can be compiled in an organizational record that is accessible to staff. In addition, an annual celebration should be held that has a singular goal of sharing staff achievement in a public forum and providing them with concrete rewards, such as certificates or prizes, for their service.

- *Retreats:* Programs should conduct periodic "retreats" in which staff have the opportunity to reflect on the work, get recharged, and reconnect with the overarching mission of the program. Ideally, such retreats should occur away from the physical location of the program in a peaceful, comfortable setting that encourages reflection and facilitates self-care. Accomplishments and challenges of the previous service period should be reviewed, with an emphasis on staff ideas and contributions to improving the quality of service to the upcoming service period.

CONCLUSION

Intervention to foster the well-being of infants and their families can only be achieved by staff who are able to execute quality services. The stress and mental health challenges that early childhood staff have been documented to experience can negatively affect their ability to intervene effectively with children and families. Organizational supports for staff psychological well-being are critical for early childhood programs to implement. An emphasis on staff nurturing within ongoing professional development and organizational activities, such as those delineated in this chapter, improves staff morale and staff capacity to deliver effective interventions.

Promoting the mental health of children and families is rooted in the support of the front-line, center-based and home-based staff who serve them. Understanding and addressing staff mental health needs promotes the parallel process that facilitates their responsive intervention with families and children. Based on our experience as practitioners and practice-oriented researchers, our firm belief is that an explicit focus on the psychological well-being of staff propels programs closer to their mission of providing high-quality services to enhance the development of young children and families.

REFERENCES

Adams, R.E., Boscarino, J.A., & Figley, C.R. (2006). Compassion fatigue and psychological stress among social workers: A validation study. *American Journal of Orthopsychiatry, 76*, 103–108.

Altman, J.C. (2008). Engaging families in child welfare services: Worker versus client perspectives. *Child Welfare League of America, 9*, 441–461.

American Psychological Association. (2008). *Listening to the early warning signs of stress.* Retrieved June 15, 2011, from http://apahelpcenter.mediaroom.com/file.php/176/WarningSigns_FINAL.pdf

American Psychological Association. (2009). *Mind/body health: Stress fact sheet.* Retrieved June 15, 2011, from http://www.apa.org/helpcenter/stress.aspx http://apahelpcenter.mediaroom.com/file.php./40/Stress+Fact+Sheet.pdf

Brandon, R.N., & Martinez-Beck, I. (2005). Estimating the size and characteristics of the United States early care and education workforce. In M. Zaslow & I. Martinez-Beck (Eds.), *Critical issues in early childhood professional development* (pp. 49–76). Baltimore: Paul H. Brookes Publishing Co.

Brookes, S., Summers, J., Thornburg, K., Ispa, J., & Lane, V. (2006). Building successful home visitor-mother relationships and reaching program goals in two Early Head Start programs: A qualitative look at contributing factors. *Early Childhood Research Quarterly, 21*, 25–45.

Centers for Disease Control and Prevention. (2009). *Coping with a traumatic event: Information for the public.* Retrieved from http://www.bt.cdc.gov/masscasualties/copingpub.asp

Chamberlain, L. (2008). Ten lessons learned in Alaska: Home visitation and intimate partner violence. *Journal of Emotional Abuse, 8*, 205–216.

Daro, D., McCurdy, K., Falconnier, L., & Stojanovic, D. (2003). Sustaining new parents in home visitation services: Key participant and program factors. *Child Abuse & Neglect, 27*, 1101–1125.

DePanfilis, D., & Zlotnik, J.L. (2008). Retention of front-line staff in child welfare: A systematic review of research. *Children and Youth Services Review, 30*, 995–1008.

Figley, C.R. (1995). Compassion fatigue as secondary traumatic stress disorder: An overview. In C.R. Figley (Ed.). *Compassion fatigue: Coping with secondary traumatic stress disorder in those who treat the traumatized* (pp. 15–28). New York: Brunner-Routledge.

Gerber, E.B., Whitebook, M., & Weinstein, R.S. (2007). At the heart of child care: Predictors of teacher sensitivity in center-based child care. *Early Childhood Research Quarterly, 22*, 327–346.

Gill, S., Greenberg, M.T., Moon, C., & Margraf, P. (2007). Home visitor competence, burnout, support and client engagement. *Journal of Human Behavior in the Social Environment, 15*, 23–44.

Gill, S., Greenberg, M.T., & Vazquez, A. (2002). Changes in the service delivery model and home visitors' job satisfaction and turnover in an Early Head Start Program. *Infant Mental Health Journal, 23,* 182–196.

Hamre, B., & Pianta, R. (2004). Self-reported depression in nonfamilial caregivers: Prevalence and associations with caregiver behavior in child care settings. *Early Childhood Research Quarterly, 19,* 297–318.

Hamre, B., Pianta, R., Downer, J., & Mashburn, A. (2007). Teachers' perception of conflict with young students. *Social Development, 17,* 115–136.

Howes, C., & Ritchie, S. (2002). *A matter of trust: Connecting teachers and learners in the early childhood classroom.* New York: Teachers College Press.

Jones, B., Flynn, D., & Kelloway, E.K. (1995). Perception of support from organization in relation to work stress, satisfaction, and commitment. In S. Sauter & L. Murphy (Eds.), *Organizational risk factors for job stress* (pp. 41–52). Washington, DC: American Psychological Association.

Jones Harden, B., Denmark, N., & Saul, D. (2010). Understanding the needs of staff in Head Start programs: The characteristics, perceptions, and experiences of home visitors. *Children and Youth Service Review, 32,* 371–379.

LeCroy, C., & Whitaker, K. (2005). Improving the quality of home visitation: An exploratory study of difficult situations. *Child Abuse and Neglect, 29,* 1003–1013.

Lieberman, A.F., & Van Horn, P. (2008) *Psychotherapy with infants and young children: Repairing the effects of stress and trauma on early attachment.* New York: Guilford Press.

National Institute of Mental Health. (2007). *Depression.* Retrieved June 15, 2011, from http://www.nimh.nih.gov/health/publications/depression-easy-to-read/depression-trifold.pdf

Phillips, D., Howes, C., & Whitebook, M. (1991). Child care as a work environment. *Journal of Social Issues, 47,* 49–70.

Saul, D., & Jones Harden, B. (2009). Nurturing the nurturer: Caring for caregivers in Head Start programs. *Head Start Bulletin, 80,* 91–93.

Schat, A.C.H., Kelloway, K.E., & Desmarais, S. (2005). The Physical Health Questionnaire (PHQ): Construct validation of a self-report scale of somatic symptoms. *Journal of Occupational Health Psychology, 10,* 363–381.

Substance and Mental Health Services Administration, Office of Applied Studies. (2007, October 11). Depression among adults employed full time by occupation category. *The NSDUH Report.* Retrieved from http://www.oas.samhsa.gov/2k7/depression/occupation.pdf

Tandon, S.D., Mercer, C., Saylor, E., & Duggan, A. (2008). Paraprofessional home visitors' perspectives on addressing poor mental health, substance abuse, and domestic violence: A qualitative study. *Early Childhood Research Quarterly, 23,* 419–428.

U.S. Department of Health and Human Services, Administration for Children and Families. (2006). *Survey of Early Head Start programs 2003–2005.* Washington, DC: Author.

Van Horn, J.E., Schaufeli, W.B., & Enzmann, D. (1999). Teacher burnout and lack of reciprocity. *Journal of Applied Social Psychology, 29,* 91–108.

Wasik, B.H., & Roberts, R.N. (1994). Home visitor characteristics, training, and supervision. *Family Relations, 43,* 336–341.

Whitebook, M., & Sakai, L. (2003). Turnover begets turnover: An examination of job and occupational instability among child care center staff. *Early Childhood Research Quarterly, 18,* 273–293.

13

Organizational Readiness

Jamell White and Brenda Jones Harden

"It takes a village to raise a child." These familiar words refer to the influence exerted by all those people and environments surrounding children as they develop. These ecological influences include those persons closest to an infant—his or her caregivers and family—as well as the people and contexts that directly and indirectly influence the infant's development and well-being, such as schools, neighborhoods, or health care providers. All of these are, in turn, influenced by less visible and tangible contexts, such as program and public policies and the greater economic climate.

For infants and families participating in early childhood and intervention programs, the commitment a program makes to address the needs of the "whole" child and family can make a critical difference in a child's immediate and long-term social-emotional well-being. This commitment is complex and requires that programs focus not only on child development, but also on caregiver mental health and on happy, healthy child–caregiver relationships. Also, this commitment plays out in multiple contexts (e.g., homes, classrooms) and through multiple partnerships (e.g., with families, within programs, with community partners).

It is an overarching assumption of this volume that programs serving infants and toddlers should have a commitment to promoting infant mental health. An infant mental health focus in early childhood programs has been aptly described as

> The promotion of optimal development and well-being in infants (prenatal to age 3) and their families, the prevention of difficulties, and intervention when infants are at-risk or have identified problems. The goal of infant mental health services is to promote positive child outcomes including secure attachments and positive inter-actions with caregivers, social-emotional development, learning and engagement

Box 13.1.   Infant mental health organizational readiness

- Organizations must be committed to addressing the needs of the whole child and family.
- Organizational readiness includes consideration of organization culture, climate, hierarchy, infrastructure, staffing, and commitment to target programs and services.
- Infant mental health programs function best with a relationship-based approach.
- Agency mission and policies need to be clearly defined.
- Qualified staff and ongoing staff training are critical to program success.
- Infant mental health organizations need to prioritize efforts to increase awareness of mental health issues of children and their families.

with their environment. It is a core mission of infant mental health services to involve families and communities in the lifelong development of young children. (Hospital for Sick Children, 2009)

Optimal development and well-being of infants and families can be a tall order for programs working with children and families experiencing multiple and serious risks, such as chronic illness, economic hardship, family or community violence, or caregiver mental health problems. As programs prepare to provide services for infants and their families, it is important that they consider their readiness to take on such a large and important endeavor. Aspects essential to an organization's readiness include its

- Culture
- Climate
- Infrastructure
- Staffing
- Commitment to addressing mental health

This chapter explores how early childhood programs can become ready to provide successful infant mental health services. The existing evidence relevant to each of the essential organizational features is briefly reviewed in the context of early childhood programs with a goal of quality delivery of infant mental health services.

ORGANIZATIONAL CLIMATE AND CULTURE

An organization's collective perspective and level of investment in the service provided is critical in shaping and establishing the success of that program or service. Evidence suggests that the climate and culture of an organization guides the perspectives and experiences of those who form or interact with an organization (Glisson, 2002; Glisson &

James, 2002). Organizational climate and culture are intertwined and, in many ways, difficult to clearly distinguish. Both contribute to the overall environment within a program. Dr. Charles Glisson, an expert in the field of organization and the delivery of social and mental health services to children and families, differentiated climate from culture, stating that "culture captures the way things are done in an organization, and climate captures the way people perceive their work environment" (2007, p. 739). The life of an organization is largely influenced by its social context, which involves both the organizational climate and culture. As Glisson (2002) described, the social context is shaped by factors that determine how members interact and collaborate with one another and with related agencies, interpret and approach their work environment, and feel about their overall job experience. Hence, an organization's social context includes aspects such as social norms, values, behavioral expectations, interpersonal relationships, and individual perceptions and attitudes (Verbeke, Volgering, & Hessels, 1998). Social context, in terms of climate and culture, addresses both qualities of the staff as well as the organization.

Specific to early childhood programs, organizations typically value young children and the mechanisms that have been found to promote their development (e.g., early childhood education centers). Although realization of the value of an infant mental health approach is still nascent in the early childhood field (Zeanah & Zeanah, 2009), the principles of such an approach, such as the importance of caregiver–infant relationships and stability of caregiving, have been emphasized in the field of infant and toddler education (Lally et al., 2003). How organizations build on these principles to deliver infant mental health services is an underexamined phenomenon. Consideration of the literature on organizational climate and culture in other related fields is informative for readying early childhood programs to take on this task.

Organizational climate refers to patterns of behavior and attitudes of employees that characterize the "life" of the agency (Isaksen & Ekvall, 2007). Researchers have made a distinction between the psychological climate and organizational climate in human service agencies (Glisson & James, 2002; James & James, 1989; James & Jones, 1974). With the individual as the unit, *psychological climate* refers to the individual's perception of the impact of the work environment on his psychological well-being (e.g., emotional exhaustion, role conflict). Organizational climate, on the other hand, is thought to be an aggregate of the shared perceptions of individual employees in the same organizational unit. The social context of an organization greatly influences the social climate, especially in the sense of the social relations among the staff (e.g., cooperation, trust).

In an environment of cooperation and trust, early childhood staff are more apt to work as a team, sharing ideas and work demands and providing support. When managers facilitate a warm and welcoming social climate, early childhood staff are likely to share ideas for organizational change and seek the support of supervisors during times of intense work stress. Such a social climate creates a direct and indirect trickle-down effect that can be experienced by the children and families that early childhood programs serve. Directly, early childhood intervention staff are more emotionally available to meet the needs of young children and families as a result of team approaches and support within the agency. Indirectly, when early childhood staff feel a sense of trust and security in their agency, they are likely to present this tone to children and families, increasing the mutual trust in the working relationship and enhancing child and family outcomes.

Organizational culture refers to a belief system or set of norms shared by members or employees of the organization, measured by both behaviors (tangible) and values (intangible) of the individuals. Hofstede described culture as "a characteristic of the organization, not of individuals, but it is manifested in and measured from the verbal and/or nonverbal behaviour of individuals—aggregated to the level of their organizational unit" (1998, p. 479). The culture of an organization tends to produce deeply entrenched values, beliefs, norms, and perspectives about the services provided by the program. Some argue that culture is conveyed and transmitted through behavioral expectations and normative beliefs rather than deeper values (Glisson, 2002; Glisson & James, 2002; Hemmelgarn, Glisson, & Dukes, 2001; Hofstede, 1998). The behavioral conformity seen in an organization's culture might be determined by external job demands (including expectations and norms of organizational leaders) more than the internalizing of organizational values. If an organization's culture reflects the leaders' deeply rooted values and assumptions, it may be difficult to change the culture of an agency short of changing the leadership. Thus, the leadership within an agency is key in passing down the organizational perspective or culture to the newer members of the agency.

The organizational culture of an early childhood program is important, because the behaviors and attitudes that emanate from that culture affect staff's response to young children and their families. It is important to consider early childhood mangers' and staff members' perspectives on and responses to their work environment and the work that they perform (Aarons & Sawitzky, 2006). Questions outside those we typically ask about our work become important, such as what feelings do staff have about the families they serve, the amount and type of duties they have, and even the physical plant of the early childhood program. These questions help us understand features of organizational culture that are critical for early childhood programs: the extent to which the culture is constructive, as exemplified by norms, values, and beliefs that support and encourage staff development and satisfaction (Cooke & Szumal, 2000; Glisson & James, 2002). Such a culture is consistent with the notion of *parallel process*, which holds that relationship experiences are similar across levels of social interaction (Saul & Jones Harden, 2009). In the context of infant mental health, experts suggest that an infant's social-emotional developmental outcomes are contingent upon the caregiving the infant experiences, which is based upon the nurturance his or her parents experience, and in turn is built on how those who intervene with his or her parents are supported (Saul & Jones Harden, 2009). (See Chapter 12 for more about parallel process as part of staff support.)

Organizational culture and climate support the health of programs, staff, and participants. Various studies demonstrate the significance and connection of climate and culture to multiple outcomes, including service quality, staff morale and turnover, and customer satisfaction. For example, findings from a study of organizational climate in child welfare systems, utilizing data from the National Survey of Child and Adolescent Well-Being, suggested that child welfare agencies with more "engaged" environments had workers who reported greater job satisfaction and realized better psychosocial outcomes among the children they served. An engaged environment is one in which staff feel high levels of personal accomplishment in their roles, and in which they feel recognized and personally involved in the service process within their agency or organization (Glisson, 2010). In addition, the Clinical Systems Project study of mental health clinics also found a link between organizational climate and worker attitudes and quality of service (Glisson, 2007).

Early childhood programs can benefit from the lessons of other service systems regarding organizational support for staff and participant well-being. From our vantage point, the evidence points to the importance of establishing open, nurturing, and relationship-based organizations within the early childhood field. In the following sections, we consider these aspects of organizational systems in turn.

Open Organizations

Another important aspect of an organization's culture and climate is whether it is an *open social system*. Such a social system is flexible and encourages new ideas and ways to implement services from all levels of the organizational hierarchy. In an early childhood or intervention program, an open system welcomes input from all people—no matter what job they perform within the program. After all, a person providing transportation to a center-based program may develop a close relationship with caregivers or be aware of the child's state or family circumstances on a given day. To the family, that person may represent the face of the program. An open system values the knowledge the transportation employee possesses and the important role this person plays providing service to a child or family.

An open system is also one that sees the benefit of interacting with other systems or outside entities for the welfare of the child or family. An early education program using an open system would also establish collaborative relations with other organizations. The necessity of open systems for programs providing an infant mental health focus is readily apparent. Developmental specialists for children with identified problems, adult mental health services, and services that address families' global needs for nutrition, housing, or health care are just a few of the collaborations that are important for addressing a child's and family's ecological needs in support of infant mental health.

It is imperative for early childhood and intervention programs to have a pulse on the families and communities they serve. Moreover, programs need to be mindful of the impact the community may have on their decision making for day-to-day program operations, which in turn have real consequences in the day-to-day lives of families and the development of children. An open system perspective honors the mutual influence that the program, outside agencies, the community, and the government exert on one another.

Nurturing Organizations

Support and nurturance for children and their families is the foundation of early childhood education and intervention, and of infant mental health. Also, there is a parallel process of support and nurturing that needs to occur within programs so that personnel are not only competent, but also confident and compassionate in serving these families. Programs have a dual responsibility of being a nurturer to the community as well as their staff (Bernstein, 2002–2003). Just as the families served by such programs are vulnerable to various stressors and risk, so is staff working with those families. Many families in need of community-based programs are those that are exposed to extreme life and societal stressors, such as poverty, trauma, or community violence (Gill, Greenberg, Moon, & Margraf, 2007; Tandon, Parillo, Jenkins, & Dugan, 2005). (See Chapter 5 for more on this topic.) In supporting these families, staff members are faced with the daily challenge of fulfilling their responsibilities within the organization, which entail obtaining resources for children and families that are often limited in availability or not accessible. This can lead staff members to feel ineffective, overwhelmed, and/or "burnt out" (Landy, 2001).

A qualitative study of Early Head Start home visitors revealed critical themes related to the barriers many staff face in working with vulnerable populations (Jones Harden, Denmark, & Saul, 2010). These workers cited concerns including the emotional toll of working with highly stressed families, limited capacity to fulfill programmatic mandates (e.g., addressing the needs of large caseloads of families), and organizational challenges (e.g., accountability for the progress of children and families with limited administrative support). It is imperative for organizations to find ways to support staff, building on their strengths and developing their professional skills, and it is important to evaluate the forces that may hinder this process within an organization. This aspect of professional development is key to the quality of the relationship between the early childhood program staff and participants, and to the child and family outcomes the program is able to achieve. How this aspect of staff development is addressed largely depends on the type of work environment the early childhood program creates; specifically, whether the organization is relationship based.

Relationship-Based Organizations

Some organizations function under an *accountability-based culture*, and as such may be results oriented and less concerned with process than with outcomes. Although appropriate supports, resources, and rewards are provided to the staff in accountability-based organizations, the emphasis is on individual responsibility, and less attention is devoted to the roadblocks and challenges faced by employees in meeting results (Prosen, 2006). In contrast, *relationship-based organizations* stress teamwork among employees. Agencies that adopt a relationship-focused culture and climate have multiple goals in mind. They strive to meet the consumer needs, to engender responsibility for individual employee performance, and to retain employees. Goals are often addressed through effective teamwork and support to the employees. Supports provided to staff include mentoring, training, supervision, and open communication among all members of the program. The process for achieving goals and objectives is explicitly supported and highly valued. In essence, relationship-based programs emphasize a climate of support and nurturance, encouraging staff well-being and emotional health (Koloroutis, 2004).

In reality, the two approaches—accountability and relationships—are not in opposition in successful infant mental health programs. Rather, healthy working relationships with families, colleagues, and partner organizations, and attention to process and continuous quality improvement, are the means to achieving accountability and successfully meeting individual and program goals.

ORGANIZATIONAL INFRASTRUCTURE

Program infrastructure typically entails several domains with various functions. Within the infrastructure are the values, policies, procedures, planning and monitoring of programs, program evaluation, human resources and staff communication, and other infrastructural supports. Each of these areas contributes to the overall functioning of the program and establishes a structure for ensuring congruency between the population served and the support needed for the staff to implement services. The organizational psychology literature informs us of the importance of a stable, flexible organizational system with effective leadership and clear lines of authority for the achievement of organizational goals and objectives (Drafke, 2009). This is particularly essential in human service and early childhood programs, in which the customers, the process, and the product each rely upon the actions and intentions of human beings.

An important feature of the organizational infrastructure is the organizational hierarchy. This refers to the structure of an organization, often represented by a chart listing positions and levels of responsibility and authority, typically used for the purpose of accountability and internal control. Hierarchies within organizations are intended to provide a clear chain of command, indicate how staff members are supported and supervised at every level, and assist in explaining and managing the complexity of an agency. Many early childhood programs find themselves managing multiple offices across numerous geographic locations, which may have different community needs that require a unique approach relevant to that particular region. When a program has an established system for accountability and internal control (e.g., assigned roles and responsibilities, periodic review of cases and outcomes), that program can more easily and effectively meet the complex and diverse needs of its children and families.

In order for early childhood education and intervention programs to carry out their missions, staff must be provided with the necessary structure and resources to effectively implement their jobs. This requires, first and foremost, a climate of transparency around the organizational mission and policies. Employees must have a clear understanding of 1) organizational boundaries regarding staff roles and responsibilities, levels of leadership, and lines of authority; 2) staff management approaches; and 3) human resource policies. All of this information should be documented and accessible through written materials such as current employee manuals, handbooks, and organizational charts. Managerial staff should continuously address interstaff roles and relationships. Likewise, staff should regularly be petitioned for feedback and input into human resource policy development.

Communication between and among various levels of management and staff is vital to the functioning of programs. Similarly, communication and two-way feedback between families and staff promotes an atmosphere of mutual support that extends beyond the organization into the community. Effective communication and transparency begins with the hiring of staff. Well-defined and detailed job descriptions need to be created for each position. As program needs and goals change, these job descriptions should be reviewed and updated. Feedback from staff about their current job roles and responsibilities needs to be elicited in order for these descriptions to accurately reflect the duties of those hired to carry out the agency's mission. Specific to programs that focus on infant mental health, it is vital that staff be hired who can work from a relationship-based perspective with children and families. (See the next section, Staff Knowledge and Qualifications, for more on staff background and skills.)

As noted earlier, organizational infrastructure includes having the necessary resources, financial and concrete, for staff to provide quality care to families. The provision of resources to staff is of utmost importance as they seek to obtain community resources for families devoid of those means themselves. There are often competing goals at play for early childhood intervention programs. Not only must they contend for fiscal resources to sustain program viability, but they are also charged to be comprehensive in their approach with families, which often requires drawing from the same (often inadequate) resources. Nonetheless, it is critical to provide staff with as many tools as possible, some of which can be low cost, to make their work more doable. Core resources for staff include

- Guides that describe explicitly how to engage and intervene with children and families from high-risk backgrounds

- Protocols regarding how to handle high-risk situations (e.g., child maltreatment, parent suicidal ideation, intimate partner violence)

- Lists of community resources for children and families

- A system for prioritizing and monitoring referrals to collaborating agencies in the community

These materials should serve as reference guides and should not replace the ongoing supervision and mentoring that needs to occur for staff working with vulnerable populations.

STAFF KNOWLEDGE AND QUALIFICATIONS

The provision of early childhood intervention services involves the participation of a team of professionals from a variety of disciplines, including social work, nursing, early childhood education, speech and language pathology, occupational therapy, psychology, and other related medical fields. Personnel vary widely in their education, professional focus, and work experience. Regardless of staff educational background, there are certain personal traits and professional qualifications that staff in infant mental health oriented programs should possess. For example, in one national survey relative to home visiting staff, program administrators identified the following characteristics as important for their home visitors to possess: positive work behaviors, helper characteristics such as empathy and flexibility, and knowledge of community resources (Wasik & Roberts, 1994). Other research has highlighted home visitors' ability to develop positive helping relationships with families as key to program engagement (Korfmacher, Green, Spellmann, & Thornburg, 2007). Staff mental health is also important for program quality and effectiveness. (See Chapter 12 for information on ways to support staff mental health needs.)

Beyond the staff's personal attributes and professional experience, it is essential that staff receive ongoing specialized training as society transforms, family needs change, and practices within their discipline modernize. Moreover, infant mental health is a complex and comprehensive field that serves families dealing with multiple risk factors such as psychiatric conditions, substance abuse, family violence, child maltreatment, poverty, and childhood disabilities. The effectiveness of service delivery depends on staff's knowledge of these factors and their potential impact on the infant's developmental trajectory. Training is, perhaps, even more critical for paraprofessional staff who have ongoing, face-to-face contact with families. Without this training, many practitioners in the infant mental health field may lack the skills and knowledge needed to work effectively with high-risk families. For example, Tandon et al. (2005) reported that, although more than half of their sample of mothers participating in home visiting programs were in need of mental health, domestic violence, or substance abuse services, only about a quarter of them received those services. The authors attributed this disparity between what mothers needed and what they received to a lack of staff training and support in ways to effectively address family risk.

Infant mental health cuts across multiple developmental domains, especially social, emotional, cognitive, and language development, and thus requires several layers of knowledge. An understanding of developmentally appropriate practice, however, is foundational (Copple & Bredekamp, 2009). Much of the focus of early childhood education has been on physical and cognitive developmental outcomes. Less attention has been paid to the social-emotional development of children. However, there is growing interest and acknowledgement of the importance of the mental health of the infant child. With an eye toward future child outcomes, policymakers are encouraging definitions of school readiness that incorporate social, emotional, and cognitive health (Johnson & Knitzer, 2005). This commitment to addressing social-emotional development in young children and the complex needs of families requires programs to provide ongoing, focused training for early childhood educators and home visitors. The importance of this commitment to training is supported by recent research describing the lack of preparation among preservice and practicing teachers for managing children who present social-emotional challenges (Hemmeter, Santos, & Ostrosky, 2008).

Early childhood staff training should include more than occasional didactic sessions on discrete topics. One important component of staff training is *reflective supervision*, which has been described as supervision that is regularly occurring, supportive and collaborative, fostering of open discussion of substantive issues and emotions related to service provision and challenges faced in one's work, and encouraging of ongoing goal setting (Landy, 2003; Levkoe, 2002–2003; Moher, 2002–2003). Reflective supervision provides guidance to help staff move beyond didactic information to practice, while supporting them during the process. (See Chapter 11 in this text.)

Shadowing is another mechanism for training and mentoring early childhood classroom teachers, family support workers, or home visitors. Shadowing allows for new staff to observe situations and ask questions that they may not have had prior to their work experience or that they would have been intimidated to ask of management. Shadowing can also occur in reverse so that the novice is observed performing his or her duties, otherwise known as *in-vivo training*. Observation holds much merit for novice early childhood staff, given the immediate feedback that can be provided. Through this mutual feedback loop, staff members learn to enhance their work with children and families, and mentors or supervisors directly observe how staff members apply what they have learned in training sessions to their actual work. Another useful strategy to support new and seasoned staff is *coaching*, in which supervisors offer concrete guidance to practitioners through joint review of videotaped intervention sessions, or when services are implemented. Ideally, supervisors or trainers should provide scaffolding (i.e., thoughtful structure and support) to new staff to allow them to gradually assume new professional roles in addition to offering more intensive practice reflection. Training for all staff needs to be flexible in addressing the myriad issues that emerge in the work with young children and families. Training topics need to thoroughly cover the salient areas for early childhood professionals, including working with children with behavioral problems or other mental health challenges, children with physical and/or cognitive disabilities, children and families who do not speak English, mothers who are depressed or have other mental health needs, and families affected by violence or substance use. In addition, programs may employ staff who do not have experiential background in all areas related to infant and family services. Early childhood educators may need more support in their interaction with parents, and family support providers may need more training regarding young child development.

ORGANIZATIONAL COMMITMENT TO ADDRESSING MENTAL HEALTH

Another feature of organizational readiness for an infant mental health approach is its commitment to meeting the full scope of children's and family's needs, including their mental health, as well as its commitment to addressing the mental health needs of program staff. A program's perspective implicitly and explicitly guides how it allocates resources to its staff to provide services. Critical questions to be considered are the following:

1. Is the program ready to fully incorporate certain services necessary to address infant, family, and staff mental health?

2. Is the program ready and willing to modify existing and incorporate new processes, while involving other disciplines and stakeholders to meet this community need?

Although the field of infant mental health is burgeoning, there has been some resistance from early education and intervention programs to adopt a mental health focus. Some of the opposition has been due to a misconception about what mental health services would entail. Early Head Start and Head Start programs' recent venture into this practice may help to dispel some of these myths. First-hand experience in programs serves as a reminder that providing mental health services is not the sole responsibility of mental health professionals. In fact, relatively few families experiencing mental health problems actually receive needed services, due to personal reticence in obtaining them, limited access to services, and shortages in the number of trained personnel. Nor is it the sole responsibility of early childhood educators who traditionally have been trained to promote child development in a more child-focused way. Rather, research in Early Head Start and early intervention programs has demonstrated that every professional can learn skills to support families' mental health needs within that professional's area of expertise and professional boundaries.

Further, infant mental health services through Early Head Start have included a variety of intervention strategies that can aid in promoting the positive mental health for families, advocacy, parent training and guidance, supportive counseling, as well as the more specialized services of infant and parent psychotherapy (Beeber et al., 2007). Moreover, programs can employ a mental health service provider as a staff person or consultant who can facilitate the quality delivery of mental health services within the early childhood program.

A commitment to mental health will affect the content and process of training and supervision that early childhood staff receives, and specifically will emphasize the mental health issues that challenge children and families. The theory of change (i.e., the specific goals and the mechanisms by which these goals are achieved) of programs with a commitment to mental health would include services and interventions designed to promote optimal social-emotional functioning in children and families. Also, as previously stated, programs with a mental health focus would also devote attention to the mental health of staff.

Family Connections, a preventive intervention project, is an example of one such approach designed to address the training needs of Head Start staff as well as the mental health needs of families (Beardslee, Ayoub, Watson Avery, Watts, & O'Carroll, 2010). This 4-year project targeted low-income families dealing with a multitude of life stressors. Program staff members were provided intensive training and consultation in supporting children and their parents, many of whom were dealing with depression. Essential components of the staff training were 1) reflective practice, 2) psychoeducation about depression and related disorders, 3) team building and increasing the engagement of parents, 4) social-emotional development in young children, 5) self-care of program staff, and 6) strengthening service provision (including home-based strategies, community information and referral services, and parent workshops and groups). At the end of this intervention project, a number of positive outcomes were noted. For example, staff reported feeling more prepared to meet the needs of families, there was a considerable reduction in staff sick days (suggesting an increase in work satisfaction), and there was an improvement in parent involvement.

Although early childhood program budgets are limited, mental health intervention needs to be a priority line item in budget planning. Activity-based budgeting is one way of ensuring that funds are appropriated to key programs. Seeking out financial support from local, state, and federal government is also critical for implementing these services. Establishing collaborations with community or university-based early childhood and mental health service professionals may result in funded grants that are designed to increase the quantity and quality of early childhood mental health intervention. In addition, utilizing other funding streams (e.g., Medicaid for mental health services) may allow programs to deliver such services without cutting into limited general program funds. Moreover, the leadership of an early childhood program, including its managerial staff and governing boards, must elevate early childhood mental health intervention to a place of primacy in the organization's mission.

CONCLUSION

The overarching premise of this volume is that high-quality programs that serve young children and their families must have an infant mental health focus. Early childhood programs must exhibit organizational readiness to provide infant mental health services. This readiness is contingent upon the culture and climate of the organization; specifically, whether it reflects a relationship-based, open, and nurturing system. The infrastructure of the organization must be solid, transparent, and supportive of the most important organizational assets—early childhood staff. Finally, there must be a commitment to addressing mental health issues that is reflected in the organization's mission, goals, services, and resource allocation. Only with stable, sound, and supportive organizations can the goal of the infant mental health field be achieved—to promote the social-emotional well-being of infants and families.

Box 13.2. Resources for infant mental health organizational readiness

Resources from Early Childhood Learning and Knowledge Center, Office of Head Start

Website address: http://eclkc.ohs.acf.hhs.gov

1. *Developing a Plan for Identifying Local Needs and Resources:* To find this resource, go to http://eclkc.ohs.acf.hhs.gov
   - Go to *Training and Technical Assistance System* tab
   - Under *Management and Administration*, click on *Community Assessment*
2. *How Do We Support Services for Infants and Toddlers in a Birth-to-Five Program?*
3. *Advantages/Considerations of the Three Budget Types:* To find these resources, go to http://eclkc.ohs.acf.hhs.gov
   - Go to *Training and Technical Assistance System* tab
   - Under *Management & Administration*, click on *Planning*
4. *Pathways to Prevention: A Comprehensive Guide for Supporting Infant and Toddler Mental Health:* To find this resource, go to http://eclkc.ohs.acf.hhs.gov/hslc/resources
   - Under *Head Start Publications*

REFERENCES

Aarons, G.A., & Sawitzky, A.C. (2006). Organizational climate partially mediates the effect of culture on work attitudes and staff turnover in mental health services. *Administration and Policy in Mental Health and Mental Health Services Research, 33*(3), 289–301.

Beardslee, W.R., Ayoub, C., Watson Avery, M., Watts, C.L., & O'Carroll, K.L. (2010). Family Connections: An approach for strengthening early care systems in facing depression and adversity. *American Journal of Orthopsychiatry, 80*(4), 482–495.

Beeber, L.S., Chazan-Cohen, R., Squires, J., Harden, B., Boris, N.W., Heller, S.S., et al. (2007). The Early Promotion and Intervention Research Consortium (E-PIRC): Five approaches to improving infant/toddler mental health in Early Head Start. *Infant Mental Health Journal, 28*(2), 130–150.

Bernstein, V. (2002–2003, Winter). Standing firm against the forces of risk: Supporting home visiting and early intervention workers through reflective supervision. *IMPrint, 35*, 7–12.

Cooke, R.A., & Szumal, J.L. (2000). Using the organizational culture inventory to understand the operating cultures of organizations. In N.M. Ashanasy, C.P.M. Wilderom, & M.F. Peterson (Eds.), *Handbook of organizational culture and climate* (pp. 147–162). Thousand Oaks, CA: Sage.

Copple, C., & Bredekamp, S. (2009). *Developmentally appropriate practice in early childhood programs serving children from birth to age 8* (3rd ed.). Washington, DC: National Association for the Education of Young Children.

Drafke, M. (2009). *The human side of organizations* (10th ed.). Englewood Cliffs, NJ: Prentice Hall.

Gill, S., Greenberg, M., Moon, C., & Margraf, P. (2007). Home visitor competence, burnout, support, and client engagement. *Journal of Human Behavior in the Social Environment, 15*(1), 23–44.

Glisson, C. (2002). The organizational context of children's mental health services. *Clinical Child & Family Psychology Review, 5,* 233–253.

Glisson, C. (2007). Assessing and changing organizational culture and climate for effective services. *Research on Social Work Practice, 17*(6), 736–747.

Glisson, C. (2010). Organizational climate, job satisfaction, and service outcomes in child welfare agencies. In M.B Webb, K. Dowd, B. Jones Harden, J. Landsverk, & M. Testa (Eds.), *Child welfare and child well-being* (pp. 378–406). Oxford: Oxford University Press.

Glisson, C., & James, L.R. (2002). The cross-level effects of culture and climate in human service teams. *Journal of Organizational Behavior, 23,* 767–794.

Hemmelgarn, A.L., Glisson, C., & Dukes, D. (2001). Emergency room culture and the emotional support component of family-centered care. *Children's Health Care, 30*(2), 93–110

Hemmeter, M., Santos, R., & Ostrosky, M.M. (2008). Preparing early childhood educators to address young children's social-emotional development and challenging behavior: A survey of higher education programs in nine states. *Journal of Early Intervention, 30*(4), 321–340.

Hofstede, G. (1998). Attitudes, values and organizational culture: Disentangling the concepts. *Organization Studies, 19*(3), 477–493.

Hospital for Sick Children. (2009). *Infant mental health promotion: Organizational policies and practices.* Retrieved November 20, 2009, from http://www.sickkids.ca/IMP/Resources/IMP%20documents/index.html#OrganizationalPoliciesPractices

Isaksen, S.G., & Ekvall, G. (2007). *Assessing the context for change: A technical manual for the Situational Outlook Questionnaire.* Orchard Park, NY: The Creative Problem Solving Group.

James, L.A., & James, L.R. (1989). Integrating work environment perceptions: Explorations into the measurement of meaning. *Journal of Applied Psychology, 74,* 739–751.

James, L.R., & Jones, A.P. (1974). Organizational climate: A review of theory and research. *Psychological Bulletin, 81,* 1096–1112.

Johnson, K., & Knitzer, J. (2005). *Spending smarter: A funding guide for policymakers and advocates to promote social and emotional health and school readiness.* New York: Columbia University, Mailman School of Public Health, National Center for Children in Poverty.

Jones Harden, B., Denmark, N., & Saul, D. (2010). Understanding the needs of staff in Head Start programs: The characteristics, perceptions, and experiences of home visitors. *Children and Youth Services Review, 32*(3), 371–379.

Koloroutis, M. (2004). *Relationship-based care: A model for transforming practice.* Minneapolis, MN: Creative Health Care Management.

Korfmacher, J., Green, B., Spellmann, M., & Thornburg, K. (2007). The helping relationship and program participation in early childhood home visiting. *Infant Mental Health Journal, 28*(5), 459–480.

Lally, J.R., Griffin, A., Fenichel, E., et al. (2003). *Caring for infants and toddlers in groups: Developmentally appropriate practice.* Washington, DC: ZERO TO THREE Press.

Landy, S. (2001, Winter). Fulfilling the promise of early intervention. *IMPrint, 32,* 2–6.

Landy, S. (2003, Spring). Reflective supervision. *IMPrint, 36,* 6–7.

Levkoe, J. (2002–2003, Winter). A practical approach to reflective practice in early childhood education. *IMPrint, 35,* 12–14.

Moher, C. (2002–2003, Winter). Putting reflective practice into practice: One program's experience. *IMPrint, 35,* 15–16.

Prosen, B. (2006). *Kiss theory good bye: Five proven ways to get extraordinary results in any company.* Dallas, TX: Gold Pen Publishing.

Saul, D., & Jones Harden, B. (2009). Nurturing the nurturer: Caring for caregivers in Head Start programs. *Head Start Bulletin, 80,* 91–93.

Tandon, S., Parillo, K., Jenkins, C., & Duggan, A. (2005). Formative evaluation of home visitors' role in addressing poor mental health, domestic violence, and substance abuse among low-income pregnant and parenting women. *Maternal and Child Health Journal, 9*(3), 273–283.

Verbeke, W., Volgering, M., & Hessels, M. (1998). Exploring the conceptual expansion within the field of organizational behavior: Organizational climate and organizational culture. *Journal of Management Studies, 35,* 303–329.

Wasik, B.H., & Roberts, R.N. (1994). Home visitor characteristics, training, and supervision: Results from a national survey. *Family Relations: An Interdisciplinary Journal of Applied Family Studies*, *43*(3), 336–241.

Zeanah, C., & Zeanah, P. (2009). The scope of infant mental health. In C. Zeanah (Ed.), *Handbook of infant mental health* (3rd ed., pp. 5–21). New York: Guilford Press.

14

Evaluating Infant Mental Health Programs

Susan Janko Summers

*A*lthough the professional field of infant mental health is itself in its infancy, every day researchers and practitioners learn more and more about infant mental health services. Elsewhere in this book, we have noted the following:

- Of children attending Early Head Start programs, 71% had experienced at least one trauma in their young lives, including serious illness or injury, a prolonged separation from their primary caregiver, homelessness, death of a close relative, and violence in the home or community (Malik, 2007).

- Children exposed to violence or neglect in the earliest years are more likely to display problem behaviors and lag significantly behind their peers in language and cognitive development (U.S. Department of Health and Human Services [DHHS], 2003).

- A national study of 17 Early Head Start programs found that more than half of mothers were struggling with feelings of depression at the time they enrolled in Early Head Start (DHHS, 2006).

- Early Head Start has been shown to have a positive influence on the parenting skills of depressed parents and on the behavior of their children. Parents used less harsh discipline and a wider array of positive strategies to cope with parent–child conflict after participating in Early Head Start. Children were less aggressive and had more positive parent–child interactions than their peers who did not receive Early Head Start (DHHS, 2006).

This information is important, because it demonstrates the stressors affecting the children and families served. It also shows that enrollment in Early Head Start programs results in positive change in high-risk infants, toddlers, and their parents. We know these facts, and the worth of our work, because of research and evaluation.

The value of program evaluation is not always so evident in the day-to-day work of early childhood programs, however. If my colleagues and I were to ask early childhood educators what they think about evaluation, we would be likely to hear statements like the following:

- It creates layers of paperwork in my already busy schedule.
- I fear being judged.
- It does not have any connection to my day-to-day work.
- We collect all this information, and it just goes into a black hole. We never hear back.
- I am afraid of what I will find. The problems families face are so big, I am not sure I make a difference.

Evaluation can at times seem equal to punishment.

If evaluation is imposed upon but not directly related to our work with children and families, those concerns can be valid. Instead, let's say program administrators invite program staff to join in planning their program. And programs give staff the time and space to gather together regularly and reflect upon their work, so that they can make sure their program is the best it can possibly be.

This is the essence of evaluation. In programs that are up and running, program evaluation is a way of taking stock of what they do in order to achieve their goals, improve their programs, and know whether they have made a difference. In programs just beginning to provide infant mental health services, evaluation can help them plan for success.

WHY EVALUATE?

Jim Yong Kim, president of Dartmouth University, shared this lament about how little people understand how and whether helping organizations actually help:

> When it comes to our most cherished social goals, not only do we tolerate poor execution, sometimes we celebrate poor execution. Sometimes it's part of the culture. You know, these folks are trying to solve this terrible problem. They can't keep their books straight. They really don't know what they're getting. They don't measure anything. But they're on the right side, so that's okay. (Kim, 2009)

Such criticisms can be pretty upsetting to early childhood educators with little training in research and evaluation. However, no matter how difficult it may be to hear, Dr. Kim's point is valid. With the precious and limited time, money, and human resources we invest in order to make meaningful differences in the lives of children and their caregivers, we must make sure that we are making meaningful differences. And we also must know how we made those differences, so we can repeat our successes and improve in areas that do not meet with success. We help ensure success through program evaluation. We evaluate our programs because we want to know that we do our good work well.

PLANNING AN EVALUATION

For the sake of simplicity, evaluation can be described as occurring in two phases: planning evaluation and doing evaluation. In truth, evaluation is not so straightforward, because evaluators and practitioners periodically go back to review and revise the evaluation plan to see if it is working and still makes sense, as they learn more about their work. A good way to begin planning an evaluation is to ask meaningful questions, ask logical questions, examine program content and create a focus, develop a logic model and theory of change, and identify ways to monitor progress and outcomes.

Ask Meaningful Questions

One reason programs shy away from evaluation is because it does not seem to make a difference in their work. This may be true in part because programs are not asking about the things that matter most to them.

Dan Pallotta is a Harvard-educated economist devoted to helping nonprofits effectively address the world's most pressing problems. Pallotta stressed the importance of asking the right questions when a nonprofit evaluates the value and effectiveness of its work, such as the following (2009, p. 10):

1. What are your goals, and what progress are you making toward those goals?
2. What challenges are you facing, and how are you trying to overcome those challenges?
3. How do you know that you're being effective?
4. Tell me what you know about the effectiveness of your work.

These questions are important to ask, because they provide information about what the organization cares about most—whether its work results in meaningful differences in the lives of children and families. These questions are also big and complex. Therefore, it is best to deconstruct them—or separate them into parts—so that they are manageable and answerable.

Take a big question of concern to all early educators: How do you know that you are being effective? Suppose your program uses pre- and postassessments of child development to show *whether* you are effective in supporting children's social-emotional growth. That is a good place to start. However, it is also important to go deeper and ask *how you know* you are effective. Here are a few examples of questions that will help you explain how you know:

1. What program services and activities support children's social and emotional development?
2. Did we provide services and activities as we planned?
3. Are all children benefiting from program services and activities?
4. What are the reasons child assessment scores did (or did not) improve?

It is important to go back and forth between asking big, general questions about whether programs are effective and more specific questions that explain how programs can be made effective.

Ask Logical Questions

In addition to being meaningful, an evaluation plan should make sense. It should lead to a reasonable explanation of how things work in a program. In other words, it should be logical and based on theory.

It is important that early childhood professionals are aware of what we ourselves believe as we plan an evaluation, because our views on subject matter express our underlying philosophies and theories about how things work (Dewey, 1938/1980). For example, in the subject of infant mental health, we hold certain things to be true:

- We believe we can gauge an infant's mental health by looking at his or her social and emotional development.

- We believe that this social and emotional development comes about as a result of past and present human relationships and social interactions, particularly with key caregivers.

- We also believe that the earliest years of human growth are particularly important and will influence a child physically, psychologically, socially, and emotionally for the rest of life.

Being aware of our beliefs and theories about infant mental health is important, because our beliefs and theories influence our daily work. When we examine them, then our resulting awareness can guide our work and tell us whether our approach to education and intervention is likely to lead to successful outcomes.

Examine Program Content and Create a Focus

How do early childhood professionals go about discovering our underlying theories and beliefs? A good way is to first identify the subject matter of our work, then work backward to examine what we already think and know about it.

What is the content or subject matter of infant mental health? This book presents what the authors and many in the field believe to be at least a portion of the subject matter. Next we review what those content areas are, some of what they include, and how they might serve to focus an evaluation of an early childhood or intervention program with an infant mental health component.

Child mental health: development, including social-emotional, language-communication, and cognitive development; behavior, including internalizing and externalizing behavior; regulation, including sleeping, nutrition and eating habits, and crying or soothing patterns; physical health

Caregiver mental health: anxiety and depression, aggression and disengagement, physical health, and exposure to trauma

Caregiver–child interaction: the consistency, promptness, sensitivity, contingency, physical touch, proximity, and emotional temperature of the caregiver's attention and responses to the child's physical and emotional needs during play and caregiving routines; the appropriateness of caregivers' expectations about child development and behavior

Risk and resilience: trauma; poverty; home and community environments including the safety, consistency, noise levels, crowding, and opportunities for exploration; access to basic needs, including food, health care, stable housing, and access to learning opportunities and materials in home and community; availability of strong and healthy social relationships between children and caregivers and between caregivers and immediate and extended family; physical and mental health of all family members

This book also covers what early childhood programs can do to support the mental health of children and families. These factors include

Professional training, development, and support, including staff competence and feelings of confidence in key content areas listed earlier; communication and relationship skills with children, families, and coworkers; recognition of professional boundaries and program protocol for consultation and referrals; identifying and coping with stress; staff retention; staff satisfaction

Reflective supervision, including regular, collaborative practice of self-reflection, critical thinking, problem solving, perspective taking, active listening, cultural auditing, and sensitivity

Mental health consultation, including information gathering, individualized service plan development and implementation, education for providers and families, emotional support for providers and families, linkages to outside services, and, possibly, direct services to families

Organization, including culture, social climate, infrastructure and staffing, and commitment to addressing mental health issues

The content areas listed above probably seem reasonable to you after reading this book, or perhaps they ring true to you based on your work with children and families. In themselves, however, these content areas are too big and not very helpful for conducting evaluation. To make these content areas useful for evaluation, we need to engage in a process of thinking about indicators (e.g., measures of social-emotional development or risk) that we can look for in our programs to determine the presence, absence, or emergence of infant mental health. Once we have identified these indicators, we can see how they fit together in actual practice.

Develop a Logic Model and Theory of Change

We have identified the subject matter of infant mental health and examined our underlying beliefs and theories about infant mental health. The next step is to design a model, or plan, that will guide our evaluation. As noted earlier, this model should identify important indicators of infant mental health (e.g., social-emotional development, positive caregiver–child relationships) and logically explain how these indicators relate to each other. Most programs use logic models to guide evaluation.

Logic Models   According to the Harvard Family Research Project's *Evaluation Exchange,* "A logical model is a tactical explanation of the process of producing a given outcome" (Anderson, 2005, p. 12). In other words, a *logic model* is something that programs construct to explain how a certain outcome (e.g., an improvement in a child's social-emotional development) happens.

Programs often present their logic model in graphic form, such as a table or drawing, to describe the relationship between program content or focus (home visits that focus on caregiver–child interactions), the activities they plan in order to achieve their stated goals (supporting caregivers in supporting their children), and the outcomes they expect (improvement in the child's social, emotional, and communication skills).

When developing a logic model, programs should start by identifying their ultimate goal, then work backward. In the example shown in Table 14.1, the goal is promoting children's social and emotional development. The proof or evidence that the program is meeting the goal is pre- and postassessments of the children's social and emotional development. To make sure these outcomes are achieved, programs must go back to planned program activities and monitor ongoing progress by looking at 1) child status (periodically observe children's behavior between formal assessments) and 2) home visits (observe parenting skills; document whether home visits occurred as planned and as often as planned; and identify individual, family, and life circumstances that support or inhibit progress along the way).

The *linked system model* described by Squires in Chapter 6 is a good example of a logic model. It includes assessment of child development in social contexts important to development and necessary for interpreting assessment results (outcome measures that link to program content), and it uses assessment results to provide essential information for designing, monitoring, and improving education and intervention (indicators of development that link to program activities and progress monitoring).

Early childhood programs increasingly use logic models to meet the demands of funders for program outcome accountability. However, as is evident in Table 14.1, logic models are equally useful in supporting program monitoring for day-to-day accountability. Logic models are well suited to programs that are complex in scope, such as those that provide two-generation (parents and children), comprehensive early childhood services that focus on infant mental health as well as on general health and development. Logic models are also well suited to programs that innovate because, rather than using a "one-size-fits-all" design, modeling lends itself to tailoring evaluations to the range of goals and activities selected by a program. (Resources for developing logic models are shown in Table 14.2.)

Table 14.1.   Program goal: The Early Care Program will promote social and emotional development among infants and toddlers through a weekly home visiting program

Program focus/content	Program activities	Program outcomes
Home visits focus on caregiver–child interactions as the basis for children's social and emotional development and well-being.	Home visitors support sensitive, responsive, and contingent caregiver–child interactions by modeling these behaviors, practicing and reflecting with parents, and encouraging parents.	The program conducts pre- and postassessments of children's social, emotional, and communication behavior. Home visitors conduct ongoing observations of child behavior and record parents' observations and concerns.

Table 14.2. Selected essential resources for logic models

Child Welfare Information Gateway: http://www.childwelfare.gov/preventing/developing/toolkit/	This web site links to the FRIENDS National Resource Center to provide a comprehensive Evaluation Tool Kit, including a Logic Model Builder, designed to guide programs in developing a program-specific logic model.
W.K. Kellogg Foundation: http://www.wkkf.org/knowledge-center/resources/2006/02/WK-Kellogg-Foundation-Logic-Model-Development-Guide.aspx	This web site provides a downloadable guide offering practical assistance to nonprofit programs wishing to develop a logic model for program planning, implementation, and evaluation.
The Evaluation Exchange, Harvard Family Research Project: http://www.hfrp.org/evaluation/the-evaluation-exchange	This web site archives past issues of the journal and makes available practical information on special issues such as Early Childhood Programs and Evaluation (Summer 2004) and Evaluation Methodology, which includes an article on logic models (Summer 2005).
Office of Planning Research and Evaluation, Administration for Children and Families, U.S. Department of Health and Human Services: http://www.acf.hhs.gov/programs/opre/ehs/perf_measures/reports/resources_measuring/res_meas_sec1.html	*Resources for Measuring Services and Outcomes in Head Start Programs Serving Infants and Toddlers* is the title of a publication that contains resources to help programs develop a program performance measurement plan, including a theory of change, and carry out data collection.

Theory of Change Part of developing a logic model is for a program to anticipate the change it thinks will occur as a result of its goals and activities and to map out how it believes change will occur. To do this, programs simply take their best guess, based on their practical knowledge and expertise, of how they can help change happen. Mapping change means describing the intermediate steps and conditions they believe will be favorable to promoting change and identifying indicators of change. This mapping process is referred to as a *theory of change* (Anderson, 2005).

All of this may sound complicated, and it does take a commitment of time and energy to create change. However, it is something that successful programs do naturally and often, even if they do not think of it as evaluation. The previous example of a logic model in Table 14.1 offers a simple theory of change. The program's theory is, We can promote children's social and emotional development through home visits.

The following program evaluation example looks at a more complicated theory of change. Programs just beginning infant mental health services or program evaluation should begin with a simple model, like that shown in Table 14.1. More advanced programs can begin to look for the underlying connections between infant mental health work and the family, community, and organizational contexts that surround them.

The following example looks at the program goal of addressing children's challenging social and emotional behaviors by providing home visits. This early childhood program uses group critical thinking to explain the content and theories underlying home visits, to revise their goal, and to map out a plan to meet their new goal. After group members identify their new goal, they describe a theory of change that will guide their program's activities and identify desired outcomes. However, their original goal of addressing children's challenging social and emotional behaviors is not as straightforward as they anticipated.

The Early Care Program—after a long history of providing classroom-based early education services for children birth to 3 years—decided to add home visits. The program was seeing an increasing number of children with challenging behavior in its toddler classrooms, and it hoped that by adding a home visit program and involving caregivers, it could support more positive child behavior. Early Care staffed the home visit program with people who were experienced infant and toddler classroom teachers.

After several months, the home visitors reported to their supervisors that they were working on child play activities during home visits, much as they had done in the classroom. However, not all of the parents seemed to catch on to what the home visitors were modeling. Further, a few parents did not seem to interact much with their children at all. Also, many parents wanted to talk about the difficult family circumstances and relationships they were experiencing rather than focus on the children. Some home visitors said they "couldn't seem to get to children's play and development" during home visits. A number of home visitors were feeling a mixture of frustration with parents and discomfort about the purpose of their work and their own professional skills.

Administrators and supervisors got together to discuss these challenges and decided to offer staff training to home visitors. First they offered a Saturday session, but only two of the seven home visitors attended, despite all of the home visitors having identified their desire for more training. So administrators invited supervisors and home visitors to join them and talk together about why home visitors did not attend the training. Early Care had an open culture of listening and caring, so home visitors felt comfortable sharing their opinions and concerns.

The training topic, Understanding Parent–Child Interactions, did not seem relevant to some home visitors, who said that their job was "working with children." Several home visitors also expressed concern about giving up part of their weekend and paying for child care for their own children.

Program administrators, supervisors, home visitors, and representatives from the parent advisory board (i.e., all "stakeholders," or people who are affected by program decisions) went back to the drawing board. They began working together with a university faculty member with expertise in infant mental health (and with whom they had a longtime, mutually respectful relationship) to identify exactly what they needed in the way of training.

The group began by identifying three underlying theories and assumptions about how home visits work:

1. Home visits should focus on parent–child or caregiver–child dyads in order to promote children's social and emotional development.
2. Staff members need to acquire new information and skills in order to work in new ways with children and families.
3. Children's and families' broad needs may have to be addressed in order for individual social and emotional goals to be achieved.

Based on these assumptions, the group members discussed again why they would like training and what they hoped to gain from it. Because logistics had been a problem, they also talked about when and where training should occur.

The group changed its goal from addressing children's social and emotional behavior problems. Instead, group members identified their overriding goal as enhancing the social and emotional development of children through home-based education. The home visitors felt comfortable with this broader, more positive goal that continued their primary focus on children.

As they "unpacked" the concepts underlying this goal, they found that focusing on children required that they think more broadly about the context in which children developed. Together, they identified what home visitors needed to learn in order to accomplish this goal. The group believed that mastery of these content areas was the key to how change would occur; in other words, it was their "theory of change." They reasoned that once program staff mastered content areas, then they would begin to change their work with children and caregivers. They identified the following content areas:

- How relationships with key caregivers relate to children's social and emotional development
- The influence of risk (e.g., stressful life events) and resilience (e.g., maternal support) on social and emotional development
- Communicating with parents, including conducting parent interviews
- Building and maintaining relationships with families
- Observing parent–child interactions during routine play and caregiving activities
- Screening and assessing children's social and emotional development in typical contexts and translating assessment information into child-centered activities and individualized intervention plans
- Sharing screening and assessment results and offering anticipatory guidance to parents about their child's development and ways to support it in the home
- Recognizing when family circumstances (e.g., violence, depression) went beyond the scope of their work and expertise (margins of authority), and how to ethically and responsibly find resources to address family circumstances (response protocols)

They realized that, as they started working in new ways, they might find new things they needed to learn. They agreed that their list was not definitive.

Home visitors also expressed the desire to have trainers or supervisors accompany them on home visits or watch videotapes of home visits so that they might get feedback and support as they worked to incorporate new knowledge and skills. At the end of the meeting, several supervisors expressed concern that they lacked the knowledge and skills they needed in order to provide the kind of supervision home visitors would need after they completed training. The group identified reflective supervision training for supervisors as the topic of the next planning meeting. Group members also identified an immediate programwide need to develop a response protocol for identifying and referring families with serious mental health needs that exceeded the program scope and their professional training.

Finally, the home visitors and supervisors devised on-site child care for their own children by pooling their resources and hiring a classroom aide who was willing to help.

What the Early Care Program thought at first would be a simple training session to support staff in providing home visits was far more complex. The true nature of children's social-emotional development means that infant mental health programs must include parents and caregivers. Including parents and caregivers means that direct service staff and supervisors need professional development opportunities to acquire new skills. Also, new program and professional developmental activities require changes in organizational infrastructure and staff support. If any one of these pieces goes missing, it is likely that the program will fail to meet the ultimate goal of training: better outcomes for children (e.g., no one will show up for training, learning in the classroom will not transfer to home visits, supervisors and home visitors with different knowledge bases will operate at cross purposes, families in crisis will not receive appropriate support). Each condition is important and connected to every other condition.

If the process of figuring out these conditions of change and how they relate to each other sounds a little messy—well, it is. As noted earlier, programs beginning infant mental health services or program evaluation will not go into this depth. Such programs should strive to keep things simple and manageable at first. Programs that are ready to deepen and expand their evaluation plan must be willing to spend time initially developing a common understanding, and program staff must not push too hard to set their ideas and plans in stone. When early childhood professionals map the conditions that may lead to successful completion of a goal, we take our best guess. We will not always be right, so it is important to consider steps toward completion as "placeholders" that can be substituted by other ideas and activities when things do not work as anticipated. Likewise, our logic models may change as our understanding and program conditions change. So programs must commit to regularly reviewing progress as a group—again with all stakeholders involved.

Identify Ways to Monitor Progress and Outcomes

A prerequisite to progress review is the selection and inclusion of *performance measures*. These measures enable programs to document the education and intervention activities they plan to use to support social-emotional development, to determine if they are providing services and activities as they intended, and to show how children and caregivers are progressing (Kisker et al., 2003).

Matching Measurement Purposes and Processes   When programs evaluate infant mental health services, they must document the range of what they do, including child and family outcomes, training, supervision, consultation, and accounting for the types and amounts of all services they offer. To do this, they need to use a variety of performance measures. The beginning of this chapter presented big questions that ask *whether* our work as early childhood professionals makes a difference. It also presented more specific questions that ask *how we know* our work makes a difference. Different

performance measures are used to answer these different questions. To answer *whether our work makes a difference*, the following measures and indicators typically are used:

- *Assessment tools* to measure growth in child development or positive changes in parent–child interactions

- *Numerical counts* to document increases in positive parenting and coping strategies and decreases in child aggressive behavior, for example

To answer *how we know our work makes a difference*, the following measures typically are relied on:

- *Ongoing formal and informal observations* of child behavior and parenting behavior that indicate progress toward goals

- *Anecdotal or case notes* that record factors that we believe help explain progress (e.g., increased family support) or lack of progress (e.g., child illness, family violence)

- *Formal observations* of the home, classroom, or organizational environment that we believe influence intervention and educational activities, or our ability to do our work as planned

This book has also mentioned times that programs may need to screen children's development, family and environment risks, and mental health (including signs of anxiety, depression, substance abuse, and posttraumatic stress) for the purposes of early identification and referral. When early childhood professionals use screening instruments, we also want to document our referral processes to see whether (and when) children and families received needed services. It is also worthwhile to remember that some of the important changes we see may be too subtle to be detected by the measures we use. For example, when a depressed mother is kept engaged so that services can be offered to her child or an isolated grandmother is helped to connect with an empathetic, supportive caregiver, it is useful to document these by taking anecdotal notes.

In the example in Table 14.3, staff members of the Early Care Program (with the help of a university partner) developed a comprehensive and ambitious plan to document the outcomes and activities they anticipated in their logic and theory of change models, and they identified a number of program performance measures to monitor progress and document outcomes. They knew they probably would not be able to implement their plan all at once, but they wanted to develop a "big picture" model, and work in stages to realize their ultimate goals.

The first column in Table 14.3 shows the program content and focus the Early Care Program plans to provide for home visitors. The second column shows content links to training activities (which are the way that the Early Care staff believe change will occur). The third column identifies corresponding program performance measurement tools and strategies that will provide evidence that change is occurring. Also in the third column, notice that the outcomes are not limited to whether the program staff learns new training content; the program is also interested in how that new content translates into new skills that result in new ways of teaching, and how new teaching approaches result in improvements in children's social and emotional development and more positive caregiver–child interactions.

Again, most programs need not start with such a comprehensive and ambitious plan. However, all programs should 1) identify meaningful program and individual child

Table 14.3. Evaluating the Early Care Program's content, training, and outcomes

Program content/focus	Training activities	Program performance measures
How relationships with key caregivers relate to children's social and emotional development	The *Promoting First Relationships Curriculum* (Barnard, 1994) is selected from a number of evidence-based curricula to train staff on-site.	Home visitors are trained to criteria for proficiency. Program evaluation focuses on videotaped observations of home visitors during home visits to determine acquisition of skills and implementation fidelity.
The influence of risk (e.g., stressful life events) and resilience (e.g., maternal support) on social and emotional development	A team of university and state and local social services providers provide didactic training.	Participants complete knowledge-based pre- and postassessments.
Communicating with parents, including conducting parent interviews	A university team works with parents, providing didactic and interactive training.	Participants complete knowledge-based pre- and postassessments and are observed by trainers during role plays.
Building and maintaining relationships with families	A university team works with parents, providing didactic and interactive training.	Participants complete knowledge-based pre- and postassessments and are observed by trainers during role plays.
Observing parent–child interactions during routine play and caregiving activities	The *Parent-Child Interaction (PCI) Feeding and Teaching Scales* (Barnard, 1994) is selected from a number of evidence-based curricula to train staff on-site.	Home visitors are trained in criteria for proficiency. Program evaluation focuses on videotaped observations of the home visitor during home visits to determine implementation fidelity. Observations during home visits document change in parent–child interactions.
Screening and assessing children's social and emotional development in typical contexts and translating assessment information into child-centered activities and individualized intervention plans	The Ages & Stages Questionnaires®, Third Edition (ASQ-3; Squires & Bricker, 2009) and the Assessment, Evaluation, and Programming System for Infants and Young Children (AEPS®), Second Edition (Bricker, 2002) are selected from a number of psychometrically sound screening and assessment tools. The AEPS is aligned with U.S. Office of Special Education Programs Child Outcomes.	Home visitors participate in a 2-day seminar to learn to administer the AEPS, and they receive a day of training on the ASQ-3. Supervisors and peers debrief actual screening and assessments and monitor goal development and intervention planning. Supervisors record observations and case notes. Home visitors complete a self-assessment survey about their experiences, successes, and challenges. Periodic administrations of the AEPS document changes in child development status. Single-subject studies and regular review of individual child education plans document progress toward goals and the relationship between intervention strategies and successful outcomes.
Sharing screening and assessment results and offering anticipatory guidance to parents about their child's development and ways to support it in the home	Home visitors receive didactic and interactive training from university and Early Care Program supervisory staff.	Participants complete knowledge-based pre- and postassessments and are observed by trainers during role plays.
Recognizing when family circumstances (e.g., violence, depression) went beyond the scope of their work and expertise and how to ethically and responsibly find resources to address family circumstances	Home visitors receive didactic and interactive training from university and Early Care Program supervisory staff.	Participants complete knowledge-based pre- and postassessments and are observed by trainers during role plays. In- and out-of-program referrals and home visitor case notes are collaboratively reviewed during reflective supervision sessions to identify what works well and why and what needs improvement.

Box 14.1. How to document a range of program activities

Program intake: Demographic forms, caregiver interviews, assessments of health and housing status, and data on family strengths and risks are commonly collected by programs. This information is useful in generating explanations for why change is or is not occurring. It also may guide the design and evaluation of services that indirectly support infant mental health by supporting families' related needs (e.g., respite care, parent-to-parent support, food and clothing). This information should be reviewed for all families several times a year to ensure that the program supports infant mental health in broad ways.

Tracking services: Programs regularly document the amount of services used by counting the number of home visits completed, child classroom attendance, and parent and family participation in education and support activities. Tracking services can also include documenting what occurs in classrooms and during home visits and measures of quality (e.g., of classroom and home environments, of supervisor observations of teaching and intervention).

Consumer satisfaction: Several times a year, programs may administer surveys that ask for caregivers' opinions about the services they receive. Another very useful way to know whether families are satisfied with services is to include open-ended questions with the surveys (e.g., "What else can you tell us that would help make the program better for your child and family?"). It is also helpful to check in with families on a regular basis during home visits and parent–teacher conferences by asking them, "How do you think things are going?" and record their responses so that you can track satisfaction with services over time and can use their responses to guide your work as you go.

Parent partnerships: We recommend that parents and family members be included in evaluation planning and review. They should be included in ways that maintain the privacy of all children and families in the program. (Team meetings using reflective consultation would not be an appropriate way to include parents and family members.) Parent partners can periodically be surveyed or interviewed to see if they found their involvement in planning and evaluation to be meaningful, how valued they felt by the program or by co-members of committees or advisory boards, the extent to which they felt supported in their work, and so on (Summers et al., 2009).

Training evaluations: Programs may assess the professional development needs of program staff by administering formal needs assessments, interviewing direct service and supervisory staff, and observing staff. Professional development activities (including individual as well as programwide professional development plans) should be checked to see if they correspond to identified needs, and staff knowledge and skills should be assessed to see if training outcomes happened as anticipated. Programs may use peer-to-peer review processes to encourage self-reflection and promote professional growth.

and family goals, 2) specify what they intend to do to reach their goals (education and intervention activities), 3) gather evidence to show their work and the effects of their work (progress monitoring and program performance measures), and 4) make decisions and draw conclusions based on that evidence. These four components are the foundation of program evaluation.

DOING EVALUATION

Once a program's staff has asked the questions that are most important to them, narrowed the focus of their inquiry, mapped how they think change will occur, and identified strategies and sources of information that will show that change is occurring, they are ready to begin evaluation. The way programs carry out evaluation is by collecting program data as they have planned and by gathering regularly to reflect upon progress, generate explanations for why progress is or is not occurring, and adjust program activities according to what is learned.

Collect Program Data According to Plan

Evaluation is not something that programs do now and then. It should be a part of everyday program activities. Program staff should regularly gather data and monitor progress toward goals to see how children and caregivers are progressing every step along the way, and to make necessary adjustments to education and intervention plans. When readministering outcome measures at the end of the year, programs are more likely to see child and family progress, because their initial measures and goals are directly connected to weekly classroom and home visit activities and progress has been monitored throughout the year. Without this constant review and adjustment to education and intervention plans, a program really cannot know how—and if—children and families are progressing.

Gather Regularly to Review Progress

Allocating time and space to meet and reflect on a program's work is necessary to support evaluation planning and implementation. Regular meetings keep the staff on track, offer a source of support from colleagues, and provide a means to professional and organizational development.

One way to review progress is through the reflective consultation process. My colleagues and I observed one early intervention program in which each week a home visitor shared a case study that she found challenging. The home visitor presented a brief summary of assessment information, educational goals, progress toward goals, parents' concerns, and contextual information that might explain progress or lack of it. Then she shared a 5-minute video showing caregiver–child interactions during a home visit, and she pointed out things that concerned or perplexed her. The program's mental health consultant supported the home visitor during the presentation by "guiding the content of the presentation through attentive listening, topical questions, and gentle prompts that help the (teacher or) home visitor fill in missing information and think aloud about the

Box 14.2.   Evidence-based practice and
practice-based evidence

To document changes in child development or child–caregiver interactions, we recommend that programs move toward using evidence-based practices when they match and support program and individual child and family goals.

What does it mean to be *evidence-based?* According to Dr. Edward Mullen, "Evidence-based practice (EBP) places emphasis on the practitioner's use of scientifically validated assessment, intervention, and evaluation procedures, as well as the practitioner's use of critical thinking when making practice decisions that matter to service recipients" (as quoted in Roberts & Yeager, 2004, pp. 4–5). In other words, Dr. Mullen urged practitioners to be discerning in the use of assessment, intervention, and evaluation procedures. Programs should select assessment tools and curricula that are reliable and valid, are supported by empirical evidence from observation or experiment, and have demonstrated their effectiveness in reaching a desired outcome with a population similar to the children and families we work with. If you choose to use evidence-based assessment tools, curricula, or intervention strategies in your program, you should also focus on using them appropriately and with fidelity, according to instructions. (A list of resources for evidence-based curricula and practices for early childhood and infant mental health is found in Table 14.4.)

Even when we use evidence-based approaches, circumstances other than our teaching and intervention can contribute to change or lack of change. To learn why change is or is not occurring, programs can also conduct research on their practice. This is called *practice-based research.* Practice-based research evaluates "the implementation of these interventions to ensure that they are being implemented as intended and the intended outcomes are achieved, with no unintended negative consequences," according to Phyllis Solomon, professor at the Penn School of Social Policy and Practice (as quoted in Roberts & Yeager, 2004, p. 5). Practice-based research is concerned with questions of effectiveness. Practice-based research might look at whether home visits occur as planned and as often as planned, whether home visitors implement a curriculum reliably and accurately, whether families like the curriculum, whether families continue curriculum activities as part of their daily routine, and so on. Learning about characteristics of intervention indirectly supports more effective intervention outcomes (P. Solomon, as quoted in Roberts & Yeager, 2004).

Both practice-based research and evidence-based practice are important in early childhood programs. Professor of psychiatry Dr. David Streiner explained,

> The link between practice and research is a two-way street. Good clinical practice must be informed by the best available evidence regarding treatment and diagnosis (evidence-based practice). However, in order for this research to be clinically relevant and useful, it must be both well executed and informed by actual clinical practice (practice-based research). (as quoted in Roberts & Yeager, 2004, p. 5)

Table 14.4. Selected resources: Evidence-based infant mental health and early childhood curricula and practices

The National Early Childhood Technical Assistance Center: http://www.nectac.org/topics/evbased/evbased.asp	This web site includes definitions, resources, and links for a number of topics related to infant mental health, such as early childhood identification, professional development, and social-emotional intervention for young children.
The Center on the Social and Emotional Foundations for Early Learning (CSEFEL): http://csefel.vanderbilt.edu/	CSEFEL is a national resource center funded by the U.S. Department of Health and Human Services Office of Head Start and Office of Child Care. This web site focuses on sharing information and providing tools that promote the social-emotional development and school readiness of children birth to age 5.
Substance Abuse and Mental Health Services Administration, National Registry of Evidence-based Programs and Practices: http://www.nrepp.samhsa.gov/AdvancedSearch.aspx	This web site is a searchable online registry of evidence-based interventions that support mental health. Searches can be conducted according to area of interest, outcome categories, geographical locations, ages, ethnicities, and settings.
The California Evidence-Based Clearinghouse for Child Welfare: http://www.cebc4cw.org/	This web site provides access to information about research evidence for selected child welfare programs, including infant and toddler mental health, adult depression, and home visiting.
Evidence-Based Practice in the Early Childhood Field. (2006). Virginia Buysse and Patricia Wesley (Eds.). Washington, DC: ZERO TO THREE: National Center for Infants, Toddlers, and Families.	This text describes the influence of evidence-based practice on research, application to real-world problems, and policy development and decision making.
Evidence-Based Practice Manual. (2004). Albert Roberts and Kenneth Yeager (Eds.). New York: Oxford University Press.	This comprehensive and technical text addresses research, evaluation, and practice issues across a range of health, social service, psychology, prevention, and education topics and settings.

educational importance and implications of her observations" (Summers, Funk, Twombly, Waddell, & Squires, 2007, p. 222). This process was followed by a group discussion during which colleagues posed questions, offered causal explanations for what they saw occurring, and made suggestions that the home visitor could use to revise and refine her work with the child and family. The process was recorded in the form of case notes that documented key information, decisions, and revisions in plans. These were reviewed at a later date in order to track and document change.

Important characteristics of this approach include the following: The entire educational team participates, so that professional development occurs not only for the person presenting the case, but also for all those participating in the review process. The focus on the individual progress of a single child and family, combined with discussion about broader educational and program issues, results in both individual child and family progress and continuous program improvement. Educators easily could (and should) use this process to share successful as well as challenging cases. (See Chapters 10 and 11 to learn more about infant mental health consultation and reflective supervision.)

Critical Friends

In the example just presented, the process of open discussion and participation did not happen by accident. This organization worked to establish a warm, open, and respectful

Box 14.3.   Single-subject studies

A sound and straightforward way to evaluate our practice as early childhood professionals is by using *single-subject studies*. Single-subject studies allow programs to document the relationship between teaching strategies and changes in child or caregiver behavior (Horner et al., 2005).

Single-subject studies are really a small experiment with one individual (a single subject). They use this model:

Antecedent	**Behavior**	**Consequence**
The teaching or intervention strategy that "occasions" the target goal	The child or caregiver target goal or objective	Something that occurs immediately after the behavior, increasing its likelihood

The following example demonstrates how the model works.

> The Early Care Program used the Assessment, Evaluation, and Programming System for Infants and Young Children (AEPS®), Second Edition (Bricker, 2002) to assess the development of a toddler, Luke, whose family recently experienced some changes at home. (The AEPS is a curriculum-referenced assessment designed to take items straight from the assessment and appropriately use them as individual child goals.) Luke, once happy and outgoing, has been crying more often, started using more "baby talk," and stopped playing with friends. On the AEPS, Luke showed a regression in communication and social skills.
>
> After the assessment, the Early Care Toddler Room teacher met with Luke's mother. Together they reviewed assessment results, talked about the mother's concerns and priorities, and chose the following goal: *Luke will initiate communication with peer.* Then they identified the behaviors they expected to see that would lead to those skills, such as playing near another child, observing another child, and so on. They talked together about how they might encourage and support Luke to begin talking and playing again with friends. They identified specific strategies that the teacher and Luke's mom could use to support this goal.

Single-subject studies require clearly defining and carefully following teaching strategies. The teaching strategies are an antecedent (i.e., they come before a behavior) that "occasion" skills or support their occurrence. In single-subject studies, the teacher must pay as much attention to her teaching strategy as to the behavior—they are causally connected. The consequence of the behavior should be naturally occurring when possible. For example, when Luke initiates communication with a peer, perhaps the peer looks and smiles at Luke or gives Luke a toy in response.

In the classroom, the toddler teacher used these teaching strategies consistently every day. Each time she used them, she observed Luke to see if he exhibited the behaviors they had identified as leading to the goal *initiates communication with peer*. When he did, she kept a careful record of changes in Luke's behavior. She did this by indicating progress toward the goal on a graph, writing down the teaching strategies she used, and carefully recording any other classroom condi-

(continued)

Box 14.3 *(continued)*

tions (e.g., which children were present, whether Luke felt tired) that might have contributed to Luke's change in behavior. In several weeks, Luke began talking and playing with friends, and the teacher knew her intervention had helped. The single-subject study was successful.

A single-subject study is well suited to education programs wishing to introduce a structure to their work that can be easily incorporated into daily routines. Single-subject studies do not present burdensome paperwork, and they provide the rigor necessary for practice-based research. Single-subject studies allow programs to document the fidelity of their treatment (by measuring teaching strategies as well as changes in behavior) so that they can have confidence that changes in child behavior resulted from treatment (Horner et al., 2005). Single-subject studies are frequently used in early intervention settings but are worth considering for early education settings as well.

Resources to Learn More About Single-Subject Studies

Hersen, M., & Barlow, D.H. (1976). *Single-case experimental designs: Strategies for studying behavior change.* New York: Pergamon.

Kazdin, A.E. (1982). *Single-case research designs: Methods for clinical and applied settings.* New York: Oxford University Press.

Odom, S., & Strain, P.S. (2002). Evidence-based practice in early intervention/early childhood special education: Single-subject design research. *Journal of Early Intervention, 25,* 151–160.

climate in which staff members felt safe questioning and problem solving aloud without fear of criticism or judgments from others. This climate takes time for programs to accomplish. One home visitor told us that at first "some bravery is required" to present a case study. Over time, program staff members came to trust and rely on each other to raise issues and solve problems collaboratively. (See Chapter 13 on organizational readiness to learn how to create just such a supportive program.)

My colleagues and I encourage programs to gather groups of "critical friends" who will openly ask questions and make suggestions in ways that deepen the way program personnel think about their work. Critical friends should think critically—that is, in careful and exacting ways. However, in all other ways, critical friends should be *uncritical;* they should be supportive and kind and come together in a spirit of solving problems together (Summers et al., 2009).

Additional Considerations

When conducting program evaluation, there are a few other things programs should keep in mind. The privacy and confidentiality of evaluation participants should be protected, and the evaluation should be practical and manageable for the program.

Scope Creep   How do early childhood professionals make evaluation broad enough to answer meaningful questions, but reasonable enough that they can accomplish the tasks associated with measuring change? When designing a logic model and describing a theory of change, it is a good idea to be comprehensive in scope. When implementing an evaluation, however, it is a good idea to prioritize which parts of the model can reasonably be implemented and evaluated given available resources. Successful program evaluations typically phase in evaluation components over time as they master each component. Once one evaluation component is going smoothly, data are reliably collected, and decisions are made according to what is learned, another evaluation component may be introduced. It is not unreasonable to design a long-term evaluation plan, for example, beginning with an evaluation planning year, followed by a year evaluating child and child–caregiver change, then a year evaluating professional development and supervision, adding a year of identifying risk and resilience among families and ways the program mediates risk and supports resilience, and finally, conducting a comprehensive evaluation of how the organization as a whole supports the activities necessary for successful infant mental health services. Programs should only do what they can manage, and do it well.

Privacy, Confidentiality, and Sensitivity   As early childhood professionals, we are used to taking precautions when we conduct research in our early childhood programs. We use informed consent to make sure that families know the risks and benefits of participating in research studies. We assure families that any data we collect will be kept under lock and key so that their privacy is protected. Also, we are careful never to share information in any way that would allow others to discover the identity of participants. Formal research studies require review and approval by institutional review boards or independent ethics committees before they can begin collecting data (DHHS, 1993).

Although we need not be quite as strict about these procedures when conducting ongoing program evaluation, we should approach our work with the same respect and care for protecting the privacy and confidentiality of all those involved in evaluation—not only children and families, but also program staff. It is always a good idea to take care with assessment results and case notes so that others do not see them, to share information only with those who need to know it for program purposes, and to check in periodically with others to make sure they feel comfortable with assessments, observations, and interviews. Remember that sensitive issues may arise during evaluation. Families may share something that is private or painful for them to express and difficult or painful for you to hear. You may hear views that are critical of you, your colleagues, or your program from consumer satisfaction surveys or interviews. Reflective supervisors and consultants can help you reframe information from "what is wrong" to "how we can improve" (Summers et al., 2009).

CONTRASTING RESEARCH AND EVALUATION

As shown earlier, program evaluation uses a variety of program performance measures that provide information for ongoing decision making and help programs determine to what extent they are meeting educational goals and objectives (Tyler, 1950). Program evaluation can also show whether a program is valued by those involved in it (Brinker-hoff, Brethower, Hluchyj, & Nowakowski, 1983; Guba & Lincoln, 1981).

In contrast, research uses scientific inquiry to acquire new knowledge and contribute to our general knowledge of the characteristics or causes of things societies view as important at a given point in time (Bogdan & Biklen, 1992). For example, there is currently a keen interest in the critical role early experience plays in shaping the brain's development, and much research has been conducted to tell us how this occurs (see Shonkoff & Phillips, 2000). *Research* is a broad term that includes many different approaches. One example, *applied research*, refers to studies designed to yield information that can be used directly to improve programs and practices (Bogdan & Biklen, 1992), such as the Early Head Start partnership studies described in the introduction to this book. A second example, *action research*, is designed to promote ongoing individual, group, or organizational change. Action research is conducted by direct service personnel, such as teachers or home visitors, in collaboration with or under the guidance of experienced researchers. Action research can be part of program evaluation such as empowerment evaluation, in which program participants conduct their own evaluations and an outside evaluator offers support and guidance throughout the process (Fetterman, 2001).

Both evaluation and research require that programs have access to experts with years of training and experience to help them design data collection strategies and carry them out. Programs will be able to carry out a well-designed evaluation plan with periodic check-ins with evaluators for guidance and support. Research, on the other hand, is best carried out by staff who will follow strict protocols to ensure reliability so that results are consistently replicable; validity so that measurements consistently measure what they purport to measure; fidelity so that procedures are applied in the precisely the same way every time; and so on. The rigor that research requires is usually beyond the available resources and expertise of early childhood programs, but such rigorous research can be of great benefit to programs and to the greater early childhood education community when done in partnership.

Research Partnerships

It is probably clear by now that in everything to do with infant mental health, partnerships are essential. Caregivers are essential partners with their children. Families are essential partners with caregivers. Home visitors work in a special partnership with caregivers called a *parallel process*, wherein the home visitor nurtures a caregiver so he or she can nurture the child. Also, program staff work collaboratively with one another as "critical friends," reflecting, questioning, supporting, and celebrating their work together.

When program staff work with outside researchers and evaluators in an effort to change and improve their program, the partnership between them is essential, too. Here are a few lessons my colleagues and I learned from our long and happy partnerships conducting research with Early Head Start and early intervention programs:

Take time to plan together. Both researchers and program administrators stressed the importance of spending extended time together before they began their research. More than one person recommended an initial planning year to allow sufficient time to form trusting relationships, to cultivate a sense of shared mission, to set goals together, and to build the necessary infrastructure to work together on infant mental health issues. During that year, researchers went into the programs and "listened to the moms, the grandparents, the teachers, and the staff" in order to learn about the challenges they faced. As one university researcher said, "The fact that we did not make this a university project where we just parachuted in has made a huge difference."

Clarify communication and expectations. Research cannot occur without ongoing collaboration, and ongoing collaboration requires clear communication and expectations. After setting goals together, researchers recommend checking back with programs by saying, "This is what I need from you. Tell me if this is too much for your staff to do." Part of making sure communication happens is being physically present on site so researchers can listen and observe—"stay close to the heartbeat of the program," as one researcher put it. In our partnerships, when conflict occurred, program personnel and researchers focused on maintaining a healthy relationship, and they used conflict to deepen their relationship by communicating the demands they faced that their partner may not have been aware of, clarifying their roles, and negotiating responsibilities.

Commit to learning with and from one another. It was clear from listening to researchers, program administrators, and direct service personnel that they valued learning from one another. One researcher explained, "A lot of the teachers come from the communities that parents and children come from. They understand them, and they know what they are dealing with. And they are really willing to teach my staff and me." Researchers and programs emphasized that each partner had unique and important knowledge and experience that was valuable to other partners. When knowledge from programs and researchers was shared and combined, the effectiveness of treatment increased.

Give back to programs and participants. Programs emphasized that they wished to realize direct benefits from their participation, beyond the general knowledge that comes from research. Programs especially wanted to receive ongoing information about the data they collected. A program mental health consultant told us that she wished she had heard back from researchers earlier in the process: "We were collecting information, but I didn't get to see it. It made me anxious." Giving back to programs by keeping people informed also kept partners involved and engaged, and presenting what was discovered as it was discovered provided opportunities to explore together the reasons why expected progress was or was not being met.

Because of the partnerships formed between universities and programs, our knowledge of infant mental health and ways we can support it has grown. Some of what the research partners learned from their collaborative work was presented at the outset of this chapter—one of many benefits that came from these research partnerships.

CONCLUSION

Learning to evaluate our work as early childhood and mental health professionals requires an up-front investment in time to learn new skills in critical thinking, reflection, and collaboration. It is really an investment in ourselves. Once we acquire these skills and practice them, they become second nature. They are ours. Evaluation also requires an up-front investment in planning and program infrastructure that will allow us to implement our evaluation plan. Once we have an evaluation plan and the program structure to support it, we become more directed, competent, and confident about our direction. Also, we are more likely to reach our goals.

I recommend that programs enjoy the journey as they conduct their evaluation. At a time in my life when I was feeling buried under the data I was collecting for a research study, my advisor plunked me down in a rocking chair, handed me a cup of tea, and began asking questions in a friendly, conversational style. This became a weekly ritual that we both looked forward to. This "rocking chair model" of reviewing one's work is exactly what programs need to do as part of evaluation. Slow down, savor your work, and question and reflect together.

This book has documented the challenges that early childhood professionals may encounter as we incorporate infant mental health services in our programs. At times we may feel we are not up to the task as we learn new skills. We cannot always meet all of the needs some children and families will have. There may even be times when we experience secondary stress or compassion fatigue in our work. More often, we will successfully support positive changes, small and large, in children and families. One final recommendation is to stop, take notice, and be thankful to play a part in such important work.

REFERENCES

Anderson, A. (2005). An introduction to theory of change. *The Evaluation Exchange, 11*(2), 12, 19.

Barnard, K. (1994). *Parent-Child Interaction (PCI) Feeding & Teaching Scales.* NCAST Programs, University of Washington, School of Nursing, Seattle.

Bogdan, R.C., & Biklen, S.K. (1992). *Qualitative research in education: An introduction to theory and methods.* Boston: Allyn & Bacon.

Bricker, D. (2002). *Assessment, Evaluation, and Programming System for Infants and Young Children (AEPS®), Second Edition: Administration guide* (Vols. 1–4, 2nd ed.). Baltimore: Paul H. Brookes Publishing Co.

Brinkerhoff, R.O., Brethower, D.M., Hluchyj, T., & Nowakowski, J.R. (1983). *Program evaluation: A practitioner's guide for trainers and educators.* Boston: Kluwer-Nijhoff.

Buysse, V., & Wesley, P. (Eds.). (2006). *Evidence-based practice in the early childhood field.* Washington, DC: ZERO TO THREE: National Center for Infants, Toddlers, and Families.

Dewey, J. (1980). *Logic: The theory of inquiry.* New York: Irvington Publishers. (Original work published 1938.)

Fetterman, D. (2001). *Foundations of empowerment evaluation.* Thousand Oaks, CA: Sage.

Guba, E.G., & Lincoln, Y.S. (1981). *Effective evaluation: Improving the usefulness of evaluation results through responsive and naturalistic approaches.* San Francisco: Jossey-Bass.

Hersen, M., & Barlow, D.H. (1976). *Single-case experimental designs: Strategies for studying behavior change.* New York: Pergamon.

Horner, R.H., Carr, E.G., Halle, J., McGee, G., Odom, S., & Wolery, M. (2005). The use of single-subject research to identify evidence-based practice in special education. *Exceptional Children, 71*(2), 165–179.

Kazdin, A.E. (1982). *Single-case research designs: Methods for clinical and applied settings.* New York: Oxford University Press.

Kim, J.Y. (2009, September). Interview with Dr. Jim Yong Kim on *Bill Moyers Journal.* Retrieved from http://www.pbs.org/moyers/journal/09112009/transcript3.html

Kisker, E.E., Boller, K., Nagatoshi, C., Sciarrino, C., Jethwani, V., Zavitsky, T., et al. (2003). *Resources for measuring services and outcomes in Head Start programs serving infants and toddlers.* Washington, DC: U.S. Department of Health and Human Services.

Malik, N. (2007, June). *Trauma exposure and intervention in Early Head Start families.* Paper presented at the meeting of the Birth to Three Institute, Washington, DC.

Odom, S., & Strain, P.S. (2002). Evidence-based practice in early intervention/early childhood special education: Single-subject design research. *Journal of Early Intervention, 25,* 151–160.

Pallotta, D. (2009, Fall). Letting nonprofits loose, Donna Stokes interview with Dan Pallotta. *World Ark.* Retrieved June 8, 2011, from http://www.heifer.org/site/c.edJRKQNiFiG/b.5402737/

Roberts, A.R., & Yeager, K.R. (2004). Systematic reviews of evidence-based studies and practice-based research: How to search for, develop, and use them. In A.R. Roberts & K.R. Yeager (Eds.), *Evidence-based practice manual: Research and outcome measures in health and human services.* New York: Oxford University Press.

Shonkoff, J.P., & Phillips, D.A. (Eds.). (2000). *From neurons to neighborhoods: The science of early childhood development.* Washington, DC: National Academies Press.

Squires, J., & Bricker, D. (2009). *Ages & Stages Questionnaires® Third Edition (ASQ-3): A parent-completed child monitoring system.* Baltimore: Paul H. Brookes Publishing Co.

Summers, S.J., Brodowski, M.L., Baker, L., Firman, C., Layden, Y., Luckie, A., et al. (2009). *Using qualitative data in program evaluation: Telling the story of a prevention program.* Retrieved June 6, 2011, from http://www.friendsnrc.org/using-qualitative-in-program-evaluation

Summers, S.J., Funk, K., Twombly, L., Waddell, M., & Squires, J. (2007). The explication of a mentor model, videotaping, and reflective consultation in support of infant mental health. *Infant Mental Health Journal, 28*(2), 216–236.

Tyler, R.W. (1950). *Basic principles of curriculum and instruction.* Chicago: University of Chicago Press.

U.S. Department of Health and Human Services, Administration for Children and Families. (2003). *Infants and toddlers in the child welfare system: Findings from the NSCAW study.* Washington, DC: Author. Retrieved June 7, 2011, from http://www.acf.hhs.gov/programs/opre/abuse_neglect/nscaw/reports/infants_todd/infants_todd.html

U.S. Department of Health and Human Services, Administration for Children and Families. (2006). *Depression in the lives of Early Head Start families: Research to practice brief.* Washington, DC: Author.

U.S. Department of Health and Human Services, Office for Human Research Protections. (1993). *IRB guidebook.* Retrieved June 7, 2011, from http://www.hhs.gov/ohrp/archive/irb/irb_guidebook.htm

Index

Page numbers followed by *b, f, and t* indicate boxes, figures, and tables, respectively.